T0092901

Text as Data

Text as Data

A New Framework for Machine
Learning and the Social Sciences

JUSTIN GRIMMER
MARGARET E. ROBERTS
BRANDON M. STEWART

PRINCETON UNIVERSITY PRESS
Princeton and Oxford

Copyright © 2022 by Princeton University Press

Princeton University Press is committed to the protection
of copyright and the intellectual property our authors
entrust to us. Copyright promotes the progress and integrity of
knowledge. Thank you for supporting free speech and the
global exchange of ideas by purchasing an authorized edition
of this book. If you wish to reproduce or distribute any part
of it in any form, please obtain permission.

Requests for permission to reproduce material from this work
should be sent to permissions@press.princeton.edu

Published by Princeton University Press
41 William Street, Princeton, New Jersey 08540
99 Banbury Road, Oxford OX2 6JX

press.princeton.edu

All Rights Reserved

ISBN (cloth) 978-0-691-207544
ISBN (pbk) 978-0-691-207551
ISBN (e-book) 978-0-691-207995

British Library Cataloging-in-Publication Data is available

Editorial: Meagan Levinson and Jacqueline Delaney
Production: Erin Suydam
Publicity: Kate Hensley (US) and Charlotte Coyne (UK)

This book has been composed in Minion Pro & Univers Lt Std

10 9 8 7 6 5 4 3 2 1

To Terese
-JG

To David
-MER

To Candi and Jerry
-BMS

Contents

Preface

Over the last decade, text as data methods have exploded in popularity in the social sciences, digital humanities, and industry. Plentiful data, new methods, and decreasing cost of computation have conspired to make it increasingly possible to unlock the valuable data in documents. These trends toward more data, better methods, and faster computers are only going to increase. Yet, these tools must be adapted to make valid inferences in the social sciences. This book is a guide to harnessing these advancements to make inferences about human behavior both now and in the future.

Prerequisites and Notation

Readers will likely come to this book with a range of technical backgrounds and interests. To speak to as broad an audience as possible, we assume only a familiarity with linear regression. To highlight the common aspects of ostensibly quite different techniques, we adhere as much as possible to a common system of notations summarized in list.

List of Notation

- N: number of documents
- i: index of documents
- M: number of tokens in a document
- m: index of tokens in document
- J: total number of features
- j: index of features
- K: total number of components
- k: index of components
- D_i: an abstract representation of document i including its text, formatting, or any additional information of interest
- W: $N \times J$ document-feature matrix
- $W_{i\cdot}$: document i row in the document-feature matrix
- $W_{\cdot j}$: column j of document-feature matrix
- W_{ij}: the cell of W at row i and column j
- Z: word level assignment to latent variables
- π: $N \times K$ matrix describing document weights/loadings on latent variables
- π_{ik}: document i's weight/loading on feature k

- μ: estimated center, factor, or other measure of central tendency
- g: a function that maps from the space of the text (denoted y_i if the text is an outcome and t_i if the text is a treatment) to the space of the representation, which is generally a K-length vector
- y_i: the target label/dimensions/category
- X: $N \times P$ matrix of non-text metadata and general covariates
- X_i: a vector of general covariates for document i of dimension P (comma is omitted because we never reference columns of X)
- $\hat{y}_i$: prediction or fitted value for y_i
- β: regression coefficients from subsequent analysis
- λ: regularization parameter or rate parameter depending on context
- σ^2: variance
- $p(\cdot)$: a generic unspecified probability distribution
- ϕ: all other nuisance parameters
- I: index for documents in the training set, or in sample
- O: index for documents in the test set, or out of sample

Uses for This Book

This is primarily a book about research design and the factors to consider when leveraging text as data. We envision three broad use cases.

In a Course. We have used earlier drafts of the book in our own advanced undergraduate and graduate courses. Many of these students have little prior exposure to machine learning methods or computational techniques. For these readers, our book provides both an introduction to techniques for working with text as data and a view on how to apply those techniques to make social science inferences. Such a course is naturally organized by following our research trajectory: representation, discovery, measurement, and inference. In each part, we illustrate with a few sample methods, but we expect courses would supplement this book with a deeper dive into the details of additional methods or the latest software implementations in the language of the instructor's choice.

A Unifying View of What Text as Data Can Do. Some readers may be familiar with some text as data techniques through either their own work or reading related articles. Our book outlines the many tasks that text as data methods can tackle and provides a starting place for engaging with this exciting literature. For those looking to explore just one task, we recommend reading Chapter 2 for our worldview and the introduction to each part for a sense of how the individual chapters within each task fit together.

Statement of Research Principles. Perhaps most importantly, we see this book as a statement about the use of machine learning methods in the social sciences. For researchers who are familiar with machine learning and text as data methods, our book provides a view about how to organize social science tasks and how to evaluate those tasks. Even readers with extensive backgrounds in machine learning may find new best practices when thinking about integrating those tools with research design. The majority of our thoughts about research design are concentrated in Chapter 2 and the chapters on principles (3, 10, 15, and 22).

What This Book Is Not

Text as data is a fast-moving field and the state of the art can easily change within the space of six months. This book focuses on research design for using texts to answer questions with social data rather than on the technical details of the latest methods or their software implementation. We understand that this may frustrate readers who want code chunks that they can run right away or a deep dive into the technical properties of a given technique. For those looking for a textbook to cover additional technical material in depth, we refer them to Murphy (2021) and Bishop (2006) for machine learning; Eisenstein (2019), Aggarwal (2018), and Jursfsky and Martin (2009) for natural language processing and machine learning with text; and Silge and Robinson (2017) for getting started with implementation. In our experience, amazing resources like these already exist for code and technical details, but there are fewer resources for explaining what is important for research and decision making in the social sciences. Our goal in this book is to highlight the logic of inference that underlies our efforts to use text as data to learn about the social world.

PART I

Preliminaries

CHAPTER 1

Introduction

This is a book about the use of texts and language to make inferences about human behavior. Our framework for using text as data is aimed at a wide variety of audiences—from informing social science research, offering guidance for researchers in the digital humanities, providing solutions to problems in industry, and addressing issues faced in government. This book is relevant to such a wide range of scholars and practitioners because language is an important component of social interaction—it is how laws are recorded, religious beliefs articulated, and historical events reported. Language is also how individuals voice complaints to representatives, organizers appeal to their fellow citizens to join in protest, and advertisers persuade consumers to buy their product. And yet, quantitative social science research has made surprisingly little use of texts—until recently.

Texts were used sparingly because they were cumbersome to work with at scale. It was difficult to acquire documents because there was no clear way to collect and transcribe all the things people had written and said. Even if the texts could be acquired, it was impossibly time consuming to read collections of documents filled with billions of words. And even if the reading were possible, it was often perceived to be an impossible task to organize the texts into relevant categories, or to measure the presence of concepts of interest. Not surprisingly, texts did not play a central role in the evidence base of the social sciences. And when texts were used, the usage was either in small datasets or as the product of massive, well-funded teams of researchers.

Recently, there has been a dramatic change in the cost of analyzing large collections of text. Social scientists, digital humanities scholars, and industry professionals are now routinely making use of document collections. It has become common to see papers that use millions of social media messages, billions of words, and collections of books larger than the world's largest physical libraries. Part of this change has been technological. With the rapid expansion of the internet, texts became much easier to acquire. At the same time, computational power increased—laptop computers could handle computations that previously would require servers. And part of the change was also methodological. A burgeoning literature—first in computer science and computational linguistics, and later in the social sciences and digital humanities—developed tools, models, and software that facilitated the analysis and organization of texts at scale.

Almost all of the applications of large-scale text analysis in the social sciences use algorithms either first developed in computer science or built closely on those developments. For example, numerous papers within political science—including many of our own—build on topic models (Blei, Ng, and Jordan, 2003; Quinn et al., 2010; Grimmer, 2010; Roberts et al., 2013) or use supervised learning algorithms for document classification (Joachims, 1998; Jones, Wilkerson, and Baumgartner, 2009; Stewart and Zhukov, 2009; Pan and Chen, 2018; Barberá et al., 2021). Social scientists have also made methodological contributions themselves, and in this book we will showcase many of these new models designed to accomplish new types of tasks. Many of these contributions have even flowed from the social sciences to computer science. Statistical models used to analyze roll call votes, such as Item Response Theory models, are now used in several computer science articles (Clinton, Jackman, and Rivers, 2004; Gerrish and Blei, 2011; Nguyen et al., 2015). Social scientists have broadly adapted the tools and techniques of computer scientists to social science questions.

However, the knowledge transfer from computer science and related fields has created confusion in how text as data models are applied, how they are validated, and how their output is interpreted. This confusion emerges because tasks in academic computer science are different than the tasks in social science, the digital humanities, and even parts of industry. While computer scientists are often (but not exclusively!) interested in information retrieval, recommendation systems, and benchmark linguistic tasks, a different community is interested in using "text as data" to learn about previously studied phenomena such as in social science, literature, and history. Despite these differences of purpose, text as data practitioners have tended to reflexively adopt the guidance from the computer science literature when doing their own work. This blind importing of the default methods and practices used to select, evaluate, and validate models from the computer science literature can lead to unintended consequences.

This book will demonstrate how to treat "text as data" for *social science tasks* and *social science problems*. We think this perspective can be useful beyond just the social sciences in the digital humanities, industry, and even mainstream computer science. We organize our argument around the core tasks of social science research: *discovery, measurement, prediction*, and *causal inference*. Discovery is the process of creating new conceptualizations or ways to organize the world. Measurement is the process where concepts are connected to data, allowing us to describe the prevalence of those concepts in the real world. These measures are then used to make a causal inference about the effect of some intervention or to predict values in the future. These tasks are sometimes related to computer science tasks that define the usual way to organize machine learning books. But as we will see, the usual distinctions made between particular types of algorithms—such as supervised and unsupervised—can obscure the ways these tools are employed to accomplish social science tasks.

Building on our experience developing and applying text as data methods in the social sciences, we emphasize a sequential, iterative, and inductive approach to research. Our experience has been that we learn the most in social science when we refine our concepts and measurements iteratively, improving our own understanding of definitions as we are exposed to new data. We also learn the most when we consider our evidence sequentially, confirming the results of prior work, then testing new hypotheses, and, finally, generating hypotheses for future work. Future studies continue the pattern, confirming the findings from prior studies, testing prior speculations, and generating new hypotheses. At the end of the process, the evidence is aggregated to summarize the results and to clarify what was learned. Importantly, this process doesn't happen within the context of a single article or book, but across a community of collaborators.

This inductive method provides a principled way to approach research that places a strong emphasis on an evolving understanding of the process under study. We call this understanding theory—explanations of the systematic facets of social process. This is an intentionally broad definition encompassing formal theory, political/sociological theory, and general subject-area expertise. At the core of this book is an argument that scholars can learn a great deal about human behavior from texts but that to do so requires an engagement with the context in which those texts are produced. A deep understanding of the social science context will enable researchers to ask more important and impactful questions, ensure that the measures they extract are valid, and be more attentive to the practical and ethical implications of their work.

We write this book now because the use of text data is at a critical point. As more scholars adopt text as data methods for their research, a guide is essential to explain how text as data work in the social sciences differs from its work in computer science. Without such a guide, researchers outside of computer science solving problems run the risk of applying the wrong algorithms, validating the wrong quantities, and ultimately making inferences not justified by the evidence they have acquired.

We also focus on texts because they are an excellent vehicle for learning about recent advances in machine learning. The argument that we make in this book about how to organize social science research applies beyond texts. Indeed, we view our approach as useful for social science generally, but particularly in any application where researchers are using large-scale data to discover new categories, measure their prevalence, and then to assess their relationships in the world.

1.1 How This Book Informs the Social Sciences

A central argument of this book is that the goal of text as data research differs from the goals of computer science work. Fortunately, this difference is not so great that many of the tools and ideas first developed in other fields cannot be applied to text as data problems. It does imply, however, that we have to think more carefully about what we learn from applying those models.

To help us make our case, consider the use of texts by political scientist Amy Catalinac (Catalinac, 2016a)—a path-breaking demonstration of how electoral district structure affects political candidates' behavior. We focus on this book because the texts are used clearly, precisely, and effectively to make a social science point, even though the algorithm used to conduct the analysis comes from a different discipline. And importantly, the method for validation used is distinctively social scientific and thorough.

Catalinac's work begins with a puzzle: why have Japanese politicians allocated so much more attention to national security and foreign policy after 1997, despite significant social, political, and government constraints on the use of military and foreign policy discussions put in place after World War II? Catalinac (2016a) argues that a 1994 reform in how Japanese legislators are elected explains the change because it fundamentally altered the *incentives* that politicians face. Before the 1994 reform, Japanese legislators were elected through a system where each district was represented by multiple candidates and each party would run several candidates in each district trying to get the majority of the seats. Because multiple candidates from the same party couldn't effectively compete with their co-partisans on ideological issues, representatives tried to secure votes by delivering the most pork—spending that has only local impact, such as for building a bridge—to the district as possible. The new post-1994 reform system eliminated multi-member districts and replaced them with a parallel system: single-member districts—where voters cast their ballot for a candidate—and representatives

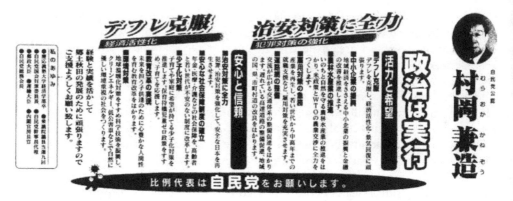

Figure 1.1. An example of a candidate manifesto of Kanezo Muraoka from 2003, Figure 3.7 from Catalinac (2016*a*).

for the whole country—where voters cast their ballot for a party and the elected officials are chosen from the party's list. This new system allowed the parties to impose stricter ideological discipline on their members and the choices of voters became less about the individual personalities and more about party platforms. Thus, the argument goes, the reform changed the legislators' *incentives*. Focusing on local issues like pork was now less advantageous than focusing on national issues like foreign policy.

The argument proceeds through iteration and induction. To begin understanding the effect of the change in electoral rules on electoral strategy, Catalinac collected an original dataset of 7,497 Japanese Diet candidate manifestos. The manifestos are nearly ideal data for her study: they are important to candidates and voters, under the control of candidates, and available for all candidates for all elections for a period before and after the shift in electoral rules. We discuss the principles for data collection in Chapter 4, but Catalinac's exemplary work shows that working with text data does not mean that we must opt for the most convenient data. Rather, Catalinac engaged in a painstaking data collection process to find the manifestos through archival visits and digitize them through manual transcription. This process alone took years.

With the data in hand, Catalinac uses an inductive approach to learn the categories in her data she needs to investigate her empirical puzzle: what elected officials are discussing when they run for office. Catalinac uses a well-known statistical model, *Latent Dirichlet Allocation* (LDA)—which we return to in Chapter 13—to discover an underlying set of topics and to measure the proportion of each manifesto that belongs to each topic. As Catalinac describes,

> Typically, the model is fit iteratively. The researcher sets some number of topics; runs the model; ascertains the nature of the topics outputted by reading the words and documents identified as having high probabilities of belonging to each of the topics; and decides whether or not those topics are substantively meaningful.... My approach was also iterative and guided by my hypotheses.
> (Catalinac, 2016*a*, p. 84)

As we describe in Chapter 4, discovery with text data does not mean that we begin with a blank slate. Catalinac's prior work, qualitative interviews, and expertise in Japenese politics helped to shape the discoveries she made in the text. We can bring this prior knowledge to bear in discovery; theory and hunches play a role in defining our categories, but so too does the data itself.

Catalinac uses the model fit from LDA to measure the prevalence of candidates' discussions of pork, policy, and other categories of interest. To establish which topics capture these categories, Catalinac engages in extensive validation. Importantly, her validations are not the validations most commonly conducted in computer science, where LDA originated. Those validations tend to focus on how LDA functions as a language model—that is, how well it is able to predict unseen words in a document. For Catalinac's purposes, it isn't important that the model can predict unseen words—she has all the words! Instead, her validations are designed to demonstrate that her model has uncovered an organization that is interesting and useful for her particular social scientific task: assessing how a change in the structure of districts affected the behavior of candidates and elected officials. Catalinac engages in two broad kinds of validation. First, she does an in-depth analysis of the particular topics that the model automatically discovers, reading both the high probability words the model assigns to the topic and the manifestos the model indicates are most aligned with each topic. This analysis assures the reader that her labels and interpretations of the computer-discovered topics are both valid and helpful for her social scientific task. Second, she shows that her measures align with well-known facts about Japanese politics. This step ensures that the measures that come from the manifestos are not idiosyncratic or reflecting a wildly different process than that studied in other work. It also provides further evidence that the labels Catalinac assigns to texts are valid reflections of the content of those texts.

Of course, Catalinac is not interested in just categorizing the texts for their own sake—she wants to use the categories assigned to the texts as a source of data to learn about the world. In particular, she wants to estimate the causal effect of the 1994 electoral reform on the shift in issues discussed by candidates when they are running. To do this, she uses her validated model and careful research design to pursue her claim that the electoral reform causes average candidates to shift from a focus on pork to a focus on national security. This is a particularly challenging setting for causal inference, because the reform changes across all districts at the same time. After showing that, in practice, there is a substantial increase in the discussion of national security following the 1994 reforms, Catalinac moves to rule out alternative explanations. She shows that there is no sudden influx of candidates that we would expect to discuss national security. Nor, she argues, does this increase in the importance of national security merely reflect an ideological shift in the parties. And she argues that there is no evidence that voters suddenly want candidates who prioritize national security.

Our brief examination of Catalinac (2016a) reveals how sequence, iteration, and induction can lead to substantively interesting and theoretically important research. Further, Catalinac illustrates a point that we will return to throughout the book, that validations for text as data research are necessary and look quite different from validations in computer science. Rather than a focus on prediction, text as data researchers are much more interested in how well their models provide insights into concepts of interest, how well measurement tools sort documents according to those rules, and how well the assumptions needed for accurate causal inference or prediction are met. These points travel well beyond political science, to other social scientists studying human behavior including sociology (DiMaggio, 2015; Evans and Aceves, 2016; Franzosi, 2004), economics (Gentzkow, Kelly, and Taddy, 2019), psychology (Schwartz et al., 2013), and law (Livermore and Rockmore, 2019).

1.2   How This Book Informs the Digital Humanities

Our view of how to apply text as data methods was developed and refined through our experience with social science research. But we will argue that our approach to text as data can provide useful insights into other fields as well. In parallel to the meteoric rise of text as data methods within the social sciences, there has been rapidly growing interest in using computational tools to study literature, history, and the humanities more generally. This burgeoning field, termed *Digital Humanities*, shares much in common with text as data in the social sciences in that it draws on computational tools to answer classic questions in the field.

The use of text as data methods has drawn considerable funding and has already made impressive contributions to the study of literature (Jockers, 2013; Piper, 2018; Underwood, 2019). Computational tools have been used to study the nature of genres (Rybicki and Eder, 2011), poems (Long and So, 2016), the contours of ideas (Berry and Fagerjord, 2017), and many other things (Moretti, 2013). To reach their conclusions, scholars working in this area follow many of the same procedures and use similar tools to those in the social sciences. They represent their texts using numbers and then apply models or algorithms that originate in other fields to reach substantive conclusions.

Even though scholars in the Digital Humanities (DH) come from a humanistic tradition, we will show how the goals of their analysis fit well within the framework of our book. And as a result, our argument about how to use text as data methods to make valid inferences will cover many of the applications of computational tools in the humanistic fields. A major difference between DH and the social sciences is that digital humanists are often interested in inferences about the particular text that is being studied, rather than the text as an indicator of some other, larger process. As a result, digital humanities have thus far tended to focus on the discovery and measurement steps of the research process, while devoting less attention to making causal inferences or predictions. Digital humanists use their large corpora to make new and important discoveries about organizations in their texts. They then use tools to measure the prevalence of those quantities, to describe how the prevalence of the characteristics has changed over time, or to measure how well defined a category is over time.

As with any field that rises so suddenly, there has been considerable dissent about the prospect of the digital humanities. Some of this dissent lies well outside of the scope of our book and focuses on the political and epistemological consequences of opening up the humanities to computational tools. Instead we will engage with other critiques of digital humanities that stipulate to the "rules" laid out in computational papers. These critics argue that the digital humanities is not capable of achieving the inferential goals it lays out and therefore the analysis is doomed from the start. A recent and prominent objection comes from Da (2019), who summarizes her own argument as,

> In a nutshell the problem with computational literary analysis as it stands is that what is robust is obvious (in the empirical sense) and what is not obvious is not robust, a situation not easily overcome given the nature of literary data and the nature of statistical inquiry.   (Da, 2019, p. 45)

Da (2019)'s critique goes to the heart of how results are evaluated and relies heavily on procedures and best practices imported from computer science (as does, it is worth noting, much of the work she is critiquing). As we have argued above, directly importing rules from other fields to studying texts in new domains can be suboptimal. When we directly import the recommendations from computer science and statistics to text-based inferences in the humanities or social sciences we might make problematic inferences, recommendations that are misguided, or misplaced assessments about the feasibility of computational analysis for a field.

Yet Da's critique is a useful foil for illuminating a key feature of our approach that departs from much of the work in the digital humanities. In Chapter 2, we offer six core principles which reflect a broader "radically agnostic" view of text as data methods. We reject the idea that models of text should be optimized to recover one true underlying, inherent organization in the texts—because, we argue, no one such organization exists. In much of the digital humanities, and Da's critique, there is an implicit assumption that the statistical models or algorithms are uncovering an ideal categorization of the data that exists outside of the research question asked and the models estimated. This approach is in tension with much of the theoretical work in the humanities, but seemingly arises because this is a motivating assumption in much of computer science and statistics, where it provides a convenient fiction for evaluating model performance.

On our account, organizations are useful if they help us to uncover a categorization of the data that is useful for answering a research question. If two models disagree on how to categorize texts, there is no sense in determining which one is any more "right" than the other. We would not, for example, want to argue that an organization of texts based on the expression of positive or negative emotion is more right than an organization based on the topic of the text. Rather, we will argue that some organizations are more useful than others for addressing a particular question. For example, we might argue that a model is particularly useful for studying genre, because it provides an organization that leads the researcher to an insight about the trajectory of books that would have been impossible otherwise. Once you have an organization, you can find the best *measurement* of that particular categorization. You can then test the measurement with extensive *validation*. But because there is a multiplicity of useful and valid organizations, a method that does not provide a "robust" answer to how texts should be organized will be less concerning than critics argue. What becomes important is the credibility of the validations once an organization has been selected and its utility in answering the research question.

We also will emphasize throughout our book that text as data methods should not displace the careful and thoughtful humanist. And there is no sense in which inferences should be made in the field of digital humanities without the reader directly involved. This emphasis on using computational methods to improve inferences will help allay some concerns about the role of digital humanities scholarship. The computational tools should not replace traditional modes of scholarship. When used well, computational tools should help provide broader context for scholars, illuminate patterns that are otherwise impossible to identify manually, and generally amplify—rather than replace—the human efforts of the scholars using them.

1.3 How This Book Informs Data Science in Industry and Government

Computational tools have also revolutionized how companies use text as data in their products and how government uses text to represent the views of constituents. The applications of these tools are nearly endless in industry. Companies use messages that users post on their website to better target advertisements, to make suggestions about new content, or to help individuals connect with elected officials. In government, there is the chance to use text as data methods to better represent the views of constituents publicly commenting on proposed rule changes at bureaucratic agencies or expressing their views to elected officials.

The stakes are high when applying text as data methods to industrial-scale problems. Perhaps the most politically sensitive application of text as data methods is content moderation: the attempt by social media companies (and sometimes governments) to regulate the content that is distributed on their platform. In the wake of the Russian misinformation campaign in the 2016 US election, social media companies faced increased pressure to identify and remove misinformation from their sites, to report on the effect of misinformation that occurred during the campaign, and to demonstrate that new procedures were fair and did not disproportionately target particular ideologies. The tools used to identify this content will appear throughout this book and will draw on a similar set of computational resources that we introduce.

Beyond the questions of political sensitivity, the application of text as data methods will also be high stakes because of the large amounts of money that will be spent based on the recommendations of the systems. For example, trading firms now use computational tools to guide their investments or to quickly learn about content from central bankers. Text as data methods also help drive advertising decisions that represent a massive share of the economy. Getting these decisions "right," then, is important for many business practices.

Our book is useful for data scientists, because these tasks are inherently social science tasks. Moderating content to suppress misinformation or hate speech is fundamentally a measurement task. When companies decide which ads will cause the largest increase in sales for their clients, they are engaged in causal inference. And when traders make decisions based on the content of documents or statements from officials, they are engaged in prediction. Recognizing the omnipresence of social science within industry is essential, because many data scientists receive their professional training outside of the social sciences. These fields do an excellent job of providing the computational tools necessary for working with the massive datasets that companies create, but often fail to expose researchers to core design principles behind the tasks those tools are built for.

This book, and indeed its very organizational structure, is designed to remove focus from the individual models and computational tools and refocus on the differences between tasks like discovery and measurement or prediction and causal inference. Identifying these differences is essential, because the different tasks imply that different models should be used, different information sets should be conditioned upon, and different assumptions are needed to justify conclusions.

1.4 A Guide to This Book

Our book spans fields within the social sciences, digital humanities, computer science, industry, and government. To convey our view on how to work with text as data in these disparate fields, we provide a different organization of our book. While most computational social science books organize the manuscript around algorithms, in this book we organize the book around tasks. We focus on tasks to emphasize what is different when social scientists approach text as data research. This also enables us to explain how the same algorithm can be used to accomplish different tasks and how validations for an algorithm might differ, depending on the goal at hand when applying that algorithm.

We organize our book around five key tasks: representation, discovery, measurement, prediction, and causal inference. Underlying this task-based focus is a set of principles of text analysis that we outline in Chapter 2. There, we explain our *radically agnostic* approach to text as data inference. We generally reject the view that there is an underlying structure that statistical models applied to text are recovering. Rather, we view statistical models as useful (and incomplete) summaries of the text documents. This view provides us with important insights into how to validate models, how to assess models that provide different organizations, and the role of humans within the research process.

In Part 2 we discuss selection and representation: the process of acquiring texts and then representing the content quantitatively. When selecting texts, basic principles of sample selection matter a great deal, even though there is a temptation to select content that is most conveniently available. When representing texts, we explain how different representations provide different useful insights into the texts and set the stage for future models in the book.

Part 3 introduces a series of models for discovery. By discovery we mean the use of models to uncover and refine conceptualizations, or organizations of the world. We show how a wide array of models can help suggest different organizations that can help researchers gain new insights into the world. We begin with methods used to uncover words that are indicative of differences between how two groups speak. These methods can be used to compare groups of documents—for example, legislators from two different political parties—or to help label categorizations inferred from other inductive methods. We then discuss some computer-assisted techniques for discovery, including models for partitioning data that exhaustively assign each observation to a single category. We then explain how clustering methods can be extended to admixture models, which represent each document as proportionally assigned to different categories. Finally, we describe methods for embedding documents into lower-dimensional spaces, which can shed light on underlying continuous variables in the data.

Part 4 describes our approach to measurement: assessing the prevalence of documents within a set of categories or assessing their location along a predetermined spectrum. We explain how to combine human judgment with machine learning methods to extend human annotations coded in a training set to a much larger dataset. When performing measurement, we explain how a discovery method can be repurposed to measure a category of interest. We include an extensive discussion of how to validate each of these measures, no matter what method produced them.

Building on the concepts and measures we have described, Part 5 explains how to apply the methods for prediction and causal inference. First, we describe how to use text as data methods to make predictions about how the world will be in the future. We discuss different types of predictive tasks and highlight how the threats to inference may vary with the setting. Next, we describe how to use the measures from texts as either the outcome or the intervention variable to make causal inferences. We explain the particular concerns that can emerge when text methods are used and provide a set of tools for assessing when a stringent set of assumptions is met.

1.5 Conclusion

There is immense promise with text as data research. With large amounts of data, complicated models, and custom measures, there is also the possibility of using these methods and getting the research wrong. Text is complicated and meaning is often subtle. The risk is that if scholars overclaim on what text methods can do, they will undermine the case for using text methods.

Our book is intended as a guide for researchers about what is feasible with text as data methods and what is infeasible. We want to help readers learn about the immense set of tasks that text as data methods can help them accomplish. At the same time, we also want to help our readers to recognize the limits of text methods. We start out on this goal in the next chapter, where we articulate the basic principles that will guide our approach to text as data research.

CHAPTER 2

Social Science Research and Text Analysis

Social scientists are increasingly using computational approaches to analyze large collections of documents.[1] This explosion of data and the new methods created to analyze it is one of the most exciting recent developments in the social sciences. These transformations in research have made it possible for social scientists to develop and test theories in ways that previously would have been infeasible.

In order to analyze these new data sources, we have found that we have to reconsider the standard deductive approach social scientists take to developing and testing claims. The most common process in the social sciences—evident in published research and conveyed to graduate students in research seminars—is that before viewing or collecting any data, authors must have a clear theory from which they derive a set of testable propositions. In this linear view, researchers must somehow a priori know the concepts that structure their variables of interest; then, they use a strategy to measure the prevalence of those concepts; finally, they develop a set of hypotheses and a research design to test the observable implications from their stated theory (King, Keohane, and Verba, 1994). This understanding of the research process is so prevalent that it is often synonymous with good research. An extreme version of this approach, particularly prominent in the early years of the twenty-first century, supposes that the theory and observable implications are determined *before* examining any original data that are collected for a project and that this theory can provide the microfoundations for model parameters that are otherwise indeterminate. Achen (2002) summarizes this (at the time) "new style" when he says that "the new style insists on starting from a formal model plus white noise errors" (Achen, 2002, 441). This approach encourages researchers to first use theory to create a formal (game-theoretic) model, next to extract predictions, and then collect data to test those predictions (Granato and Scioli, 2004, 315). Indeed, each of us has written several papers that follow this research model.

This standard deductive approach has many virtues both inside and outside academia and can be particularly powerful when there are known or established theories that have testable implications. It encourages analysts to reflect on their beliefs about the mechanistic processes that underlie the phenomenon they seek to understand. If followed explicitly, the deductive approach helps to reduce false discoveries

---

[1] Parts of the introduction of this chapter and Section 2.5 are drawn from Grimmer, Roberts, and Stewart (2021).

that can occur as the result of researcher discretion. This is the thought process behind pre-registration of hypotheses and analysis procedures before running an experiment.

However, forcing researchers to use data to test theories that were developed before the data arrived also has substantial weaknesses. Scholars in the social sciences have acknowledged the importance of more inductive forms of analysis in qualitative research, including full-cycle research design, grounded theory, and nested analysis (Lieberman, 2005; Glaser and Strauss, 1967; Chatman and Flynn, 2005). In our experience, researchers often discover new directions, questions, and measures within their quantitative data as well. If the standard deductive procedure is followed too closely and data is only collected at the very last minute, researchers might miss the opportunity to refine their concepts, develop new theories, and assess new hypotheses. A great deal of learning happens *while* analyzing data. Even when a research project starts with a clear question of interest, it frequently ends with a substantially different focus. This is what happened with one of our own projects, an analysis of Chinese social media by Gary King, Jennifer Pan, and Margaret Roberts (King, Pan, and Roberts, 2013). The initial study sought to validate an automated text analysis method, ReadMe. It was only after examining the data and understanding what it could measure that the authors were able to iteratively refine their research to focus on a different question: what is the strategy behind the Chinese government's censorship of social media? Had the researchers rejected an *inductive* approach and refused to alter their question after looking at the data, they would have missed exploring an important phenomenon: censorship.

If adopted too restrictively, the deductive approach to research leads analysts to miss important opportunities to discover interesting questions and measurement strategies from the data. Aversion to induction may also cause scholars to avoid new theory building at the end of a series of empirical tests, for fear that it may be viewed as post-hoc justification to build a model based on the results in a paper.

Anecdotally, we find that many researchers inductively discover interesting patterns and theories in data, but because the deductive style of research is so widely accepted, discussions of how they made their discoveries are rarely emphasized in published articles. Regardless of how the research was actually conducted, standard practice of writing articles begins by stating the theory, its observable implications, and the measurement strategy; then the dataset is introduced. This poses a problem for inference if a researcher—even unintentionally—presents a theory as if it is being applied to a fresh dataset when in fact the same data is being used both to develop and to test the theory of interest.

Not discussing the role of induction in research hinders our ability to improve the methods of discovery and measurement. This is problematic because scholars are likely able to improve their theories if they embrace the notation that they are learning inductively from their data. As we explain below, there is nothing inherently wrong with an inductive approach in research. In fact, a lot of important learning we do in our life and in science is inductive. Acknowledging that we regularly engage in induction to refine the methods of discovery and then rigorously test these discoveries would greatly improve how we conduct social science. It would also allow us to avoid missteps in using induction in research, for example using the same dataset to both develop and test a theory.

Rather than continue entertaining the fiction of the standard deductive model of social science research, in this book we emphasize the recursive nature of the research process and explain how thinking iteratively is the best approach for analyzing text as data (Figure 2.1). As in the standard model, we begin with an interesting question,

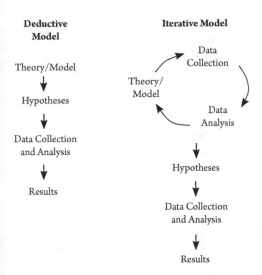

Figure 2.1. Flowcharts for the standard deductive model of research (left) as compared to the iterative model of research (right).

insight, or specific dataset. But rather than suppose that our theories are completely developed before looking at data, we emphasize that iteratively examining data and refining theories help us to clarify our theoretical insights. After this inductive process, the researcher must then obtain new data on which to test the refined theories. This new dataset ensures that researchers avoid the concerns of p-hacking, forking paths, and researcher degrees of freedom that social scientists have been trained to associate with inductive research.

The need for a more inductive model of social science research is not new; nor is it specific to text. However, because of the high informational content and richness of text data, an inductive approach can be helpful at the early stages of a research project—when scholars are formulating their intuitions—as well as at the later stages of the research process. Furthermore, by explicitly acknowledging discovery as a part of the research process, we can design text analysis methodologies that help us pursue this specific goal as well as the goals of measurement and testing.

We explain how methods to analyze text as data can contribute to inference at three stages of the research process: discovery, measurement, and inference. In the last of these, inference, we include causal inference and prediction. Before turning to each stage in detail, we want to emphasize that a research project need not proceed through all stages to be useful. For example, a study that suggests a new way of looking at the world or a new measure for a well-known concept may be very useful. Or, a study that uses off-the-shelf concepts and measures to estimate an important causal effect or make a prediction clearly advances the goals of social science research. And, as we explain below, research need not proceed sequentially from discovery to measurement and to analysis. Rather, studies might move across the different stages of the research process in various orders. While we present the research process in the order of discovery, measurement, and inference, an inferential task may cause us to reconsider our measures or discover a completely new research question.

2.1 Discovery

At the earliest stages of the research process, analysts are focused on *discovery*. The primary goal during discovery is to develop the research question. This includes the task of deciding what you want to measure from the data and your goal of inference. Deciding what you want to measure from the data involves developing a *conceptualization*—a way of organizing the world—that helps us make sense of the complex word we live in. The conceptualization will help you simplify the highly complex world that we live in to study one or two specific aspects of it. For example, say you wanted to study a set of social media posts. What aspects of these posts are important and interesting to you for your analysis? Do you want to measure their topical content, sentiment, readability, informativeness, or civility? Or is there another important dimension of social media posts that you are unaware of, that might be captured by a different concept or way of organizing the posts? The issue of which concepts you want to use as elements of your analysis are worked out at the discovery stage.

Text analysis helps us develop conceptualizations by pointing out new ways to organize a collection of documents. This organization can come from identifying clusters—that is, groups of text that are similar to each other and distinct from other groups. The organization can also come from identifying an underlying spectrum within a collection of documents—a low-dimensional summary of the data in which texts that are close to each other are more similar to each other than texts that are farther apart. And text analysis can aid in understanding what these clusters mean by identifying words that characterize and describe different groups of texts. Of course, not all of these new organizations will be useful, and researchers will have to use what they know about the context of the data and current theories in the literature to distinguish between more and less useful concepts and ways of slicing the data. But by pointing out new ways in which documents can be organized, text analysis can prompt social scientists to read the texts differently and draw connections between texts that they otherwise would have missed. These conceptualizations can be used later on in the research process for description, causal inference, and prediction.

Discovery is often left out of the standard quantitative research model, even though it is an important part of every research project. Methods for discovery have been underdeveloped, partly because research questions can come from so many different origins—the results of a previous analysis, an opportunity to study a new dataset, or even a research mistake that uncovers a new direction. Qualitative methodologists have developed techniques like grounded theory that are explicitly designed to facilitate discovery from new data (Glaser and Strauss, 1967). Acknowledging the role of discovery in the research process enables the development of methodologies that facilitate future discoveries and gives license to scholars to explicitly describe the discovery stage of their research in publications.

2.2 Measurement

With concepts in hand—from a discovery stage, from a theoretical model, or from intuition—scholars often want to *measure* the prevalence of particular concepts in their data or to characterize where individuals or texts fall on a spectrum. For example, Jones, Wilkerson, and Baumgartner (2009) were interested in learning the amount of legislation that falls within a broad range of policy agendas. Two of the most successful data gathering projects, the Policy Agendas Project and the Comparative Agendas Project, measure the prevalence of different topics in party manifestos around the world. Other projects assign documents to categories. For example, scholars are interested in the effect of negative campaign advertisements on election turnout (Ansolabehere and Iyengar, 1995). To explore this, scholars have to develop reliable and accurate measures of negativity in advertisements.

The prevalence of text data and the preponderance of methods for measurement have led to an explosion of interest in measuring quantities from text in increasingly diverse ways and from collections of increasing size. Novel and larger sources of text mean that the measures are often granular, providing insights into behavior otherwise difficult to detect. Measurement is the essential ingredient for description: an important goal in itself that is too often dismissed in social science research. If done well, description provides valuable summaries of the data, which in turn may inform theories, provide the measures necessary for causal inferences, or characterize the state of the world. To accomplish these goals, researchers have to demonstrate that their method of measurement does indeed describe the concept or behavior they want to measure—that is, they have to validate their measures and provide evidence that the described quantities are relevant to the theoretical quantity at hand. If the measure does not reflect the concept, this is an indication that we should refine the measure, or in some cases through the process of measurement redefine the concept. In either case, the resulting measure should reflect as closely as possible a concept of theoretical interest and importance.

2.3 Inference

Once a concept is discovered and the measures are constructed, researchers can use those measures to make *predictions* about events in the future or *causal inferences* about the effect of an intervention. For example, researchers might use texts to forecast values of stock prices or the locations where political conflict is likely. These are predictive questions because they ask how the information available today helps us to understand what will happen tomorrow. Researchers might also assess the causal effect of going negative in a campaign—an intervention—on the news coverage about the campaign. Or they might be interested in how certain types of political content affect users' engagement in online forums. These are fundamentally causal questions because they ask how the world will change in response to some intervention. Repeatedly in this book, we will pay close attention to whether we are using prediction or causal inference in our analysis, and this will be important because we will use very different approaches to research design in each case.

2.4 Social Science as an Iterative and Cumulative Process

Our experience is that paying attention to where we are in the research process—whether we are making a discovery about concepts of interest or measuring the prevalence of those concepts, and then estimating their effect or making a prediction about the world—is crucial to fully leveraging the potential of text data. Importantly, in the process of discovery, iterating between data analysis and theory will help us develop more insightful research questions and concepts of interest. While working with text data, researchers will discover new typologies and concepts from the texts that can be usefully integrated into social science theories. After identifying these new concepts, classifying documents into the categories associated with these concepts forces researchers to be attentive to their measurement strategies. And both of these exercises—discovery and measurement—are crucial for making good inferences, whether they are descriptive, causal, or predictive.

But even studies with the best research design should not have the final say on a research question. Throughout this book, we also pay particular attention to the *cumulative* nature of the research process. After a study is published, researchers can use the findings of that study to redefine the concepts or question of interest, refine the measurement strategy, or replicate the prediction or causal inference on a new set of data. Because the social world is constantly evolving, this cumulative nature of social science research should also be in the forefront of our minds while conducting research.

In fact, we think being aware of this iterative and cumulative research process is so useful for text analysis that we organize the book around the steps of this process. In this book we will introduce new methods in order to explain how they can be used to accomplish tasks at each phase of the research process. This is a departure from how other works describing text analysis techniques are organized, including journal-length overviews that some of us have written (Grimmer and Stewart, 2013). In most settings, they are organized around the technical capabilities of different models, such as how the model is trained and whether the model suggests a statistical data generation process. These organizations are important and throughout the book we will explain how various approaches that we introduce fit within the more traditional typologies of text analysis methods.

We choose to organize this book around the stages of the research process because the key decisions about which method to apply to a text collection, how to interpret a method's output, and how to validate the product of a method all depend on where we are in the research process. In other words, models can serve multiple purposes. For example, methods that can be used to classify documents—a typical measurement task—may also be used to discover words and phrases that characterize a group of documents—a discovery task. Methods like Latent Dirichlet Allocation (LDA) that were designed to *discover* an organization can be repurposed to quickly *measure* a concept of interest. Crucially though, the particular task or goal of a method strongly shapes the way the methods are interpreted, validated, and deployed. We will treat the same statistical model very differently in the context of discovery than in measurement because the *task* is distinct.

More broadly, we organize the book around the components of the research process because while the *tools* used to analyze texts will change, the *tasks* will remain unchanged. If we attempted to make this book a comprehensive list of the state-of-the-art methods, it would be obsolete before it was in print. Instead, we focus on the stages of the research process because social scientists who understand how to perform each stage will be able to adopt new techniques as they come along.

In this chapter, we introduce six core principles that guide how we analyze text data to make social science inferences. In part, the principles follow from basic statistical properties and from insights into how research designs developed for non-text data perform when researchers are using text data. But the insights also come from our experience conducting dozens of text analysis projects across numerous academic, industrial, and nonprofit settings. As a meta point about how we view research, then, our principles for how to conduct text analysis research were learned inductively.

2.5 An Agnostic Approach to Text Analysis

The six core principles that we advance reflect our *agnostic* approach to using text analysis to make social science inferences. By agnostic, we mean that our general view is that in many instances there are no "true" values for us to target with text-as-data methods, or no one best model that can be used for all applications of a corpus. The consequences of this view are numerous, profound, and extend to almost all the tasks that we discuss in this book. For example, our agnostic view provides guidance on how we evaluate the quality of our findings from all our models, it informs how we choose between models to perform the same basic task, and it suggests when it is reasonable to aggregate findings for a more accurate model and when model aggregation is likely to obscure the key content of interest.

Our agnostic view contrasts most sharply with a structural approach to text analysis. As the name suggests, a structural approach posits that there is an underlying "true" data-generating process, even in the discovery phase. The clearest and most influential statement of the structural view is found in Denny and Spirling (2018), an insightful paper on how to think about different ways to preprocess texts. As we will see, if we assume that there is some underlying true model or organization of texts, problems like model selection are much more straightforward. But this approach will often force us to make assumptions that we might find uncomfortable. For example, we may have to assume that there is a true underlying set of categories or a "right" organization of our data, which might makes little sense in some applications.

To see why, consider a simple example: suppose we want to organize campaign advertisements for a study of how political candidates present themselves to the public. For some applications, we might be interested in the tone of the advertisement—whether the advertisement is positive or negative. Other times we might be interested in the topic of the advertisement. And still other times we might find that a nested conceptualization—with coarse topics comprised of more granular organizations of the text—is most useful to our question.

There is no sense in which any of these organizations are "correct" unless we have more information *beforehand* about the goal of the research question. Critically, text methods can help researchers to discover and identify different organizations, which in turn could lead to new research questions, hypotheses, and insights into political campaigns. So, during the discovery phase, we might prefer methods that fail to be "consistent" or "unbiased" because they yield the most useful insights for researchers.

Once the research question is defined and the researcher is performing measurement, we can assess how accurate a method is at recovering the specific concept of interest to the researcher. Because there were many different things about the document that the researcher could have chosen to measure, we do not assume there is a single model that captures a true data generating process, but hopefully there are options that help us capture what we need for our research question. In other words, we are agnostic about which particular model is used for measurement, as long as the model can accurately and reliably measure the concept of interest. This perspective leads us to place a heavy emphasis on validations that provide evidence that our models measure what we claim they measure. These validations often involve careful reading of the documents, codebooks with category definitions, and/or application-specific criteria, rather than model-fitting diagnostics, because, consistent with our agnostic perspective, the model is only a useful approximation.

We want to highlight that the contrast with the structural view is not intended to detract from the important work in this area. We make this distinction to highlight a key difference in how text analysis techniques are presented in this book. We view the structural approach as useful and important for social science. We simply disagree that there is one "best" set of concepts for a corpus text or underlying organization of text that we should try to approximate.

In the next section, we step through an example of a research program and illustrate the separate steps of discovery, measurement, and inference. We then step back and offer six principles that will guide our discussion of text analysis throughout the remainder of the book.

2.6 Discovery, Measurement, and Causal Inference: How the Chinese Government Censors Social Media

In our experience, research programs rarely emerge as a straightforward product, even though they are often reported that way in papers. While papers portray thoughtful questions and specific hypotheses as emerging after careful non-data-driven contemplation and observation about the world, the reality is that those questions and hypotheses often emerge from an initial inspection of data. This inspection is usually guided by substantial background knowledge and preexisting theories of how the world works, which inform the discovery of a theoretical tension or empirical puzzle when looking at data. Such an examination can bring to light a previously unknown feature or pattern, which the researcher then seeks to explain. Text data is particularly amenable to such examinations because reading documents allows for deep explorations of the phenomena they embody.

In order to highlight how different tasks come together, we describe the development of King, Pan, and Roberts (2013) (KPR hereafter), which showcases the value of not adhering to a standard research process when using text data. In this article, the authors successfully use an iterative and sequential process to yield theoretically interesting insights. KPR's initial research agenda was to extend tools of automated text analysis for the Chinese language. To this end, KPR downloaded millions of posts from more than 1,400 social media websites. In doing so, the researchers returned to the original web pages of the posts using URLs logged in their data to better understand the context of the social media posts. When they returned to the sites, however, they noticed something surprising: many of the posts were now missing. In their place, KPR now found notices proclaiming that the content had been removed—an indication of government censorship.

By exploring their data, KPR had accidentally stumbled upon a new research question—what was the target of government censorship? They had also discovered one way to organize the texts: they were either censored or not censored. In their subsequent analysis, they drew on their general knowledge of the phenomenon of censorship in authoritarian regimes. While the question itself certainly could have occurred to a researcher who was not in possession of one million social media posts, what KPR's initial data exploration revealed was an approach to studying government censorship.

The question that KPR were ultimately interested in was causal: what types of social media posts caused government censorship? To generate a hypothesis, they again turned to the data. At first, they grouped posts by topics that they expected to have varying degrees of sensitivity. But the topics did not have much variation in censorship. A computer-assisted examination of censorship over time gave them the impression that censorship rates tended to be much higher for posts associated with collective action events in China. This hypothesis suggested a different unit of analysis—the event—and a different key quantity of interest to measure: whether or not the event was related to collective action. Critically, this exploration stage gave KPR reason to believe that other conceptualizations would be less useful for answering their causal question. Not only topic, but sentiment (whether the post was critical or supportive of the government) also did not seem to explain censorship decisions. If they were right, then the decision to censor a text would be unrelated to whether the post was critical of the government or not and instead would depend on whether the post related to a protest event.

This process illustrates how KPR used a subset of their data and statistical methods to discover their question of interest, generate a hypothesis, and formulate the implied conceptualization. This is what we mean by *discovery*. We will describe a general process to facilitate discovery in Part 3: Discovery.

KPR then set out to *measure* the texts according to their conceptualizations. That is, they imposed a particular organization and then sought to assess the presence and prevalence of their categories. KPR identified 87 events based on bursts of social media posts in 85 different topic areas. They then manually categorized whether or not each burst was related to collective action. Measuring whether a post was censored was straightforward, based on their own records of the post. It was less straightforward, however, to measure the post's sentiment toward the government. As often happens with social science research, their goal was not to characterize each individual document's sentiment, but rather to characterize the proportion of documents that were critical or supportive within the categories censored and not censored. For this task, they used a supervised learning algorithm—ReadMe (Hopkins and King, 2010), which we cover in Part 4: Measurement—to measure whether censored posts were supportive or critical of the government. Specifically, KPR sampled posts and hand-labeled them as critical or supportive of the regime. They then used ReadMe to extrapolate from the hand-labeled documents to the entire collection of posts to measure the proportion of documents that were supportive of the government.

With the measurement in hand, KPR now turned to the task of estimating a social science causal effect of interest: the average effect of a post being about collective action on the probability that the post is censored. They also wanted to estimate the average effect of sentiment on the probability of censorship.

KPR found that posts in bursts about collective action events were censored at an extremely high rate—strong evidence that the government was censoring posts about events related to public protest. They also found that the government's decision to censor posts was essentially unrelated to whether the post supported the government. Their conclusions provide evidence that the government's censorship rules were not designed to suppress online dissent against the regime but were intended to avoid mass protest. Their study also provides an example of how text can be used to make a causal inference. In Part 5: Inference, we describe a general approach for causal inferences with texts, including when text is the intervention, outcome, or confounder.

In King, Pan, and Roberts (2013), KPR make a case based on observational data that censorship focuses on collective action. However, KPR's observational data necessarily excluded posts that were automatically censored and never posted. Further, because they could not manipulate the subject of the post directly, there remained the possibility that discussion of collective action is not the property of the text that is causing the censorship. The ability to randomly assign the intervention of interest (in this case, the subject of the post) was crucial for capturing the full censorship process and for making the most credible causal inferences. Thus, KPR produced a second study, King, Pan, and Roberts (2014), that used a randomized field experiment to provide further evidence for their theory of censorship. They created accounts on one hundred social media sites across China and submitted text to these sites, randomly varying 1) whether the text discussed protest events or events not related to protests and 2) whether the post was critical or supportive of the government. These experimental results produced the same conclusion as the observational results, providing further verification that protest-related topics were causing censorship.

KPR's insights into the Chinese government's strategy on removing dangerous speech began with a completely different research question related to automated text analysis. But this does not mean that their research design is overfit, atheoretical, or devoid of usefulness to social science. Importantly, their initial exploration of the data was based on a subset of that data. This ensured that KPR would have the opportunity to demonstrate that they were right or wrong by analyzing new data where a different pattern might occur. Also noteworthy is the important role theory plays in KPR's research design. They began with a simple theoretical account of why the Chinese government censors certain posts. That theory led them to pose a new question that emerged from their data. Their initial work inspired a second study which sought to reinforce theoretical claims with data collected in a more controlled laboratory-like environment. Finally, while KPR did not solve or test a formal model of government censorship in their articles, their results have inspired other researchers to create new formal, theoretical models that seek to explain and contextualize KPR's findings (Chen, Pan, and Xu, 2016; Lorentzen, 2014). Importantly, the research program of KPR didn't appear in a single paper; it was developed cumulatively over multiple studies and extended through work by a broader community of scholars.

Using KPR's experience as a reference, in this chapter we describe the research process when using text as data. While we focus on decisions that must be made when working with text data, our argument is more general and illuminates one model of how empirical social science can proceed.

2.7   Six Principles of Text Analysis

We offer six principles to guide the use of text analysis. Table 2.1 provides a statement of each principle, which we then detail in the referenced sections below.

2.7.1   SOCIAL SCIENCE THEORIES AND SUBSTANTIVE KNOWLEDGE ARE ESSENTIAL FOR RESEARCH DESIGN

The fundamental goal of social science is to develop theories that explain how the social world works. To do this, researchers use substantive knowledge and empirical evidence to develop and refine their theories. We understand "theory" as a broad term that refers to explanations of systematic facets of social science processes. Theory can

Table 2.1. Key Principles for Text Analysis

1) Social science theories and substantive knowledge are essential for research design. (Section 2.7.1)
2) Text analysis does not replace humans—it augments them. (Section 2.7.2)
3) Building, refining, and testing social science theories requires iteration and cumulation. (Section 2.7.3)
4) Text analysis methods distill generalizations from language. (Section 2.7.4)
5) The best method depends on the task. (Section 2.7.5)
6) Validations are essential and depend on the theory and the task. (Section 2.7.6)

be expressed in many ways, including as formal mathematical models or a written sentence. Theory is important to the research process because it determines what data are relevant, how to interpret results, and why the results are important for understanding the world.

To see the role of theoretical thinking, it is useful to begin at the start of a research project. In some instances, scholars are building on a rich theoretical literature that has already defined basic concepts and generated hypotheses. For example, an extensive literature has examined the effects of negative campaign advertisements. In this literature, the definition of "negative advertisement" is understood as advertisements that cast opponents in unfavorable terms. Researchers use this categorization to understand how negative advertisements affect various dimensions of voter behavior as well as the behavior of other candidates. In this situation, theory explains how to measure a concept of interest and suggests hypotheses that should be empirically investigated by positing that "negative advertisements" have measurably different effects than other types of advertisements.

In other instances, however, scholars are investigating topics where the theoretical concepts are much less precise or the research question has not yet been articulated clearly. This is how KPR started their research project. For example, the study of social media in China was a relatively new field when KPR began studying it in 2009. KPR quickly developed a general topic of interest: how is public opinion expressed in authoritarian China? There is a rich literature on how citizens in repressive regimes express their political preferences, but that literature offers only limited guidance when attempting to understand how citizens engage in social media, KPR's data of interest. Because of this ambiguity, KPR used text analysis techniques to explore a subset of their data to help them understand broad themes in the online posts.

Interpreting the output of those initial exploratory models—the categories of text that the models identified and the trends they uncovered—in a way that is useful for research requires thinking about the incentives actors face when posting to social media, how the government constrains what social media companies can do, and the online culture in China. This is where theory and substantive knowledge come in. KPR used their understanding from the academic literature of the Chinese government behavior with their theoretical understanding of authoritarian governments' positions on public expression to come up with hypotheses that explained the patterns in their data.

Furthermore, theory and substance were essential for KPR's discovery that they had a dataset for studying how censorship occurs in China. When validating and interpreting their first models, KPR realized that some of the posts were no longer available. After ensuring that they had not erroneously stored the URLs, KPR recognized they had captured the Chinese government's practice of censoring social media posts. There is a clear sense in which the statistical and algorithmic tools made it possible to develop this dataset. But it is also the case that the authors had to be attentive to the substance of their problem—they had to know about the practice of censorship, how it could be detected, and why it was important for understanding public opinion and expression.

KPR's example shows that even the most massive collections of text analyzed with the most sophisticated algorithms require social scientists to theorize about systematic relationships and to know their topic deeply. Indeed, the onslaught of massive collections of texts and new statistical models makes theoretical reasoning more, not less, important. Rather, these massive datasets help researchers to think more precisely about their theoretical relationships because the increase in data often allows them to test hypotheses that previously they would have had too little data to test.

This fact—that combining data, statistical algorithms, and substantive knowledge leads to deeper and richer theoretical insights—contrasts with recent pronouncements that big data would change how social scientists operate and obviate the need for theory development. Writers have proclaimed that big data and machine learning algorithms would lead to "The End of Theory: The Data Deluge Makes the Scientific Method Obsolete" (Anderson, 2008). The argument was that large datasets would eliminate the need for theoretical thinking because we could replace any work that theorizing does in a project with more data. These pronouncements are wrong, because they overstate what any algorithm can provide. There is an amount of interpretive work that is essential to the functioning of these approaches that simply cannot be automated (at least in the foreseeable future). Contextual knowledge is also essential to asking important research questions and ensuring we are abiding by ethical guidelines. Quite contrary to proclamations that theory will end and humans will be obsolete, many of the models we introduce in this book are useful only with deep and close interpretation from analysts.

2.7.2 TEXT ANALYSIS DOES NOT REPLACE HUMANS—IT AUGMENTS THEM

Text data is already pervasive in the social sciences and has been for quite some time. For centuries scholars have analyzed books, laws, documents, and interview transcripts to learn about the world. Qualitative methodologists have developed methods to improve how researchers read to ensure that the information in the texts is reported reliably and to increase the transparency of the research (Corbin and Strauss, 1990; King, Keohane, and Verba, 1994; Caporaso, 1995; Glaser, 2002). At the core of these methods is a researcher who not only carefully consumes the content in a text, but also adds analysis and insights to reach a conclusion. Consider, for example, McQueen (2018), who argues that great political thinkers, including Machiavelli, Hobbes, and Morgenthau, were influenced by apocalyptic movements of their time. To situate her intellectual history, she analyzes thousands of documents to better understand the context in which those thinkers wrote.

It would be a mistake to suppose that new computer-assisted text analysis could replace this long research tradition by eliminating the need for careful and close readings of texts or otherwise obviating the need for human analysis. Rather, computer-assisted text analysis *augments* our reading ability. New text analysis methods help us read differently, not avoid reading at all. This amplification of human effort improves the analyst's ability to discover interesting organizations, measure key quantities of interest, estimate causal effects, and make predictions.

To better understand why new text analysis methods augment rather than replace human readers, we use the "hay" analogy from Hopkins and King (2010). Suppose that our texts are like straws of hay. When we look at the texts, what we see is a field full of hay. Our task might be to analyze a particular straw of hay in that field. We might want to understand its beauty, describe its particular features, or characterize its color. We can apply this analogy to text analysis. We might want to analyze a particular poem and describe its linguistic beauty, we might engage with a particular line of text to appreciate its meaning, or we might examine the words that are not written to better understand an author's complete message (Strauss, 1952; Melzer, 2014). While humans are often very adept at this sort of deep reading, new text analysis methods are rarely designed to be helpful with this specific task. The methods we describe typically fail to identify features of small or isolated documents.

Now consider a separate task. Suppose that we want to identify features of the straws of hay and sort them into piles of similar hay straws. Humans, as it turns out, are ill equipped for this sort of task. This is because we have tiny active memories, we tend to get distracted when performing the same task for a while, and we might make errors because we fail to interpret the instructions correctly. In contrast, algorithms work incredibly well at sorting, provided there is a well-defined objective function or human guidance that a computer can replicate. When applied to text, this implies that computers work well when discovering new organizations and compressing texts into lower dimensions.

New text analysis methods, then, are best suited to accomplish tasks that humans find difficult. The methods we describe in this book are complements, not competitors, to close readings of texts. For example, at the discovery stage, new text analysis methods can guide and assist close readings of texts with computer-discovered organizations, helping to reveal new concepts that are then interpreted by experts. Blaydes, Grimmer, and McQueen (2018) analyze a large collection of advice for rulers written in Muslim and Christian countries from 1000–1600 CE. To analyze the large of collection of texts, Blaydes, Grimmer, and McQueen (2018) introduce a method that discovers coarse and granular topics and applies them to the texts. Using the organization of the texts as a guide, they characterize the divergent evolution of themes in the Christian and Muslim texts. In Christian texts, the authors show that there is a secularization that occurs, where religion occupies a smaller and smaller share of the texts. Meanwhile, in Muslim texts the share of religious content remains constant. Based on this evidence, the authors theorize that the divergence that occurred between governments in Muslim and Christian kingdoms is due in part to the importance of religion for just rule. To establish the divergence, the authors rely on the results of both computer-assisted sorting and their own close reading of the texts.

New text analysis methods make some research tasks cheaper, which augments human research by making more research projects feasible within realistic cost constraints. This is particularly true for classification methods. A large class of methods develops rules to assign documents to predetermined sets of categories. Rather than engage in expensive and time-consuming hand coding, supervised methods reduce the amount of human intervention that is necessary to do the classification. Other classification methods eliminate human coding altogether and instead use proxies to classify documents. Supervised scaling methods, such as WordScores (Laver, Benoit, and Garry, 2003), similarly embed documents into a low-dimensional space with anchors predetermined by the researcher.

Machine learning algorithms applied to text clearly have a speed advantage. This is true even for relatively small collections of text, which can still lead to high-dimensional problems. To see why, suppose we are interested in classifying 100 open-ended survey responses to identify the most interesting partition—an organization that assigns every text to one and only one category—of the documents. This is a relatively small dataset. Hanna Wallach calls corpora this size "artisanal data," a reference to a dataset's smaller size and the careful curation of text collections. However, carrying out this simple-sounding goal on this small dataset still requires a search over a massive domain. We can characterize the number of potential partitions from a collection with the *Bell Number*. For example, if we have two documents $\{A, B\}$ then the Bell number is 2—AB assigned to the same partition and A, B

assigned to different partitions. With three documents the Bell number is 5—ABC; A, BC; AB, C; AC, B; A, B, C. With 100 documents, the Bell number is $10^{115.68}$—an incomprehensibly large number. By comparison, scientists estimate that there are approximately 10^{80} atoms in the known universe. Clearly, then, even with only 100 documents there is a truly massive space of possible organizations that computational methods can help us explore.

Ultimately, text analysis serves a fundamentally qualitative task: to extract meaning and analysis from collections of text. The methods and research designs that we introduce in this book bridge the quantitative and qualitative divide. Throughout the book, we suggest that researchers engage in deep reading of the texts, understanding the context in which the texts were produced and the people who produced them. Automated text methods are useful because their statistical and algorithmic foundations help humans read, organize, and analyze documents. In this way, when used in combination with theory, new text analysis methods catalyze discovery, make measurement more efficient, and facilitate our estimation of causal effects.

2.7.3 BUILDING, REFINING, AND TESTING SOCIAL SCIENCE THEORIES REQUIRES ITERATION AND CUMULATION

As we describe above, the goal of social science is to build robust theoretical explanations for social phenomena. But theory building is rarely as simple as accumulating evidence from theoretical deductions and then revising the theory according to those deductions. The perception that social science theory building is almost exclusively deductive is a product of a time when acquiring data, running surveys, conducting experiments, and interviewing subjects was expensive and thinking was comparatively cheap. The cost of thinking has stayed relatively constant over time, but the cost of data collection and analysis has plummeted. The result is that it is now practical for social scientists—even those on the smallest of budgets—to include new data acquisition as an explicit part of even the initial stages of the research process. This means that initial samples of data can be used for exploration, which may lead researchers to find new ways that data can be organized. New organizations suggest new measurements and eventually new questions. This leads us to pursue new research designs, which we then use to estimate causal inferences or to make predictions about what will happen in the future.

Importantly, the iterative and cumulative approach to social science that we advocate is not atheoretical. Rather, each stage of the research process is informed by theory. The process can also help us build new theoretical explanations and then test those explanations. For example, developing a conceptualization requires knowing how prior theoretical work organized the world and the extent to which an organization is new. Measures are interesting insofar as they correspond to theoretical quantities of interest. Estimated causal effects can help us to build new theories and to test existing theories by revealing the extent to which observable implications are found in a dataset and which observable implications are not present.

Learning from data, updating theories, and then testing those revised theories is a big move away from how social science is typically *taught*. But, we argue, it actually aligns with how social science is typically *practiced*. We see this iterative and cumulative description of social science as a more accurate account of how social science research tends to be done. The increased transparency makes clear the value of different methods at particular phases of the research process and enables us to design new methods to support individual research tasks. For example, we describe discovery methods in Part 3 of this book, which tend to get little attention in the social sciences. We think this is due, in part, to the tendency to ignore how conceptualizations are produced before the real research begins.

As we will emphasize throughout the book, the iterative nature of research leads us to regularly recommend that analysts split their sample into a training set and a test set. At nearly every stage of the research process—discovery, measurement, causal inference, and prediction—we encourage sample splitting. In discovery, this is essential to learn whether a particular pattern or organization is prominent only in one subsample or if it holds in the whole set. In measurement, the use of a split sample ensures that the functions that are used to classify objects are not overfit and the fresh data ensures that we can accurately evaluate the performance of our classifier on new data. In Part 5: Inference, we show that the training/test split is essential for using machine learning methods in causal inference. The training stage enables us to tune our method, discovering conceptualizations that are likely to give rise to interventions that exert a causal effect on some outcome of interest. The test stage enables us to credibly evaluate the size of the causal effect while avoiding some of the common problems with fishing in causal inference. Sample splitting is perhaps most common in applications of prediction, where it plays a vital role in assessing accuracy.

The role of sample splitting in the discovery and measurement phases is worth highlighting because it helps to solve one of the biggest concerns in empirical analysis: that analysts will discover results by running large numbers of statistical tests on their data that, because of multiple testing, will not be generalizable to other datasets. Because the deductive approach to research assumes discovery is already complete before data is acquired, the current popular solution to this problem is for researchers to register their hypotheses in a pre-analysis plan. However, sample splitting provides a better solution, particularly for text data. Pre-analysis plans are often only effective when others are present to regulate their content and notice that deviations have occurred. Researchers often lack the time to check pre-analysis plans and current resources for pre-registering studies often makes it difficult to connect a final paper to an initial pre-analysis plan. Pre-registration sources exacerbate this problem by allowing researchers to amend their pre-analysis plan. Split samples avoid these pitfalls in large part because they are transparent to readers.

The recommendation to split samples is usually met with two different objections. The first objection is that a particular experiment might be very costly and the decrease in power to split the sample is not justified. As we explain in more detail in Part 5: Inference, we do not believe that any loss in power objection outweighs the risks of *not* splitting the sample. Especially in instances where stakes are high, interventions are expensive, and the consequences for public policy are clear, we want to have the most confidence possible in the effects we estimate. A split sample provides robust detection of overfitting while also ensuring our data cleaning rules take into account the realities of a particular dataset. The second objection is that some historical data may occur only once and therefore splitting a sample can happen only once. In some cases this will be true: some events only occur once and therefore provide us with only one dataset (and therefore one sample split). But as Fowler and Montagnes (2015) suggest, this happens less often than people realize, as there are often analogous interventions that can be studied. For example, they examine the compelling finding in Healy, Malhotra, and Mo (2010) that college football scores affect Congressional elections by examining the effect of National Football League (NFL) games, finding no indication that NFL scores affect election outcomes. This related study is useful because if the logic in Healy, Malhotra, and Mo (2010) is correct, we would expect to see a similar effect from NFL games. Thus even with historical collections of texts that may feel unique, there are likely analogous interventions in different times or in different places.

2.7.4 TEXT ANALYSIS METHODS DISTILL GENERALIZATIONS FROM LANGUAGE

Text is a complex form of data. Consider one of the greatest speeches in American political history. On the eve of his assassination, Martin Luther King, Jr., delivered a speech entitled "I've Been to the Mountaintop" in Memphis, Tennessee. In the rousing speech, King confronts the threats on his life, closing with a prophetic declaration:

> Like anybody, I would like to live a long life. Longevity has its place. But I'm not concerned about that now. I just want to do God's will. And He's allowed me to go up to the mountain. And I've looked over. And I've seen the Promised Land. I may not get there with you. But I want you to know tonight, that we, as a people, will get to the promised land!

"I've Been to the Mountaintop" is a rich, complex text. It makes a vivid allusion to biblical stories, in particular the Book of Exodus. King is implicitly comparing himself to Moses, the Black audience members to the enslaved people escaping Egypt, and the quest for equal rights and justice to the escaped slaves finding a land of their own. Part of the speech's power comes from when it was delivered and who delivered it: on the eve of his assassination, an iconic civil rights leader discusses his vision of the future. All of this context is important to understand King's message and why the speech is an important moment in United States (US) history. No text analysis method could hope to fully capture this level of complexity and context, much of which does not even come from the text alone.

The goal of text analysis methods is to develop a distillation that reduces this complexity to something simpler. We will often talk about this in the language of mathematics, referring to text as *high-dimensional* because any dataset that could represent all of each text's information in numbers would need many, many features or columns. This is in stark contrast to many common datasets in the social sciences, where features such as a survey respondent's income, age, or opinion about an issue might each be stored in a single number. Text analysis methods are about compressing high-dimensional information in the text to a lower-dimensional representation, where that representation retains the content that is useful for a particular social science research agenda. This could be as simple as representing a movie review as positive or negative and as complex as annotating a legislative bill along dozens of categories.

There are many reasons to reduce information and extract only the content of the text that is relevant to the researcher. First, distilling information can make the text interpretable and generalizable in a way that would otherwise be difficult. Distilling the information in a text allows us to relate it to other texts on some dimension. In the discovery phase, reducing the complexity of text may provide an organization of the documents that then informs the way the researcher reads those documents. When performing a measurement, the reduction of information enables us to understand what we are measuring and why it might be relevant as a quantity of interest. For example, reducing political legislation together with roll call voting decisions to a single dimension of ideology or partisanship can be incredibly useful for summarizing political decisions.

A second reason for reducing the dimensionality of text is for statistical properties. When we attempt to use texts to make predictions, infer how texts affect an individual, or try to determine the similarity of two texts, we are unable to work with the entire text because there is simply too much information. This curse of dimensionality can manifest in several statistical applications of text analysis methods. If we fail to reduce the dimensionality when attempting to make predictions we will overfit and our forecasts will perform poorly. If we do not reduce the dimensionality when attempting to infer the causal effects we will lack the basic information necessary to reliably estimate causal effects of interest. The only way to proceed, then, is to reduce complexity.

A third reason to reduce the dimensionality of text is that most social science theories are about relatively low-dimensional concepts. For example, many theories in political science suppose that political conflict happens along a low-dimensional ideological spectrum (Downs, 1957). In order to test the observable implications of these theories, we need measures of individuals along that spectrum. One way to do this using text analysis, for instance, would be to categorize a person's online posts as very conservative, conservative, centrist, liberal, or very liberal.

Given the importance of reducing dimensionality, we will focus our efforts in this book on understanding the particular distillation we are using, what properties it has, and how we know if we are doing a good or bad job. The distillations that we use will take several forms. The most familiar one for many social scientists will be using research assistants to hand code documents into a set of categories. We also introduce several computer-assisted distillations. First, we use samples of manual codings to statistically learn a distillation that places previously unseen documents and assigns them to known categories. Second, we take a collection of documents, partition them into a set of categories, and then assign documents to categories. Third, we use a distillation to discover the treatments that are present in a collection of documents. Any of these approaches will require the loss of information—and that's okay. In fact, the compression is the point of the exercise.

2.7.5 THE BEST METHOD DEPENDS ON THE TASK

While our overarching goal is always to distill texts into the most useful content possible, there is no single method that is best for all text analysis tasks. Indeed, even for a single task, there may be a handful of different methods that could be useful. Nor do we argue that the algorithms and statistical models we ourselves have produced are superior to all others. Rather, we take a pragmatic, task-specific approach: researchers should try several methods, evaluate their performance, and select the one that best helps them accomplish their goal.

We advocate for a pragmatic approach based on our experience working with different kinds of texts to accomplish different tasks. In fact, this is the primary reason for our agnostic approach to using text analysis methods. The performance of different methods often varies substantially across the types of texts we analyze, which vary in length, content, formality, and grammatical structure. For example, our experience has been that topic models, which we discuss throughout the book, tend to perform extremely well at the task of topic extraction when analyzing newspaper articles or well-prepared statements from political or social elites. While topic models can work well in other settings, their performance can be uneven when dealing with shorter statements or more informal language. Texts' great diversity makes it difficult to know how any one method will perform across all types of texts.

We also advocate for a task-specific approach to applying text analysis methods because the features of interest vary based on what we want to learn from the text. For example, the content that we would want to extract from a text if we are interested in learning its topic is qualitatively different from the content we would extract if we are interested in learning its sentiment. Identifying the ideology of a text is quite different from identifying its author (a task from the field of stylometry). The types of quantities that social scientists hope to extract from texts are diverse and constantly growing.

There is also diversity in the tasks themselves. Discovering an organization of texts is fundamentally different from classifying documents into preexisting categories, which is different from inferring the causal effect of a text. The multitude of demands that social scientists place on their methods ensure that there is no one right way to do text analysis across all research questions. In this book we focus on presenting different options and describing specific methods where we expect they will perform well.

Another reason that the best method to use depends on the task at hand is because the methods that are applied to text data tend to lack the statistical theory found in many other areas of statistics. There are important and deep statistical theoretical properties for the estimators that we discuss in this book, which help us evaluate the performance of methods. Yet, even the most theoretically well-developed methods have few theorems that relate the performance of the method back to natural language *as it is spoken* or tie performance to particular social science tasks. This represents another key reason to use an agnostic approach to text as data methods. We always work with *representations* of the text, rather than the spoken language itself. So, even if we assume that there are structural parameters that govern how text is constructed, the statistical properties are proven conditioning on a (generally very simplified) representation of the text and are relevant to tasks that may not quite align with our uses in the social sciences.

Thus, in general, our confidence in the methods that we apply to our data is not based on proofs of their statistical properties. Rather, our confidence is based on empirical evidence of how the methods perform when applied to actual texts: we adopt those methods that have performed well across a range of problems. As we explain in the next section when we discuss validation, this means that *every* application of text analysis methods requires extensive evaluation, because we cannot be sure beforehand that the method will perform well at our desired task with our specific data.

2.7.6 VALIDATIONS ARE ESSENTIAL AND DEPEND ON THE THEORY AND THE TASK

Our agnostic and pragmatic approach to text analysis is essential because of the complexity of language, the variability of tasks, and the difficulty of connecting the statistical properties of text analysis methods to natural language. As a consequence, there are few (if any) theorems that justify text analysis methods as applied to natural language. Perhaps unsurprisingly, then, every application of text analysis methods requires that we validate the properties of the measures that our models produce. Validations are necessary because the primary justification for using text analysis methods is empirical: we use methods that have worked well in the past when applied to similar problems. Of course, we may suspect that the dataset we are working with has features similar to other text collections on which the method has performed well in the past. However, text collections may differ from each other in a great many ways, and it is often hard to understand how those differences could affect the performance of a method before validating the results.

Given that most justifications for methods in the text analysis literature are empirical, validation is critical to establish that a method performs well on a particular dataset. But performing the literal task that we set out is neither necessary nor sufficient for a method to accomplish our ultimate goal: making a valid social science inference. A method might perform well on the specific task, but when we aggregate up the low-level measures to a unit of interest, bias could accumulate, resulting in an inaccurate measure of some aggregate, unit-level behavior. And, even if our method is able to produce accurate unit-level measures, we still have to validate that we are measuring our concept of interest. Thus, research projects will typically involve several validation steps.

The first validation assesses whether our method correctly performs the specific task it is designed to perform. This sort of validation is most obvious with supervised classification methods, where our task is to replicate human coding decisions, and with predictions, where our task is to accurately forecast a variable in the future. To assess the performance on both tasks, we ask, can we replicate the task on data where we know the answer? In Part 4: Measurement, we describe how validation datasets and cross-validation can assess how well our method classifies documents into categories. In Part 5: Inference, we discuss the conditions under which data we hold out from the main analysis can help us assess the accuracy of our forecasts.

A variety of tools have also been developed to evaluate unsupervised models that we use for discovery (Part 3: Discovery), for measurement (Part 4: Measurement), and to facilitate causal inferences (Part 5: Inference). These validations work in various ways. Some involve the researcher manually reading texts assigned to a particular category and deciding if the organizations from a distillation are coherent. Other validations involve examining the features that are indicative of a category or latent dimension to evaluate if those features are coherent and correspond to an identifiable quantity of interest for the researcher. Another approach is to use quantitative measures of model fit that assess how well a particular text analysis method fits the data.

One feature that is common to many of the validation methods we describe is that they place "humans in the loop," explicitly relying on human judgment in a partially automated process that incorporates two key insights. First, for many tasks we want to assess models based on how humans use the information the model provides. Second, to include human information we need to carefully design experiments to ensure that researchers avoid arbitrary criteria when choosing the model. With these insights in mind, we describe how to use experimental evidence to assess the quality of topics and clusters from a wide array of text analysis methods.

Another step that requires inspection is the way in which measures are aggregated across documents. For example, imagine that you had an email classifier for spam which sometimes let spam emails into your inbox but only very rarely sent an important message to your spam folder. This is a property that most people would like in a spam filter, but it also means that the probability that an email is not spam is likely systematically overestimated. If we then aggregated these estimates to assess the total proportion of emails that are spam, we would get an upwardly biased estimate of the spam emails we receive. Thus, even beyond assessing individual classifications, we need to demonstrate that combining individual level decisions avoids introducing systematic bias, which would make our measures less useful.

It is also often useful to establish that measures have *face validity*. That is, we should expect that, at a minimum, our measures pass the inspection of a subject expert. Moving beyond face validity is difficult. *Hypothesis validity* is a demonstration that a dataset adheres to an expected set of patterns. This provides a formal mechanism for assessing the quality of our measures. Of course, there might be a blurred line between a measure failing a hypothesis validation and a research finding. It is essential to select hypotheses that are so obvious that it would be difficult to explain a negative finding. For example, in order to demonstrate the accuracy of his topical classification of Senate press releases, Grimmer (2013*b*) shows that committee chairs are more focused on issues under their committee's jurisdiction than an average senator. This finding is both obvious and would be difficult to explain if it were shown to not be true.

A final validation provides an assessment that the label we have attached to our compression of the text corresponds to what the measure is actually capturing from the text. This assessment of label *fidelity* is essential to establishing the viability of a particular text compression for a research task. When hand coding or using a supervised method, the key to establishing fidelity is providing transparency about how categories are defined in the codebook and demonstrating that the coders adhered to the coding rules. Demonstrations of fidelity for unsupervised methods can be more challenging. Some techniques are straightforward—providing sample text to the reader, for example. And it is always an option to validate the discovered categories using hand coding and supervised methods. That is, we can take the measures that were originally discovered using a method without predetermined categories and then demonstrate that we can recover those categories with a codebook defined by a researcher.

2.8 Conclusion: Text Data and Social Science

In this book we advocate for a research process in which data and algorithms are deployed at each stage—from the earliest stages when research questions are being formulated to the estimation of causal effects. Of course, using such techniques is standard practice when it comes to assigning texts to categories, measuring the prevalence of specific topics in the texts, and assessing causal effects. But we also advocate that researchers use text data and algorithms at the earliest stages of a research project to refine their research questions, develop measures for key concepts, and generate hypotheses. Our experience has been that we are able to formulate better questions, obtain better theories, and articulate clearer concepts when data and statistical models assist us in the earliest stages of our research.

This is an exciting moment for text analysis. The number of studies deploying text analysis is increasing, and new methods for conducting text analysis are emerging rapidly. As a result, some methods that we describe here might already be out of date in a few years time. However, we don't view that as a significant limitation for our overarching project. Our model for social science inference does not depend on any specific methods that are used at any one point in time. Rather, the tasks that we outline are long-standing features of social science projects. And our approach of being transparent about how social science inferences are made means that new methods have a clear place within the research process. We also provide a set of validations to assess the performance of the methods—even methods not yet developed at the time this book was written.

To that end, in the next chapter we begin introducing tools for analyzing text data. We describe a set of methods for representing text as quantitative data, which can later be used for discovery, measurement, and inference.

PART II

Selection and Representation

Once you start to see text as a source of data, new opportunities to study the social world open up everywhere. Firms use company earnings reports and consumer complaints to guide investment decisions and improve customer service. Governments use safety inspection reports and transcripts of emergency dispatch to improve government services. Economists gain insights into economic growth and marketing through transcripts of Federal Reserve meetings and advertisements. Political scientists answer questions about representation, accountability, and political competition with speeches, press releases, and debates. Sociologists measure culture, track demographic changes, and map the digitized footprints of diverse communities. Outside the social sciences, historians leverage vast archives of historical documents, public health scholars investigate electronic health records, and English professors study the broader patterns of literature. In each of these cases, our goal is more than fitting a statistical model to data; we want to learn something about the human processes that documents record and represent.

In this part, we discuss the first step in the text analysis process: the collection and representation of text. We begin in **Chapter 3: Principles of Selection and Representation** by providing four principles that provide a framework for the rest of the chapters in this part. We then move to **Chapter 4: Selecting Documents**, which explores why a principled approach to gathering and sampling text is imperative for making inferences. Here the goal is to construct a *corpus*—the collection of documents to analyze. **Chapter 5: Bag of Words** provides an initial default recipe for representing the documents numerically based on the "bag of words" model. This simple, yet powerful, representation of texts treats each document as simply a collection of word counts—as though we threw all the words into a bag and shook them up so their order was no longer preserved. Although this representation loses a lot of information, it can be highly effective for many tasks and is a useful default approach.

The bag of words representation lends itself to a probabilistic modeling strategy based on the multinomial distribution. **Chapter 6: The Multinomial Language Model** introduces the multinomial language model that will form the foundation of many of the statistical models that we will cover throughout the book. **Chapter 7: The Vector Space Model and Similarity Metrics** introduces the idea of interpreting the bag of words representation as a vector space. This provides a foundation for the algorithmic models in much the way that the multinomial model provides a foundation for the statistical ones.

Chapters 5–7 use a representation of words that makes no initial assumptions about how similar words are to each other: `cat` and `kitten` are treated as equally distinct as `cat` and `ecclesiastical`. The next two chapters discuss how we can use external information to enhance our understanding of words. Using large text collections such as Wikipedia or the Common Crawl of the internet, we can learn distributed representations of words that encode the idea that some words are more similar than others. These "word embeddings" are described in **Chapter 8: Distributed Representations of Words**. While word embeddings leverage an external corpus to gain semantic information, **Chapter 9: Representations from Language Sequences** overviews several approaches from natural language processing that can be used to extract different kinds of information from documents such as the roles that words play in a sentence. These techniques include text reuse, part-of-speech tagging, named entity recognition, dependency parsing, and other information extraction tasks.

We assume throughout that documents are already machine readable. Documents that aren't natively digital can be made machine readable through *optical character recognition*—the process of converting pictures of text into characters that a machine can read. While not perfect, these technologies are the best solution for making text machine readable for large corpora where transcribing the documents by hand would be prohibitively time consuming.

CHAPTER 3

Principles of Selection and Representation

As we have discussed in previous chapters, text data reflects social interactions, economic transactions, and political processes. In order to use this wealth of information to ask and answer interesting questions, the researcher must first carefully curate the corpus of interest and then represent those documents numerically. While more complicated because of the sheer amount of information stored within texts, decisions on how to collect and numerically represent text are similar to the decisions researchers make to numerically represent other social science variables of interest. Collecting a corpus is analogous to identifying a sample from a population of interest. Numerically representing text is similar to how social scientists might use a metric like GDP to represent the economic activity of a country. These decisions simplify more complicated phenomena into numbers that can be analyzed quantitatively.

Not all of the information encoded in the text will be useful to our question – the challenge is deciding what information is relevant and what can be discarded. In this part, we overview a few different recipes for representing texts—from the "bag of words" model to distributed representations—that can be adapted to individual research questions and tasks. Often, theory will not be able to guide us to selecting the best representation, and the choice will require extensive validation.

We stress throughout this part that our goal is not to find one right model of language or one correct representation of the text for all research questions. As social science researchers, we are not studying the text itself, but rather the political, economic, and social processes that are reflected in it. Thus, what information we retrieve from the text will depend on what we want to discover, measure, or infer. And that will depend on the goal of our research.

We begin by building off Chapter 2's six principles to emphasize four specific principles that inform how we decide to collect and represent a corpus. We then introduce the examples that we use throughout the part that show how research-driven representation of text can be effective in uncovering social phenomena and answering historical questions.

3.1 Principle 1: Question-Specific Corpus Construction

The usefulness of a corpus depends on the question the researchers want to answer and the population they want to study.

Whether or not a corpus is useful will depend on the research question. The analysis of Twitter data, for example, might not be the most accurate way to gauge US public opinion about climate change because only a minority of the population uses the platform and, of those, few tweet about climate change. However, it could be a useful way to study how elected officials interact with their constituents online, or to measure how activist groups try to change the conversation.

When the research question is well defined, we urge researchers to articulate the quantities of interest and a population of interest before beginning to collect documents. They can then evaluate the utility of potential corpora by judging whether a corpus reflects the population they are interested in and whether the quantities they are interested in can be measured from the text. This doesn't mean biased or incomplete corpora always need to be completely discarded. Incomplete corpora can also be useful, if the researcher understands the sources and consequences of incompleteness and can articulate them to the audience.

As we cover extensively in the Discovery part of this book, researchers may not always begin to explore a corpus with a well-defined research question. For example, a researcher might have a corpus on hand and not know what is in it or what it could measure. Exploring the corpus both by conducting some quantitative analyses paired with in-depth reading could lead to new insights and theories that could later be tested. In these cases, we suggest that as researchers refine their question, quantities, and population of interest, they revisit the corpus selection step and collect new data once they have decided on a question.

3.2 Principle 2: No Values-Free Corpus Construction

> *There is no values-free construction of a corpus. Selecting which documents to include has ethical ramifications.*

Constructing a corpus requires special attention to ethical issues about representation and privacy. As we will discuss extensively in this section of the book, corpus construction may inaccurately reflect the population of interest because of differences in resources and incentives of individuals to write and make available text data. Even when texts have been produced, institutional and governmental policies might skew data retention and availability. The case of internet censorship, discussed in the previous chapter, is a particularly extreme version of this kind of selection. When researchers focus on text, they often end up focusing on the population producing the documents, a shift in focus that is important to acknowledge. Failure of the corpus to equitably reflect the population can lead to inaccurate conclusions and inaccuracies of the models for subgroups of the data (Olteanu et al., 2019; Tatman, 2017).

Text corpora also represent language as it used by the document authors and not in a neutral way. In certain settings authors use harmful language, such as of racial stereotypes or hate speech. In some applications, identifying this language (for example, to remove it) is the intention of the research task itself. In other applications, such as predictive language models, inclusion of harmful language in training data can perpetuate the problem in downstream applications (Bolukbasi et al., 2016). While certainly not the only cause of systems that perpetuate unfair outcomes, the data used can be an important part of the process.

Text frequently contains personal or identifiable information. This creates complexity in two distinct kinds of situations. When documents are generated explicitly for the purposes of research—for example, for an open-ended response in a survey—researchers should follow standard procedures in academic research for obtaining consent, ensuring the removal of obviously identifying personal information, and protecting human subjects from harm. These concerns are particularly pressing when the text data is being merged with other sensitive data because it is especially difficult to know what details in text might be identifying. Lundberg et al. (2019) offers an informative example of how to conduct a privacy threat analysis for sensitive social data.

More frequently, documents are collected from some public source and are generated without the intention of their being used in research, often without any simple way to obtain informed consent. Many researchers reason that because the author chose to publish a document, it is ethically permissible to use it for research. Yet, there may also be reasons to believe that the dichotomy of public and private oversimplifies privacy concerns in the social media age (boyd and Crawford, 2012). Nissenbaum (2020) reasons about these issues through the lens of "contextual integrity," which considers not just whether the text is public but also the contextual norms under which its authors expected that information to be accessed. The ethical situation becomes even more complex in the context of information that is only semi-public, such as that available through a closed Facebook group or a mailing list that requires a sign-up form. Salganik (2018, Chapter 6) provides an excellent discussion of common frameworks for thinking through these privacy concerns in the more general setting of data in the digital age.

3.3   Principle 3: No Right Way to Represent Text

> *There is no one right way to represent text for all research questions.*

Just as the corpus depends on the research question, so does the representation. There is no one right way to represent text for all questions. In some cases—as we'll detail more below—the researcher may only be interested in one word, and representing the text will only involve an indicator for whether that particular word is included in the text. In other cases, a researcher may want to include indicators for most words within the text, but exclude common words such as the and and. In other cases, the only words of interest might be these common words. For other questions, not only whether a word is included, but also a representation of how that word is related to other words might be required, or information about the context of the word as well as the word itself.

We suggest that researchers choose the simplest representation that will contain sufficient information about the what they hope to measure in the text. What quantity is the researcher trying to measure? How might this social phenomenon manifest itself in the text? In some cases, a simple representation will adequately reflect the phenomenon the researcher is trying to capture. In other cases, a more complicated representation may be required to measure the quantity of interest. In many cases, we will not know ahead of time what the best representation is. In these cases, we will use a representation that includes many different features from the text and then use a model to extract those that are most important according to a particular measure of what we are interested in studying.

3.4 Principle 4: Validation

> *The best assurance that a text representation is working is extensive validation.*

There are many different decisions that need to be made in order to represent text as numbers. In many cases, the number of ways to represent the text in a corpus will be too many to enumerate. How will researchers know that they have selected the "right" representation for their research question?

Here, we suggest that researchers rely extensively on validations that we detail throughout the book. We will know that our representation is working in a measurement model if the measures that we have created using that representation align with validated, hand-coded data and facts that we know about the social world. We will know that representations are working in a prediction model if we achieve high accuracy. And we will know that a particular representation is working in causal inference if we can replicate the experiment and achieve the same results. If our validations show that our measures, predictions, and inferences are not working, we will need to revisit our approach—both our representation and our model—to understand why.

We do not believe that a research finding must be robust to the many different ways that the text could be represented, as is common practice in other areas of social science. Some representations will be more appropriate for different tasks—achieving better accuracy or facilitating better discoveries. Evaluating the robustness of our findings over many different representations is not necessary if one representation clearly dominates the others. Instead, we suggest that researchers use external validations to find the best representation for the quantities they are interested in measuring and ignore representations that are not useful to their question.

Having laid out our four principles, we now provide a brief preview of two example applications. While we will reference many applications throughout Chapters 4–9, we will return to these two particular applications several times.

3.5 State of the Union Addresses

Throughout this section, we will use a corpus of 236 State of the Union addresses from 1790–2016.[1] Given to the US public each year by the president in either written or spoken form, the State of the Union (SOTU) corpus provides a snapshot of the policy priorities of the US executive branch throughout its over 200-year history.

Several studies have used the SOTU corpus to examine trends in the nature of political speech over time. For example, Rule, Cointet, and Bearman (2015) use a variety of text analytic techniques to detect shifts in the language of these political speeches. In doing so, they argue that the discourse of the SOTU corpus shifted after 1917, when the topics of "Statecraft" and "Political Economy" morphed into broader discussions of "Foreign Affairs" and "Public Policy."

In another example, Benoit, Munger, and Spirling (2019) analyze the SOTU speeches in the context of readability. They develop a measure of textual complexity which they apply to the SOTU corpus. They find, overwhelmingly, that the textual complexity of speeches has decreased substantially over time. Comparing SOTU speeches given in the

---

[1] Data was obtained from Arnold and Tilton (2017).

same year in written and spoken form, they find that textual complexity is much higher in written speeches, and the increasing likelihood of presidents giving the SOTU in spoken form might explain some of the trend to less complexity.

In the following section, we will use the SOTU corpus to introduce how to represent text as data.

3.6 The Authorship of the Federalist Papers

In one of the earliest instances of quantitative text analysis, Mosteller and Wallace (1963) set out to identify the authors of the unsigned Federalist Papers. The Federalist Papers are 85 documents written by a combination of Alexander Hamilton, John Jay, and James Madison in the late 1700s supporting the American Constitution, which was then under debate. The first 77 of the papers are of interest to Mosteller and Wallace (1963) and were published anonymously between 1787 and 1788 in New York newspapers in support of ratifying the Constitution.

While all the documents are unsigned, the authorship of 73 (of the 85) of them are uncontested. For twelve documents, it is believed that they were written by either Hamilton or Madison. For an additional three documents, it was known that they were written jointly, but which author wrote which section has been disputed (Mosteller and Wallace, 1963). This is partly because the authors themselves provided conflicting lists of authorship. Hamilton provided a list of which individual authored each paper two days before he died in a duel with Aaron Burr in 1804. Madison, however, provided a different list of the authors in 1818 (Adair, 1944).

Like many of the studies we will describe in this book, according to Mosteller's biography, the idea to study the question of authorship in the Federalist Papers came from a conversation between himself, a statistician, and a political scientist, Frederick Williams.[2] Inspired by this conversation, Mosteller and Wallace (1963) set out to use statistical methods to try to distinguish the authors on the basis of their writing style, rather than the content of the essays. They made the observation that what they called `filler words` distinguish the two authors—Hamilton and Madison use words like upon, by, and to at different rates in documents known to be written by the two authors.

They split the documents into blocks of text of about 200 words each, in order to be able to distinguish joint authorship within one document. They then represented the text by counting the use of filler words in each of these blocks. Unlike the technology we have today, simply counting the words in the Federalist Papers proved quite challenging in 1959–1960. In Mosteller's words:

> The words in an article were typed one word per line on a long paper tape, like adding machine tape. Then with scissors the tape was cut into slips, one word per slip.... When the counting was going on, if someone opened the door, slips of paper would fly about the room.   (Mosteller, 2010, pp. 53–54)

Once the words were finally counted, the authors created a statistical model that uses the filler words to predict the authorship of papers using existing documents known to

---

[2] "When I worked at the Office of Public Opinion Research . . . I got to know Frederick Williams, a political scientist. One day in 1941, Fred said, 'Have you thought about the problem of the authorship of the disputed *Federalist* papers?' I didn't know there were *Federalist* papers, much less that both Hamilton and Madison had claimed authorship of them." (Mosteller, 2010, p. 47)

be written by the two authors. Essentially, for a given 200-word passage, the model asks whether the rates at which the filler words occur are more like those from known Hamilton documents or known Madison documents. The model distinguishes authorship in the unknown documents quite decisively—attributing all 12 documents with unknown authorship to Madison.

Keeping in mind the image of cutting one word at a time from a text and placing it into piles, we use Mosteller and Wallace (1963) as a simple example of the bag of words approach to representing text—where each document is represented by how many times each individual word of interest appears within the text. However, the example is also useful because it illustrates the way the decision of how to represent a text depends entirely on the research question of interest. While for many social science research questions, the rate at which a text contains the word upon is not useful information, for this particular question, these "filler words" are most important.

3.7 Conclusion

In this chapter we've covered the principles of corpus selection and representation that will guide our thinking in Chapters 4–9. These principles parallel our six main principles from Chapter 2, placing a focus on the question-specific nature of the corpus construction, urging researchers to abandon the notion that there is a single right representation for all purposes, and in light of that to focus on validation. We now turn to selecting documents (Chapter 4) followed by our first algorithm for representing text as data (Chapter 5). We will return to the State of the Union and the Federalist Papers examples throughout.

CHAPTER 4

Selecting Documents

Text analysis always begins with a process of choosing the documents to analyze. Sometimes this choice is dictated by availability. Particularly before a research question is developed, researchers may grab as many documents as they can in a particular domain to begin searching for interesting ideas. In other settings the goal of the analysis might be to understand the contents of a particular document collection. In the immediate aftermath of disclosure of large sets of documents, such as the 250,000 US State Department cables leaked in 2010 or the 11 million financial documents in the Panama Papers, the goal for many journalists and researchers was to explore those specific collections of documents. Similarly, the Mosteller and Wallace (1963) analysis of the Federalist Papers is focused on an authorship attribution-specific corpus of text, and does not draw inference to other documents beyond it.

Many of the examples we cover in this book, though, are cases where researchers have or develop a well-defined question of interest and select the corpus to answer their particular question. For example, Catalinac (2016a), whose work we discussed in Chapter 1, was interested in understanding how the electoral strategy of candidates running for office in Japan changed in response to the electoral reform. She decided to use a corpus of electoral manifestos because these manifestos are made in the same format by all candidates, are directly given to voters, and have not changed in their design over time. Therefore, they are representative of her population of interest—candidates—and also what she was interested in measuring—candidates' strategy of persuading voters to vote for them.

In other cases, the researcher's goal shifts over time and so too does the collection of documents. As we described in Chapter 2, after King, Pan, and Roberts changed their research topic to measuring censorship, they switched their data collection method to a stratified sample based on keywords that they believed would be associated with censorship. As we emphasize throughout the book, the research process isn't always a strictly linear progression through the research steps, and corpus construction may need to be done more than once as researchers iterate toward the most interesting question and the most compelling answer.

In this chapter, we begin by discussing the population and quantity of interest. Once you've decided on a question, population, and quantity of interest, how well you can measure these quantities will depend on whether your corpus represents this population well. We then examine four types of bias that might influence how reflective a particular corpus is of a given population.

4.1 Populations and Quantities of Interest

The usefulness of a corpus depends on the question the researchers want to answer and the population they want to study. Without digging into the data, the researchers may not know what they *can* measure, or how the corpus relates to key questions in their area of expertise. At this stage in the process, the analysts are in the discovery phase; they must explore, read, and describe the texts to better understand what questions can be answered. Eventually, they will develop a research question and revisit how well the sample reflects the population they are interested in, which will typically require subsequent data collection or refinement of the sample.

Other times, the researcher begins with a question of interest, which will make it more clear at the outset whether or not the texts are relevant. Questions of interest typically reference or imply a *population of interest*. For example, if the question of interest is, "How do likely voters in the United States feel about the President?", the population of interest is likely voters in the United States. The question clarifies whether or not the corpus at hand reflects this population. Using a corpus of tweets to answer this question may result in *sample selection bias* because, among other reasons, users of Twitter skew substantially younger than likely voters.

The research question suggests how the texts should be compressed or summarized to be used in analysis. We often refer to these summaries as the *quantities of interest*. A quantity of interest is a numeric value (or set of values) that is of particular interest to the researcher. In the Twitter example, an analyst might be interested in how much users talk about a particular topic or how many tweets about the president are positive versus negative. The population and quantities of interest inform how well a corpus can answer the question of interest. If the corpus does not reflect the population of interest, or the quantity of interest cannot be calculated from the texts within the corpus, then answering the research question will be difficult with that particular corpus.

Researchers ask questions that focus on a wide variety of populations, domains, and time periods. For some research questions, text data may be used similarly to population surveys, where researchers hope to reflect the underlying opinions, activities, or demographics of a country's people. For example, scholars have begun to use social media data on platforms like Twitter to describe everything from political opinions (O'Connor et al., 2010) to movie preferences (Asur and Huberman, 2010), to the spread of the flu (Lampos and Cristianini, 2010), and personal happiness in a population (Golder and Macy, 2011; Dodds et al., 2011). To accurately gauge underlying quantities of interest in the broader (both online and offline) population, these analyses depend on accurately accounting for the ways in which online populations are different from offline populations. Even within online populations, those who choose to engage in discussions about politics may be very different from those choosing to engage in discussions about entertainment, all which must be taken into account when generalizing to the population that does not discuss the topic within the data (Barberá and Rivero, 2015).

In other cases, the population of interest is a much smaller subset of the entire population. For example, Blaydes, Grimmer, and McQueen (2018) explore the divergence in political thought between Muslim and Christian societies. To reflect both Muslim and Christian political thinkers, they gather political advice texts from the sixth to the seventeenth centuries from both the Islamic tradition and Christian Europe. The authors' goal is not to gather *all* Muslim and Christian writings, or to reflect all thoughts on these subjects within these populations, but rather to reflect those with the most influence on political thought in this time period. In the digital humanities, analyses may be focused on exploring thematic trends in a particular genre, for example, Danish ghost stories (Abello, Broadwell, and Tangherlini, 2012). Appropriate selection of texts in these cases will often rely on the ability to distinguish between stories that contain a subject like ghosts from those that do not.

Even if the corpus is not representative, careful analysis can lead to valid insights about the population of interest. Gill and Spirling (2015) use historical records and leaked data to understand what types of information the United States government keeps secret and what types it declassifies. Of course, the authors do not have access to *all* classified information; they only see declassified or leaked records. But in comparing information that is unclassified to that which was classified at some point, the authors can infer some of the types of topics that remain secret, and can offer insight into what might be missing.

4.2 Four Types of Bias

Once the researchers have a question, a population, and quantities of interest, meaning that they have moved from the discovery to the measurement, causal inference, or prediction stage of the analysis, they should think carefully about the potential sample selection biases in their corpus. In this section, we provide a starting checklist of common sources of sample selection bias that researchers might consider when they have a question and candidate corpus of interest. Not all of these sources of bias will pertain to all research questions and certainly some of the factors we consider may be *beneficial* for answering some types of questions. However, we have found that for many questions and populations of interest, the four types of sample selection bias below reappear frequently when analysts use text for social science inference.

4.2.1 RESOURCE BIAS

Texts are expensive to produce, gather, and collate. *Resource bias* refers to the fact that texts often better reflect populations with more resources to produce, record, and store documents. This issue is especially salient when access prevents entire portions of the population from being represented at all. Illiteracy, limited access to the internet, or barriers to entry can render large swaths of a population invisible to scholars studying texts.

Recording and preserving historical activity is a costly process that can require substantial resources. Events are more likely to be recorded if the press is present (Snyder and Kelly, 1977; Danzger, 1975). Archives might only contain documents that citizens found convenient to store and may be woefully unrepresentative of the population of interest. Texts may have been lost, burned, or not stored, and stories may have never been transcribed. Communities and individuals with the capabilities to store and preserve texts will likely be very different than those without, and as such historical documents should not be considered a random sample of a larger set. For example, Pechenick, Danforth, and Dodds (2015) point out that the Google Ngrams corpus, a large collection of English texts, contains increasingly disproportionate amounts of scientific texts over the course of the twentieth century.

Government document availability may also reflect local resources. Some governments may have the personnel to transcribe meetings and make them available to the public; others will not. For example, Sandhya Kambhampati, a journalist at ProPublica, writes about requesting information from the state of Illinois via the Freedom of

Information Act. She notes that documents from some agencies were not already digitized. Because of scanning costs, some of these records could not be made available to the requester.[1]

4.2.2 INCENTIVE BIAS

Incentives and strategic behavior can also drive the production and retention of documents, a process we call *incentive bias* (Herrera and Kapur, 2007). Social interaction is performative (Goffman, 1959) and individuals as well as organizations have incentives to fail to record or to hide or destroy evidence that could cast them in a negative light. Individuals may be more likely to post social media that reflect the happiest or most successful aspects of their lives. For researchers studying interactions on social media, this concern may not be an issue, but for those who are trying to measure true emotional states of users, how individuals portray themselves may bias results. Similarly, politicians and governments may force removal of news and social media that undermines them, censoring others or self-censoring to frame political conversations (House, 2015; Boydston, 1991; Gup, 2008; King, Pan, and Roberts, 2013; MacKinnon, 2008).

While transparency laws and initiatives make texts more accessible to researchers, they also change the incentives of those whom it affects. Email transparency within organizations may create incentives for members of these organizations to talk on the telephone about sensitive issues or hold informal meeting where discussions are not recorded. Transparency initiatives might make government leaders curtail their political participation if they are afraid of making missteps (Malesky, Schuler, and Tran, 2012). These initiatives might also be more likely in certain political contexts; for example, Berliner and Erlich (2015) show that states in Mexico with more political competition passed transparency laws earlier than states without political competition.

When researchers are interested in using documents as a reflection of government internal workings, researchers should seek to understand the incentives behind document collection and the process through which the data are made available. A brilliant example of this is Cheryl Schonhardt-Bailey's *Deliberating American Monetary Policy: A Textual Analysis*, which examines transcripts of the Federal Open Market Committees (FOMC) and Congressional committees on banking to understand the role of deliberation in making monetary policy (Schonhardt-Bailey, 2013). Schonhardt-Bailey (2013) uses unsupervised machine learning to explore and measure deliberation and strategies of persuasion in these transcripts. However, she then goes one step further and interviews many of the individuals who appear in the transcripts. Many of the questions she explores in the interviews relate not only to her research question but also to what the transcripts represent—how candid members of the FOMC felt they could be in their discussions, whether their remarks were pre-prepared, and how transparency of the transcripts themselves affected their deliberation (Schonhardt-Bailey, 2013, p. 370).

4.2.3 MEDIUM BIAS

The technologies and types of mediums in which texts are recorded will play an important role in the types of content that will be reflected in them; we will call this *medium bias*. Until 2017 Twitter only allowed 140 characters in one tweet, necessitating users to use abbreviations and links for further treatment of the topic. However,

---

[1] Kambhampati, Sandhya. "I've Sent Out 1,018 Open Records Requests, and This Is What I've Learned." *ProPublica*. Jan. 4, 2018. https://www.propublica.org/article/open-records-requests-illinois-foia-lessons

140 characters has very different implications across languages—in languages that require fewer characters per word, like Chinese and Japanese, users will be able to express more content in one post than in languages that necessitate many characters for each word like English (and notably when the character limit was doubled in November of 2017, the other languages were not included). Further, the mode of expression in social media changes with advances in technologies. As users have been able to incorporate pictures, videos, and live streams, the role of the accompanying text changes. Users interested in text analysis in social media should be aware of other types of data—links, pictures, and videos—when describing their content and how technological capabilities have changed over time.

The technology and evolution of the medium can create different cultures for users so that the text can only be understood in the context of the platform. Snapchat, a social media platform where posts are generally only accessible briefly before being destroyed, will create a different environment for users than Twitter, where posts are public and more permanent. Because online platforms tailor their website to individual users' predicted interests, users may all have a different experience of the content on the platform, which might be reflected in their posting behavior. Researchers should consider biases that might be produced from different experiences users have between platforms and within individual platforms to understand the underlying data generating process of how the texts were produced.

Text outside of social media is similarly influenced by its medium. Meeting transcripts or notes may reflect the content of the conversation, but not tone of voice, body language, or other forms of expressed emotion (Schonhardt-Bailey, 2017; Dietrich, Enos, and Sen, 2019). Handwritten notes may contain drawings or doodles. Text messages may contain emojis, which are central to content. When possible, researchers should read and interact with texts in their original context to understand how the social events of interest are translated by the medium into text, even if text analysis tools only take the text into account.

4.2.4 RETRIEVAL BIAS

As texts are sometimes selected using statistical methods, *retrieval bias* can sometimes affect the selection of a corpus. For example, Abello, Broadwell, and Tangherlini (2012) use computational methods to analyze Danish ghost stories. For their work, they use a hand-collected set of stories from the 19th century collector and Danish schoolteacher Evald Tang Kristensen, categorized by Kristensen as "ghost stories." It's truly remarkable to have such a hand-curated dataset, although of course what is included in the dataset reflects Kristensen's own social network and categorization scheme.

As an alternative, imagine trying to retrieve a global list of ghost stories with keywords.[2] To do so, you might select every book in the library that includes in the title ghost, but such a strategy would be riddled with errors. Some book titles that contain the word ghost may have nothing to do with ghost stories; for example, *Hungry Ghosts: Mao's Secret Famine* deals with the famine in China rather than with ghost stories. Similarly, many books that don't contain the word ghost may still be ghost stories, *A Christmas Carol* is a ghost story without ghost in the title. While these errors may

---

[2]The authors go through this thought experiment in their article, and develop statistical methods that allow for more efficient exploration of the collection.

at first seem random, they are often systematic. `ghost` may orient the analysis toward one type of genre, missing books about phantoms, which may have different themes.

This type of keyword selection of corpora is a frequent problem in the analysis of text because researchers often have a focused population of interest—like ghost stories—that is a subset of a larger, unwieldy corpus—such as all books. The problem is made worse by the fact that humans often have difficulty thinking of words off of the top of their head. Limited recall means that an analyst may miss some of the most important words on which to select. One approach is to take a computationally driven approach to corpus selection by applying machine learning to the problem of selecting documents, using many of the same techniques we will introduce in the measurement part of the book (King, Lam, and Roberts, 2017; D'Orazio et al., 2014; Abello, Broadwell, and Tangherlini, 2012). Regardless, researchers should be transparent about how they selected the texts and what potential biases this might produce in what population the text reflects.

While keywords are a simple algorithm for retrieving documents in theory, the reality is often more complicated because researchers often rely on third parties to provide data for them. Data access through Application Programming Interfaces (APIs) or other search functions may not have a transparent underlying process translating search queries into results. This could be for reasons as simple as some interfaces ignoring capitalization while others being case-sensitive. Some systems may return only a random selection of the relevant document, or only the most relevant selection. The process through which the API makes documents available will affect the population the text represents and the research questions the text can reliably answer.

4.3 Considerations of "Found Data"

Often, text corpora are a form of "found data," data not collected by purposeful sampling of a larger population, but instead made available by governments, individuals, or other institutions. What data is made available is dictated not by the research design, but by the resources and incentives of the institutions and individuals producing them. This type of data has frequently been criticized because it may not represent the population of interest, leading researchers to draw flawed or even flat-out wrong conclusions from the data (Harford, 2014).

Despite these limitations, the use of data in a research project is dictated by data availability and must be subject to ethical and legal constraints, as we discussed in Chapter 3. For any dataset, researchers should clearly communicate to the reader the logic of selecting that dataset to answer the question of interest, as well as what relevant information the dataset may not contain or represent.

4.4 Conclusion

Selecting documents is a crucial part of the analysis process but is subject to many constraints based on availability, medium, and ability to retrieve them out of a larger collection. The core challenge is to create a corpus that is representative of the population of interest. This is, of course, notably challenging if you have not chosen a population of interest. Are you interested in sentiment on Twitter or in the US population? Do you care about the political preferences of everyone or just likely voters?

These challenges may be further exacerbated by the need to draw comparisons across time or source. Social media platforms like Twitter and Facebook are constantly changing their policies, which make resource bias, incentive bias, medium bias and retrieval bias all moving targets. Indeed the very nature of the phenomenon itself might be changing (Munger, 2019). Larger cities might have more established newspapers that can do more investigative reporting. Does this mean that corruption—to choose one example—happens more in big cities than in small localities or just that we know more about it? A quite common problem we have observed in practice is that with document collections over a multi-decade time horizon there are essentially always more documents later than earlier.

These challenges are question-specific and the temporal or source inconsistencies that plague one research question might be exactly the object of interest for another. How problematic these issues can be also depends on the particular method used to analyze the texts. We will return to this issue throughout the book.

CHAPTER 5

Bag of Words

In the previous chapter, we covered some of the key biases to watch out for when curating a new collection of documents. In order to apply the tools of text analysis we need to give those documents a numerical representation. In this chapter we introduce the "bag of words" model. This representation provides the foundation for the multinomial language model and the vector space model, which we cover in Chapters 6 and 7 respectively.

As we introduced in Chapter 3, we will use the State of the Union corpus to introduce the bag of words model to show how the expression of the policy priorities of presidents in the US has changed over time. We use this corpus in part to show how to represent texts as data, but we also hope to convey how even simple quantitative analyses of text used in conjunction with deep knowledge of social science can be powerful for social science research.

5.1 The Bag of Words Model

The most common text representation is called the *bag of words* model. The core idea is simple: we will represent each document by counting how many times each word appears in it.

For example, we might be interested in how Presidential focus on the manufacturing sector has changed over time. We take two sentences including the word `manufacturing` from the State of the Union corpus. For now, let's treat each of these short sentences as documents: and represent them in a matrix.

	undoubtedly	power	congress	seriously	affect	agricultural	manufacturing	interests	france	passage	laws	relating	trade	united	states	make	sure	foreign	company	advantage	american	comes	accessing	financing	new	markets	like	russia
Doc 1	1	1	1	1	1	1	1	1	1	1	1	1	1	1	1	1	0	0	0	0	0	0	0	0	0	0	0	0
Doc 2	0	0	1	0	0	0	0	1	0	0	0	0	0	0	0	0	1	1	1	1	1	1	1	1	1	1	1	1

Example 5.1. Two example sentences that include the word `manufacturing` from the SOTU corpus.

> Doc 1: It is undoubtedly in the power of Congress seriously to affect the agricultural and manufacturing interests of France by the passage of laws relating to her trade with the United States. (President Jackson, 1831)
>
> Doc 2: And this Congress should make sure that no foreign company has an advantage over American manufacturing when it comes to accessing financing or new markets like Russia. (President Obama, 2012)

This is a *document-feature matrix* where each row represents a different document and each column defines a feature that we use to represent the document. This throws away a lot of information—most notably word order—but provides the researcher with a parsimonious representation of the document that is useful for many purposes.

While the core idea of a bag of words is quite simple, there are a multitude of small decisions that have to be made to create a representation like the one above. In this chapter we lay out a default recipe for the bag of words model and in later chapters we introduce some more of the complexities. In total the full recipe is:

1. Choose the Unit of Analysis
2. Tokenize
3. Reduce Complexity
   - Lowercase
   - Remove Punctuation
   - Remove Stop Words
   - Create Equivalence Classes (Lemmatize/Stem)
   - Filter by Frequency
4. Create the Document-Feature Matrix

5.2 Choose the Unit of Analysis

After digitizing the text, the analyst must decide on the *unit* of analysis. In many cases, the unit of analysis is the document—some researchers want to measure such quantities as topics and sentiments in anything from newspaper articles to social media posts to journal articles. However, in some cases the unit of analysis might be smaller or larger than the document—the analyst may want to break apart a newspaper article into headlines and paragraphs, or combine all the tweets written by a single author in one day. For our example, we will use sentences as the unit of analysis because they are short and are therefore more useful for expository purposes.

There are three things to consider when choosing the unit of analysis: the logistics of splitting, the model, and the question.

Documents—especially documents that are difficult to access—don't always come in the form we would ideally like. For example, the *Chronicling America* project from the Library of Congress collects and digitizes historical newspapers from 1789 to 1963.

These documents are scanned from newsprint and then digitized using optical character recognition (OCR) technology. Because newspapers tend to print in columns and
news articles often jump across pages, it is difficult to actually access the text that goes
with a particular news article even if it is the relevant unit of analysis. Instead, as a
compromise to the logistics of splitting up the articles, we might analyze the newspaper
page (Young, 2012). Logistical issues also arise when we want to split a text into sections
but those sections are not uniformly labeled or otherwise easy to detect.

The second consideration is how the unit of analysis affects the model. We will discuss this issue in more depth in the coming chapters, but in some cases splitting up
a single text into many documents can substantially increase or decrease the computational cost of fitting a model. It also may make the model more or less statistically
efficient. In the digital humanities, researchers often analyze long texts like novels and
split them up into chunks of a few hundred words to improve model fits (Jockers, 2013).

The final—and most important—consideration is the question itself. Just as
researchers with a question about when countries go to war should use countries or
country dyads rather than provinces as the unit of analysis, researchers interested in
how the plot of a novel varies over time should study a novel instead of individual
chapters or sentences. This can create a conflict between what is computationally expe-
dient and what best addresses the question of interest. These trade-offs don't always
have obvious answers. Sometimes the model can be fit on small chunks of text and the
results aggregated to estimate properties of the question-relevant unit, but depending
on the model this might not be straightforward. The decisions need to be made on a
case-by-case basis.

For the rest of the book, for ease of understanding, we will typically refer to the unit
of analysis—whether novels, paragraphs, or tweets —as the "document." We want to be
clear that this does not mean we always expect the researcher to be using a full document
as the unit of analysis.

5.3 Tokenize

Having chosen the unit of analysis, we are ready to move to the second step, tokenization. While choosing the unit of analysis is about breaking up the corpus into discrete
documents, tokenizing is about breaking up a document into discrete words. In our
initial example, we split our two short sentences (henceforth "documents") into their
constituent words. The bag of words model retains only the number of times each word
appears in each document. Each individual word in the document is a *token* and the
process of splitting a document into its constituent words is called *tokenization*. More
generally, *tokens* are the individual units we split our document into before counting
them up. Each token is of a particular *type* (in this context the name of the column).
We will often refer to the set of *types* as the vocabulary.

In English, distinct words are separated using white space. This means from a code
perspective, tokenization is essentially as simple as splitting the text up by white space.
This approach will work for most languages. However, in some languages, such as
Chinese, Japanese, and Lao, words are not separated by spaces; instead, words are
inferred by the reader from the context within the sentence. For these languages we need
a model, called a word segmentation model, to split the characters into their constituent
words.

It is worth considering why we choose to divide documents into words at all. On one
extreme we could split documents into individual letters. This would have the advantage

of there being only 26 possible types, one for each letter from A to Z (in English at least). This probably wouldn't be a great representation of the document because the letter K has no meaning on its own. On the other extreme we could split documents into individual sentences. Sentences generally contain a complete idea, but any given sentence is probably unique even in a corpus of millions of documents—that is, there are far too many types. Words are a compromise because they individually contain meaning but there are a limited number of types.

Yet sometimes even the single word can be too narrow because some concepts bridge words. A common example is white house, where some important meaning is lost when the phrase is tokenized into white and house. We can recover some of this meaning by using *n*-grams, an ordered set of *n* words, as our features. We call single words *unigrams*, ordered pairs *bigrams*, and ordered triples *trigrams*. Using higher order *n*-grams substantially increases the number of unique types, but can aid our text analysis by retaining more information.

Researchers can include n-grams in two ways. First, they could include all consecutive sets of two words that appear in the corpus, in addition to or instead of unigrams. This will result in a very large number of types and thus many columns in our final document-feature matrix. We will discuss ways to reduce the number of unique types in Section 5.4.5 on filtering.

Alternatively, researchers might find it useful to retain a list of particular bigrams and trigrams that they anticipate will be useful to their analysis. For example, Rule, Cointet, and Bearman (2015) use some multiword phrases such as national security and local government in their analysis of SOTU speeches. We will visually denote this by placing an underscore between two words that are being treated as an *n*-gram. When the list of *n*-grams to be extracted is small, this solves the problem of the large vocabulary, but it requires an *n*-gram list.

A common way to produce lists of *n*-grams (and also the approach taken by Rule, Cointet, and Bearman (2015)) is based on statistical tests. There are many variants but they share a common logic. Imagine that we are trying to create a list of bigrams that have a meaning separate from their constituent parts. We can use the probability of seeing this pair of words relative to the probability of seeing them each independently. For example, if the chance of seeing white house is high enough relative to seeing white and house separately, we add it to our list of bigrams. There are other strategies for identifying *n*-grams that are based on grammatical patterns in

Example 5.2. Example of tokenization for a sentence from the SOTU corpus. United States is converted to United_States to make it a bigram.

```
It is undoubtedly in the power of Congress seriously
to affect the agricultural and manufacturing interests
of France by the passage of laws relating to her trade
with the United States.

It is undoubtedly in the power of Congress seriously
to affect the agricultural and manufacturing interests
of France by the passage of laws relating to her trade
with the United_States.
```

language. We defer a discussion of these until Chapter 9 on structured representations of language.

In Example 5.2, we show how the first document from Example 5.1 could be tokenized. We have included the bigram United States as an *n*-gram that we want to treat as a single token.

5.4 Reduce Complexity

Once the words in the document have been tokenized, we could immediately jump to the fourth step of the recipe and count them up and construct our document-feature matrix. However, for many applications this will lead to a vocabulary that is far too large to be productive. Thus, in bag of words models there is usually a stage where we drop some word types in order to reduce complexity. Reducing complexity will help us with computation and make downstream analysis parsimonious. In this section we identify five common steps and identify the many decisions that go into each one. At each stage we update our running example.

5.4.1 LOWERCASE

Often the first step after tokenizing identifies the individual words is to replace all capital letters with lowercase letters. The idea is that the word In is no different than in for most applications and research questions. A variation of this strategy is to only lowercase words when they begin a sentence.

Original: It is undoubtedly in the power of Congress
seriously to affect the agricultural and manufacturing
interests of France by the passage of laws relating to
her trade with the United States.

Before Lowercase: It is undoubtedly in the power of Congress
seriously to affect the agricultural and manufacturing
interests of France by the passage of laws relating to
her trade with the United_States.

After Lowercase: it is undoubtedly in the power of congress
seriously to affect the agricultural and manufacturing
interests of france by the passage of laws relating to
her trade with the united_states.

5.4.2 REMOVE PUNCTUATION

The second step is to remove all punctuation. Again for many research questions, researchers are often not interested in how many commas, apostrophes, or periods appear within the text, and thus choose to delete them. The researcher may also want to get rid of formatting cues that often exist within data from other sources. For example, section headings, page numbers, and html tags, may not be important to the purpose of the research, and, if so, should be discarded before the analysis. On the other hand, certain forms of punctuation, for example the # symbol on Twitter,

may be essential to retain the meaning of the original work. For certain tasks, such
as sentiment analysis, this step must be done carefully as common punctuation-based
emojis, such as :) , and exclamation marks can be strong predictors of sentiment. Note
that we are careful here not to remove the underscore as we are using it to indicate
the bigram.

Original: `It is undoubtedly in the power of Congress`
`seriously to affect the agricultural and manufacturing`
`interests of France by the passage of laws relating to`
`her trade with the United States.`

Before Punctuation Removal: `it is undoubtedly in the power of`
`congress seriously to affect the agricultural and`
`manufacturing interests of france by the passage of`
`laws relating to her trade with the united_states.`

After Punctuation Removal: `it is undoubtedly in the power of`
`congress seriously to affect the agricultural and`
`manufacturing interests of france by the passage of`
`laws relating to her trade with the united_states`

5.4.3 REMOVE STOP WORDS

After lowercasing and removing unwanted punctuation, the only content left in the
document is the words themselves. The analyst may decide to remove *stop words*—
common words used across documents that do not give much information about the
task at hand.[1] In English, common words such as `and`, `the`, and `that` may be removed

---

Original: `It is undoubtedly in the power of Congress`
`seriously to affect the agricultural and manufacturing`
`interests of France by the passage of laws relating to`
`her trade with the United States.`

Before Stop Word Removal: `it is undoubtedly in the power of`
`congress seriously to affect the agricultural and`
`manufacturing interests of france by the passage of`
`laws relating to her trade with the united_states`

After Stop Word Removal: `undoubtedly power congress seriously`
`affect agricultural manufacturing interests france`
`passage laws relating trade united_states`

---

[1] The idea of omitting a specific list of common words appears to have originated in the early information
retrieval work of Harold Luhn while proposing keywords in context (Luhn, 1960). Barbara Flood recounts
that in 1961 she was compiling biological abstracts and they had decided to try the new keywords in context
approach to indexing. She was given reams of printouts to look through manually and decided to delete
highly common words in the index such as `of` and `in`. Because these were going to be literally stopped
from printing, she called them the "stop list" (Flood, 1999).

from the documents to reduce the size and complexity of the feature set. Removing stop words often removes an extremely high fraction of the corpus's *tokens* while removing very few of the *types*, which—if those words carry little or no meaning—can result in huge computational savings. This reflects the empirical fact that in most languages a few words are extremely common. The idea is that even though these tokens account for a large fraction of the words, they account for only a small fraction of the meaning. Lists of stop words in many languages are available in software packages that provide text analysis tools.

5.4.4 CREATE EQUIVALENCE CLASSES (LEMMATIZE/STEM)

Shifting everything to lower case, removing punctuation, and dropping stop words will substantially reduce the number of types in the vocabulary. However, there can still be cases where many words carry the same information because they share a common root. For example `family`, `families`, and `family's` (with the apostrophe possibly dropped) are all distinct types in the vocabulary but for some tasks it may be effective to map them all to a common form. A *lemma* is the canonical form (such as one might find in a dictionary) of a set of words that are related by inflection (i.e., modifications due to case, number, tense, etc.). Lemmatization is the process of mapping words to their lemma. This is an equivalence assertion—a statement that for our purposes we will treat all variants of the word the same.

Sometimes identifying the lemma is relatively simple, as in the case of variants of `family`, but it can also be quite complex. For example, in English, many common words (e.g., `see`) have an irregular past tense (e.g., `saw`). Even exactly the same token can have two different lemmas depending on the part of speech. For example, a piece of writing would have the lemma `writing` while the act of writing would have the lemma `write`. Lemmatization can be cumbersome because it often requires a dictionary lookup (to map `saw` to `see`) and part of speech tagging (to distinguish the two lemmas of `writing`). A popular approximation to lemmatizing that also maps related forms together is *stemming*. In stemming, we simply discard the end of a word using a few simple rules. In the case of `family`, all of our variants above would be mapped to `famili`. While stemming is often quite effective and substantially faster than lemmatization, it does fail to deal with words that have more complex forms

---

It is undoubtedly in the power of Congress seriously to affect the agricultural and manufacturing interests of France by the passage of laws relating to her trade with the United States.

Before Stemming: undoubtedly power congress seriously affect agricultural manufacturing interests france passage laws relating trade united_states

After Stemming: undoubt power congress serious affect agricultur manufactur interest franc passag law relat trade united_states (such as the see and writing examples). Stemming can also sometimes reduce two words to a common stem that may have quite distinct meanings such as secure and securities.

There are many stemming algorithms available in a wide range of software; among the most common is the *Porter* stemming algorithm (Porter, 1980). Stemming is still substantially more popular than lemmatization, likely due to a combination of speed, accessibility across languages, and momentum. Depending on the language you are working in and the computational resources available, lemmatization may be more or less preferred to stemming. In either case, the goal is to simplify the analysis by bringing down the number of types by treating the variants of a word as equivalent in our document-feature matrix.

5.4.5 FILTER BY FREQUENCY

The final step of reducing complexity before creating the document-feature matrix is to remove words that are very rare (or sometimes, very common). If a word appears only once in the corpus, we are unlikely to use it effectively and, depending on the model, removing all such words from the corpus might yield substantial computational savings. Due to the properties of language there are often many such rare words in a corpus.

In other cases we may want to remove words that have incredibly high frequency. A word that is used in every document is unlikely to be useful in helping us discriminate between documents. We like to think of these as application-specific stop words and they often appear when the corpus was explicitly selected on presence of a keyword or when the corpus is on a particular topic with a common vocabulary.

In total, the recipe we have given is tokenize, lowercase, remove punctuation, create equivalence classes, and filter by frequency. It is worth noting that the order in which these steps are taken matters as well. For example, if stop words are removed before tokenization, the analyst will end up with different bigrams and trigrams than if they are removed before. The analyst must use her best judgement to decide which preprocessing steps to take and in what order. When the preprocessed data are used in analyses downstream, validation will be needed to ensure that the preprocessing retained the information relevant to the researcher's question of interest. We will talk more extensively about validation in later parts of the book.

5.5 Construct Document-Feature Matrix

Now that we have tokenized the corpus and reduced its complexity somewhat, it is time to turn the text into numeric data. We will use N to delineate the number of unique text units within your dataset, and i to index each of these units. After preprocessing these units, you can identify the number of types within your dataset, which is the size of your vocabulary and which we will delineate with J and index by j. The result of this is what we call a document-feature matrix, which we will call W, an $N \times J$ matrix. Each element W_{ij} of this matrix is the number of times that each type appears in the document. In general, since most documents only contain a few of the many unique types within a corpus, the document-feature matrix is relatively *sparse*—that is, it contains mostly zeros.

We return to our two example sentences from the SOTU corpus, below:

SOTU example corpus

Doc 1: `It is undoubtedly in the power of Congress seriously to affect the agricultural and manufacturing interests of France by the passage of laws relating to her trade with the United States.` (President Jackson, 1831)

Doc 2: `And this Congress should make sure that no foreign company has an advantage over American manufacturing when it comes to accessing financing or new markets like Russia.` (President Obama, 2012)

We could then put them through the same preprocessing routine as we did above. This would create two documents, each having been converted to lowercase, had punctuation removed, had stop words removed, and been stemmed. After doing this, we would document the number of unique types within the corpus, the *vocabulary*. Overall, after being preprocessed, these three documents have 28 unique words. W would therefore consist of two rows (one for each document) and 28 columns (one for each unique word). The entries of those rows would count the number of times each word appeared in each document; see below.

Once we have W, there are many operations we can perform on it that can help summarize the text. To take two simple examples to start, if we sum each of the columns of W, we will have a summary of how many of each unique type appear within the corpus.

Or, we could sum each of the rows of the document-feature matrix, which would tell us how many tokens each document has (after preprocessing). The maximum of this sum would be the length of the longest document, and the minimum of this sum would

Table 5.1. Document-feature matrix W from two sentences containing the word `manufacturing` from the SOU corpus.

	undoubt	power	congress	serious	affect	agricultur	manufactur	interest	franc	passag	law	relat	trade	unit	state	make	sure	foreign	compani	advantag	american	come	access	financ	new	market	like	russia
Doc 1	1	1	1	1	1	1	1	1	1	1	1	1	1	1	1	1	0	0	0	0	0	0	0	0	0	0	0	0
Doc 2	0	0	1	0	0	0	1	0	0	0	0	0	0	0	0	0	1	1	1	1	1	1	1	1	1	1	1	1

Table 5.2. Result of summing the columns of W, the document-feature matrix.

undoubt	power	congress	serious	affect	agricultur	manufactur	interest	franc	passag	law	relat	trade	unit	state	make	sure	foreign	compani	advantag	american	come	access	financ	new	market	like	russia
1	1	2	1	1	1	2	1	1	1	1	1	1	1	1	1	1	1	1	1	1	1	1	1	1	1	1	1

Table 5.3. Result of summing the rows of W, the document-feature matrix.

Doc 1	15
Doc 2	15

be the length of the shortest document. While these are basic examples, much of the rest of this book describes algorithms that perform operations on representations like this document-feature matrix.

5.6 Rethinking the Defaults

The default procedure that we outline above is simply that, a default procedure. It doesn't work for all cases and is primarily designed for settings where our task is to cover the general subject matter of the documents, as in the examples from the SOTU corpus. There are two types of settings where you may want to abandon one or more of these procedures. The first is where the procedures are inappropriate for the type of problem and the second is where the data is sufficiently large that the procedures are harmful.

5.6.1 AUTHORSHIP OF THE FEDERALIST PAPERS

To see how the default procedure we describe can be inappropriate for particular problems, we return to Mosteller and Wallace (1963)'s analysis of the Federalist Papers that we described in Chapter 3. Mosteller and Wallace (1963) tackle the problem of unknown authorship of a set of the Federalist Papers, documents written in support of the American Constitution by a combination of Alexander Hamilton, John Jay, and James Madison in the late 1700s. While the authors of many of the papers are known, the authorship of 12 particular papers is disputed.

Mosteller and Wallace (1963) show that the writing style of Jay, Hamilton, and Madison differed significantly through their use of *filler words*—particularly words like upon, by, and to. These are precisely the kinds of words we would filter out as stop words because they don't contain any meaningful content about subject matter. In this context though, that was exactly the objective. In his autobiography, Mosteller recalled that they wanted "words whose use is unrelated to the topic and may be regarded as reflecting minor or perhaps unconscious preferences of the author" (Mosteller, 2010, p. 56).

This kind of conflict between the default recipe and substantive problem is restricted not just to the author attribution problem. Social scientists of all types have shown the importance of text features that the default recipe can treat as content-free (Biber, 1991; Chung and Pennebaker, 2007; Breiger, Wagner-Pacifici, and Mohr, 2018). For example, Monroe, Colaresi, and Quinn (2008) show that gender pronouns like he and she are highly associated with the political party of the speaker in speech in the US Congressional Record. Since these pronouns are included in nearly every English stop word list, we might miss a valuable insight by just dropping all stop words without thinking about it. Denny and Spirling (2018) demonstrate that variations in many of the steps we describe above can impact the results of downstream analyses and suggest

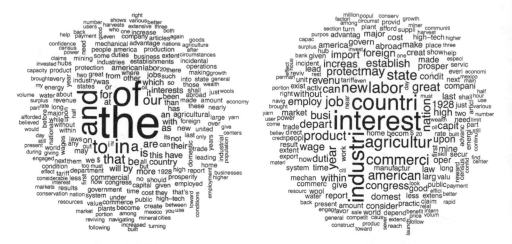

Figure 5.1. Word clouds of the most common words in the sentences in the SOTU corpus containing the word `manufacturing`. The left panel shows the word cloud with only punctuation removed. The right panel shows the word cloud with the default recipe. In both cases, we remove the word `manufacturing` since it is most prevalent by design.

testing several different combinations to see if the outcomes differ. We will return to this argument later in the book.

5.6.2   THE SCALE ARGUMENT AGAINST PREPROCESSING

Many of the steps in the default recipe are about reducing the size of the vocabulary. There are essentially two reasons for this: aesthetics and efficiency.

When we make word clouds or visualize model results, not removing stop words can make those visualizations less informative. Figure 5.1 shows two word clouds of the SOTU corpus sentences that contain the word `manufacturing`. The left panel does not do any removal besides punctuation, and the right panel follows the default recipe. We see immediately that the right panel is much more informative about the subjects of the sentences that contain the word `manufacturing`, while the left panel highlights common and uninformative words such as `of` and `the`. While the aesthetic consideration is an an important practical reality, it can be addressed by changing our visualizations rather than changing our inputs. For example, we could always include stop words in our document-feature matrix but explicitly omit them from the visualization. When we discuss separating words in the Discovery part of the book, we will return to this issue of how to find representative words that are less susceptible to the clutter of uninformative words.

The second reason to reduce the size of the vocabulary is efficiency of the subsequent data analysis. Stemming and lemmatizing make an assertion that two related words like `car` and `cars` can be treated exactly the same. If they have close enough to a common meaning, baking in that knowledge will be helpful because it means fewer types in the vocabulary to deal with. However, the salience of this advice arises from a pragmatically understandable focus on corpora with relatively few documents. Yet, as social scientists move from analyzing collections of thousands documents to routinely analyzing collections of millions of documents, it may not be as important to assert that any subsequent analysis treat `car` and `cars` the same because our models have enough information to figure out these relations on their own. Indeed, we could even be wrong about the two words conveying similar information. If we are predicting the wealth of the author, mentioning `cars` may mean something different on average than `car`.

A recent line of work by Alexandra Schofield and David Mimno has documented that for topic models—a popular class of models that we will discuss in Discovery where these procedures are almost always applied—the application of default stemming and stop word removal can actually be harmful for model performance when the corpus is large (Schofield and Mimno, 2016; Schofield, Magnusson, and Mimno, 2017). The more general lesson here is that folk wisdom and heuristic advice of the sort represented in default recipes is always a product of its time. It is a sign of text analysis maturing as a field that the community is beginning to reexamine those defaults.

5.7 Conclusion

In this chapter we walked step by step through the basic recipe of the bag of words representation of text. While any default recipe will have some limitations—and we explored some of those in the previous section—the bag of words model is shockingly powerful for something that throws away so much information! In the next two chapters, we present two different frameworks for building methods on top of the bag of words representation, the multinomial language model and the vector space model.

CHAPTER 6

The Multinomial Language Model

This book describes models with two types of foundations: *probabilistic* and *algorithmic*. In this chapter we will consider the multinomial distribution, which builds off the bag of words representation from the last chapter and provides the foundations for many of the probabilistic models we will consider in this book. In the next chapter we provide an alternate algorithmic framework with the vector space model.

In probabilistic models—the most common in the field of statistics—we tell a story about how the data came to be generated using probability. This data generating process is based on a set of unknown parameters or unobserved latent variables which we can infer using the data that we actually observe. For example, in analyzing the Federalist Papers example, we will tell a story about how each author generates function words in given texts at different rates. After positing the story, we can use the attributed Federalist Papers to reverse that process and infer the unknown rates for each author. This in turn allows us to calculate the probability that Hamilton or Madison authored a disputed paper by comparing their inferred rates to the real unattributed text.

These models are attractive because they offer a clear statement of assumptions about when the models would perform ideally (i.e., when the assumptions about the data generating process are accurate), and they are easy to extend to new situations by modifying the data-generating process. Perhaps most importantly, specification of a probability model provides access to a wealth of recipes in statistics for optimization and quantification of uncertainty. Blei (2014) provides an accessible overview to this style of model, where he advocates a loop of building models, computing parameters, critiquing the findings, and then repeating.

These probabilistic foundations are in contrast to algorithmic approaches which specify a series of steps, usually in the form of an objective function to optimize. This is best thought of as a different language for describing a similar thing. For example, many models, such as linear regression, might be described from a probabilistic perspective (a normal linear model) or from an algorithmic perspective (minimize the sum of squared errors). The difference between these two foundations is often overstated. A probability model implies an objective function and many objective functions imply an algorithmic model.

We start by introducing the multinomial distribution, a popular distribution for count data. We then describe its application to a basic probabilistic language model— a model that predicts a sequence of words. We then show how to extend this simple setup by building a hierarchical model. This strategy of building hierarchical models will form the foundation of the probabilistic clustering, admixture, and classification models that appear later in the book.

6.1 Multinomial Distribution

We start by formulating an improbable model of language creation that accords with the bag of words representation of text that we developed in the previous chapter. We begin with the highly simplified setting where we have a three-word vocabulary (cat, dog, fish) and each document contains only a single token (i.e., an instance of a type). We will encode each token with a vector of the same length as the vocabulary that contains only a single 1 (indicating the category) with the rest of the entries being 0. Thus we represent each word with the following vectors, which also happen to be the three possible unique documents:

$$\texttt{cat} = (1, 0, 0)$$
$$\texttt{dog} = (0, 1, 0)$$
$$\texttt{fish} = (0, 0, 1)$$

This is called a "one-hot encoding" in machine learning, although social scientists may be more familiar with the term "dummy variable."

When each document is only one token long, we can think of the document as a draw from a *categorical distribution*. The categorical distribution assigns a probability to realizing each category such that the document $\mathbf{W}_{i,} \sim \text{Categorical}(\boldsymbol{\mu})$, where $\boldsymbol{\mu}$ is a vector containing the probability of each individual type. For example, say that the cat document is twice as likely as dog and fish; we have the vector

$$\boldsymbol{\mu} = (.5, .25, .25).$$

We can write the probability mass function as

$$p(\mathbf{W}_{i,}|\boldsymbol{\mu}) = \prod_{j=1}^{J} \mu_j^{W_{ij}}. \tag{6.1.1}$$

This generalizes naturally to the case of documents that are longer than one word using the multinomial distribution. The multinomial has an additional parameter M, an integer that controls the number of tokens (i.e., the length of the document). We can thus say that $\mathbf{W}_{i,} \sim \text{Multinomial}(M_i, \boldsymbol{\mu})$, and when $M_i = 1$ this reduces to the categorical distribution. This model has a probability mass function

$$p(\mathbf{W}_{i,}|\boldsymbol{\mu}) = \frac{M!}{\prod_{j=1}^{J} W_{ij}!} \prod_{j=1}^{J} \mu_j^{W_{ij}}. \tag{6.1.2}$$

A draw from this distribution will still be a vector but now instead of a single 1 and the remainder 0, it will be all nonnegative integers, which sum to M_i. For example, for the document (fish, cat, fish), we can provide the vector representation and calculate the probability of drawing it under our previously stated parameter vector of

$\mu = (.5, .25, .25)$ by plugging it into our probability mass function above.

$$(\texttt{fish}, \texttt{cat}, \texttt{fish}) = (1, 0, 2)$$

$$p(\texttt{fish}, \texttt{cat}, \texttt{fish} \mid \mu) = \frac{3!}{(1!)(0!)(2!)} (.5)^1 (.25)^0 (.25)^2$$

$$= .09375$$

Under the multinomial distribution each word is generated independently of all other words. It is equivalent to taking M independent draws from the categorical distribution with parameter μ and summing the resulting one-hot encoding vectors. This provides a simple generative story that matches the bag of words representation where order is irrelevant, and we represent documents by the count of the words it contains.

The parameter μ can't take on any value: it must be within the $J-1$ dimensional simplex. A $J-1$ dimensional simplex is a vector of J values that sum to 1 and are all nonnegative—intuitively, it is a set of proportions. Figure 6.1 visualizes the two-dimensional simplex for our three-word vocabulary using a triangle.

PROPERTIES

The advantage of specifying a probability model is that it immediately comes with a set of known results that are a consequence of the modeling assumptions. For example, the following properties about the expectation, variance, and covariance arise from the model:

$$E[W_{ij}] = M_i \mu_j \qquad (6.1.3)$$

$$\text{Var}(W_{ij}) = M_i \mu_j (1 - \mu_j) \qquad (6.1.4)$$

$$\text{Cov}(W_{ij}, W_{ij'}) = -M_i \mu_j \mu_{j'} \qquad (6.1.5)$$

Note that under the multinomial model, the variance and covariance are fixed functions of the parameters that determine the mean.

In practice we typically observe the word counts $W_{i,}$ and want to estimate the underlying parameter μ ($M_i = \sum_{j'=1}^{J} W_{ij'}$ is effectively observed as it is the number of tokens in the document). The probability model also provides straightforward approaches to computation. The maximum likelihood estimate for a given element μ_j is just the number of times word j is used divided by the total number of tokens.

$$\hat{\mu}_j = \frac{W_{ij}}{M_i} \qquad (6.1.6)$$

μ can be interpreted as the fraction of each type of word that would be used in an infinite length document.

Now imagine that we have N documents that share the parameter μ. That is, each document $W_{i,} \sim \text{Multinomial}(M_i, \mu)$. We can visualize this process using the graphical model depicted in the left panel of Figure 6.2. As we build more complex models, the notation will get cumbersome, and so we will represent the model using plate notation (right panel). The idea is that each plate indicates repetition, with the index in the bottom right corner of the plate indicating the number of replicated nodes sharing the same relationships. In this case, because W is inside the plate and μ is outside the plate,

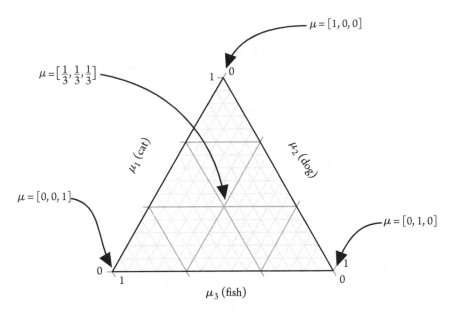

Figure 6.1. A visualization of a 2-D simplex. Each element of μ corresponds to a word (e.g., μ_1 provides the probability of cat). Each point inside the triangle corresponds with a value of the vector μ. Four individual points are labeled (the three corners and the center).

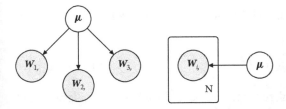

Figure 6.2. A graphical model and the plate diagram for a simple multi-nomial model with $N = 3$.

we know there are N documents, but only one parameter μ. The node containing W is shaded to indicate that it is observed data.

Because each token in the multinomial is drawn independently, we can also sum over all the documents to create a single multinomial random variable. That is, $\sum_i W_i, \sim$ Multinomial($\sum_i M_i, \mu$). Under the model assumptions, we can treat all the documents sharing the parameter μ as one large document for the purposes of estimating μ.

The multinomial distribution effectively tells a story about how documents are produced. The assumption that the word counts arise from a multinomial distribution with a common parameter μ brings with it a number of useful statistical results. In the next section we show how this connects to the idea of a language model.

6.2 Basic Language Modeling

A *language model* is a model that assigns a probability to observing a particular sequence of tokens given some set of parameters. Language models are building blocks that underlie many of the more complicated models that we will consider in later chapters. For now, we will consider cases where we are calculating the probability of

Table 6.1. Word counts from our three-word vocabulary for Federalist Papers attributed to each author and Federalist #49, one of the disputed essays.

	by	man	upon
Hamilton	859	102	374
Jay	82	0	1
Madison	474	17	7
Disputed Essay	15	2	0

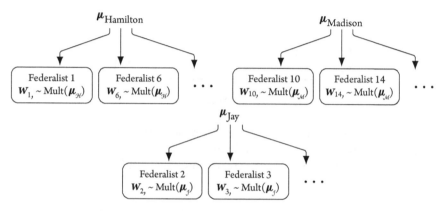

Figure 6.3. Flowchart showing the data generating process for the multinomial language model.

an unordered set of tokens and return to the question of ordered sequences in later chapters.

To consider how this would be useful, recall the work of Mosteller and Wallace (1963) on trying to identify the authors of the disputed Federalist Papers. For simplicity, let's consider a highly simplified setting that only has a three-word vocabulary: by, man, and upon. The word counts for papers known to be from each author as well as Federalist 49 ("Method of Guarding Against the Encroachments of Any One Department of Government by Appealing to the People Through a Convention"), which is disputed, are given in Table 6.1. These are our raw data.

The multinomial language model provides us with one way to assess the probability that the disputed essay was written by each author. We will assume each author uses his own multinomial distribution and posit a generative process for the documents shown in Figure 6.3.

Because the sum of multinomials with the same μ parameter is also multinomial, the model in Figure 6.3 can be written formally as follows (denoting each author with a stylized subscript of his last initial):

$$W_{\mathcal{H},} \sim \text{Multinomial}(1335, \mu_{\mathcal{H}})$$
$$W_{\mathcal{J},} \sim \text{Multinomial}(83, \mu_{\mathcal{J}})$$
$$W_{\mathcal{M},} \sim \text{Multinomial}(498, \mu_{\mathcal{M}})$$

We can then estimate a value for each author-specific μ given the data (his attributed collection of documents). This in turn will let us calculate the probability that the disputed essay arose from each of the three.

Applying formula 6.1.6, we can estimate the μ vector for each author.

$$\hat{\mu}_{\mathcal{H}} = \left(\frac{859}{859 + 102 + 374}, \frac{102}{859 + 102 + 374}, \frac{374}{859 + 102 + 374} \right)$$

$$= (.64, .08, .28)$$

$$\hat{\mu}_{\mathcal{J}} = \left(\frac{82}{82 + 0 + 1}, \frac{0}{82 + 0 + 1}, \frac{1}{82 + 0 + 1} \right)$$

$$= (.99, 0, .01)$$

$$\hat{\mu}_{\mathcal{M}} = \left(\frac{474}{474 + 17 + 7}, \frac{17}{474 + 17 + 7}, \frac{7}{474 + 17 + 7} \right)$$

$$= (.95, .035, .015)$$

Now if we want to assess the probability of the disputed essay coming from Hamilton or any of the other authors, we can simply plug in $\hat{\mu}_{\mathcal{H}}$ for μ and W_{Disputed}, for $W_{i,}$ in the formula for the probability mass function:

$$p(W_{\text{Disputed},} | \hat{\mu}_{\mathcal{H}}) = \frac{17!}{(15!)(2!)(0!)} (.64)^{15} (.08)^2 (.28)^0$$

$$= 0.001$$

$$p(W_{\text{Disputed},} | \hat{\mu}_{\mathcal{J}}) = \frac{17!}{(15!)(2!)(0!)} (.99)^{15} (0)^2 (.01)^0$$

$$= 0$$

$$p(W_{\text{Disputed},} | \hat{\mu}_{\mathcal{M}}) = \frac{17!}{(15!)(2!)(0!)} (.95)^{15} (.035)^2 (.015)^0$$

$$= 0.077$$

This calculation clearly favors Madison as the author of the disputed essay—the same conclusion that Mosteller and Wallace (1963) come to. Note that this model assigns zero probability to Jay—an overly confident conclusion we will come back to momentarily.

Here we have set up the problem as having a separate data generating process for each author. We can formulate these under one model by introducing an indicator π_i, which is a length 3 one-hot encoding that denotes which author wrote document i. For example, Federalist Paper 1 would have $\pi_1 = (1, 0, 0)$ because it was written by Hamilton. We can then stack all $\mu_{\mathcal{H}}, \mu_{\mathcal{J}}, \mu_{\mathcal{M}}$ alongside each other into a matrix μ. This allows us to write the model as

$$W_{i,} \sim \text{Multinomial}(M_i, \mu \pi_i), \qquad (6.2.1)$$

where π_i has the effect of choosing which column of μ, and thus which one of $\mu_{\mathcal{H}}, \mu_{\mathcal{J}}$, and $\mu_{\mathcal{M}}$ to use in the multinomial. This can be depicted using the plate notation in Figure 6.4.

This is a mixture model where (as indicated by the shading) the component is known. We can then perform inference directly on π_{Disputed}, but we will come back to this approach in Chapter 19 when we discuss supervised classification. A similar structure with an unobserved π will generate a clustering model that we cover in Chapter 12.

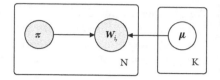

Figure 6.4. A plate diagram for the multinomial mixture model with observed labels.

6.3 Regularization and Smoothing

Recall that the model puzzlingly assigned zero probability that the disputed text was written by John Jay. This was because in the five articles attributed to John Jay, he never once uses the word man; thus, the maximum likelihood estimate of $\mu_{J,\text{Man}}$ is 0. When the word man appears in our disputed essay, we conclude that the disputed essay belonging to Jay is a zero probability event. This seems like an overly strong conclusion. In reality, we simply have fewer documents by Jay and so it seems more likely it is just by chance that he didn't ever use that word and not that he would *never* use the word.

The nature of language means that rare words are quite common and therefore so is this particular problem. A valuable approach is to include *regularization* in our estimator, which draws the estimate toward a particular value. Regularization is a non-data piece of information or a constraint that is added to the model to draw estimates toward a particular value. The idea is that this can help prevent overfitting, such as concluding that the probability of Jay writing the word man is zero.

One of the most common approaches to this problem is to simply add some fixed amount, α, to the count of each word type for each author. This essentially adds pseudo-data and pushes the estimates away from zero. In our running example, we might imagine setting $\alpha = 1$, which would move Jay's word counts to (83, 1, 2). This changes the probability of man from 0 to .02 and the probability that Jay would generate the words in the disputed text from 0 to .008—unlikely, but no longer impossible. The effect on Jay's estimates are larger than for Hamilton or Madison because as the amount of real data increases, the amount of pseudo-data stays constant, and thus it has a smaller and smaller impact on the estimate. This strategy for regularization is called *Laplace smoothing*.

Laplace smoothing is an add-on fix that exists outside the probabilistic model, but we can also include regularization in the model itself through a *prior distribution*. This essentially gives the parameter (e.g. μ) a data generating process of its own. The result is a Bayesian hierarchical model and it induces regularization in much the same way as Laplace smoothing. Recall, though, that the parameter μ must lie on the simplex, and thus to add a prior, we need a distribution where each draw results in a point on the simplex. The most common distribution of this sort is the Dirichlet distribution, which we discuss in the next section.

6.4 The Dirichlet Distribution

The Dirichlet distribution provides us with the tools to specify a data generating process for a parameter on the simplex, such as μ. This may seem like a more cumbersome process than simply adding a bit of pseudo-data to the real data, but it will provide a much more general infrastructure for building more complex models. We can write out the full data generating process as,

(1) sample word probabilities for each author

$$\mu_k \sim \text{Dirichlet}(\boldsymbol{\alpha}) \text{ for } k \in 1, 2, 3 \qquad (6.4.1)$$

(2) stack author-specific word rates in columns of matrix

$$\boldsymbol{\mu} = [\mu_1, \mu_2, \mu_3] \qquad (6.4.2)$$

(3) sample the text using the author's word probabilities

$$W_i | \boldsymbol{\mu}, \pi_i \sim \text{Multinomial}(M_i, \boldsymbol{\mu}\pi_i) \qquad (6.4.3)$$

The parameter vector $\boldsymbol{\alpha}$ defines the Dirichlet distribution and is of the same size as the μ vector for each author (thus in our running three-word vocabulary example, it is of length 3). Each value of $\boldsymbol{\alpha}$, α_j is a positive number but is otherwise unconstrained. As we will show below, $\boldsymbol{\alpha}$ corresponds to the amount of pseudo-data added under the Laplace smoothing regularization.

PROPERTIES

The properties of the Dirichlet distribution give us some sense of what typical draws of μ will look like depending on $\boldsymbol{\alpha}$. We can write the properties in terms of $\boldsymbol{\alpha}$, defining for convenience a term α_0, which is equal to the sum of the elements of $\boldsymbol{\alpha}$: $\alpha_0 = \sum_{j=1}^{J} \alpha_j$.

$$p(\boldsymbol{\mu}|\alpha) = \frac{\Gamma(\alpha_0)}{\prod_{j=1}^{J} \Gamma(\alpha_j)} \prod_{j=1}^{J} \mu_j^{\alpha_j - 1} \qquad (6.4.4)$$

$$E[\mu_j] = \frac{\alpha_j}{\alpha_0} \qquad (6.4.5)$$

$$\text{Var}(\mu_j) = \frac{\alpha_j(\alpha_0 - \alpha_j)}{\alpha_0^2(\alpha_0 + 1)} \qquad (6.4.6)$$

$$\text{Cov}(\mu_j, \mu_{j'}) = \frac{-\alpha_{j'}\alpha_j}{\alpha_0^3 + \alpha_0} \qquad (6.4.7)$$

$$\text{Mode}(\mu_j) = \frac{\alpha_j - 1}{\alpha_0 - J}, \qquad (6.4.8)$$

where Γ is the gamma function. Roughly speaking, the relative size of the values of $\boldsymbol{\alpha}$ control the typical size of the proportions of μ, and the size of α_0 controls the variance of μ. The densities for Dirichlet distributions with different values of $\boldsymbol{\alpha}$ are shown in Figure 6.5.

The Dirichlet distribution is one of the core building blocks of the more complex probabilistic models that we will consider throughout this book. In Bayesian inference, we characterize the posterior $p(\mu_k | \boldsymbol{\alpha}, W_i)$. The Dirichlet distribution is the *conjugate prior* for the multinomial distribution, which means that the conditional posterior distribution will have the same form as the prior. For our purposes it means that Bayesian computation is comparatively simple (relative to a nonconjugate prior) and that $\boldsymbol{\alpha}$ has an interpretation as pseudo-data when estimating the values of μ.

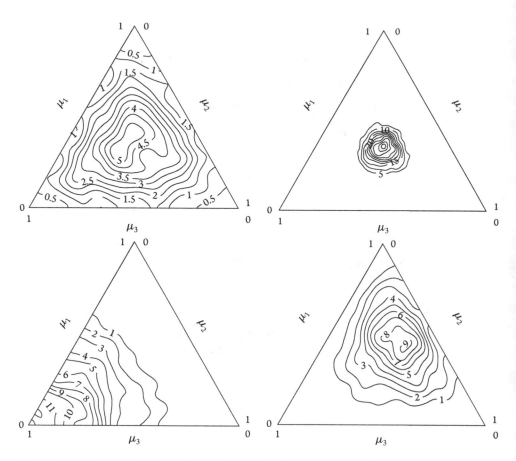

Figure 6.5. Contours of draws from a Dirichlet distribution with four different values of $\boldsymbol{\alpha}$. Top left: $\boldsymbol{\alpha} = (2,2,2)$, Top right: $\boldsymbol{\alpha} = (20,20,20)$, Bottom left: $\boldsymbol{\alpha} = (1.2,1.2,4)$, Bottom right: $\boldsymbol{\alpha} = (4,3,2)$. Note that as α_0 gets large the values become more concentrated while having a particular value of α_j be larger than the others pushes the draws into that corner of the simplex.

Returning to our example from the Federalist Papers, imagine we had estimated $\boldsymbol{\mu}_{\mathcal{H}}$, $\boldsymbol{\mu}_{\mathcal{J}}$, and $\boldsymbol{\mu}_{\mathcal{M}}$ under the language model

$$\boldsymbol{\mu}_k \sim \text{Dirichlet}(\boldsymbol{\alpha} = (1, 1, 1))$$

$$W_{i,}|\boldsymbol{\mu}, \boldsymbol{\pi}_i \sim \text{Multinomial}(M_i, \boldsymbol{\mu}\boldsymbol{\pi}_i),$$

which is depicted in plate notation in Figure 6.6. This has the form

$$\boldsymbol{\mu}_k|\boldsymbol{\alpha}, W_{i,} \sim \text{Dirichlet}(W_{i,} + \boldsymbol{\alpha})$$

$$E[\boldsymbol{\mu}_k|\boldsymbol{\alpha}, W_{i,}] = \frac{W_{i,} + \boldsymbol{\alpha}}{\sum_{j=1}^{J}\left(W_{i,j} + \alpha_j\right)}.$$

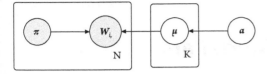

Figure 6.6. The multinomial mixture model with observed labels and a prior for the language model.

Our estimates (based on the posterior mean) would then take the form

$$\hat{\mu}_{\mathcal{H}} = \left(\frac{859 + 1}{859 + 102 + 374 + (1 + 1 + 1)}, \frac{102 + 1}{859 + 102 + 374 + (1 + 1 + 1)}, \frac{374 + 1}{859 + 102 + 374 + (1 + 1 + 1)} \right)$$

$$= (.64, .08, .28)$$

$$\hat{\mu}_{\mathcal{J}} = \left(\frac{82 + 1}{82 + 0 + 1 + (1 + 1 + 1)}, \frac{0 + 1}{82 + 0 + 1 + (1 + 1 + 1)}, \frac{1 + 1}{82 + 0 + 1 + (1 + 1 + 1)} \right)$$

$$= (.97, .01, .02)$$

$$\hat{\mu}_{\mathcal{M}} = \left(\frac{474 + 1}{474 + 17 + 7 + (1 + 1 + 1)}, \frac{17 + 1}{474 + 17 + 7 + (1 + 1 + 1)}, \frac{7 + 1}{474 + 17 + 7 + (1 + 1 + 1)} \right)$$

$$= (.95, .035, .015).$$

Notice that this looks like our previous estimate under the multinomial model, but as if we had observed an additional one count of each word type. While this adjustment does not change the values of $\mu_{\mathcal{H}}$ or $\mu_{\mathcal{M}}$ much, it keeps the estimate of $\mu_{\mathcal{J},\text{man}}$ from being exactly 0. Overall, it draws our estimates of μ toward α/α_0, but as we increase the amount of observed real data, as we have done with Madison and Hamilton, the effect of this pseudo-data on our estimate becomes negligible. Our final estimate of $p(W_{\text{Disputed},i}|\hat{\mu}_{\mathcal{H}}) = .001$, $p(W_{\text{Disputed},i}|\hat{\mu}_{\mathcal{J}}) = .008$, and $p(W_{\text{Disputed},i}|\hat{\mu}_{\mathcal{M}}) = 0.077$. While the model now assigns a positive probability of authorship to John Jay, the ultimate conclusion we make of assigning authorship of the disputed paper to Madison does not change.

In the example above we simply chose the value of α. We could also build the model even further by giving α a probability model itself. By stacking layers of latent variables together we can create hierarchical models. These models offer a few important advantages: they allow us to borrow information across documents and shrink estimates toward a particular point; we can use them to extend our model to include known corpus structure such as author or time and we can use them to build more complex models for discovery and measurement that we will discuss in later chapters.

6.5 Conclusion

In this chapter we have laid out the probabilistic foundations for a bag of words model based on a Multinomial distribution. We have also shown how to build a simple hierarchical model using the conjugate prior for the Multinomial—the Dirichlet distribution. These models are attractive because, once specified, they allow researchers to build off a wealth of results in statistics and computer science that enable computation and establish theoretical properties (Bishop, 2006; Murphy, 2021; Gelman et al., 2013).

In the next chapter we outline another approach for building models based on the bag of words representation—the vector space model. While these foundations look quite different from the multinomial model, we emphasize that probabilistic and algorithmic models are often using two quite different languages to describe a common set of techniques.

CHAPTER 7

The Vector Space Model and Similarity Metrics

The previous chapter offered a way of thinking about the bag of words representation that was based on thinking of each row in the document-feature matrix as a random draw from a multinomial distribution. In this chapter, we describe the *vector space model*, which views each row of the document-feature matrix as a vector in a high-dimensional space. Just as the multinomial interpretation gave us a rich set of results from probability theory and statistics, the vector space model allows us to leverage a rich set of results from linear algebra and will generalize more straightforwardly to weighted representations of the word counts. The vector space model provides the foundation of many of the *algorithmic* approaches that we will consider throughout the book.

The vector space model was originally developed in the context of information retrieval (for an excellent survey of vector space models of semantics see Turney and Pantel, 2010). A core task in information retrieval is to take a query and return all documents that are relevant to that query—in other words, documents that are "relevant" or "close" to the query. In the vector space model, closeness is determined by the similarity of the vectors. Even though we aren't often implementing information retrieval systems in the social sciences, assessment of the closeness between sets of documents is central to nearly all the methods in this book. For example, the methods we cover in Discovery partition documents such that documents within the cluster are as close as possible. In Measurement, unlabeled documents are assigned labels based on the labeled documents they are closest to. But what it means for two documents to be close doesn't have an obvious answer. Because these methods were developed in the context of information retrieval, they tend to emphasize a definition of closeness that returns documents that are about a common subject matter. This may or may not be consistent with the definition of similarity most relevant to a particular research question.

Thinking of documents as vectors in a space allows us to use measures of similarity and distances drawn from linear algebra. In the next section we start with a discussion of some of similarity metrics and then distances. We then discuss a common approach to weighting the words when constructing the vector space.

7.1 Similarity Metrics

A central challenge in text analysis is comparing pairs of documents and assessing how "close" they are to one another. What closeness ought to mean depends largely on context. Are a positive and negative review for the same movie more closely related than two positive reviews for different movies? It largely depends on whether you care more about the sentiment of the review or the subject matter. Consistent with our agnostic view, there is in general no single correct notion of similarity, but there are only metrics that are more or less effective for tackling individual tasks.

In the previous chapter we thought about closeness of documents implicitly based on a probability model. The disputed Federalist 49 is closest to Madison because it had the highest probability of being generated by a language model with parameters estimated based on Madison's attributed documents. In this chapter, we will think about closeness in terms of metrics operating on the document vectors. Each of these vectors contains the count of each of the features included in each document, and the vectors themselves are collected in our document-feature matrix.

There are a few properties that we might like a measure of similarity to have. First, the maximum similarity observed should occur when comparing a document to itself. Second, any two documents that share no words in common (this implies the two vectors are orthogonal) should have the minimum similarity. Third, similarity should increase as more of the same words are used. Fourth, we might want to impose symmetry—document a is always as close to document b as document b is close to document a.

One way to measure similarity between documents that arises naturally from the vector representation is to compute the inner product. The inner product of two vectors a and b is the projection of a onto b times the length of b (it is symmetric, so equivalently the projection of b onto a times the length of a). The inner product is calculated by summing the element-wise multiplication of the vectors. Thus for some generic vector $a = (a_1, a_2, \dots)$ and $b = (b_1, b_2, \dots)$ the inner product is

$$a \cdot b = a^T b \tag{7.1.1}$$

$$= a_1 b_1 + a_2 b_2 + \dots. \tag{7.1.2}$$

This has a simple interpretation for a special dichotomized document-feature matrix where each element is only 0 (if a given document does not contain a feature) or 1 (if a given document contains the feature). In this case, the inner product between two rows would be the number of words that the two documents share in common—a reasonable first notion of similarity.

For illustration with the more general term counts, we return to our three-word vocabulary vectors from the Federalist Papers in Table 6.1. We can compute the inner product of the entry for Hamilton with the disputed document:

$$W_{\text{Hamilton,}} \cdot W_{\text{Disputed,}} = (859, 102, 374) \cdot (15, 2, 0) \tag{7.1.3}$$

$$= 859 \times 15 + 102 \times 2 + 374 \times 0 \tag{7.1.4}$$

$$= 13089 \tag{7.1.5}$$

Because these terms are all composed of nonnegative numbers (recall the cells are word counts), the more nonzero terms in the two vectors overlap, the larger the resulting measure of similarity will be.

A potential problem with the inner product is that its result depends on the magnitude[1] of the two vectors. For example, imagine that we were trying to use our similarity metric to evaluate whether or not the disputed essay was closer to Hamilton's writing or to Madison's. Hamilton's vector is substantially larger in magnitude and the inner product is sensitive to this difference.

$$W_{\text{Madison,}} \cdot W_{\text{Disputed,}} = (474, 17, 7) \cdot (15, 2, 0)$$

$$= 7144$$

The resulting similarity between the disputed essay and Madison's work appears to be lower than between the disputed essay and Hamiliton's work, but this is an artifact of how many more essays we have attributed to Hamilton. One way to address this problem is to normalize by each vector's magnitude before taking the inner product.

We can use the inner product operator to compute the magnitude of the vector (denoted $\|a\|$), which is just the square root of the inner product with itself. For example, the magnitude of Hamilton's vector is,

$$\| W_{\text{Hamilton,}} \| = \sqrt{W_{\text{Hamilton,}} \cdot W_{\text{Hamilton,}}}$$

$$= \sqrt{859^2 + 102^2 + 374^2}$$

$$= 942.42.$$

This is substantially larger than the magnitude of Madison's vector, 474.36.

The inner product of two magnitude normalized vectors is the cosine of the angle (denoted θ) between the two vectors. This is the cosine similarity metric between the vectors.

$$\text{cosine similarity}(a, b) = \cos \theta \tag{7.1.6}$$

$$= \frac{a}{\|a\|} \cdot \frac{b}{\|b\|} \tag{7.1.7}$$

$$= \left(\frac{a}{\sqrt{\sum_i a_i^2}} \right) \cdot \left(\frac{b}{\sqrt{\sum_i b_i^2}} \right) \tag{7.1.8}$$

$$= \frac{\sum_i a_i b_i}{\left(\sqrt{\sum_i a_i^2} \right) \left(\sqrt{\sum_i b_i^2} \right)} \tag{7.1.9}$$

The core intuition here is that the angle between vectors is invariant to the magnitude of the vectors; only directions they are pointing in matter. To get a visual intuition for this, see Figure 7.1, which shows three example document vectors for a two-word vocabulary. As we extend one of the vectors while maintaining the direction, the angle between the vectors stays constant.

The cosine of the angle provides a nice measure of similarity because it normalizes the measure between 0 and 1 (formally it is between -1 and 1, but with nonnegative

---

[1] The magnitude is the length of the vector; however, we avoid the word length here to avoid confusion when we talk about the magnitude of a document. The length of a document is generally thought of as the number of words in the document, but this is not the same as the length of the document's vector.

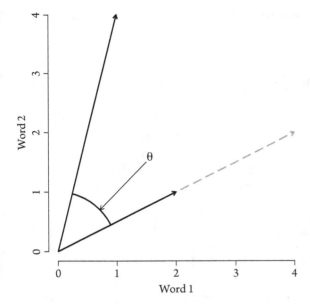

Figure 7.1. Three documents in a two-word space. Document 1 (at coordinates 1,4) is compared to document 2 (at coordinates 2,1) and document 3 (at coordinates 4,2). Documents 2 and 3 have the same ratio of words 1 and 2 but have different magnitudes. The angle θ is constant between the first document and the second/third. Thus, while the inner product between documents 1 and 2 and documents 2 and 3 are different, the cosine similarity is the same.

features like our word counts, the values cannot be smaller than 0), with 0 being the most different and 1 being the most similar.

We apply this technique to the Federalist Papers and reconsider which author the disputed document is closet to.

$$
\begin{aligned}
\text{cosine similarity}(W_{\text{Hamilton,}}, W_{\text{Disputed,}}) &= \frac{W_{\text{Hamilton,}} \cdot W_{\text{Disputed,}}}{\lVert W_{\text{Hamilton,}} \rVert \, \lVert W_{\text{Disputed,}} \rVert} \\
&= \frac{(859, 102, 374) \cdot (15, 2, 0)}{\lVert (859, 102, 374) \rVert \, \lVert (15, 2, 0) \rVert} \\
&= .918
\end{aligned}
$$

$$
\begin{aligned}
\text{cosine similarity}(W_{\text{Madison,}}, W_{\text{Disputed,}}) &= \frac{W_{\text{Madison,}} \cdot W_{\text{Disputed,}}}{\lVert W_{\text{Madison,}} \rVert \, \lVert W_{\text{Disputed,}} \rVert} \\
&= \frac{(474, 17, 7) \cdot (15, 2, 0)}{\lVert (474, 17, 7) \rVert \, \lVert (15, 2, 0) \rVert} \\
&= .995
\end{aligned}
$$

The results now show that the disputed document is much more similar to Madison's prior writing. Because we have normalized by the magnitude of the vectors we no longer prioritize Hamilton.

7.2 Distance Metrics

We can also compare documents by treating them as points in space and calculating the distance between them. Distance metrics will play a central role in the clustering algorithms that we cover in Discovery.

If you are familiar with one distance metric, it is likely the Euclidean distance, which can be defined as:

$$\| \boldsymbol{W}_{i,} - \boldsymbol{W}_{i',} \| = \sqrt{\sum_{j=1}^{J} (W_{ij} - W_{i'j})^2}. \qquad (7.2.1)$$

Euclidean distance shares some of the same problems that the inner product has in that it is very sensitive to document magnitude. Although it may not be immediately obvious, cosine similarity is closely related to Euclidean distance when the points have been normalized. We can relate the two normalized vectors by

$$\| \boldsymbol{W}_{i,} - \boldsymbol{W}_{i',} \| = \sqrt{\| \boldsymbol{W}_{i,} \| + \| \boldsymbol{W}_{i',} \| - 2 \left(\boldsymbol{W}_{i,} \cdot \boldsymbol{W}_{i',} \right)} \qquad (7.2.2)$$

$$= \sqrt{1 + 1 - 2 \left(\boldsymbol{W}_{i,} \cdot \boldsymbol{W}_{i',} \right)} \qquad (7.2.3)$$

$$= \sqrt{2 \left(1 - \text{cosine-similarity} \left(\boldsymbol{W}_{i,}, \boldsymbol{W}_{i',} \right) \right)}, \qquad (7.2.4)$$

where the second line follows because we have normalized the vectors to have magnitude 1. In other words, the cosine similarity and a normalized version of Euclidean distance are closely related. Sometimes for text analysis, researchers will use "cosine distance," which is simply 1 minus the cosine similarity (so that larger numbers indicate more dissimilar documents).

Beyond Euclidean distance there is a wide range of possible distance metrics. One example is called the Minkowski family. Minkowski distance metrics are those that have the form

$$d_p(\boldsymbol{W}_{i,}, \boldsymbol{W}_{i',}) = \left(\sum_{j=1}^{J} \left| W_{ij} - W_{i'j} \right|^p \right)^{1/p} \qquad (7.2.5)$$

for a given value of p. The Minkowski distance for $p = 2$ is Euclidean distance. More generally, as p gets larger the word counts with the largest differences will contribute more to the distance. The extreme is when $p = \infty$, which is known as Chebyshev's metric and returns as the distance the largest absolute difference on any single feature ignoring all other features.

Another special case that often arises is the Manhattan distance, which occurs when $p = 1$. The idea behind Manhattan distance is that it measures the distance between two points in space when you can only travel in right angles. Euclidean distance is the distance as the crow flies, Manhattan distance is the distance as a taxicab would drive in Manhattan (this is why it is also sometimes called the "taxi cab metric"). This metric will tend to be more robust to large differences between counts of individual words.

The choice of distance metrics comes down to an assumption about what kind of difference is most important to consider. Normalization using the cosine distance will deprioritize document magnitude, and different versions of Minkowski distance can be used to emphasize the relative importance of individual components of the vector. Because different measures of distance correspond to different notions of what it means for two documents to be similar, algorithmic methods can be substantially altered by swapping out one distance metric for another. We will see later that many algorithmic clustering methods allow the distance metric to be set as a user-specified parameter, providing substantial flexibility.

7.3   tf-idf Weighting

Up until now we have been assuming that the vectors are the counts of individual words in a document; however, one of the advantages of the algorithmic framework is that we can reweight words to make the distance metrics more informative. In fact, we have already discussed one extreme form of weighting—removing words entirely. This first came up in the context of removing stop words when they were believed to have little informational content. In the analysis of the Federalist Papers, we took the opposite approach, focusing only on stop words and removing everything else. Removing a set of words is equivalent to giving them weights set to 0. Whether these weights are exactly 0 or something else, the goal is to amplify the signal of interest.

A common theme in the computational linguistics literature is that the greatest signals from words are those in the goldilocks region—neither too rare nor too frequent. Highly frequent words are essentially the glue that holds language together and they offer few clues about what the text as about. Rare words on the other hand might contain a lot of useful information, but they appear so infrequently they aren't useful for making generalizations about the text. The key is the words in the middle.

This insight is enshrined in *term frequency inverse document frequency weighting* or *tf-idf* for short. After computing the document-feature matrix, tf-idf scales each term count by a measure of its inverse frequency within the whole corpus. This has the effect of down-weighting frequent words. While there are many version of the penalty, the most common form of tf-idf takes the form

$$W_{ij}^{tf-idf} = \underbrace{W_{ij}}_{\text{word count}} * \overbrace{\log\frac{N}{n_j}}^{\text{penalty for frequent words}},$$

where N is the number of documents in the corpus and n_j is the number of documents that contain word j. The core idea is to prioritize the words that are highly frequent in the document, but rare in the corpus over all.

The tf-idf heuristic is surprisingly robust. In the Federalist Papers example, even using tf-idf on stop words can reveal information about the authorship of the disputed papers. To show this, we created a document-feature matrix of the Federalist Papers, but included only stop words and words that Mosteller and Wallace (1963) identified as very common within the papers.[2] Figure 7.2 shows word clouds of simple counts of the words within the corpus. The left figure shows the counts from the papers known to be authored by Madison. The right figure shows the counts from the papers known to be authored by Hamilton. The center figure shows the word cloud from the unknown paper of interest so far in this book, #49. As you can see, word clouds of simple counts

---

[2]We use the stop words list in the tm package in R (Feinerer, Hornik, and Meyer, 2008) in addition to words from Tables 2.5 and 2.6 from Mosteller and Wallace (1963). The data for the Federalist Papers comes from the Project Gutenberg, cleaned and made available in this blogpost by Patrick Perry: http://ptrckprry.com/course/ssd/lecture/federalist.html.

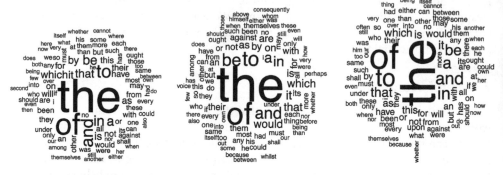

Figure 7.2. Word clouds of stop words and common words in the Federalist Papers. Left: papers known to be authored by Madison. Center: unknown Paper #49. Right: papers known to be authored by Hamilton

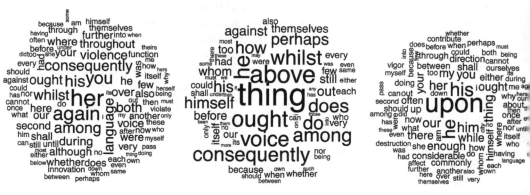

Figure 7.3. Word clouds of stop words and common words in the Federalist Papers, weighted by tf-idf. Left: papers known to be authored by Madison. Center: unknown paper # 49 Right: papers known to be authored by Hamilton.

do not reveal the words that distinguish the authors because they are overwhelmed by the most common of the stop words.

However, if we weight the words using tf-idf, the distinct voice of each author begins to emerge. Figure 7.3 shows word clouds of the weighted tf-idf counts of the same words. We see on the left that the papers authored by Madison contain a disproportionate use of words like her, again, and, importantly, consequently, whilst, and ought. In contrast, Hamilton's papers overwhelmingly use upon in comparison to other papers, as well as his and him. The disputed paper #49 clearly looks most attributable to Madison, with disproportionate use of consequently, whilst, and ought.

In the case of the Federalist Papers, the tf-idf weighting also makes the distance metrics more informative. Using the simple counts of our document-feature matrix, the cosine similarity between the Madison word counts and paper #49 is 0.9899, while the cosine similarity between the Hamilton word counts and paper #49 is 0.9848, a miniscule difference. However, using the tf-idf weighted counts, the cosine similarity between the Madison papers and paper #49 is 0.5545, while the cosine similarity between the Hamilton papers and paper #49 is 0.4981.

We also note that tf-idf weighting is most important for distance/similarity calcula-tions and methods based on distance/similarity calculations rather than methods like linear regression. Because linear regression using a document-feature matrix to predict some outcome would be invariant to a linear feature-level rescaling, the tf-idf weights won't matter.

7.4 Conclusion

The vector space model conceptualizes documents as vectors in space and then uses results from linear algebra to make comparisons between them. We briefly cov-ered some of the main similarity measures, distance metrics, and weighting results. In each case the goal is to amplify the signal of what is interesting about the documents to make later methods for discovery and measurement more successful. These ideas can be extended further with methods such as string kernels, which capture similarity that preserve word order—see, for example, Spirling (2012) for an application in political science.

While the vector space model seems quite different from the multinomial model reviewed in the last chapter, one of the recurring themes of this book is that many seem-ingly unrelated models are actually tightly connected. The vector space model compares documents by computing distances on the document vectors, while probability mod-els compute relative probabilities of being generated under a given model. This seems like a different foundation on which to build methods to compare documents. Yet, many probability models imply a notion of distance. For example, the cosine similarity measure covered in this chapter is closely related to the von-Mises Fisher distribution (Banerjee, Merugu, Dhillon, and Ghosh, 2005). More generally, many common prob-ability distributions have strong connections to common distance metrics (Banerjee, Merugu, Dhillon, and Ghosh, 2005). We will explore these connections more when we discuss clustering in Chapter 12.

One of the tremendous strengths of the models that we have considered so far is that they don't rely on any knowledge about what the individual words mean, instead making inferences based on how often the same words are used across documents. This is advantageous because it assures us that the same techniques will work across different languages and even with other forms of high-dimensional count data (such as found in genetics data or consumer purchase data). Yet the downside is that it becomes possible to miss the similarity between two documents which use different words to convey the same idea. In the next chapter, we consider representations based on distributed word embeddings. This approach leverages large external text corpora to capture information about the meanings of words, which can then be used to assess similarity in a way that smooths across words.

CHAPTER 8

Distributed Representations of Words

In the last few chapters, we have examined representations where every document is represented by a (possibly weighted) sum of the words it contains. In these models the representation of a word is a one-hot encoding—a vector with one dimension per unique word in the vocabulary containing a single 1 for that word and 0 for all the others. A consequence of this representation is that every word is treated uniquely and two documents which have no words in common will have a similarity of 0 by essentially any metric (as indicated by the fact that the two documents will have a 0 inner product).

Yet, we know in practice that many words have highly similar meanings. We encoded this knowledge in Chapter 5 by lemmatizing or stemming—taking two words such as writer and writers and collapsing them into the same feature—implicitly making an assertion that, for our purposes, they contain *identical* information. The distributed representations covered in this chapter generalize this idea by learning from external data the semantic relationships between words like writer and author even when they don't share a common lemma or stem.

In this chapter, we will cover how massive quantities of text can be used to learn *distributed representations* of words—dense vectors that replace the one-hot-encoding representation of words that build in some measure of similarity. Instead of representing a word (for example, cat) using the one-hot-encoding representation with a vector of length the size of the vocabulary J and an indicator for the word cat,

$$\mathbf{cat} = (0, 0, 0, 1, 0, 0, 0, 0, \dots, 0),$$

we will instead use data to estimate a dense vector of length K, where $K < J$, to represent cat, for example:

$$\mathbf{cat} = (1.3, .2, \dots, .45).$$

Because these techniques embed words into a common low-dimensional space (relative to the size of the vocabulary), they are called *word embeddings*. These vectors have the desirable property that they encode the similarity between words—for similarity metrics like the one we discussed in Chapter 7, similarity(cat, dog) will reflect the closeness of cat and dog and will likely be larger than similarity(cat, planet). These representations are generally learned by appeal to the *distributional hypothesis*, which suggests that the context in which words are used provides a clue to their meaning.

First we will make the case for why word embeddings are an appealing representation before moving on to how they are estimated. We will then discuss the challenge of aggregating the word-level representations into a representation of the document. We briefly discuss techniques in computer science literature for validating word embeddings and conclude with a brief discussion of recently developed contextualized word embeddings.

8.1 Why Word Embeddings

The bag of words representations that we have covered so far implicitly treat every word as having a distinct, unique meaning. In many respects, this preserves the most information about the word and—given sufficient data for our downstream task and a flexible model—we can learn whatever we need to learn about each word. In practice though, even moderate size corpora can have tens or hundreds of thousands of unique words in their vocabularies. Each of these words is represented by a highly sparse vector containing a single 1 that has length matching the size of the vocabulary. Even when aggregated over documents, most documents do not contain most words, and so the document-feature matrix will be very sparse. The practical upshot is that the downstream problem is often very high dimensional and the feature matrix may well have columns (features) that exceed the number of rows (data points).

The core insight of *distributed representations* is to represent a word as a *dense* vector in a low-dimensional space learned from unlabeled data. This is a case of *unsupervised learning*—similar to the topic models used in Amy Catalinac's work discussed in Chapter 1 and in more detail in the next part of this book. By using a large corpus of text data to *discover* a numeric representation of each word, we can *estimate* (rather than specify a priori) which words are used in similar ways. The hope is that the embeddings learned from a large general-purpose language corpus will capture information about the meanings of words that will be helpful in performing a context-specific task where there is only limited available labeled data. This idea of using information from a large corpus of texts to help in a different setting is called *transfer learning* and rests on the idea that the meaning of words is relatively stable across different corpora. The idea of distributed representations of text have been around since at least the 1980s (Hinton, 1986), but they have only recently started to take off in popularity as researchers have developed approaches to estimation which would allow the distributed representations to be learned on corpora at the scale of hundreds of billions of tokens.

Embeddings represent meaning by leveraging the distributional hypothesis of language, an idea that goes back to at least Wittgenstein (1953). The distributional hypothesis has been succinctly summarized by an oft-repeated quote in this literature: "you shall know a word by the company it keeps" (Firth, 1957). It posits that we can learn something about the semantic meanings of words on the basis of the words that appear frequently in a small context window around the focal word. This is an idea with tremendous potential because it suggests that we can learn about the meanings of words *without* labeling data by hand, instead using the patterns of word co-occurrence from large *unlabeled* collections that are readily available.

Word embeddings offer three key advantages compared to the word count features that we considered in previous chapters:

1) they encode similarity,
2) they allow for "automatic generalization,"
3) they provide a measure of meaning.

Encoding Similarity. In the opening to Mikolov, Chen, Corrado, and Dean (2013) the authors write:

> Many current NLP systems and techniques treat words as atomic units—there is no notion of similarity between words, as these are represented as indices in a vocabulary. This choice has several good reasons—simplicity, robustness and the observation that simple models trained on huge amounts of data outperform complex systems trained on less data.

Under the bag of words representations of the last several chapters, the inner product of the representation for any two different words will always be 0. This means that there is no notion that two semantically similar words are closer together than two completely unrelated words. By contrast, the distributed representations of words have vectors which point in similar directions for words with similar meaning. These relationships are so strong that word embeddings have been used to solve analogy tasks by simply adding and subtracting the vectors together. In Mikolov, Yih, and Zweig (2013), the authors famously demonstrated that King − Man + Woman yields a vector which is quite close to Queen. This straightforward vector offset method provides surprisingly strong performance even though the embedding model was not explicitly trained to solve analogies.

Automatic Generalization. By encoding similarity in the representations of the words, word embeddings offer "automatic generalization" (Hinton, 1986)—learning something about one word allows us to *automatically* learn something about related words. For example, imagine that we are trying to classify the sentiment of movie reviews using a series of hand-labeled examples (more on this style of task in Chapter 19). Because the hand-labeled example is small, perhaps we never see the word fantastic but we do see the word great. Under a bag of words representation, we might learn that great is associated with positive reviews but—because it never appears in the labeled set—we won't be able to use the word fantastic when classifying new unseen documents. Now consider approaching the problem with a representation based on word embeddings. Because great and fantastic often occur in similar contexts in broader language corpora, their embeddings will be quite similar. This is helpful because when we see the word great appear frequently in positive reviews, we aren't really learning an association between great and positive reviews; we are learning an association between great's *location in the embedding space* and positive reviews. Because the word fantastic is in a similar location in the space as great, our ability to predict the review is positive *automatically generalizes* to fantastic even if we never observe that particular word in any movie reviews. The relationships captured in word embeddings can even be more subtle, because relative positions in the space have meaning as indicated by the King is to Man as Queen is to Woman analogy example. This means that more complex reasoning between words is possible.

In short, the embeddings provide an efficient way of sharing information *across words*. The benefits will be particularly noticeable in small corpora (or with short documents), but given the nature of language, even large corpora will have a large fraction of relatively rare words.

Measuring Meaning. Following the idea of the distributional hypothesis, word embeddings learned on large corpora have also been used as a measure of the word's meaning. This has allowed researchers to investigate research questions about the meanings of words and how those meanings change over time or across speakers (Caliskan, Bryson, and Narayanan, 2017; Garg et al., 2018; Kozlowski, Taddy, and Evans, 2019; Rheault and Cochrane, 2020; Rodman, 2020). It is worth emphasizing here that we are referencing a very specific sense of *meaning*. Two words are considered to have the same meaning when they are used in similar contexts. Often this accords with our intuitive sense of meaning, but it is useful to keep in mind the limitations of this conception.

All three of these strengths derive from the ability of distributed representations to reach beyond the analyst's corpus to leverage a notion of a word's meaning estimated using a larger preexisting corpus. We now turn to how these embeddings are estimated in practice.

8.2 Estimating Word Embeddings

There are many different word embedding algorithms. Each converts the idea of the distributional hypothesis into a slightly different objective function which is used to learn the embeddings from a corpus of documents. In this section, we briefly walk through the idea of self-supervision, which powers most of the word-embedding algorithms, and then describe some of the choices that users need to make. We then delve into the estimation of a few different techniques.

8.2.1 THE SELF-SUPERVISION INSIGHT

Hand-labeled data is expensive. It takes time for a researcher to define a labeling scheme, it takes time for coders to annotate the data, and it takes time to evaluate the labels for quality. This means that high-quality, labeled data is hard to come by.

Yet valuable information can still be learned even when labeled data is unavailable. The *self-supervision insight* is the idea that we can create a supervised task where the label is provided by the data itself. In the context of word embeddings this often involves using the words around a focal word to predict that word. The self-supervision insight is that the information needed to do this prediction well will also be helpful for completing other tasks.

8.2.2 DESIGN CHOICES IN WORD EMBEDDINGS

There are four choices that need to be made by a researcher looking to use word embeddings. Rodríguez and Spirling (N.d.) provide an article-length account of and evaluation of these choices aimed at social scientists.

1) Data Source. Word embeddings need to be trained on text and the particular text selected can have a large impact on the kind of representation learned. A lot of data is necessary to learn stable embeddings—probably at least several million tokens (Zhang et al., 2021). One of the central advantages of word embeddings is that they can be trained on large external corpora. Many collections of pretrained embeddings are available for download that have been learned on corpora that have billions of tokens drawn from Wikipedia, news articles, and web pages. However, it is important to note that the embeddings will reflect the language used in these documents. Rodríguez and Spirling (N.d.) argue that widely available pretrained embeddings perform about as well at capturing political meaning as embeddings trained on political speech.

2) Context Window Size. The distributional hypothesis supposes that we can understand the meaning of a word by examining nearby words. The first choice an analyst has to make then is what is meant by "nearby." Usually this is operationalized as a symmetric window around the embedding word of some fixed size, e.g., five words to the left and five words to the right. The size of this window dictates the kind of information that the embedding will capture. When the window sizes is very small, it will tend to capture some syntactic meaning and when the window is larger it will tend to capture semantic meaning.

3) Dimension of the Embedding. Word embeddings are vectors in a low-dimensional space that encode information about the contexts a word appears in, generally only a relatively small number of dimensions—usually 50 to 500. It should be initially surprising that this can work—the vocabularies of these models can be in the millions of words and the word embedding for a focal word has to predict the co-occurence pattern with all of them. Yet, the effectiveness of relatively low-dimensional embeddings is one of those findings that has stood the test of time.

4) Algorithm. Given a dataset, a context window, and the dimension of the embeddings, the analyst needs to select an algorithm to learn the embeddings from the data. We step through three popular algorithms below.

8.2.3 LATENT SEMANTIC ANALYSIS

While word embeddings have recently taken the natural language processing community by storm, they have been around for some time. Latent Semantic Analysis (LSA), proposed by Deerwester et al. (1990), is a special case of word embeddings that learns the embeddings using a truncated singular-value decomposition on the (possibly tf-idf weighted) document-feature matrix. This means that the entire document is the context window and thus the recovered embeddings generally capture semantic content (hence the name!).

The core algorithm is a truncated singular-value decomposition, which is a general approach to learning a low-rank matrix factorization. Roughly speaking, the idea of a low-rank factorization is that a matrix can be decomposed into the product of smaller matrices (Figure 8.1). Each column in the matrix on the right represents a continuous embedding for a word in the vocabulary where similar words will have similar embeddings, indicating that they are likely to appear in the same kind of documents (this can be either because they frequently co-occur or because they are substitutes).

While this strategy is simple and effective, it has limitations. The entire document may prove too wide a context window, and when the number of documents or the size of the vocabulary grows large, the computation can become infeasible.

8.2.4 NEURAL WORD EMBEDDINGS

Modern word embeddings are often called neural embeddings as they are based off the architecture of neural networks. While these models were proposed as far back as Bengio et al. (2003), they really took off with the specific approaches proposed by

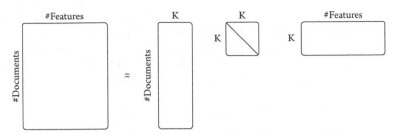

Figure 8.1. A low rank decomposition approximates a matrix as the product of three lower-dimensional matrices. The second matrix is a diagonal matrix indicated by the thin line along the diagonal.

Mikolov and coauthors (Mikolov, Chen, Corrado, and Dean, 2013; Mikolov, Sutskever, Chen, Corrado, and Dean, 2013) due to their computationally efficient learning algorithms. These techniques are often called word2vec after the software released to implement them.

word2vec is actually an umbrella term for two distinct objective functions—the continuous bag of words (CBOW) model (Mikolov, Chen, Corrado, and Dean, 2013) and the skipgram model (Mikolov, Sutskever, Chen, Corrado, and Dean, 2013)—as well as the optimization routine that makes it computationally feasible—negative sampling (Mikolov, Sutskever, Chen, Corrado, and Dean, 2013). CBOW is premised on the idea of setting up a prediction problem where a focal word is predicted by the context around it. For example, "the quick brown fox [blank] over the lazy dog" would use the average of the estimated word vectors of "the, quick, brown, fox, over, the, lazy, dog" to predict the word in the blank. The vector for the word that actually fills the empty spot—jumps—is set to maximize the equation

$$\underset{\mu_{\text{jumps}}}{\text{argmax}} \frac{\exp(\mu_{\text{jumps}} \cdot \bar{v})}{\sum_j \exp(\mu_j \cdot \bar{v})}, \tag{8.2.1}$$

where $\bar{v}$ denotes the average of all embeddings in the context (in this case the average embeddings of the, quick, brown, fox, over, the, lazy, and dog) and j indexes over the entire vocabulary. In the alternative skipgram model the prediction problem is the other way around—the context words are predicted one at a time from the focal word. Both objectives have the property that the two words will have similar embeddings when they appear in the context windows of the same types of words.

The challenge of Equation 8.2.1 is that the denominator involves a sum over a very large number of terms. In the word embeddings released by Google for the word2vec project, there are over three million terms and phrases in the vocabulary, which means that the denominator is a sum over three million terms. Negative sampling is an approximate estimation technique designed to solve this problem (Mikolov, Sutskever, Chen, Corrado, and Dean, 2013). In negative sampling, the denominator is approximated using a (weighted) random sample of a few words (two to 20 in Mikolov, Sutskever, Chen, Corrado, and Dean (2013)) from the vocabulary that were not the focal word.

The negative sampling approximation is closely related to a weighted version of the matrix factorization technique used in LSA (Levy and Goldberg, 2014). The GloVe method introduced by Pennington, Socher, and Manning (2014) builds off of this foundation to tackle the matrix factorization problem directly. GloVe forms a square matrix of word co-occurrences C such that the cell $C_{jj'}$ equals the number of times that words j and j' appear in the same context together. This model is factorized using a weighted objective that down-weights highly frequent co-occurrences.

8.2.5 PRETRAINED EMBEDDINGS

A central advantage of word embeddings is that large collections of pretrained embeddings are readily available to be downloaded from Google (word2vec), Stanford's Natural Language Processing Group (GloVe), and Facebook (fastText). These embeddings were often trained on ten to hundreds of billions of tokens. They are also available in languages beyond English—e.g., fastText currently has pretrained models for 157 different languages from Afrikaans to Zeelandic (discussed more below).

8.2.6 RARE WORDS

Even when trained on billions of tokens, there will always be a long tail of words which show up infrequently, and these embeddings will be noisier as a result. In many cases, social scientists may find when applying pretrained embeddings to their own corpus that many of the words used in their documents don't have trained embeddings at all. This is particularly likely to occur with domain-specific vocabulary and jargon that might be of particular interest to the researcher. We briefly outline three strategies for dealing with this problem that lean on different sources of information: retrofitting to external semantic lexicons, using character-level information, and inducing embeddings.

Retrofitting is a strategy introduced by Faruqui et al. (2015) to leverage large community databases of semantic information. Projects like WordNet (Miller, 1995), FrameNet (Baker, Fillmore, and Lowe, 1998), and the Paraphrase Database (Ganitkevitch, Van Durme, and Callison-Burch, 2013) provide readily available resources about semantic relationships such as synonyms, common semantic frames, and paraphrase relationships. These resources can be used to create a graph of relationships where words are linked to related words (for example, a word might be connected to all its synonyms). The retrofitting procedure takes as an input pretrained word embeddings and this graph of relationships and returns a refined set of embeddings which have been encouraged to assign similar embeddings to neighbors in the graph. This helps to ensure that the embeddings reflect the known relationships as reflected in the semantic databases.

A second strategy is to drop down from the word level to the character level. This is based on the insight that words are often compositional. For example, even if you hadn't heard of retrofitting before, you might have been able to guess something about its meeting by breaking the word into parts (`retro-`, `-fit-`, `-t-`, `-ing`). This subword information is not exploited by the embedding strategies we have discussed so far. Bojanowski et al. (2017) introduced *fastText* embeddings, which use character n-grams as the atomic unit of analysis (see also, Schütze, 1993; Wieting et al., 2016). In fastText, each word is represented by the sequence of character n-grams (of sizes 3, 4, 5, and 6) it contains and the resulting embedding of the word is the average of all the character n-gram embeddings in that word. This has the distinct advantage of allowing fastText to embed words it has never seen and share information across words which have similar sequences of characters in common.

Our third strategy considers the setting where we want to induce an embedding for a new word based on a few samples of its usage. This could arise because the pretrained embeddings didn't contain a word that appears in our corpus or because we have reason to believe that the word would have a corpus-specific meaning. Khodak et al. (2018) introduce *à la carte embeddings* as a way to induce a new embedding based on a set of pretrained word embeddings and samples of the new word's use in context. The core insight is that while we may not have an embedding for the rare word, we have pretrained embeddings for all the words that appear in the context around it. Using a transformation of the average of those embeddings, Khodak et al. (2018) show it is possible to induce an accurate embedding even from only a single instance of the word.[1] The à la carte embedding strategy is particularly helpful because it can be used to learn embeddings for *n*-grams and capture contextually specific meanings of words in social science settings (Rodríguez, Spirling, and Stewart, 2021).

8.2.7 AN ILLUSTRATION

Two words have different embeddings when they are used in the close proximity of different kinds of words. This difference in *usage* suggests a difference in *meaning* through the distributional hypothesis. Researchers can train embeddings on a large corpus or make use of pretrained embeddings to explore relationships between words or even within different uses of the same word (e.g. different parts of speech, different speakers, or different time periods). When analyzing a document collection such as our State of the Union corpus, researchers can make use of the techniques for rare words to contrast word meanings.

To demonstrate, we consider the use of the word manufacturing in State of the Union addresses between 1900 and 1959 and contrast with the use of manufacturing between 1960 and 2016. The meaning of the word manufacturing hasn't changed in the sense of the dictionary definition, but the bundle of activities it refers to has drifted over this period. This is a difficult task because there are only 53 uses of the word manufacturing in total, approximately evenly split between the two time periods. Using the à la carte embedding strategy described in the last section, we are able to produce a time-period-specific embedding for manufacturing using only those few instances and pretrained embeddings for the words that appear within the context window for manufacturing.

While this produces two embeddings for manufacturing (one pre-1960 and one post-1960), each is (in our case) a 300-dimensional vector that has no obvious meaning. To provide a sense of what the embedding means, we present the nearest neighbors using cosine distance. The top five nearest neighbors for the pre-1960 period include exportation, oil-related, concomitant, detriment, and war-relate, with neighbors further down the list including energy-intensive, import/export, defense-related, and capital-intensive. The nearest neighbors for the post-1960 period reflect a different discussion of manufacturing, with the top five neighbors retool, retooling, jobs, downtowns, and offshoring, with neighbors further down the list including outsourced, globalized, low-skilled,

---

[1] The average of the embeddings in the context is not itself a good embedding because it overstates the common dimensions of the embedding space. Using theory drawn from Arora et al. (2018), Khodak et al. (2018) show that it is possible to learn a linear transformation of the average that provides an effective estimation strategy.

retraining, and workforce. Even with only a small number of instances, the embeddings have captured the difference in the way manufacturing is used in the post-1960 era, leveraging words around it. This information can both be interesting in its own right and also provide a useful representation of the text for downstream tasks like classification and clustering.

While the associations with nearby words can help researchers learn about the meanings of words or build better feature representations of their data, the embeddings reflect the associations as they appear in the corpus, which can lead the researchers to reflect not only on the meanings of words but also on negative associations and stereotypes. Recent research demonstrates that large pretrained embeddings have problematic content like associations between gendered pronouns and certain occupations (Bolukbasi et al., 2016), gender stereotypes (Caliskan, Bryson, and Narayanan, 2017) and ethnic stereotypes (Garg et al., 2018). The presence of these harmful associations in the data reflects the way language is used in the large corpora used to train these embeddings—a point we made in principle 2 of Chapter 3 on the ethical ramifications of corpus construction. For social scientists, this can serve as an opportunity to study these biases. Garg et al. (2018) characterize the evolution of ethnic stereotypes over the course of a century using trained embeddings. However, when embeddings are used in real-world systems, they risk exacerbating harmful racial and gender inequalities in these settings (Benjamin, 2019). Just as our embedding didn't know anything about the true meaning of manufacturing, only the words used around it, the embedding for the word doctor does not know that the job can be held by a person of any gender rather than having a meaning specifically associated with men.

While there has been research attempting to "debias" embeddings to remove these associations, they cannot address the root concern that embeddings reflect the language being trained on, that language does not exist in a vacuum, but is instead of a product of a social process. We must still be vigilant about these problems so that we do not amplify existing inequalities, but to us the presence of bias requires a careful consideration of the research goal and the data we use to address that goal.

8.3   Aggregating Word Embeddings to the Document Level

In the default Bag of Words recipe of Chapter 5, each token was represented as a one-hot encoding and the associated document representation was as easy as summing over the token representations. While word embeddings provide a rich representation of the words themselves, it is less obvious how to use them to represent the document even though this is the level of analysis most social scientists are working at.

A reasonable first approximation would be to average the embeddings of every word in the document. This can be improved using Smooth Inverse Frequency (SIF) embeddings, which first weight the sentences and then remove a common component by taking out the first singular vector (Arora, Liang, and Ma, 2017). This strategy builds on the tf-idf strategy described in Chapter 7 by weighting in a way that de-emphasizes the common signal. A variant of this strategy using the à la carte embeddings can also include word order information by leveraging induced n-grams.

Alternatively, at the cost of doing some additional training, document embeddings can be learned from the data itself. Le and Mikolov (2014) introduce the *doc2vec* model to learn representations at the paragraph level. doc2vec employs a similar model as the skip-gram algorithm, but in addition to the word vectors includes a paragraph-level vector in the prediction model that is optimized to aid in the prediction.

All the models mentioned so far use word order only very lightly (through n-grams and n-gram-like information in the case of doc2vec). Models based on recurrent neural networks are able to produce order-sensitive document representations at the cost of being substantially more difficult to train and fit (Socher et al., 2013; Kiros et al., 2015). When the goal is classification, several approaches based on deep learning only require token-level representations and create the document-level representation implicitly during the classification process.

It is worth noting that most of the computer science work done to aggregate word embeddings is primarily focused on sentences or paragraphs. While these are likely to work effectively for short texts, longer documents may not have as high a performance.

8.4 Validation

In the computer science literature, validation of word embeddings is often split into two categories: *extrinsic* evaluations, which assess performance on a downstream natural language processing task, and *intrinsic* evaluations, which assess whether the embeddings are able to capture similarities between words. The most important validation for social scientists is how that text representation helps to accomplish their specific tasks (Kozlowski, Taddy, and Evans, 2019; Lauretig, 2019; Rheault and Cochrane, 2020; Rodman, 2020). However, we briefly overview some of these additional approaches as they provide context for how such methods are evaluated in the literature.

Most of the excitement around word embeddings in the natural language processing community is that they enable substantial performance gains in downstream systems. Thus, prior work has demonstrated that such embeddings boost accuracy rates of core tasks like noun phrase chunking, part of speech tagging, and named entity recognition (Pennington, Socher, and Manning, 2014). We cover these topics in the next chapter. Such embeddings have also been shown to improve accuracy in different classifications when using simple linear classifiers.

Intrinsic evaluations have focused on whether embeddings are able to capture meaningful notions of word similarity. The exact structure of these tasks takes many forms, including word pair similarity assessments (Finkelstein et al., 2001), analogy solving (Mikolov, Sutskever, Chen, Corrado, and Dean, 2013; Levy, Goldberg, and Dagan, 2015), and clustering tasks designed to see if a clustering recovers the correct partition of words into semantically coherent groups (Baroni, Dinu, and Kruszewski, 2014; Schnabel et al., 2015). Many of these tasks are based on comparing a set of words to some query word and using cosine similarity to pick the closest.

While a high score on an intrinsic evaluation is an indication that the word embeddings are picking up *something*, there are many ways in which the tasks themselves are not ideal. Word similarity tasks are inherently subjective, cannot account for polysemy, and lack some of the standardized features of machine learning benchmarks, such as train test splits, and are likely underpowered (Faruqui et al., 2016; Card et al., 2020). Further complicating matters, Schnabel et al. (2015) show that extrinsic and intrinsic validations often conflict with each other. This just underscores our broader theme that there is never going to be a single correct representation for all tasks.

In their review of word embeddings for applied social scientists, Rodríguez and Spirling (N.d.) develop a Turing style test for word embeddings, which expands on the intrinsic evaluations in the computer science literature. In their design they provide a set of crowd workers on Amazon MTurk ten political words and ask them to produce a set of ten nearest neighbors. They then use those same words to generate machine nearest neighbors by finding the most cosine similar vector using word embeddings. They then enlist a separate set of humans to look at a prompt word and two possible nearest neighbors (one from the humans, one from the machine, but unlabeled) and ask them to choose the best. This allows them to compute a metric on how often the human-generated words are selected over the machine-generated ones by other humans. They find that off-the-shelf pretrained embeddings often perform on par with or exceeding human-generated words.

8.5 Contextualized Word Embeddings

In all the embeddings we have discussed so far, the embedding of a word is fixed independent of its context. That is, the word bat has some embedding regardless of whether it is in a sentence with cave and night or a sentence with ball and pitch. Polysemic words like bat tend to be located at the average of the word-specific senses (Arora et al., 2018).

A recent flurry of publications in natural language processing has demonstrated the enormous potential of contextualized word embeddings (Peters et al., 2018; Devlin et al., 2019; Liu et al., 2019; Brown et al., 2020). These models are premised on the same self-supervision insight as standard word embeddings, but use much more complicated deep learning language models to learn the embeddings. These models have the advantage that a pretrained model can be used to produce a context-specific embedding for every word in a document—that is, an embedding that captures not just the word but also the relation it has to other words around it. Because many of these models are based on either Recurrent Neural Networks (Rumelhart, Hinton, and Williams, 1986) or the Transformer architecture (Vaswani et al., 2017), they are the first models we have considered to truly capture word order information.

A number of pretrained models are readily available for use, including BERT (Bidirectional Encoder Representations from Transformers) by Devlin et al. (2019) and GPT-3 (Generative Pre-trained Transformer) by Brown et al. (2020). These models can further be fine-tuned[2] to the particular corpus the researcher is working with, although even this partial training process can be computationally intensive.

Most word embeddings covered in this chapter can be feasibly trained by individual social scientists (e.g. Rodríguez and Spirling trained numerous models with up to 700 million tokens in three hours using eight CPU cores). However, the contextualized word embeddings are costly on a completely different scale, effectively requiring the use of Graphics Processing Units (GPUs) and taking days, weeks, or even months to train. In a paper on the energy and cost implications of training these models, Strubell, Ganesh, and McCallum (2019) estimated that each training instance of BERT takes 79 hours and costs $4–12K in cloud compute time. In a case study for the paper they describe how for a single paper, building a similar model, they used 27 years' worth of GPU time (60 GPUs running continuously for six months) for an estimated cloud compute cost of $100–350K.

---

[2]Fine-tuning is a process of continuing to train a model on some new data for a limited number of iterations. Fine-tuning alters the model slightly to better accommodate the task at hand but must be done carefully to avoid overfitting.

8.6 Conclusion

In this chapter we have covered word embeddings as an alternate approach to the default bag of words recipe described in Chapter 5. While a bag of words produces a large sparse vector representation for each document, word embeddings produce a comparatively small, dense representation for every word, which must then be aggregated to the document level.

A key idea in word embeddings is the self-supervision insight, where the representation for each word is selected to improve the ability to predict a target (either a word from its context, the context from the word, or just the co-occurence of words). This gives embeddings the ability to capture similarity between words, allowing models to generalize across distinct words in a way that isn't always straightforward with bag of words representations.

Crucially, these models can be learned in large, preexisting language corpora and then used in the researcher's specific research context, an idea called transfer learning. Many off-the-shelf embeddings exist for just this purpose including word2vec, GloVe, and fastText. Newer contextualized word embeddings that are able to capture information about word order can also be downloaded pretrained.

CHAPTER 9

Representations from Language Sequences

You can get shockingly far in text as data projects while ignoring word order. Such analyses are attractive because they are relatively simple and computational tractable. As such Chapters 5–8 focused on how semantic information could be gleaned from individual words. In this chapter, we show how to make use of natural language processing techniques that more explicitly focus on the role of words within a sequence. Rather than exploring how these models are estimated, we focus on how their outputs can be useful for improving social science applications.

We begin the chapter with a discussion of text reuse—the process of identifying exact or approximate copying of text between documents. We then discuss part of speech (POS) tagging—a method that annotates the part of speech of each individual word within a sentence—and demonstrate how it can be used to detect noun phrases. In the third section, we review named entity recognition (NER), which allows researchers to extract the names of people, organizations, and locations and other types of structured information from texts. And in the last section, we discuss dependency parsing, which maps the syntactical relations between words in a sentence. In each section, we summarize the method and describe applications that have used these approaches in the social sciences. This chapter only scratches the surface of what is possible and we recommend Eisenstein (2019) and Jursfsky and Martin (2009) for a more detailed treatment of this topic.

9.1 Text Reuse

Building on the core technology behind plagiarism detection, social scientists have begun to explore the implications of *text reuse*. These algorithms identify common sequences of text that appear across a pair of documents that are sufficiently long that it is improbable they appeared by chance. This is generally because one document was copied from the other or they both were copied from a common source. Understanding how these patterns of copying arise can be quite revealing for political and social processes across a variety of contexts, from history (Smith, Cordell, and Dillon, 2013) to scientific writing (Citron and Ginsparg, 2015), to memes (Leskovec, Backstrom, and Kleinberg, 2009) and literary studies (Bamman and Crane, 2009).

In a project that we will discuss more in the Discovery part of the book, Grimmer (2010) wanted to understand how US senators related to their constituents. To do so he collected 24,000 press releases put out by Senate offices in 2007. A key challenge in this work was establishing that the information in these press releases actually reflected the information that reached news consumers (since most news consumers are not reading the daily press releases from their senator's office). Using off-the-shelf plagiarism detection software, Grimmer (2010) showed that local newspapers reprint large sections of Senate press releases essentially word-for-word (see also Grimmer, 2013*b*). For smaller local papers as many as 30% of a given state's senator's press releases might be copied, and even large papers, such as the *San Francisco Chronicle*, quoted from 6–7% of the California senators' press releases.

Bail (2012) also applies this technique to track the influence of fringe civil society organizations on the mainstream media coverage of Muslims in the United States after the 9/11 attack. He identified mainstream newspaper and television news coverage that substantially reused text from civil society press releases. He then combined these press releases with additional qualitatively coded information to explain why some press releases spread and others did not. He finds that media outlets amplified the message of both well-resourced civil society organizations as well as fringe organizations that promoted angry and fearful frames about Muslims (see also Bail, 2014*a*). Bail's work establishes that far from simply establishing that copying has occurred, text reuse can be an important innovation in the measurement of culture (Bail, 2014*b*; Mohr et al., 2020).

Finally, Wilkerson, Smith, and Stramp (2015) trace the evolution of legislation in the US Congress by tracking the progression of policy ideas through the reuse of text across previously failed bills. They use these insights to provide new evidence about the history of the Patient Protection and Affordable Care Act (Obamacare), which drew ideas from 232 previously introduced bills, including those sponsored by Republicans, who would later vote against the bill. The possibilities are arguably even richer at the state legislature level, where organizations like the American Legislative Exchange Council explicitly distributed legislative text to be adopted across states (Hertel-Fernandez and Kashin, 2015; Burgess et al., 2016; Jansa, Hansen, and Gray, 2019; Hertel-Fernandez, 2019). In recent years, scholars have just started tapping the potential for text reuse as a tool to understand influence in lawmaking (Linder et al., 2020; Gava, Jaquet, and Sciarini, 2021).

The challenge of these methods is that they can be quite computationally costly. By construction, these methods make use of pairwise comparisons between documents which means that even a moderate size corpus can lead to an infeasible number of comparisons without further approximations. For example, Wilkerson, Smith, and Stramp (2015) have nearly 120,000 individual bill sections to compare, which would require over seven billion comparisons using a naive approach. Ultimately they are able to leverage preprocessing techniques that reduce the number of comparisons by three orders of magnitude, which makes these techniques possible to use. As tools to do these comparisons become more widely available, we anticipate that studies will become even more common.

9.2 Parts of Speech Tagging

Parts of speech (POS) tagging is the task of assigning a grammatical tag to each word within a document, for example, tagging it as a verb, noun, preposition, or adjective. Words are tagged either by a rule-based algorithm or by a machine learning algorithm that classifies each word based on a manually tagged training dataset (Jursfsky and Martin, 2009, p. 297). The Penn Treebank, a corpus of 4.8 million words from a variety of

English language sources tagged with 45 different parts of speech tags, is often used as a training set for POS tagging in English (Marcus, Marcinkiewicz, and Santorini, 1993) although different approaches exist for other mediums of writing, such as Twitter (Gimpel et al., 2011) and online conversations (Owoputi et al., 2013).

POS tagging is an important input to a number of other techniques and can also be used as a way to subset document-feature matrices to focus on properties of interest. For example, if researchers are primarily interested in sentiment content in their documents, it may be advantageous to remove all parts of speech except adjectives and adverbs, which are more likely to convey cues about sentiment. Part of speech tags can also be useful for separating out word senses when those senses are separated by parts of speech.

An important practical application for POS tagging is identifying phrases or n-grams that can be included in feature sets or to visualize texts. For example, we can identify noun phrases—a group of nouns and the words that modify it. These phrases, such as health care and World Cup, often indicate cases where the set of words means something substantially more than the sum of the constituent unigrams. One way to identify such phrases is through the use of particular grammatical patterns (Justeson and Katz, 1995; Handler et al., 2016). To identify noun phrases, researchers first use POS tagging to annotate each word. Then, they take all phrases of a certain length within the text, for example, all phrases with length 4. They then identify whether any given phrase fits a particular grammatical pattern, which is typically written in a regular expression so the matching can be automated. For example, a simple noun phrase might be a noun (N) with either a noun (N) or an adjective (A) coming before it:

$$(N|A)+N$$

The | sign indicates an OR. This grammatical pattern would pick up phrases such as New York, World Cup, and old songs.

Noun phrases also might contain prepositions after the noun that describe the noun, for example, woman from New York, or airplane over the Pacific Ocean. Therefore, another more complicated grammatical pattern to select noun phrases uses prepositions (P) and determiners (D):

$$(N|A)+N(P+D^*(A|N)^*N)^*$$

where $*$ indicates that the previous clause is optional. Thus $(P+D^*(A|N)^*N)^*$ reads that the phrase can optionally include a preposition and a noun, the latter of which can optionally have an adjective or a noun before it, and optionally a determinant before that. Noun phrases of many variations have been used in many other applications, such as for enhancing search in digital libraries (Frantzi, Ananiadou, and Mima, 2000), discovering biographical information in text (Bamman and Smith, 2014), and identifying partisan language (Handler et al., 2016). Similar strategies can be used to identify verb phrases, which can be useful as a basis for identifying events.

9.2.1 USING PHRASES TO IMPROVE VISUALIZATION

In a number of the preceding chapters, we have used word clouds in order to visualize corpora. While plenty of criticism can and has been made against word clouds, they often provide a quick, visually appealing view of a corpus. Noun phrases can be useful not only for precisely extracting information from text, but also for improving the

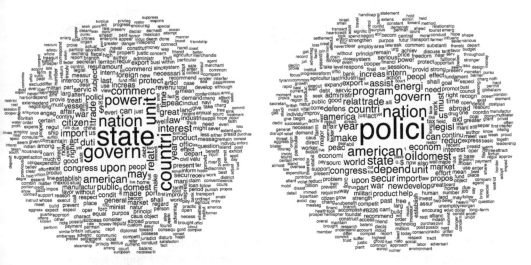

Figure 9.1. Word clouds of sentences from the State of the Union corpus containing the word `foreign`. Left: Sentences from before 1917. Right: Sentences 1917 and after.

interpretability of word clouds and similar visualizations. In a study of text visualization, Chuang, Manning, and Heer (2012) asked human coders to write down keyphrases that summarize dissertation abstracts. They found that the coders were very likely to select noun phrases as useful keyphrases. Even though noun phrases only accounted for 13% of all phrases in the abstracts, they accounted for 65% of the keyphrases selected by humans (Chuang, Manning, and Heer, 2012, p. 8). Crowdsourced ratings of word cloud visualizations similarly showed that human judges found the word clouds with phrases more informative.

To demonstrate how this would work we return to one of our running examples. We explore the claim in Rule, Cointet, and Bearman (2015) that the way in which foreign policy was described in State of the Union addresses changed in 1917, around the time of the US entry into World War II. Rule, Cointet, and Bearman (2015) show that the topical cluster that they label "statecraft" declines and is replaced by the topical cluster "foreign policy."

To investigate this through a simple analysis of word counts, we extract all sentences from the State of the Union corpus that contain the word `foreign` and examine the differences in the word clouds produced by these sentences before 1917 as opposed to after 1917. Figure 9.1 shows a word cloud of all the unigrams, as in Chapter 5, but now split over time with uses before 1917 on the left and uses after 1917 on the right (note: we removed the word `foreign` itself so it didn't dominate every other word since it is in every sentence by construction). Our findings reflect Rule, Cointet, and Bearman (2015)'s high-level finding that foreign policy became a much more dominant term after 1917 (`polici` being the most common word post-1917) while discussion of `states` was perhaps more common before 1917. Beyond this rephrasing, however, it is more difficult to distinguish between the use of the words in these two periods.

In Figure 9.2 we construct the same figures using the newly identified noun phrases rather than the individual tokens of Figure 9.1. This new figure is arguably substantially more informative. One of the primary conclusions from this plot is the increase in discussion about foreign oil and foreign aid after 1917. It also reflects the changing

Figure 9.2. Noun phrase word clouds of sentences from the State of the Union corpus containing the word `foreign`. Left: Sentences from before 1917. Right: Sentences after 1917.

geographic focus of US foreign policy—the first word cloud contains the word `Great Britain`, while the second word cloud contains the word `Middle East`.

Here we have demonstrated just one example of phrase detection and, more generally, part of speech tagging. Part of speech tagging is relatively fast and—for formal text such as news articles—has quite high accuracy. Thus we anticipate that there are more opportunities for social scientific use of these techniques waiting to be discovered.

9.3 Named-Entity Recognition

In natural language processing, part of speech tagging is an important input to other processes like named-entity recognition (NER). NER is the process of tagging people, organizations, and places within texts (Manning et al., 2014). In some specialized contexts, these systems can be learned to tag additional information such as dates, drug names or chemical reactions. Like part of speech tagging, modern named entity recognition systems tend to be built on sequence-based machine learning models and for settings with formal writing are fairly accurate out of the box.

Jaros and Pan (2018) use named-entity recognition software in official Chinese newspapers to better understand the distribution of power among political elites in China. Many had speculated that after he took office in November 2012, General Secretary Xi Jinping consolidated power more than his predecessor, Hu Jintao (Mulvenon, 2015). Other experts observed that the Party had consolidated more power relative to the government in China (Lampton, 2015) and that anti-West sentiment seemed to be on the rise in China.[1]

However, power is difficult to measure, particularly in China, where much of politics takes place behind closed doors. Jaros and Pan (2018) note that previous research has shown that official newspapers in China often reflect the consolidation of power within the CCP, as they signal to citizens and elites the allegiances of those controlling the paper

---

[1] Wong, Edward. 2014. "In new China, 'hostile' West is still derided," *New York Times*, 11 November.

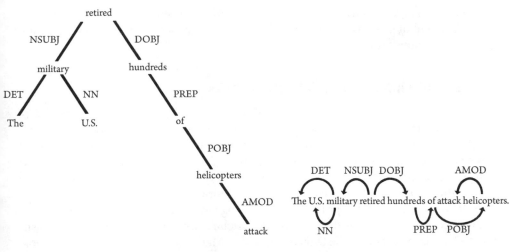

Figure 9.3. Two different representations of the dependency parse of "The U.S. military retired hundreds of attack helicopters."

(Shih, 2008; Huang, 2015; Zeng, 2016). Therefore, entities with more power would be mentioned more frequently in newspapers than those with less power.

To measure power, Jaros and Pan (2018) used NER in Chinese official provincial newspapers to recognize all people and organizations named in Party newspapers. They then used the number of times an entity was mentioned within official newspapers, as a proportion of all other entities mentioned, as a measure of power. They found that the official newspapers reflected many of the hypothesized trends. Xi Jinping was much more frequently mentioned in Party newspapers than his predecessor was during his time in office. Party institutions also gained prominence over the time that Xi was in office. However, they showed unexpectedly that there was not a decline in mentions of foreign organizations.

9.4 Dependency Parsing

Part of speech tagging and named entity recognition both tag individual words, but it is also possible to extract information about the way words relate to the entirety of the sentence. Dependency parsing is the process of extracting a directed graph that explains the way words and phrases are syntactically connected to each other within a sentence (Jursfsky and Martin, 2009, Chapter 14). Dependency parsing identifies a root word (often the primary verb) and then describes the other words in relation to that word and to each other. For example, in the sentence, "The U.S. military retired hundreds of attack helicopters," the nominal subject of the sentence is "The U.S. military" and the main verb of the sentence is "retired," which would be identified as the root of the sentence. The direct object of the root "retired" is "hundreds of attack helicopters." The nominal subject and direct object can then be broken down into dependencies, as shown in Figure 9.3.

Because dependency parses contain information about which words modify other words, they can be incredibly useful when attempting to determine sentiment (Socher et al., 2013), identify semantic relationships between actors and issues (Van Atteveldt, Kleinnijenhuis, and Ruigrok, 2008), or measure the political complexity of a text

(Benoit, Munger, and Spirling, 2019). However, for social scientists dependency parsing isn't an end in itself, as much as it enables a broader array of information extraction tasks that we now consider.

9.5 Broader Information Extraction Tasks

Information extraction is the process of identifying discrete, structured pieces of information from a text. Many of the approaches in this book are focused on characterizing document-level properties of a text while information extraction is often about three types of information: *entities* in a text, the *relations* between entities, and *events* that occur between those entities. We have actually already seen one instance of an information extraction task—named entity recognition.

Relation extraction is the process of identifying particular relationships between the established entities, such as that Barack and Michelle Obama are married, that Washington D.C. is the capital of the United States, that Mark Zuckerberg founded Facebook, or that Hamilton, Madison, and Jay are the authors of the Federalist Papers. The result of relation extraction tasks is often a list of facts that places entities into a fixed number of slots.

The third broad type of information extraction is about finding events. Event extraction denotes a particular action occurring at some period of time usually between two or more entities. While relations typically exist between two particular entities, events often have a great deal more information attached to them that we want to recover, such as the time of, location of, nature of, and participants in the event. One branch of event extraction looks at templates that have specific slots that must be filled in to identify the event.

In one example that brings many of these techniques together, Keith et al. (2017) use NER and dependency parsing to extract names of people killed by the police from news articles. Federal datasets of individuals killed by the police are incomplete, and therefore current efforts to create a dataset of individuals killed by the police rely on manual extraction of names from news articles. Keith et al. (2017) seek to automate this process. First, they use NER to extract all potential targets. Then, from each sentence they extract dependency paths that include the target. They use these dependency paths with other features to train their model to identify sentences indicating a particular event—the target had been killed by the police. Over a six month test period, Keith et al. (2017) identified 39 individuals killed by the police who were not included in *The Guardian*'s database "The Counted," indicating that this automated approach could be used to improve existing datasets.

POLITICAL EVENT DATA

Despite the fact that event extraction is an incredibly difficult task, it was one of the earliest examples of text as data in sociology and political science. Scholars were attempting to code complex interactions between social and political actors as far back as the 1980s (Schrodt, 1986; Franzosi, 1989; Schrodt and Gerner, 1994; King and Lowe, 2003; Schrodt, 2006). These interactions—records of the form someone did something to someone else in the international sphere—have been demonstrated to be useful in forecasting (Brandt, Freeman, and Schrodt, 2011; Bagozzi, 2015; Chadefaux, 2017; Chiba and Gleditsch, 2017). While early systems were primarily based on part of speech tagging, modern systems use dependency parsing and attempt to record substantially more information about the event (Beieler et al., 2016; Halterman, 2017; Lee, Liu, and Ward, 2019; Halterman, 2019).

Early approaches captured directional information using pattern matching with a fixed dictionary of possible actors (like `Russia` and `United States`) and events (like `attack`). These approaches were often foiled by complex sentence structures, for example, "The U.S. embassy in Baghdad suffered an attack." Dependency parsing provides a way forward because it captures the structure of the sentence, allowing the analyst to identify 1) whether the sentence involves `attack` as its root and 2) the actor doing the attacking, even if this actor doesn't appear just before the word `attack`. The sentence can then be effectively rearranged so that pattern matching can be used again (Beieler, 2016). This still leaves the central problem that dictionaries are expensive to create and maintain, with event dictionaries often trying to cover every conceivable phrasing for hundreds of types of events. Some work has explored the ability to automatically learn actions by using some of the techniques we will discuss in the chapters on Discovery (O'Connor, Stewart, and Smith, 2013). This is an area in which a community of social science scholars are actively pushing forward the state of the art using the latest techniques in natural language processing (Salam et al., 2020; Halterman, 2020).

An open challenge for these systems moving forward is incorporating different types of media. In the study of protests, Zhang and Pan (2019) build a classifier which extracts protest events in China from social media and find that both the text and photographs provide more information than text alone.

9.6 Conclusion

In this chapter we covered a series of related tasks that treat language as a sequence—from finding copies of that sequence to using parses of that sequence to extract valuable information. Many of the techniques covered here were quite different those covered in Chapters 5–8, but techniques like part of speech tagging and parsing are relatively underutilized in the social sciences.

This is also the conclusion of our part on Representation. In this section we showed how to turn text into numbers in a wide variety of different ways. The purpose of most text as data methods is to estimate a measure for the unit of text, and aggregate this measure to reflect the whole corpus, arriving at the quantity of interest. The representation is a choice about which information in the text to keep and which to discard, and thus it will be intrinsically connected to the specific research question and where the researcher is in the process.

If you do not know what the text contains and don't have a question of interest yet, you might try a few different ways of representing the texts to apply the discovery methods we will talk about in the next part of the book. These methods in turn might help describe the data, uncover new concepts, and guide the next steps of your research process. Representing texts at the discovery stage can help you apply models that can point you to interesting texts in the corpus to read or groups of text that may have substantive meaning. It may be that the more creative you can be about the way you represent text at this phase, the more likely you will be to discover new ways of organizing or thinking about the corpus or the social science question of interest.

If, on the other hand, you already know what your population and quantities of interest for your analysis are, then your representation of the text should be driven by the quantity you are interested in measuring. In other words, what information from the text do you want to measure, what will your quantities of interest be? Texts are complex — they encode meaning through word choice, phrasing, and the organization of concepts. However, not all of the complexity of text is necessary for any particular analysis, and trying to retain that complexity can be a barrier to success. Because quantitative analyses of text are often focused on characterizing a few general characteristics of a large document set—characterizing the haystack instead of a straw of hay—our analyses and quantities of interest will not typically require us to retain all information from the texts. Reducing the complexity of the text is a key step in allowing the analysis to focus on only the aspects of the text that are important to the task at hand.

PART III

Discovery

Social research is often presented as if the basic concepts we use to organize the empirical world are given. Consider an example from recent research. McGhee et al. (2014) examine how moving from a closed primary—where only members of a party can vote—to an open primary—where any eligible voter can cast a ballot—affects ideological polarization in state legislatures. On its face, this question is clear and corresponds with deep questions about how to reform American politics. But it also implies a particular organization of the world. Primary elections have to be categorized according to who is eligible to vote and members of the legislature have to be placed in an ideological space.[1]

In Chapter 2, we related the story of the circuitous route through which King, Pan and Roberts (KPR) came to study censorship in China. Their work showed that the Chinese government censors social media posts not on the basis of criticism of the government, but instead on the potential for collective action. This work relies on defining myriad concepts—censorship, criticism of the government, collective action potential, and various topics of posts used in their analysis. Of course, this is not the only way the social media posts could have been organized. Indeed, subsequently scholars have argued that a finer categorization of criticism would add explanatory power to understanding the Chinese government's censorship policies (Shao, 2018; Gueorguiev and Malesky, 2019). For other questions outside of censorship, for example public opinion analysis, researchers might come up with a completely different organization for the same posts.

In these cases as well as numerous others, concepts form the entire structure of the research project. They define what measures are necessary to construct and what those

---

[1] Parts of this introduction are drawn from Grimmer, Roberts, and Stewart (2021).

measures are trying to achieve; what questions can be asked and what constitutes an answer; and ultimately, what conclusions can be reached about the world. Yet, quantitative researchers have traditionally spent too little time examining their concepts—how they arrived at them and what alternative ways might exist to organize the world. This is a shame because concepts are integral to research findings. It is not as though social science lacks a way to think about developing new concepts. There is a long tradition in qualitative research of developing methodology for the creation of new concepts. Grounded theory (Corbin and Strauss, 1990) and abductive analysis (Tavory and Timmermans, 2014), to give two examples, provide iterative frameworks for moving, in a principled way, from initial field notes and interviews toward the generation of concepts and new hypotheses. Several scholars have offered frameworks for using quantitative methods to enhance these qualitative methodologies, already scoping out a place for quantitative methods in what has traditionally been a qualitative task (Baumer et al., 2017; Nelson, 2020; Karell and Freedman, 2019).

In this section, we offer a methodology for discovering and applying new ways of organizing observations. In particular, we show how the combination of texts, quantitative methods for discovery, and careful reading can facilitate uncovering new ways of organizing the world, reemphasize the importance of existing organizational schema, and facilitate new theoretical innovations. The new organization leads us to measure new quantities, refine theories, infer relationships, and even offer policy prescriptions. This process can be iterated repeatedly to provide new evidence on longstanding questions of interest and to consider entirely new questions.

Chapter 10: Principles of Discovery provides the foundation of our framework for discovery. The next four chapters that make up the part highlight the four classes of methods that we think are most effective for discovering new concepts: discriminating words, clustering methods, topic models, and embedding techniques.

A central challenge in discovery is making sense of an organization of texts once we have it. This could be because an organization exists in the world (for example, organizing documents by speaker) or because we have uncovered a new organization using one of the unsupervised methods we discuss in Chapters 12–14. Regardless of how the organization came about, we often want to characterize what is distinctive about an organization to help us make sense of it. In **Chapter 11: Discriminating Words**, we describe methods to identify words that are used disproportionately by a given group of documents.

The next three chapters describe different ways of discovering new organizations of texts. Unsupervised clustering analysis methods, the subject of **Chapter 12: Clustering**, produce a *partition* of the texts: every document is assigned to one of K categories. Rather than assume the categories are known beforehand, unsupervised clustering analysis methods discover the categories, attempting to assign documents such that similar documents share a cluster and clusters are as distinct from each other as possible. **Chapter 13: Topic Models** describes a related class of methods for discovering a set of K categories where documents hold proportional membership in all categories (rather than being entirely a member of one). This conceptual difference allows topic models to more faithfully represent documents that cover a complex mix of themes. **Chapter 14: Low-Dimensional Document Embeddings** presents the final set of approaches that locate a document in a real-valued space. Unlike the constrained representations in clustering (membership in one category) and topic models (proportional membership across categories), embedding locations are unconstrained. This often makes these techniques particularly useful for visualization (when embeddings are low dimensional) or for calculating similarity of documents when absolute position is less important (when embeddings are high dimensional). All three of these approaches suggest new organizations to facilitate discovery by extracting underlying systematic patterns in the texts that may not be apparent to human readers!

Each of these four classes of methods could be the subject of its own large manuscript (and several already are). Here, we focus on the intuition behind each class of method and explain how these particular techniques can support conceptual discovery. Once the reader has an intuition for the particular class of method, it can be generalized to other models in the general class (including models that may not even exist yet at the time of writing).

CHAPTER 10

Principles of Discovery

Most of the conventional rules of scientific research came from a time when data was sparse, but thinking was comparatively cheap. When data is very limited it is important to theorize in advance of examining the data to preserve as much information as possible for evaluating theories. The absolute cost of thought has not changed, but data are now more readily available. This deluge of data allows us to use data-driven approaches to discovery on one set of documents and then use a *different* set of documents to develop measures and evaluate claims. This approach avoids the common critiques of data mining—that it will be circular, will overfit, or be meaningless. As we will explain below, once we have a conception in hand, it is ours and it is *irrelevant* how it was developed. What matters is that the concept provides an insightful way to look at our problem and that we use fresh data moving forward. This origin-independence of the concept frees us to use whatever technique produces the best insights for us without worrying about the underlying assumptions.

This chapter outlines the four principles that guide our computational approach to discovery. We then provide an example of how concepts can shape not just one piece of work, but the research of an entire field. We conclude with an argument for why explicitly studying discovery is so important.

10.1 Principle 1: Context Relevance

> *Text as data models complement theory and substantive knowledge. Contextual knowledge amplifies our ability to make computational discoveries.*

The methods in this chapter are designed to aid the researcher—to suggest new ways of organizing data, or to confirm that existing organizations are present in data. The methods that we present in this chapter are not, however, a substitute for substantive knowledge. We want to be clear from the outset: there is no replacement for careful study and deep knowledge of social structures. This might be surprising if we take seriously claims from optimistic futurists in articles like "The End of Theory: The Data Deluge Makes the Scientific Method Obsolete" (Anderson, 2008).

These declarations overstate the power of machine learning algorithms and understate the importance of qualitative human analysis. Before applying any model we have to identify interesting data to analyze, which requires substantive knowledge. Interpreting the output of any of the models we discuss requires deep understanding of the case at hand. And knowing what to make of the findings from any model—and how those findings revise our understanding of the world—still requires that we have an organizing theory and knowledge of our case.

Take for example, identifying a surprising category, pattern, or concept, often known in the qualitative literature as abductive analysis. As we will show in Chapter 13 through Karell and Freedman (2019)'s analysis of documents produced by Afghan radical groups, recognizing a surprising category requires being aware of existing theoretical organizations of radical rhetoric. Similarly, in Chapter 11 we describe Nelson (2020)'s use of computational grounded theory to analyze literature produced by feminist organizations. Nelson's understanding of the geographical structure of these organizations allows her to use computational methods to elucidate new distinctions between political strategies that existing frameworks cannot.

Rather than viewing the methods in this chapter as supplanting traditional theorizing, we argue that the methods we introduce are best thought of as complements to the traditional social scientific theory building process. By unifying theorizing and exploration, we can refine our theories in light of discovered categories in data. The methods in this chapter therefore contribute to the iterative nature of the scientific process, where the goal is theory development, and deep substantive knowledge is a prerequisite for inference. While they cannot replace substantive knowledge, they can facilitate discovery of new findings about a substantive case and highlight tensions in previous theories.

10.2 Principle 2: No Ground Truth

> *There is no ground truth conceptualization; only after a concept is fixed can we talk meaningfully about it being right or wrong.*

It makes little sense to discuss the "true" conceptualization because different organizations of our data merely imply different ways of viewing the world. There is no sense in which there is a single true or false way of grouping documents. For example, we might organize texts based on their topic, their tone, or the author. It is difficult to ask which conceptualization is "right" because different organizational schemes are more or less useful for answering different questions.

While there is no true way to group our data, it does not mean that all organizations of the data are equally useful for all tasks. To give an extreme example, the index to this book is ordered alphabetically to facilitate easily finding a particular entry, but that wouldn't be a useful order in which to present the topics covered in this book. In a less obvious choice, the presentation of methods in this book is organized by research task rather than by the foundations of the technique. This has the effect of emphasizing the research design components of the text and de-emphasizing the statistical and algorithmic foundations of the methods—a choice that is appropriate for our book but would be less helpful for a book aimed at a different audience. The usefulness of the organization will depend on the question or problem we are trying to solve.

Once we have arrived at a conceptualization, there will be more and less accurate methods to *measure* those concepts—this is the subject of Part IV of the book. For example, we can—and should—validate how accurately our method identifies "criticism" in a document. However, what categories to use ("criticism" and "praise" versus "effusive" and "curt") will depend entirely on the research question.

10.3 Principle 3: Judge the Concept, Not the Method

The method you used to arrive at a conceptualization does not matter for assessing the concept's value—its utility does.

The value of a particular conceptualization is derived from what those concepts help the researcher accomplish and not the method used to develop them. Regardless of where the organization comes from, once the researcher has the organizational schema in mind, she can use it to create measurements, test hypotheses, and update theories appropriately. In this sense—as with our general principle of text analysis methods—there is no "best" method for discovery.

This implies that the only meaningful way to evaluate a conceptualization is based on its usefulness for the particular application. For example, we might ask if the organization helps us to better understand the primary goal of censors when limiting posts on social media, the rhetoric of radical groups, or the way that advocacy groups shape the media landscape. But there is no meaningful sense in which we can make an application-independent declaration that organizing the topics of social media is "better" than organization according to sentiment. The value comes from the particular application.

Given that all that matters for a conceptualization is its usefulness to any application, there is no reason to prioritize where the idea for the organization comes from. On the one hand, this frees the researcher to do all the exploration she wants when deciding how to organize her data. On the other hand, though, it means that evaluating the methodology for discovery is extremely difficult. There are no proofs that we could write down that would show some methods are better at discovering organizations of data than others. There are no analogous simulations that could show that one method does better on average than another. And perhaps most problematically, demonstrating that the method has produced insights once for the researcher—the real goal of the method—holds no guarantee that the method will produce comparable insights in the future or for other research teams.

This all implies that when attempting to discover new research conceptualizations, researchers should be prepared to explore many different methods and many different ways of organizing the data. Statistical methods and computational algorithms based on clear and precise assumptions about the underlying organization can yield insightful ways of organizing data; but so can something radically different like going for a walk in the woods. There are many ways to implement similar ideas about what constitutes a good organization and many intuitive properties we might want conceptualizations to have. Varying these properties is essential to uncovering more interesting and useful ways of organizing the data. And it also means that there is a real sense in which the properties of the model don't matter—other than in their ability to produce useful organizations. Once researchers have a conceptualization, they can use it for whatever purpose they choose and apply it to whatever new dataset they would like to use.

10.4 Principle 4: Separate Data Is Best

> *Ideally, after data is used for discovery it should be discarded in favor of new data for confirming/testing discoveries.*

If we want to use our conceptualization in other points of the research process, for measurement and inference for example, the data we used to arrive at the conceptualization should be discarded for freshly collected or previously held-out data. The use of external data ensures that the categories we discover are not merely artifacts of the particular dataset in which they were discovered and the labels that we place on the categories or dimensions mean what we claim they do. This is particularly true when using text as data methods to make causal inferences. If we fail to divide the data into two distinct datasets we run the risk of violating core causal inference assumptions, as we discuss in more detail later in the book.

In practice, there is plenty of research in the text as data space that has not used a separate dataset for confirmation and testing (including work that we like, believe, and/or have written). In certain projects data is highly limited and the value of separating the discovery and testing stages hasn't always been recognized (perhaps in part because discovery itself isn't talked about as frequently). Many pieces of work remain highly compelling due to their careful validation and investigation of the dataset. Yet, when possible, it is difficult to understate the value of having separate data to evaluate the results of new discovery, particularly when exploring the data with many different techniques and using the agnostic view of discovery that we espouse here.

10.5 Conceptualizing the US Congress

To motivate how statistical models can facilitate new insights, inferences, and theories in text, we turn to a discussion of how similar methods have inspired a literature based on Congressional roll call voting data—a form of high-dimensional data not all that dissimilar from the bag of words representation from Chapter 5. In particular, we explain how a new conceptualization, generated using a statistical model, led to new insights into the behavior of legislators in the US Congress and how this conceptualization leads directly to new research questions, new theories, and ultimately a better understanding for society about how the US Congress behaves.

Scholars of American political institutions develop theories to explain how legislators' diverse preferences are aggregated to reach decisions in order to understand when and how Congress shapes public policy. In order to study how Congress works, scholars have contributed numerous ways of conceptualizing its members, the votes taken in the institution, and the salient dimensions of conflict. Each conceptualization contributes a distinct organization of members, votes, and dimensions of conflict, which itself implies a particular view on how Congress creates public policy. For example, MacRae (1965) argues that underlying Congressional roll call votes are six to eight voting blocs that emerge depending upon the legislative content of a piece of legislation. Other conceptualizations emphasize ephemeral coalitions that emerge occasionally, such as the "conservative coalition" that would emerge around civil rights issues in the 1960s. There is also a long tradition in American politics to describe politicians along an ideological spectrum. Politicians are often assessed, declare that their opponents are, or declare themselves to be "far-left liberal," "liberal," "moderate," "conservative," or "far-right conservative." Each label corresponds to a location on the ideological spectrum.

The most consequential conceptualization of US legislators' voting records for modern day political science comes from the VoteView project (Poole and Rosenthal, 1997). Beginning with seminal work published in the early 1980s, Keith Poole, Howard Rosenthal, and collaborators developed low-dimensional measures of where legislators fall on an ideological spectrum based on their Dynamic Weighted Nominal Three-Step Estimation (DW-NOMINATE) algorithm for compressing legislative voting data. This summarized each legislator with a two-dimensional score—the first dimension, which is often the only one used, is said to correspond to the ideological position of the legislator (Poole and Rosenthal, 1985). The first dimension is visualized in Figure 10.1. There is a close connection between DW-NOMINATE scores and spatial models that are common in political economy models of politics. Political economy models suppose that actors and policies are located in a policy space, with politicians located at their "ideal point" or the point in policy space that the politician prefers more than any other option. DW-NOMINATE supposes that politicians vote for proposals that are closer to their ideal points than the status quo; therefore, the estimates from DW-NOMINATE can be interpreted as a measure of legislators' ideal points. Thus, there is a direct connection between spatial models and the estimates from DW-NOMINATE.

The organization was viewed as audacious when it was first introduced: there was deep skepticism that only two dimensions could capture the salient ideological dimensions of conflict within Congress (Poole and Rosenthal, 1997). Even among those who agreed that a low-dimensional representation could capture Congressional behavior, there was a deep divide about why. The evidence for this organization and assertion came from a discovery of where legislators fell in the ideological space. This particular conceptualization emphasized a representative's "ideal point" but suppressed a large number of other features of Congressional conflict and compressed the entire roll call voting record to a single point in a two-dimensional space. Not surprisingly, numerous scholars objected to the conceptualization as too simplistic to understand how Congressional conflict worked.

And yet, after over 30 years of analysis, the VoteView project has become the default conceptualization of members of Congress. It is utilized in nearly every quantitative paper about the US Congress written in political science and forms the basis for understanding how Congress works. It has even provoked new theory that seeks to explain why the voting in the US Congress is so low dimensional and has inspired attempts to recreate the literature in legislatures outside of the US (Snyder Jr., 1992). The same core techniques have been used to measure ideal points of candidates for office (Shor and McCarty, 2011), donors (Bonica, 2013), social media users (Barberá, 2014; Bond and Messing, 2015), and voters (Bafumi and Herron, 2010). The work has spread outside of political science, generating a healthy literature in computer science that seeks to improve ideal points by combining the voting information with the text of the bill being voted on (Gerrish and Blei, 2011, 2012; Nguyen et al., 2015; Kraft, Jain, and Rush, 2016; Vafa, Naidu, and Blei, 2020). Through the technique, the conceptualization of Congress has spread to other types of phenomena, other scientific communities, and other modes of data.

The organization of legislators that comes from the VoteView project is developed inductively, but it has been instrumental for further developing deductive theories of the US Congress. That is, even though the dimensions of DW-NOMINATE are not specified a priori, it has still become a vital tool for the work of theoretical studies of

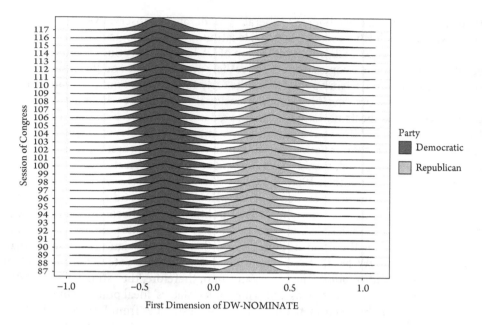

Figure 10.1. A visualization of the distribution of Congressional ideology over time, using the first dimension calculated by the DW-NOMINATE algorithm based on the voting record of the legislators.

Congress. For example, it is used to assess theoretical innovations about the organization of Congress (Krehbiel, 1998), the structure of inter-branch bargaining (Cameron, 2000), and the nature of political representation (Canes-Wrone, Brady, and Cogan, 2002). In turn, the use of DW-NOMINATE to assess theoretical models has pushed scholars of other legislatures to develop analogous measure of legislators' ideological positions using a variety of data sources, including political speech (Laver, Benoit, and Garry, 2003; Slapin and Proksch, 2008).

Of course, there are other important ways to organize members of Congress and their actions—organizations that suggest different research questions and different inferences about the way Congress operates. For example, legislators are organized into leadership, they are placed on committees that have more or less power, or they are members of party caucuses. Organizing legislators in this way leads to different questions and measures. For example, Berry and Fowler (2016) ask whether legislators who are on the Appropriations Committee are able to deliver more money to their district. Other work includes a number of conceptualizations on legislator behavior. We might ask how leaders came to be powerful (Powell, N.d.). A rich literature asks how representative Congressional committees are of the institution—questions that depend on organizing legislators based on the committees they sit on and their place in the ideological spectrum (Krehbiel, 1990).

Still other conceptualizations are based on the way legislators communicate with their constituents. Fenno (1978) organized legislators based on the kinds of issues they engaged in with their constituents. In a research project we will return to in this chapter, Grimmer (2013b) employs a similar organization of senators, placing them on a spectrum ranging from senators who focused their rhetoric on broad national issues to senators who focused on claiming credit for money delivered to their district.

This organization leads to other important measurements—where do legislators fall on the pork/policy spectrum—and questions that lead to inferences about why legislators adopt particular styles, how those styles affect the way constituents evaluate their elected officials, and how differences in who adopts those styles affects contributions to debates.

Each of the examples also demonstrates that social science inferences depend upon our conceptualizations. To study the origins of polarization, we assume that legislators can be located in an ideological space and that this space is defined by the organization of legislators in it. Likewise, to study how legislator appeals affect constituents' evaluations, we need a map for organizing what legislators say and how they say it. The particular organization that we assume facilitates certain hypotheses, while also making other questions impossible or nonsensical. This is why the particular organization is essential: all of our conclusions depend upon how we decide to organize the world from the start.

Conceptualizations have a pervasive influence in research, and yet, very little quantitative work engages methods for developing new conceptualizations. Even in the literature on the US Congress, the application of DW-NOMINATE scores has far outpaced attempts to develop new organizations to explain the structure of Congressional conflict. The lack of attention to developing new conceptualizations is problematic because it severely limits what the field studies about Congress. It is limiting because the lack of methods, time intensity, or the anxiety about producing new schema means that scholars will adopt organizations that prior researchers have used, or adopt conceptualizations that are well established from the institution. Certainly, it is important that scholars accumulate evidence and share a common perspective—having no shared conceptualizations in a field leads to its own kind of dysfunction. But focusing on only one conceptualization will also necessarily limit the questions researchers ask and therefore limit the inferences they can make from data.

10.6 Conclusion

We simply don't talk about discovery enough, even though it is an implicit part of every research project. Consider this quote from the methodological appendix of Mitch Duneier's award-winning ethnography *Sidewalk*:

> The fact that I did not know my specific research question at the start may seem counter to the way sociologists are supposed to operate. I take a different view, however. In much of social science, especially much of quantitative research using large datasets, a research design often emerges after data has been collected. Of course, survey instruments themselves require design, which requires some sort of theoretical agenda or conceptual foundation to begin with.... But a well-designed survey allows the research to raise a variety of questions and topics later on, some of them unanticipated. ... Like quantitative researchers who get an idea of what to look at from mulling over existing data, I began to get ideas from the things I was seeing and hearing on the street.   (Duneier, 1999, p. 341)

Most of the time the discovery phase of work is invisible in published research, but as Duneier notes it is the way much of quantitative work proceeds.

In this chapter we have outlined a view of what discovery is, the principles on which it should proceed, and an account of how novel conceptualizations can substantially alter the path of research in a field. In the next chapters we will outline a set of techniques that can help produce computationally assisted discoveries. In this concluding section we outline three ways we think that discussing discovery more could improve empirical practice.

First, once we acknowledge discovery as part of the research process, we can set about developing methods explicitly designed to facilitate it. This has been most clearly pursued in the qualitative research design literature (Strauss, 1952; Tavory and Timmermans, 2014) and several computational social scientists have worked to import those insights into the text as data literature (Baumer et al., 2017; Nelson, 2020; Karell and Freedman, 2019). In order to develop new models that would maximize the chance of interesting discoveries, it is necessary to have frank discussions about how the process of discovery works, what the barriers to success are and how we would know a good discovery when we saw one.

Second, explicitly portraying discovery provides a more accurate representation to students in the field about what the scientific process is like. Too often we present novel conceptualizations as simply springing from the minds of brilliant scholars unbidden. This is, of course, a difficult process to replicate and can be discouraging to new entrants into the field.

Finally, acknowledging discovery allows scholars to be clearer about the nature of their evidence and where results are most credible. Articles which establish the plausibility of an interesting discovery are inherently important, but it is useful to know whether that discovery has been validated on external data or was hypothesized based on the same evidence used to confirm it. In Chapter 21: Repurposing Discovery Methods, we return to the use of the techniques discussed in this part of the book to discuss how they can be used for the task of measurement. An assessment of that sort is only possible when we clearly separate the discovery and measurement tasks and acknowledge the different types of evidence they require.

In the next chapter, we begin with the discussion of our technique for discovery: discriminating words, which provides a set of methods for discovering what is interesting or distinctive about a particular organization of text.

CHAPTER 11

Discriminating Words

In this chapter we describe methods for discovering words that characterize the language use in a given organization of documents. These work by identifying a set of words that convey the distinct content of a particular observed category—such as an author's gender, partisanship, or ideology—or a learned category—such as clusters induced by the methods we will discuss in the next chapter. Unlike the approaches that follow in this part, we will suppose that a set of categories already exists. In political science and economics, a common application of these methods is to understand how rhetoric in Congress differs between Republicans and Democrats—an organization of the text that exists by virtue of the partisan affiliation of the speaker (Monroe, Colaresi, and Quinn, 2008; Gentzkow, Shapiro, and Taddy, 2019). Similar analysis has been applied across a variety of categories and texts to understand differences in ideology (Diermeier et al., 2012), gender (Cunha et al., 2014), and geography (Eisenstein et al., 2010). These methods are an important part of the computer-assisted methods of discovery that will follow because they provide the tools to quickly understand newly discovered organizations of text.

Discriminating word methods are widely used, in part because they have a strong intuitive appeal. Language that one group disproportionately uses is often thought to be indicative of the kind of arguments the group wants to make or to characterize the linguistic frames that group employs. Applications often validate this intuition, demonstrating that methods that uncover distinctive words do often provide valuable insight into how a group communicates. The results can also be surprising in a way that sparks genuine discovery.

However, there is a key tension in discriminating words, because there is an inherent tension between words that are *distinctive* between groups of documents and words that are *prevalent* within that group. Thus the challenge emerges from how distinctive words are measured. Discriminating word approaches tend to focus on the most distinctive words but some attention is needed to prevalence to ensure the relevant words are still representative of the group as a whole. Different ways of making this trade-off leads to different definitions of "discriminating" and thus to different results.

In this chapter, we will present a variety of approaches for calculating discriminating words starting with an information-theoretic measure, mutual information. We will then cover a probabilistic method motivated by the multinomial model of Chapter 6 called Fightin' Words (Monroe, Colaresi, and Quinn, 2008). Finally, we will describe an approach to this problem based on predictive models of the group labels. We call these settings *fictitious prediction problems* because we are predicting a piece of information that is already known by construction. The goal isn't the prediction itself, but identifying the words that are the most effective predictors.

Throughout we will use a running example from Nelson (2020). Nelson uses discriminating word algorithms to discover the "cognitive frameworks" of feminist movements in the United States. While existing literature on the topic distinguishes primarily between first wave and second wave feminist movements, Nelson (2020) explores geographical differences in women's movements, particularly between movements located in Chicago and those in New York.

To do this, Nelson (2020) collects documents that originated in four women's organizations, in each of the two different locations and each of the different time periods: Hull House (first wave, Chicago), Heterodoxy (first wave, New York City), Chicago Women's Liberation Union (CWLU) (second wave, Chicago), and Redstockings (second wave, New York City). Nelson (2020) infers from her analysis that both Chicago organizations (Hullhouse and CWLU) were focused on concrete policies, such as education, medicine, and access to abortion, while both New York organizations (Heterodoxy and Redstockings) were focused on abstract and general ideas about feminism. She validates these results using both topic models, which we will cover in later chapters, and by careful reading. Nelson's application provides a great example of how discriminating words can be a springboard for discovery, which can enhance further reading.

Finally, we note that while we will talk about these techniques in terms of a feature set based on individual words, it is also feasible and often preferable to use *n*-grams or phrases detected using some of the methods described in Chapter 9. While multi-word phrases will necessarily have lower frequency than single words, the combination of words together can often be substantially more informative than individual words alone (Chuang, Manning, and Heer, 2012).

11.1 Mutual Information

As a first measure of word separation, we use a measure from information theory that assesses the *mutual information* between words and the category of a document y_i (Shannon, 1949). Mutual information is an unsigned measure of how strongly a word is related to documents in a particular category. For this discussion we will assume that our documents are sorted into a set of K discrete categories and thus, $y_i \in \{1, 2, \ldots, K\}$. The mutual information between words and a value of y_i is an information-theoretic measure that describes how much knowing a particular word resolves our uncertainty about whether a document belongs to a particular category. To motivate the use of mutual information, suppose we were given the task of guessing a randomly selected document's value of y_i. Mutual information for word j measures how much the presence or absence of word j informs our guess.

As a baseline, consider the *unconditional* uncertainty, which in information-theoretic terms is the entropy for a category. Suppose that π_k represents the proportion of documents that fall in category k and let $\pi_{-k} = 1 - \pi_k$ be the probability that a document does not belong to category k. π_k also represents the proportion of time we would be correct in guessing category k for a randomly selected document. Define the entropy for category k as

$$H(k) = -\pi_k \log_2 \pi_k - \pi_{-k} \log_2 \pi_{-k}, \tag{11.1.1}$$

which is a measure of our uncertainty about our guess. When every document is in category k, guessing category k would be right every time and the entropy would be 0. Entropy is at its maximum when $\pi_k = \pi_{-k}$, which is when we are most uncertain.

We might be able to make a better guess if we knew whether a word j was present in the document or not. Define $\pi_{k,j}$ as the proportion of documents that are both in category k and have word j, and $\pi_{k|j}$ as the proportion of documents in category k given that word j is present. We can then define conditional entropy as:

$$H(k|j) = - \sum_{k,-k} \sum_{j,-j} \pi_{k,j} \log_2 \pi_{k|j},$$

where $\sum_{k,-k}$ indicates that we sum over documents in k and not in k. The conditional entropy describes how much our uncertainty about the document's category decreases after we condition on a word. If a word is a perfect predictor of the document's category, then the uncertainty will go to zero, and if a word is orthogonal to a category, then the measure will merely return the entropy. This property motivates the Mutual Information between category k and word j,

$$\mathrm{MI}_{kj} = H(k) - H(k|j),$$

which intuitively can be read as the unconditional uncertainty minus the conditional uncertainty. When the word perfectly predicts the category, the mutual information will be at a maximum, and when a word has no predictive power, it will be zero. We can apply this procedure repeatedly across each category and each word to get a list of words with the highest mutual information for each category.

To give a sense of how this performs, we can compare to Nelson (2020). To identify distinguishing words, Nelson (2020) uses the difference in proportion. That is, for each word, she calculates the proportion that word was used in each organization. Then she orders words by the largest differences in proportions between each organization. We replicate her analysis in the left four columns of Table 11.1.[1]

As shown in the left four columns of Table 11.1, both Chicago organizations (Hull House and CWLU) use words like work, classes, school, and medical whereas for the New York organizations (Heterodoxy and Redstockings), particularly the second wave Redstockings, most distinctive words are more abstract, such as consciousness, theory, revolution, and political. To provide a different perspective on the same problem, we use mutual information. We find a similar pattern in the right four columns of Table 11.1, which perhaps even centers more clearly some of the abstract words of the First Wave New York organization (Heterodoxy) with words like suffrage and liberty coming higher on the list.

A core challenge with the mutual information metric is that it doesn't take into account uncertainty in the estimation of the probabilities. It also only considers whether a word appears or doesn't appear in a document, discarding information about words which are used repeatedly. We can address both of these concerns by moving to a fully probabilistic model.

---

[1] Our words are slightly different because we use slightly different preprocessing than Nelson (2020). However, the substantive results are unchanged.

Table 11.1. Replication of Nelson (2020) difference in proportions between feminist organizations (left) and mutual information words (right).

| Difference in Proportions (Replication) | | | | Mutual Information | | | |
| First Wave | | Second Wave | | First Wave | | Second Wave | |
Hull House	Heterodoxy	CWLU	Redstockings	Hull House	Heterodoxy	CWLU	Redstockings
hullhouse	woman	chicago	movement	hullhouse	man	womankind	feminist
club	man	children	women	miss	woman	get	male
miss	women	center	men	club	masses	chicago	movement
school	life	union	radical	given	say	union	radical
given	know	school	feminist	mr	upon	say	political
members	world	work	male	members	world	working	revolution
chicago	like	cwlu	political	mrs	matter	us	womens
year	sanger	vietnam	history	residents	sanger	can	women
mr	men	nixon	womens	evening	shall	health	liberation
classes	get	people	feminism	year	yet	office	redstockings
house	said	office	revolution	house	thing	job	even
boys	home	day	love	clubs	business	help	power
work	just	health	feminists	school	think	cwlu	female
social	say	city	left	neighborhood	tell	control	really
held	dont	working	power	held	suffrage	center	oppression
clubs	little	vietnamese	oppression	various	mind	workers	woman
mrs	way	legal	class	classes	believe	jobs	consciousness
residents	think	war	female	chicago	hand	lives	men
room	never	care	personal	years	true	page	personal
children	must	womankind	woman	music	great	medical	feminists
many	things	government	really	charge	come	day	supremacy
evening	want	workers	consciousness	large	liberty	women	oppressed
neighborhood	sex	south	consciousnessraising	summer	know	pay	must
italian	right	medical	group	hall	little	home	theory
building	one	home	theory	hundred	whole	together	real
various	masses	hospital	groups	room	dear	government	feminism
summer	make	abortion	action	boys	right	around	like
plays	thing	rape	new	italian	wife	cont	just
city	go	help	oppressed	social	margaret	call	actually
association	good	pay	supremacy	bowen	ever	just	way
						care	

11.2 Fightin' Words

Building on the multinomial model we reviewed in Chapter 6, Monroe, Colaresi, and Quinn (2008) introduce a method to identify words that systematically separate categories, called Fightin' Words. In their paper, they slowly build up their method starting with the difference in proportions method used in Nelson (2020) and show results from adding each subsequent piece of the method. The core intuition is that by creating a probabilistic model of word use, they can account for the different levels of uncertainty that arise from words having different frequencies.

The Fightin' Words method also introduces explicit *regularization* of the estimates—that is, it shrinks coefficients toward some common value. Common words will be able to move away from this common value if they are truly distinctive, but rare words used only occasionally will be shrunk to the average. As we will see, regularization is essential to identifying the words that are indicative of how a particular group uses language and will recur through later methods.

We use $y_i \in \{1, 2, \ldots, K\}$ to denote whether the document arises from one of the four feminist groups studied in Nelson (2020). For each level k we can compute the probability that a document belonging to category k uses a particular word. Define the total number of tokens that documents from category k include as $n_k = \sum_{j=1}^{J} \sum_{i=1}^{N} I(y_i = k) W_{ij}$, and call $W_{jk}^* = \sum_{i=1}^{N} I(y_i = k) W_{ij}$. We can then construct a regularized estimate of the probability a document from category k (i.e., has $y_i = k$) uses word j with

$$\widehat{\mu}_{jk} = \frac{W_{jk}^* + \alpha_j}{n_k + \sum_{j=1}^{J} \alpha_j}, \tag{11.2.1}$$

where α_j represents a small value used to *smooth* the estimates. As in Chapter 6, we can motivate this estimate of the proportion using a Bayesian multinomial model with a Dirichlet prior. If we suppose that $\boldsymbol{\mu} \sim \text{Dirichlet}(\boldsymbol{\alpha})$ and that $W_k^*, \sim \text{Multinomial}(n_k, \boldsymbol{\mu}_k)$, the estimate corresponds to the expected value of the posterior distribution $p(\boldsymbol{\mu} | W)$ after observing the words.

With a probability model in hand, Monroe, Colaresi, and Quinn (2008) are now able to estimate relative measures of word use by groups while including uncertainty. They opt for a standardized log odds ratio. Specifically, they first calculate the log odds a particular word is used and compare usage in group k to other groups,

$$\text{log odds ratio}_{kj} = \log \underbrace{\left(\frac{\mu_{kj}}{1 - \mu_{kj}} \right)}_{\text{odds in group } k} - \log \underbrace{\left(\frac{\mu_{-kj}}{1 - \mu_{-kj}} \right)}_{\text{odds in other groups}}.$$

To standardize the ratio, they suggest using an approximation of the variance of the odds ratio, $\text{Var}(\text{log odds ratio}_{kj}) \approx \frac{1}{W_{kj}^* + \alpha_j} + \frac{1}{W_{-kj}^* + \alpha_j}$. Using this variance, they calculate the standardized log odds ratio, which is their suggested measure of word separation.

$$\text{Std. Log Odds}_j = \frac{\text{log odds ratio}_{kj}}{\sqrt{\text{Var}(\text{log odds ratio}_{kj})}} \tag{11.2.2}$$

Table 11.2. Example from Nelson (2020) using the Fightin' Words algorithm of Monroe, Colaresi, and Quinn (2008).

First Wave		Second Wave	
Hull House	Heterodoxy	CWLU	Redstockings
club	man	center	radical
miss	can	children	feminist
school	us	union	male
year	know	school	political
given	world	vietnam	men
mr	said	nixon	history
members	like	office	feminism
classes	sanger	cwlu	women
chicago	just	health	revolution
house	get	city	oppression
boys	women	vietnamese	love
social	think	legal	left
work	dont	south	consciousness
years	say	day	female
held	way	rape	feminists
mrs	must	womankind	personal
room	things	hospital	theory
clubs	sex	childcare	l
children	never	medical	class
many	right	car	oppressed
evening	life	north	consciousnessraising
two	want	care	liberal
summer	home	maternity	analysis
residents	thing	welfare	supremacy
city	go	war	power
association	masses	government	really
various	birth	gonorrhea	womens
number	control	pm	action
committee	wife	pay	groups

This formulation both explicitly regularizes the probability of using a particular word and standardizes it to address uncertainty in estimation. The results in the Nelson (2020) data are shown in Table 11.2.

Yet, there are some challenges remaining. For example, the Monroe, Colaresi, and Quinn (2008) model is difficult to apply with a continuous category, such as ideology of a speaker, rather than with the discrete categories we have considered so far. To address this we will turn to a more general formulation of this process: the *fictitious prediction problem*.

11.3 Fictitious Prediction Problems

To identify the discriminating words, many methods set up a *fictitious prediction problem*. A word's distinctiveness is measured in the context of a prediction problem that is never of direct interest. For example, Gentzkow, Shapiro, and Taddy (2019) identify the words that best predict whether a member of Congress is a Republican or a Democrat. Obviously, predicting a member of Congress' political party is never of interest—members of Congress publicly self-identify with a party. And while they might change sides or identify with another party, we never need to make a prediction about any serious candidate's or legislator's party affiliation.

Rather than building the model to perform some future prediction or classification, the fictitious prediction problem is used for analytic convenience. Entertaining the fiction that there is a prediction problem is useful, because it enables researchers to repurpose prediction methods that can more easily handle cases like continuous underlying organizations (as in the case of ideology) or other more complex settings. The premise is that a word that is useful at predicting the outcome will also be discriminating in a sense useful for discovery.

Recognizing that prediction is only fiction is important, because it shows that demonstrating that a model performs well at prediction is insufficient to show that the words provide an accurate distillation of the rhetoric of a particular group. In the next part we will show that procedures to measure predictive accuracy, like cross-validation, are essential for assessing the performance of classification methods, because they provide an estimate of how the method performs on the central task. But cross-validation is less useful here, because we might prefer models that are less predictive but do a "better" job of identifying words that are indicative of particular categories. Rather, the validations we use will necessarily be less direct and require subject matter expertise to assess the extent to which the measures of words help us to understand the key distinguishing features.

Fictitious prediction problems also highlight a potential risk when identifying discriminating words. We set up the problem to identify words that are associated with a particular category, but there might be other characteristics of the document correlated with the category. For example, Taddy (2013) analyzes Congressional speech to find words associated with Democrats and Republicans. But many Republicans represent states where there are large allocations of space to public lands and, therefore, models tend to identify words associated with national parks as Republican words, even though discussions about these issues are not particularly partisan. This connects back to our more general point about the role of theory in analysis—we need a rigorous conception of what partisanship is in order to contextualize what we find.

The conflation of public land discussion and partisanship highlights the core tension we raised earlier. Words that distinguish categories might be distinct from the words that are indicative of a category. That is, words that are particularly partisan—indicative of how Republicans and Democrats talk when they convey their party's stance—might not overlap completely with the set of words that distinguish Republican and Democratic rhetoric. Taddy (2013) recommends including covariates, but raises the question of which covariates to include and why.

The framing of the fictitious prediction problem also provides some context for understanding the need for regularization when finding discriminating words in terms of overfitting the prediction problem. The extreme case of overfitting occurs because in any dataset any word that is spoken only once will perfectly classify the speaker as either a Republican or Democrat. Note that this is true regardless of the partisan content of the word—this will happen merely because the word is rare. And this problem persists even if we eliminate words that are spoken only once. Whenever there are rarely used words, there is the possibility those words are used by just one group, solely by chance. If this happens, then we are no longer identifying words that are used systematically more often by one group, but rather whatever words just happen to align with a particular set of categories.

As a simple first example of the prediction problem approach, we describe a simple procedure based on test statistics that are commonly used in the field of Statistics. We then move to a more complex probabilistic model built for this purpose—Multinomial Inverse Regression (MNIR) (Taddy, 2013).

11.3.1   STANDARDIZED TEST STATISTICS AS MEASURES OF SEPARATION

Again we will start with some attribute y_i—the feminist organization in our running example. However, we will now allow that y_i to be any type of variable including continuous measures (like income or ideology) or categorical measures (such as partisan affiliation or feminist organization). We compute an ordinary least squares regression, predicting the outcome (in the case of a categorical variable you can imagine using a dichotomous variable for whether the document is in category k),

$$y_i = \mu_0 + \mu_{1j} W_{ij} + \epsilon_i.$$

Using the output from the regression, we compute the test statistic that corresponds to the null hypothesis that $\mu_{1j} = 0$ and then use this test statistic as our measure of separation:

$$\text{Standard}_j = \frac{\widehat{\mu_{1j}}}{\widehat{\text{SE}(\mu_{1j})}},$$

where SE indicates the standard error. This measure prioritizes words that discriminate between the categories better, where the discrimination is scaled by the estimated standard error of the coefficient. The more positive the test statistic, the more discriminating a coefficient is, scaled by its variance. Cast in terms of the test statistic, under the null of a coefficient of 0, a larger test statistic corresponds to a lower p-value.

Using this approach in Table 11.3, we again find a similar pattern with more specific and concrete words associated with the Chicago organizations and the more abstract and general words associated with the New York organizations. The words give us an even clearer picture, with words associated with actual events such as attendance, music, and entertainment being used disproportionately in the Chicago organizations, and words like analyzing, thinking, and evaluating being disproportionately used in the New York organizations.

11.3.2 χ^2 TEST STATISTICS

Gentzkow and Shapiro (2010) suggest a related procedure in their study of words that political parties in Congress use disproportionately. To construct this measure they use a χ^2 statistic from a χ^2 test of equal distribution across categories in a table. We will focus on the two-category case, but the idea generalizes naturally to the multi-category

Table 11.3. Discriminating words from Nelson (2020) based on standardized linear regression test statistics.

First Wave		Second Wave	
Hull House	Heterodoxy	CWLU	Redstockings
hullhouse	woman	womankind	analyzing
miss	can	chicago	antiwomanism
given	like	union	belief
club	way	office	classic
members	know	cont	cross
chicago	right	th	daring
school	think	day	evaluating
various	man	health	examining
neighborhood	thing	school	expressing
residents	said	belmont	false
year	never	s	fear
held	believe	home	finding
evening	us	help	glorification
house	yet	city	going
clubs	go	children	history
music	just	month	ongoing
number	world	pm	personal
childrens	say	nixon	reasons
attended	things	working	recognizing
bowen	anything	page	relating
director	kind	t	romantic
room	get	cwlu	selfblame
classes	women	illinois	speaking
membership	means	center	starting
evenings	tell	three	stop
several	see	two	taking
entertainment	must	weeks	thinking
january	rather	care	able
attendance	now	e	abused
meetings	life	year	adequate

setting. To construct the statistic, call $W_{j1}^* = \sum_{i=1}^N W_{ij}^* I(y_i = 1)$, or the total number of times observations in group 1 uttered word j, and $W_{-j1} = \sum_{m \neq j}^J \sum_{i=1}^N W_{im} I(y_i = 1)$, or the total number of words not j uttered by individuals in group 1. We can then define W_{j0}^* and W_{-j0}^* analogously. The χ_j^2 statistic is then defined as

$$\chi_j^2 = \frac{W_{j1}^* W_{-j1}^* - W_{j0}^* W_{-j0}^*}{(W_{j1}^* + W_{j0}^*)(W_{j0}^* + W_{-j0}^*)(W_{j1}^* + W_{-j1}^*)(W_{-j1}^* + W_{-j0}^*)}.$$

Table 11.4. Discriminating words from Nelson (2020) based on Multinomial Inverse Regression (Taddy, 2013).

First Wave		Second Wave	
Hull House	Heterodoxy	CWLU	Redstockings
hullhouse	sangers	belmont	redstockings
entertainments	adrian	cont	radicalism
addams	tad	morse	analyze
gymnasium	mike	graphics	supremacist
entertained	hewitt	counselling	iust
hull	harwood	daley	hanisch
auspices	grefesaunders	lutheran	reformist
ewing	staley	thei	wlm
riddle	bullet	joins	oppressors
polk	dora	vietnams	sarachild
concerts	mickey	janitresses	authentic
dante	sweetheart	saigon	oppressing
stereopticon	mirah	restructuring	beauvoir
gratifying	teh	midwest	assumptions
recreative	commonwealth	latins	clarity
orchestra	sanger	thieu	manipulation
howe	suffragette	bacteria	writings
britton	abstract	augustana	liberalism
hamilton	instinct	retraining	wilh
generously	physiology	auto	friedan
decorated	comrade	l0	opportunists
recreation	forbidden	laos	bul
benedict	bourgeoisie	haiphong	scef
nancrede	suffragists	janitors	gage
pelham	prevention	urine	sncc
signor	correspondence	payments	retreat
programme	sentenced	negotiate	nonviolent
syrian	cheapest	thi	koedt
loaned	comstock	locations	matriarchy
countrymen	graft	complications	allfemale

Using this measure, we are able to identify words that are disproportionately used by individuals in group 1 or 2, consistent with a lower p-value under a null hypothesis of equal use across the categories.

With either standardized regression coefficients or χ^2 statistics, we might be concerned that the method could confuse a rarely used word that happens to separate groups with a more regularly used word that captures a systematic difference in language usage across the categories. We could address this issue manually, removing words that are used that fall below a threshold of use. However, this threshold can be difficult to determine.

Rather than manually remove words, we will turn again to models that explicitly regularize the parameter estimates. As we will see, the amount of shrinkage will depend on the information available in the data to form the estimate. Rare words that just happen to coincide with a particular category will be smoothed toward the common value. But words that are used regularly and distinguish the categories will only have a small amount of shrinkage.

11.3.3 MULTINOMIAL INVERSE REGRESSION

In Section 11.3.1 we regressed the label, y_i, on the words W. Of course, regressing on all J features simultaneously is problematic. One problem is that if $J > N$ then the regression coefficients are not identified. And even if we are able to compute the regression coefficients, including all J features may lead to noisy estimates that produce unhelpful comparisons across categories. In Section 11.3.1 we avoided this by including each word one at a time in the regression.

Taddy (2013) introduces Multinomial Inverse Regression (MNIR) to perform a similar regularization task as Fightin' Words, while ensuring that we are able to include continuous Y_i. As the name suggests, MNIR inverts the regression problem: rather than regressing y_i on the features, it regresses the features on y_i. Using this framework, Taddy (2013) introduces a multinomial regression model. That is,

$$W_{i,} \sim \text{Multinomial}(n_i, \theta_i)$$

$$\theta_{ij} = \frac{\exp(\mu_{0j} + \mu_{1j}y_i)}{\sum_{l=1}^{J} \exp(\mu_{0l} + \mu_{1l}y_i)}. \tag{11.3.1}$$

To address the problem of rare words creating chance differences in word usage, Taddy (2013) uses a Gamma-Laplace prior—which provides regularization related to the regularization in Lasso regression (Hastie, Tibshirani, and Friedman, 2013). Using the MNIR, we can use the estimated coefficients as measures of how well particular words separate the categories.

Examining the words produced in Table 11.4 for our running example, we can see a dramatic difference in the kinds of words produced. These words are substantially rarer than those from the previous methods, but still correspond to robust distinctions in language use between the groups. These words still reflect Nelson's (2020) underlying theory of group differences; they simply provide an alternative view of those differences. Most notably the more abstract concerns of the New York first wave feminists (Heterodoxy) are substantially clearer in this list than in prior lists.

11.4 Conclusion

Examining discriminating words across groups of documents can be a powerful way to discover insights in collections of documents. By drawing attention to contrasts between different segments of the corpus, word lists of this sort provide a sense of language representative of different communities. This can be used to spark interesting ideas, which can then be confirmed by deeper engagement with the texts.

We also highlighted the core tension in discriminating words between prevalence and distinctiveness. There is no optimal trade-off between prevalence and distinctiveness when trying to determine which words best represent a particular corpus. One implication is that there is no single best method and we have provided here a mix of approaches that yielded different views of the Nelson (2020) corpus.

The approaches here are only a small sample of the many techniques that exist (some of which we will discuss in later chapters as well). Part of the strength of the fictitious prediction problem framework is that essentially *any* supervised learning method can be used to generate labels. There are numerous techniques that allow for simple summaries to be extracted from even complex predictive models that could serve as the basis of a discriminating word list (Ribeiro, Singh, and Guestrin, 2016).

In the next three chapters we describe techniques for discovering new organizations of text based on clustering, mixed-membership topic models and document embeddings. The techniques covered in this chapter can be invaluable tools for helping make sense of the patterns that these other algorithms discover, and we will return to them for help with the process of labeling and interpretation.

CHAPTER 12

Clustering

The process of discovery is a process of engaging with the data, conceptualizing, and then re-engaging in iteration. Qualitative researchers have proposed numerous frameworks for this process, including open coding, where properties of the text are assigned annotations that organize or otherwise describe the text (Corbin and Strauss, 1990). By reading closely and accounting for different dimensions of similarities between observations, the researcher can build concepts and categories from the ground up. Our goal in computational-assisted discovery is to amplify the reader's ability to engage with the text by suggesting feasible groupings, directing reading to documents representing different ideas, and guiding the analyst's interpretive work.

In the previous chapter, we discussed how to characterize an existing grouping of texts. In this chapter we will consider how to produce partitions of documents—mutually exclusive and exhaustive categorizations—using unsupervised clustering analysis. Many of the ideas here about how to approach model selection and how to interpret clusters will carry over to our discussion of topic models and document embeddings.

Clustering algorithms for text data take as an input a collection of texts and output a set of K categories and document assignments to each of those K categories, creating a partition of the data. This facilitates discovery because the way that the documents are organized is estimated as part of the process, rather than being assumed. For each document we will estimate its cluster assignment π_i is a one-hot encoding where $\pi_{ik} = 1$ if the document belongs to cluster k, and 0 otherwise. π_i is chosen so that similar documents are in the same cluster or category and dissimilar documents are assigned to different clusters. This basic task may seem straightforward, but there is inherent ambiguity in several key steps, leading to a proliferation of methods for partitioning data—notably the way that similarity is measured, the way those similarities are aggregated to assess the overall quality of the solution, and the approach to solving the implied optimization problem.

The automated part of the clustering involves the creation of the categories, but the researcher is still heavily involved in choosing the inputs and clustering procedure and then through interpreting the results after the fact. A small class of clustering methods involves the researcher interacting during the clustering process, exploring many different organizations of the text, with a final partition emerging only after exploring and considering many potential partitions (Grimmer and King, 2011).

To focus our intuition and to provide a reference for our general discussion of clustering algorithms, we begin with the canonical k-means clustering algorithm in Section 12.1. We then step back to break down the various components of the clustering process, including the representations we choose for the text (12.2), the different approaches available to do clustering (12.3), the way to make choices about the model (12.4), and approaches to interpretation and interaction (12.5).

12.1 An Initial Example Using k-Means Clustering

Scholars of Congress have long been interested in how members of Congress portray themselves. Famously, Mayhew (1974) categorized Congress members' communications into three conceptual types: credit claiming, position taking, and advertising. As a running example, we will conceptually replicate an exercise in Grimmer and King (2011), using 558 press releases issued between 2005 and 2007 by US Senator Frank Lautenberg's office. Lautenberg was a US senator from New Jersey who served for a total of 28 years during the period from 1982 until his death in 2013. Our goal is to discover different and new ways of conceptualizing how members of Congress describe their activities to their constituents.

We will start by walking through one of the most widely used clustering algorithms, k-means.[1] Before beginning the clustering process, we need to choose a representation for our documents. Using the bag of words recipe described in Chapter 5, suppose that we have represented our $N = 558$ documents so that each text is a $J \times 1$ count vector that indicates the number of times each feature appears in the document. Because there are substantial differences in document lengths, we first divide each count vector by the total number of tokens in the document, such that W_i, now represents the proportion of each token type in the document. We end up with 7,118 unigrams total.

Our goal is to partition our documents into a set of K categories, where documents with similar rates of word usage are assigned to the same cluster and dissimilar documents are assigned to different categories. We will suppose that each of the K categories has a $J \times 1$ mean vector $\mu_k = (\mu_{1k}, \mu_{2k}, \ldots, \mu_{Jk})$ that characterizes the center of all the documents in the kth cluster. In this case, because we are using normalized word counts, this will describe the average rate that documents that belong to the kth cluster use the jth feature. Our goal, restated, will be to find a set of cluster centers μ and a partition of our documents π so that documents are close to their assigned cluster centers.

To get to k-means, we need to make this intuition precise. We suppose that we will measure the dissimilarity between a document and the cluster center as the squared Euclidean distance:

---

[1] The k-means formulation that people recognize today was circulated in a draft to scholars at Bell Labs on July 31, 1957 by Stuart Lloyd as a method for pulse-code modulation (a method for converting analog signals into digital ones as in audio). This manuscript was later published in the *IEEE Transactions on Information Theory* as Lloyd (1982). In the same period, Forgy (1965) proposed essentially the same method. MacQueen (1967) introduced the term k-means, provided an analysis of the convergence properties, and cited out a complex web of related work in different fields including notes added in proofs about independently discovered insights. One of those mentions is a paper by Geoffrey Ball, which aimed to provide an introduction to "cluster-seeking techniques" for use in the social sciences that were amenable to new "computer-oriented" ways of doing computation (Ball, 1965). Hartigan and Wong (1979) provided what is probably the most popular algorithm, which the programming language R uses as a default.

$$d(W_{i,}, \mu_k) = \sum_{j=1}^{J} (W_{ij} - \mu_{jk})^2. \qquad (12.1.1)$$

Using this measure of dissimilarity, we can assess the quality of any partition π and any set of cluster centers μ. The k-means algorithm makes *hard* assignments, so that each document is assigned to only one category (and thus only one element of the vector π_i equals 1 and the rest are 0). We can write the objective function—the function that reflects the quality of each solution and that our optimization algorithm will minimize—as:

$$f(\pi, \mu, W) = \sum_{i=1}^{N} \sum_{k=1}^{K} \sum_{j=1}^{J} \underbrace{\left(W_{ij} - \mu_{jk}\right)^2}_{\text{dissimilarity measure}} \overbrace{\pi_{ik}}^{\text{Cluster indicator}}. \qquad (12.1.2)$$

In words, the objective function measures the dissimilarity of documents from their assigned cluster centers, using the definition of dissimilarity from Equation 12.1.1.

Given this definition of the objective function, we try to find the partition (or set of partitions) and corresponding set of cluster centers that provide the best answer in terms of minimizing the squared Euclidean distance (i.e., sum of squared errors) between the cluster center and the documents assigned to that cluster. Unfortunately, optimizing Equation 12.1.2 with respect to the cluster assignments and cluster centers is difficult. Because cluster assignments are discrete, the kinds of optimization methods used for common social science tools like generalized linear models are not available. Instead, the k-means algorithm relies upon an iterative algorithm to optimize Equation 12.1.2.

We begin with a random initialization of the cluster centers. We will call this collection of parameters μ^0. Given this initial set of cluster centers, we assign each document to the center it is the closest to (in terms of squared Euclidean distance). We call this set of cluster assignments π^1. Then, given those new cluster assignments, we update the cluster centers. The update for the kth center, μ_k^1 is:

$$\mu_k^1 = \frac{\sum_{i=1}^{N} \pi_{ik}^1 W_{i,}}{\sum_{i=1}^{N} \pi_{ik}^1} \qquad (12.1.3)$$

which is simply the average along each dimension of the documents assigned to the kth cluster center. Based on the new location of the cluster centers (μ^1), the closest center may have changed for a number of documents and so we reassign to get π^2. We continue updating these two sets of parameters until the change in the objective function, Equation 12.1.2, drops below a small threshold. The algorithm then returns estimates of the optimal cluster centers and partition μ^*, π^*. Figure 12.1 provides pseudo-code for the algorithm.

There is no guarantee that the algorithm we just described will provide the solution that globally minimizes the objective function. Rather, it will produce an approximation of the globally optimal (in the sense of minimizing the sum of squared Euclidean distances) partition. This has important implications for our analysis: the iterative algorithm we just described will often get stuck in local optima (a point the algorithm will converge to that does not minimize the objective function globally), causing instability

Input: W (documents), K (number of desired clusters)

- Initialize a set of K cluster centers, μ^0
- While the change in the objective function (the sum of squared errors) remains above the threshold,
  - Set $\pi_{ik}^t = 1$ if document i is closest to center k in terms of squared Euclidean distance, set to 0 otherwise
  - Set $\mu_k^t = \frac{\sum_{i=1}^N \pi_{ik}^t W_{i,}}{\sum_{i=1}^N \pi_{ik}^t}$
- Return μ^* and π^*.

Figure 12.1. Pseudocode for the k-means Algorithm

Table 12.1. Applying k-means to the Press Releases

	Proportion	Words
1	0.17	s, presid, bush, administr, u, elect, compani, opec, tax, mr
2	0.16	senat, lautenberg, frank, r, statement, press, washington, comment, d, question
3	0.28	new, jersey, menendez, secur, million, fund, grant, chemic, nj, feder
4	0.39	sen, epa, bill, act, legisl, safeti, famili, protect, requir, victim

in the solutions across repeated runs of the algorithm (Roberts, Stewart, and Tingley, 2016). There are numerous approaches to initialization that result in less instability and better solutions—as measured by the objective function (Pena, Lozano, and Larranaga, 1999; Arthur and Vassilvitskii, 2007; Celebi, Kingravi, and Vela, 2013).

However, even if the solution that we are given is not the global minimum, it can still be useful for discovering new organizations. Remember that there is no one *correct* organization of the texts, and therefore the objective function is just a useful tool for grouping similar documents together—an organization that is only locally optimal for a given objective function may well be the most substantively interesting and insightful. Therefore, even the approximation can give us interesting organizations of texts that may lead to useful conceptualizations for our research.

Now, with a solution in hand, we can look at the results. In Table 12.1 we provide a brief summary of the clusters from applying the k-means algorithm setting $K = 4$. We discuss procedures for labeling clusters below, but for now for each cluster, we take the difference between the mean vector μ for that cluster and the average of the mean vectors of the other clusters. We label the clusters with the 10 words with the largest positive difference—words that are overrepresented by the μ_k for cluster k relative to μ_{-k}. We discover almost immediately that even after a first cut the clusters are loosely similar to the framework for understanding Congressional representation described in Mayhew (1974). Documents in cluster 4 tend to discuss the position of the lawmaker, such as that titled "Lautenberg Specter Introduce Bill To Give Justice To Victims of State Sponsored Terrorism—Measure Would Empower Victims To Pursue Assets of Countries Like Iran That Sponsor Terror"; documents in cluster 3 are mainly credit-claiming documents about funds the senator has secured for New Jersey, such as "Lautenberg and Corzine Secure Over 12 Million for New Jersey Agriculture Programs"; and documents in cluster 2 seem to relate to advertising legislative successes, such as "Homeland Security Chief Follows Lautenberg's Lead, Announces Risk Will Trump Politics for DHS Grants, Change Will Make America Safer Lautenberg Says."

The words in cluster 1 don't neatly fit into this categorization, with documents, such as "Lautenberg Reacts to Republican Incompetence After Republicans and President Bush Posted Nuclear Weapons Information Online," that largely make negative comments about the Republican party and the Bush administration in particular. Grimmer and King (2011) found a similar category and proposed it as a new category of Congressional speech, "partisan taunting." They defined the speech act as an explicit, public, and negative attack on another political party or its members. Having discovered the category, they show that category is widespread by developing a classifier to identify partisan taunting (using tools we show in the Measurement part) and applying it to 64,033 press releases from 301 senator-years. They find a full 27% of the press releases in this out-of-sample dataset are classified as partisan taunting.

Having given a brief overview of how k-means can lead to a discovery in practice, we now step back to explore each part of the clustering process, including the many different approaches we might have chosen instead of k-means.

12.2 Representations for Clustering

This chapter is about clustering, but it is worth emphasizing that *what* you are clustering is often a great deal more important than how the clustering is done. This means that the processes of document selection and representation that we described in Part 2 are particularly important here. For example, instead of using word counts we could have represented documents using word embeddings as described in Chapter 8, or we could add in grammatical or named-entity tags as described in Chapter 9.

To provide an example, we used pretrained GloVe word embeddings to represent the words within the Lautenberg press releases.[2] We represented each document as the average of the embeddings of the words contained in it. We then used this representation of the documents as an input into the k-means algorithm, with $K=6$. Table 12.2 show the top words for each cluster.[3] We see very similar clusters appear: transportation and security (cluster 1), statements about awards and honors (cluster 2), taunting of President Bush and Republicans (cluster 3), credit claiming for grants in New Jersey (cluster 4), legislation related to healthcare (cluster 5), and legislation related to the environment (cluster 6).

12.3 Approaches to Clustering

The two clusterings we just described are only two of countless ways that the same documents could be organized. While k-means is a straightforward and intuitive solution to the unsupervised clustering problem, the inherent ambiguity involved in forming a "good" partition has given rise to a massive literature on clustering methods, with substantial differences in how the individual methods are justified, what assumptions the models and algorithms make about the underlying structure of the

---

[2] We obtained word embeddings from https://nlp.stanford.edu/projects/glove/
[3] Here we use a test statistic approach described in Chapter 11 to identify top words.

Table 12.2. *k*-means clusters using word embeddings representation.

Cluster	Words
1	passenger, amtrak, rail, security, gas, lott, stronger, preempt, approved, billion
2	court, she, demint, burr, mi, nc, nomination, r, was, medal
3	iraq, dc, american, president, united, taxpayer, issued, following, statement, senator
4	funds, for, announce, county, million, will, river, grants, project, hudson
5	income, care, drug, children, health, coverage, programs, beneficiaries, medicare, deductibles
6	epa, pollution, residents, dangerous, near, environmental, data, safety, agency, chemicals

data, and how well the methods scale to larger datasets. There are generally two flavors of clustering methods: statistical mixture models, which specify a data generating process using the language of distributions, and algorithmic clustering methods, which specify a series of steps for generating a solution.

Before diving into different choices, we describe the components of every clustering method followed by an overview of some of the main stylistic differences that occur across models. We then discuss probabilistic models that build on and extend the multinomial representation introduced in Chapter 6, algorithmic methods, and the connections between these approaches.

12.3.1 COMPONENTS OF A CLUSTERING METHOD

Regardless of the foundations of the clustering method or the language used to describe it, there are three components of all clustering approaches that are either specified explicitly or fixed implicitly: 1) a notion of document (dis)similarity, 2) an objective function to measure the quality of a proposed partition, and 3) a method for optimizing over the set of partitions. We describe each component, relating back to *k*-means, and then explain how they matter for the partitions that are obtained.

Component 1: Document (Dis)similarity

The first component is a measure of document similarity/distance between two documents. This measure makes precise what it means for two documents to be similar. In the *k*-means algorithm, dissimilarity is measured using the squared Euclidean distance. Other methods can make use of a much broader set of distance measures, like those that we discussed in Chapter 7. For example, we might use a measure of cosine similarity between documents, calculate the Manhattan distance between documents, or use a kernel to measure the similarity of a pair of documents. These are just different ways of precisely defining what it means for two documents to be "similar" to each other.

All clustering methods invoke a notion of document dissimilarity even if they only do so implicitly. Statistical mixture models specify probability distributions to describe the generative process for documents, and the different probabilities of seeing each document under these distributions imply a measure of document dissimilarity. *k*-Means uses squared-Euclidean distance, but we can also express that through a probabilistic model by using a mixture of Normal distributions (Fraley and Raftery, 2002). As we will discuss below, cosine similarity also has a corresponding probabilistic interpretation through a distribution called the von Mises-Fisher distribution (Banerjee, Merugu, Dhillon, and Ghosh, 2005). More generally, there is a one-to-one mapping between a broad class of probability distributions and dissimilarity measures (Banerjee, Merugu, Dhillon, and Ghosh, 2005).[4]

Choosing the similarity measure is one of the most challenging tasks in text analysis. Intuitively, it seems easy to envision what it means for documents to be more or less similar. But implementing this intuitive notion of similarity into an explicit measure is challenging. After all, humans are accustomed to reasoning about language through a complete text, but we are providing computers with a very different—and more limited—representation of the document. Because unsupervised methods are often fast and easy to run, rather than carefully considering the measure beforehand, it will often be easiest to run several methods and compare the output after the fact to determine which was the most useful.

Running several models and choosing the best subjectively might raise alarm bells for researchers used to traditional approaches to statistical testing. Yet, discovering conceptualizations is a completely different task where such an approach is not inherently problematic. As we noted in the Chapter 10, it does not matter *how* you arrive at a conceptualization since there is no universally "true" conceptualization. Our goal in discovery is to find some useful representation of the observations. As long as new data are used to assess the ultimate quantity of interest and make inference, there is no concern about researchers "fishing" for new conceptualizations.

Component 2: Measure of Partition Quality

Given a notion of document (dis)similarity we can measure the quality of a partition, as measured by the similarity measure. As we described above with k-means, intuitively we know that a good partition of our documents will tend to group together documents that are similar and separate documents that are different. Making this intuition concrete, however, requires assumptions about which features of a partition we will measure and which features of a partition are less important. For example, with k-means we measure partition quality by summing up each document's dissimilarity from its cluster center. This achieves part of our intuitive objective—grouping together similar documents. But it does not include information about the distinctiveness of different clusters, which we might want to explicitly take into account in the objective function.

Objective functions provide us with a clear standard for measuring the quality of partitions, but they do not provide us with an absolute measure of cluster quality that we can use to make comparisons across different methods. Further, we can never suppose that a clustering is optimal because it comes from a particular method. Without clear knowledge about what is in the dataset or about the general goals of an analysis, it is *impossible* to distinguish between two partitions. This is because the objective functions are on different scales, are often based on different notions of document similarity, and might be useful for researchers engaged in different kinds of projects. What objective functions do provide are relative measures of cluster quality, which are good

---

[4]Formally, Banerjee, Merugu, Dhillon, and Ghosh (2005) establish a bijection between the regular exponential family and regular Bregman divergences, which unifies a broad class of methods.

for selecting the "best" partition given a specific notion of best—whether that is set explicitly or implicitly through a probability model. Adjudicating between the different objective functions will be an essential clustering task.

Component 3: Optimization Algorithm

The final feature of a clustering method is an algorithm to optimize the objective function—that is, to actually find the solution given a set of data. Optimization algorithms are necessary because finding the best partition according to an objective function is almost never straightforward. One reason optimization is difficult is that finding the best partition requires searching over discrete partitions, where the usual helpful rules from calculus are not applicable. The second reason is that the number of ways to partition even small sets of objects is massive. As we explained in Chapter 2, the number of ways to partition 100 documents is greater than 4.75×10^{115}. This means that it is impossible to brute force search over all potential solutions to choose the best one.

Finding the partition that is the global maximum, then, would require such a monumental effort that it would render the methods useless. Methods generally use approximate optimization approaches. While this means we often give up on the guarantee of a best solution, it does mean that clustering methods can be run in real-world settings. There are a wide variety of approximation methods that include the iterative relocation scheme used for k-means. A vast literature introduces new methods for optimization, and throughout the book we will introduce the algorithms as they are necessary to present the material we introduce. Unfortunately, the particular optimization can matter quite a lot in practice even when used on the same dissimilarity measure and with the same measure of partition quality.

The use of approximation algorithms often comes at more cost than just giving up on the globally optimal solution. Approximation algorithms will often result in unstable solutions, which means that running the same algorithm twice will sometimes result in different solutions. We can stabilize the approximations with careful starting values. But, as we discuss below, this instability is less problematic when we're using clustering methods for discovery because we are looking for interesting new ways of organizing our data. Even if a partition is only locally optimal, it can still be useful for conceptualization.

In Table 12.3, we cluster the same press releases using the same method as in Table 12.1, but beginning at different starting values. While overall, the clusters look similar, you will notice that there are some differences. In particular, in Table 12.3 we see two familiar clusters—the credit claiming cluster is now cluster 1, and cluster 2 is some combination of the taunting and advertising clusters; perhaps we could interpret it as a "statement" cluster. Clusters 3 and 4 are new, however. Cluster 3 is mostly related to legislation generally, and cluster 4 is primarily focused on chemical and transportation security, reflecting Senator Lautenberg's work on container security.

12.3.2 STYLES OF CLUSTERING METHODS

While every clustering method has some version of the three components listed above, there are also a number of other stylistic features that substantially change how clustering methods behave and the kinds of information they return. The variety of methods is astounding. In general, any attempt by us to pretend we could characterize all of this variation would be a fool's errand—the breadth of the field means we will necessarily miss important distinctions and the rate of new method production means we

Table 12.3. Applying *k*-means to the press releases, with different starting values than Table 12.1.

	Proportion	Words
1	0.28	new, jersey, menendez, fund, project, feder, million, program, counti, nj
2	0.21	senat, lautenberg, frank, r, statement, s, presid, comment, press, follow
3	0.42	american, famili, victim, legisl, epa, act, libya, terror, sponsor, report
4	0.08	secur, chemic, homeland, port, law, risk, protect, administr, dhs, bill

could never be comprehensive. More importantly, the arguments in favor of a particular class of clustering method are often overstated, particularly when we use clustering methods to engage in discovery. Rather than list all the methods, then, instead we focus on the most prominent types of clustering methods and then provide a few examples.

Probabilistic vs. Algorithmic

As with many of the methods discussed in this book, the most salient division is between probabilistic and algorithmic approaches. Probabilistic clustering methods specify a data generating process and then use the data to reverse this process and learn the hidden parameters. Algorithmic models are often motivated by an appeal to intuition about what constitutes a useful clustering and then derive theorems based on metaphors about the clustering procedure. Each of the approaches to clustering implies objective functions on what constitutes a good clustering and procedures to optimize the objective function. We discuss this distinction more below, but in short there is a great deal to learn from both types of models.

Soft vs. Hard

A separate dimension along with clustering algorithms differs in whether it provides a soft or hard partition of the data. A hard partition of the data assigns each document to one and only one cluster. A soft clustering (sometimes called fuzzy clustering) method expresses uncertainty by assigning a document to a particular cluster with some probability. Algorithmic approaches in general tend to use hard clustering while model-based approaches tend to use soft clustering. In general, the difference is less significant than it might seem on its face. Soft clustering methods nudge every document toward one cluster, so even the fuzzy methods tend to place most of the probability on a single cluster for most documents.

Means vs. Mediods

The way the center of a cluster is defined constitutes yet another difference across clustering methods. In some methods, like *k*-means and mixture models, the cluster center is an average of the documents assigned to the cluster. For example, in *k*-means we saw that the center of the documents are the averages of documents assigned to the cluster. In contrast, in mediod methods the center of the cluster is constrained to lie exactly on top of a document assigned to the cluster (much like a median is constrained to be a number in the set, barring ties). For example, *k*-mediods has an estimation procedure similar to *k*-means, but in the step where the cluster center is relocated, it is set as the document that minimizes the distance to other documents assigned to the cluster.

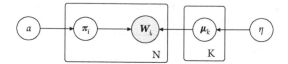

Figure 12.2. The structure of a typical probabilistic mixture model. π is the vector which denotes cluster membership and *w* is drawn for each document for some distribution parameterized by a set of parameters μ that are cluster-specific. α and η act as regularizing priors on the membership and cluster parameters respectively.

Flat vs. Hierarchical

Clustering methods also differ in whether they are flat or hierarchical. Flat clustering methods are the methods that we have considered so far—they produce a single clustering of the data. Hierarchical clustering methods provide a nesting of observations. At the top of the hierarchy all the methods are grouped together, at the bottom the observations are in their own clusters. In between, hierarchical methods nest observations to create increasingly coarse clusters as we move up the tree.

12.3.3 PROBABILISTIC CLUSTERING MODELS

Now having characterized some of the properties of clustering methods, we briefly review a few specific instances. The usual approach in probabilistic clustering methods is to use a mixture model that supposes that each data point arises from a set of unknown probability distributions. This is similar to how in Chapter 6 we viewed the disputed Federalist paper as arising from one of three possible multinomial distributions (one for each author). The key difference is that in the authorship problem, we had some documents attributed to each author and so we could learn each multinomial distribution from a particular author—the clustering problem has no such labels. Instead we will infer the labels for all documents, iteratively refining the assignments of documents to clusters and the features of the distributions, much as we did with k-means.

Mixture models typically have a common form that reflects the data generating process in Figure 12.2 and follows the following data generating process.

- for each cluster, $k = 1$ to K
  - sample the parameters defining the cluster (μ_k)
- for each document, $i = 1$ to N
  - sample a cluster for that particular document (π_i) from a multinomial distribution
  - sample the data from that cluster using the distribution parameterized by $\mu \pi_i$

This is a very flexible model that can behave quite differently depending on the distribution that we choose to sample the data from. Common mixture models that are used include mixture of multinomial distributions (Nigam et al., 2000), mixtures of normal distributions (Fraley and Raftery, 2002), and mixtures of von Mises-Fisher distributions (Banerjee, Dhillon, Ghosh, and Sra, 2005). Probabilistic mixture models are attractive because they come with statistical infrastructure that provides principled ways to extend the model, perform model selection, and estimate parameters. For example, estimation is generally possible through an Expectation-Maximization (EM) algorithm (Dempster, Laird, and Rubin, 1977) or through variational inference (Wainwright and Jordan, 2008).

Mixture of Multinomials

The mixture of multinomials clustering model is a probabilistic, soft, mean-based, and flat clustering method. It is also the straightforward generalization of the multinomial model described in Chapter 6 to the case without labeled data. The data generating process is,

$$\mu_k \sim \text{Dirichlet}(\alpha) \tag{12.3.1}$$

$$\pi_i \sim \text{Multinomial}(\eta) \tag{12.3.2}$$

$$W_{i,}|\mu, \pi_i, M_i \sim \text{Multinomial}(M_i, \mu\pi_i). \tag{12.3.3}$$

This model is helpful in its own right (Nigam et al., 2000), but it also serves as a building block to the models we discuss in Chapter 13 on Topic Models.

Often probability models require a particular form of input data. In the case of the multinomial mixture model, it takes the counts of words and implicitly accounts for document length by including the M_i parameter. Thus, as in the k-means case using the proportion of words per document, the multinomial mixture model will group documents which have a similar rate of word use rather than a similar number of words. One advantage of the multinomial here is that it preserves information about the number of tokens in each document and thus can accurately reflect that there is more information in a longer document than in a shorter document.

Mixture of von Mises-Fisher

The mixture of von Mises-Fisher model of Banerjee, Merugu, Dhillon, and Ghosh (2005) is similar to the mixture of multinomial model but it replaces the multinomial distribution for word counts with a von Mises-Fisher distribution—a distribution for directional data related to the cosine similarity metric described in Chapter 7. The von Mises-Fisher distribution assumes that the data is normalized by the magnitude of the vector. Defining the count data as W_i, the von Mises-Fisher will work with the data,

$$W_{i,}^* = \frac{W_{i,}}{\|W_{i,}\|} \tag{12.3.4}$$

$$= \frac{W_{i,}}{\sqrt{\sum_{j=1}^{J}(W_{ij} - W_{i'j})^2}}. \tag{12.3.5}$$

The full data generating process is then,

$$\mu_k \sim \text{Dirichlet}(\alpha) \tag{12.3.6}$$

$$\pi_i \sim \text{Multinomial}(\eta) \tag{12.3.7}$$

$$W_{i,}^*|\pi_i, \mu \sim \text{von Mises-Fisher}(\phi, \mu\pi_i). \tag{12.3.8}$$

Table 12.4. Applying mixtures of von Mises-Fisher distributions
to Lautenberg press releases.

Cluster	Top Words
1	sen, d, bill, victim, famili, terror, militari, libya, r, american
2	secur, chemic, homeland, port, risk, law, dhs, protect, tsa, rail
3	new, jersey, fund, menendez, feder, project, nj, million, program, counti
4	senat, s, lautenberg, presid, bush, frank, releas, statement, unit, iraq

The von Mises-Fisher distribution is analogous to the normal distribution but on the surface of a sphere, making it appropriate for directional data. μ_k is the center of the distribution and ϕ is analogous to the precision of a distribution.

This data generating process provides the three key pieces of information to characterize the clustering method. The von Mises-Fisher distribution measures the cosine of the angle between the document and the cluster center. The complete data generating process defines a likelihood model that provides the objective function. And there are numerous methods for optimizing the likelihood—with the EM algorithm among the most widely used methods (Dempster, Laird, and Rubin, 1977).

Table 12.4 describes four clusters from a model of the Lautenberg press releases based on a mixture of von Mises-Fisher distribution. Cluster 1 (partisan taunting) and cluster 2 (statements and legislation) from the k-means clustering are clustered together by the von Mises-Fisher clusters into cluster 4. Cluster 1 of the von Mises-Fisher clusters about military legislation is one part of the position, taking cluster from k-means, cluster 4. Cluster 3 from both clusterings—the credit claiming cluster—aligns quite strongly across the two clusterings.

The von Mises-Fisher mixture model has a very similar structure to the mixture of multinomials but conceptualizes similarity differently. For example, while the multinomials consider the rate of word use in each document, the von Mises-Fisher looks at the direction in which the normalized vector is pointing. Neither of these is right or wrong, but they take into account a different notion of document magnitude.

Other Probability Models

There are many other possible probability models, including the mixture of Gaussians (Fraley and Raftery, 2002), which is closely related to k-means and the mixture of Bernoullis, which may be familiar to social scientists as a form of latent class analysis (Lazarsfeld and Henry, 1968). By changing the probability distribution in the mixture model we alter both the document dissimilarity and the measure of partition quality, but as long as we stay within a well-behaved set of distributions, the optimization algorithm will continue to be relatively straightforward (McLachlan and Peel, 2004). Another advantage of these models is that they can form the building blocks of more complex hierarchies of data, including nesting documents within time (Quinn et al., 2010) or author (Grimmer, 2010). We will return to these ideas in Chapter 13.

12.3.4   ALGORITHMIC CLUSTERING MODELS

Algorithmic clustering methods do not make explicit assumptions about the data generating process. Instead they define a specific algorithm (e.g., k-means) and define performance relative to some explicit objective function.

Table 12.5. Applying affinity propagation to the Lautenberg press releases.

Cluster	Top Words
1	rail, bill, amtrak, passeng, year, lautenberg, system, improv, servic, transport
2	presid, statement, iraq, bush, tax, follow, william, unit, white, troop
3	secur, new, chemic, jersey, safeti, administr, million, s, law, bush
4	state, d, jersey, new, feder, sen, menendez, health, nj, r

Affinity Propagation

Affinity propagation is an algorithmic, hard, mediod-based, and flat clustering method (Frey and Dueck, 2007). The model takes an arbitrary *similarity* matrix—a matrix where the cell at row r and column c measures the similarity from document r to document c, using measures such as those discussed in Chapter 7. Every cluster has a particular document as its center and the algorithm tries to maximize the similarity between documents and their center. The model optimizes cluster assignment by iteratively determining the fitness of a document as an exemplar and assessing which documents are likely to serve as exemplars for other models. One substantial advantage is that affinity propagation can use a huge range of similarity measures with the same algorithm.

Affinity propagation is also different from the algorithms we have seen thus far in that the number of clusters is set indirectly rather than explicitly. The diagonal elements of the similarity matrix are the self-similarity and determine the chance that a particular document is selected as an exemplar. When this number is low, there will tend to be few clusters, and when the number is high, more documents will break out and form their own clusters. Of course, this doesn't solve the problem for the user of setting the number of clusters, since her or she still has to set the self-similarity measure. It does, however, allow for the possibility that different documents have different levels of self-similarity (and thus are more or less likely to serve as exemplars).

We give an example using cosine similarity in Table 12.5, where the self-similarity is set to -7 which results in four clusters. Affinity Propagation provides a quite different clustering to k-means. Clusters 1 and 2 from k-means—taunting and statements—cluster mainly into the second Affinity Propagation clusters. However, where clusters 3 and 4 from k-means split Senator Lautenberg's work by national versus New Jersey policies, clusters 3 and 4 from Affinity Propagation split the work topically, between safety and healthcare.

Hierarchical Clustering

Hierarchical clustering is really a class of different algorithms that are a world unto themselves (Ward Jr., 1963). Rather than returning a single partition of documents into clusters, hierarchical clustering returns a tree where clusters are successively split from a single cluster at the top to each individual document in its own cluster at the bottom. Much like affinity propagation, these methods often allow for a wide variety of different similarity measures (although in this case they are typically constrained to be symmetric).

Because the algorithm always returns a hierarchy, we don't explicitly set a number of clusters. However, we need to "cut" the tree at a particular height in order to interpret

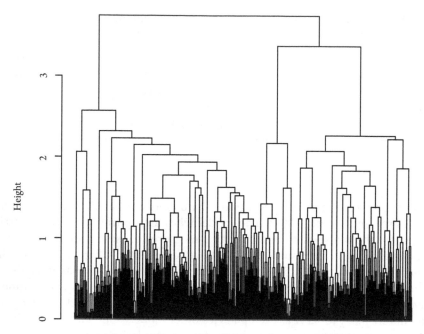

Figure 12.3. Hierarchical clustering of the Lautenberg press releases using Ward's minimum variance method.

Table 12.6. Applying hierarchical clustering to the Lautenberg press releases.

Cluster	Top Words
1	american, dc, kill, unit, compens, bipartisan, john, legal, r, md
2	jersey, menendez, new, nj, robert, resid, communiti, project, garden, contact
3	secur, chemic, homeland, stronger, dhs, preempt, port, adopt, deem, attack

the clusters. To see this example, see Figure 12.3, a hierarchical clustering of the Lautenberg press releases. At the leaves of the tree, the clusterings become more and more specific. But by cutting the tree horizontally at height 3, we get three distinct clusterings. Table 12.6 shows the most distinctive words for these three clusters. Reading a sample of the documents, these clusters have distinct interpretations—cluster 1 is legislation and position taking, cluster 2 is credit claiming, and cluster 3 relates to national and homeland security. If we were to cut at a different height, we would see further subdivisions of these clusters.

Other Algorithmic Approaches

There are other algorithmic approaches, many of which address the clustering problem by transforming it into a related problem. For example, one popular class of algorithms, spectral clustering, has a close analogue to graph-cutting algorithms—procedures that attempt to find closely connected communities in a network (Ng, Jordan, and Weiss, 2001). From a practical perspective the algorithmic approaches are often attractive because they don't place as many restrictions on the representation of the data that can be used; however, they don't come with the same statistical infrastructure as their probabilistic counterparts.

12.3.5 CONNECTIONS BETWEEN PROBABILISTIC AND ALGORITHMIC CLUSTERING

The differences between probabilistic and algorithmic clustering are smaller than they appear to be, based on the substantial differences in language used to describe them. For example, k-means is a limiting case of a mixture of normals as the covariance matrices in the normal distributions go to zero (Kulis and Jordan, 2012; Broderick, Kulis, and Jordan, 2013). Further, as we have shown above, distinct clustering algorithms also produce quite similar solutions.

This distinction is particularly important for the way that we talk about assumptions when using clustering methods. k-means is often discussed as making no assumptions about the underlying data, while a mixture of normals is seen as assuming the data are distributed multivariate normal within the cluster. While it is technically true that k-means will seek to minimize the sum of squared errors from documents to their centers regardless of the data generating process, it is worth emphasizing that Gaussian mixture models are also based on minimization of sum of squared errors. The distributional assumptions encoded in the probabilistic mixture models are really just encoding the document dissimilarity and measure of partition quality that are given in k-means. Much as linear regression can be understood as a well-defined approximation even when the data are not conditionally normally distributed (Aronow and Miller, 2019), so too can probabilistic mixture models. Of course, consistent with our Principle 3: Judge the Concept Not the Method in Chapter 10, we are far less concerned about assumptions than identifying interesting insights and then validating them in new data.

12.4 Making Choices

While analysts don't set the labels ahead of time in clustering, they still must make a lot of choices, including: the representation, the clustering method, the number of clusters, and often additional consequential hyperparameters. In this section, we talk about how to make those choices. We start with some general advice on model selection and then discuss the most common parameter that must be set, the number of clusters.

12.4.1 MODEL SELECTION

What metrics can we use to decide what clustering method is more useful for our particular application? Although there is no one "right" conceptualization, we might be able to decide on metrics that can tell us what organization of texts will be more useful for a particular task at hand. In this section, we describe some strategies to evaluate cluster quality, relying on both statistical guidance and human evaluations.

Determining the most useful clustering necessarily requires the researcher to consider quantitative evidence, but also to consider the particular problem she is confronting, the substantive goal of the project, and to evaluate distinct clusterings. This means that no one statistic is going to be sufficient to drive model selection, but statistics can still be useful. Rather, our preferred procedure will make use of statistics that proxy for the usefulness of clusters, experiments that help us elicit credible human evaluations outside of the research team, and a manual deep inspection of different potential clusterings.

Statistics

We introduce two additional statistics that are useful for selecting a particular clustering: exclusivity and cohesiveness (Roberts et al., 2014; Mimno et al., 2011). The focus on exclusivity and cohesiveness comes from our intuition about what might make a "useful" clustering. Typically our goal will be to put like documents in the same group, and so we will identify groups of documents that have the same cohesive use of language: the content of documents in the same group are similar. Of course, as the number of clusters increases, the groups of documents within each cluster will be more cohesive, but there might be several clusters that repeat the same basic content. Typically, we are interested in creating distinct clusters. Thus, a second property of a useful clustering is that the clusters are exclusive: several clusters don't replicate the same basic content.

We follow discussions in the appendix of Roberts et al. (2014) and Mimno et al. (2011) to formalize this intuition. First, consider a definition of exclusivity. We will say that a cluster is exclusive if the "top" words that describe membership in one cluster do not also describe membership in other clusters. Specifically, suppose that each cluster has a center vector $\boldsymbol{\mu}_k = (\mu_{1k}, \mu_{2k}, \ldots, \mu_{Jk})$, where μ_{jk} describes the probability of appearance attached to the jth word in cluster k. For each cluster we can select the M largest weights and collect the indices for the words that have the M largest weights into $\mathcal{M}_k$. For each word $m \in \mathcal{M}_k$ we can define the exclusivity as

$$\text{Exclusivity}_{mk} = \frac{\mu_{mk}}{\sum_{k=1}^{K} \mu_{mk}}.$$

If a word is as exclusive as possible—it is only used in one cluster—then the exclusivity is 1. If the word is not exclusive at all and used equally across the clusters, then the score will be $\frac{1}{K}$. And if it is used more often in other clusters, the score will be even smaller.

We can then aggregate up the exclusivity scores for the clusters by summing across the words and across clusters. For a particular clustering with K clusters, we can describe its average exclusivity as

$$\text{Average Exclusivity} = \frac{1}{K} \sum_{k=1}^{K} \left(\sum_{m \text{ in } M_k} \text{Exclusivity}_{mk} \right).$$

To measure cohesiveness we use the strategy adopted in Mimno et al. (2011) and examine the extent to which two words that indicate that a document belongs to a cluster actually co-occur in the documents that belong to that cluster. Call the function $D()$ a function that counts the number of times its arguments occur in documents. For example, if we provide the indices m_1 and m_2 then $D(m_1, m_2)$ will count the number of times the words m_1 and m_2 co-occur in documents, while $D(m_1)$ counts the number of documents in which the word m_1 appears. If we again collect all top M words into the set $\mathcal{M}$, we can then define cohesiveness of a cluster as

$$\text{Cohesion} = \sum_{n=1}^{M} \sum_{l=1}^{l-1} \log \left(\frac{D(m_n, m_l)}{D(m_l)} \right). \qquad (12.4.1)$$

And we can take the average across clusters to compute a clustering-level measure of cohesiveness.

As Roberts et al. (2014) note, we cannot compare cohesiveness and exclusivity across models with different numbers of clusters, because different clusters imply different constraints. Further, increasing the exclusivity necessarily will result in a drop of cohesiveness, so the statistics are unable to provide a specific recommendation on the single model to choose. But the measures of cohesiveness and exclusivity can ensure that we end up on the cohesiveness/exclusivity *frontier*: the sets of models that do the best job of managing the cohesiveness and exclusivity trade-off.

Experiments

Statistics are useful to guide decision making, but we can also incorporate credible human evaluations of the clustering. We examine two such experiments here: topic-intruder detection and overall cluster evaluation. Each attempts to inject human evaluation of the clustering while being attentive to cognitive limitations of humans as they engage with the content of clusters.

We consider first the topic-intruder experiment, first introduced in Chang et al. (2009). The intuition for the topic intruder experiment is that if a set of clusters is both cohesive and exclusive then we should be able to easily detect language that does not belong with a particular cluster. Suppose again that we have word weights that are indicative of a cluster μ_k and suppose again that we have identified the top M words for each cluster. If a cluster is grouping together documents that have cohesive and exclusive language, then we should expect that we could detect a top word from another category if it were accidentally mixed with these M words. To test this, we randomly select an intruder. Specifically, we randomly select a different cluster and then we randomly select one of the top words from that other cluster as the intruder. We then have a list that contains $M + 1$ words, M from our particular topic and one intruder word from the other topic.

The key to the topic-intruder experiment is asking experiment participants to identify the intruder word. The higher the proportion of topic intruder words detected, the better the model performs under this human evaluation. The number of examples that are necessary to code to make meaningful comparisons depends on the topic-intrusion rate for the comparison models. In general, the lower the topic intrusion detection rate for clusterings, the more examples that require coding. This is because the variance of the topic intrusion rate is very low when the topic intrusion rate is very high. Ying, Montgomery, and Stewart (2019) generalize these designs and develop new tasks which help to validate the human-chosen label for a cluster as well.

Grimmer and King (2011) suggest a different approach to estimating the quality of a clustering and making comparisons. The intuition behind this cluster quality measure is that high-quality clusterings should group together pairs of documents that readers evaluate as similar and separate pairs of documents that are dissimilar. To evaluate this idea with human reading, the first step is to sample pairs of documents that are both assigned to the same cluster and pairs of documents that are assigned to different clusters. Then, evaluators are asked to rate the pairs of documents on a three-point scale. Documents are given a 1 if they have no similarity, a 2 if there is some similarity, and 3 if they are very similar.[5] Using the evaluations from coders, the average evaluation for documents assigned to the same cluster is calculated and the average evaluation for documents assigned to different clusters is calculated. Finally, a cluster

---

[5] If the analyst has a particular conceptual grouping of interest, then more direction could be given to defining "similar."

quality calculation is made:

$$\text{Cluster Quality} = \text{Average Same Cluster} - \text{Average Different Cluster}$$

Clusterings will have higher cluster quality when documents assigned to the same cluster are evaluated higher than clusterings assigned to different clusters.[6]

12.4.2 CAREFUL READING

Armed with measures of exclusivity and cohesiveness, and potentially experimental measures of particular clusterings, we are close to ready to make a final selection of a particular clustering. Of course, the statistics alone are insufficient. This might be because the statistics and the experiments might offer contradictory recommendations. In particular, a subset of the clusterings might remain as potentially viable organizations. The only way to adjudicate between the clusterings is to carefully consider the organizations, what they mean, and their implications for further analysis.

Reading the documents, guided by the organization and our own substantive knowledge of the research question, is essential for understanding the meaning of the clusterings. In our running example of press releases, for example, some research questions might require measuring attention to chemical and transportation security from Table 12.3, while for other questions that cluster would be largely irrelevant. For other questions, partisan taunting or credit claiming might be more useful concepts. Closely engaging with the text and reading the documents in light of the organization tends to provide new insights and conceptualizations about how to observe the world.

12.4.3 CHOOSING THE NUMBER OF CLUSTERS

We have so far assumed that we know the number of clusters to include in our analysis, but often this is a quantity that individuals want to discover (along with the content of the clusters). In this section we first review common methods used to set the number of clusters in a clustering. We then discuss their shortcomings and an alternative way to view selecting the number of clusters.

Common Strategies for Determining the Number of Clusters

At first glance it might appear that the objective function used to obtain clusterings provides information to set the number of clusters. It might be tempting to try and use the machinery of clustering methods to make this determination. For example, it might (intuitively) seem that we could use the objective function from k-means to compare the partitions that we obtain from k-means. Unfortunately, in-sample fit is unable to provide a guide on how many clusters to include. This is because the k-means objective function, like many other statistical models, improves as more cluster components

---

[6]If we are merely comparing two clusterings, then we only need to calculate cluster quality for pairs of documents where the two clusters disagree. This is because any pairs that are either placed in the same cluster in both or different clusters in both will not contribute to a final difference between the two evaluations. Further, note that any pair of documents can be used to calculate the cluster quality.

(parameters) are added.[7] If we follow the advice from the objective function alone, we receive the unhelpful suggestion of placing every document into its own cluster.

There are numerous quantitative methods that attempt to provide guidance on the number of clusters to include (Fraley and Raftery, 2002). The core intuition of the numerical approaches to determining the number of clusters is that a penalty term can be used to balance two competing concerns. On the one hand, we would like to have a sufficient number of clusters to capture the major variation across our documents and to find substantively interesting groups of texts. On the other hand, we would like to avoid too much model complexity: creating a large number of clusters that divide up very similar texts or create several clusters that group together essentially the same "type" of document. The statistical methods take several approaches to this problem. Perhaps one of the most prominent groups of methods for determining the number of clusters builds on the objective function from clustering and embeds a penalty for additional cluster components. For example, when using a mixture model to cluster data there are easily available statistics such as the Akaike Information Criterion (AIC) and the Bayesian Information Criterion (BIC) (Fraley and Raftery, 2002) that penalize the addition of new clusters. This penalty ensures that to add a new clustering component we know that the improvement in model fit outweighs the penalty for additional parameters.

As an alternative, several methods attempt to estimate the number of clusters as part of the estimation process. For example, affinity propagation does not require the researcher to set the number of clusters, but the self-similarity parameter determines the number of clusters that are likely to emerge (Frey and Dueck, 2007). Nonparametric Bayesian methods provide the comparable approach in statistical models. The most widely used nonparametric Bayesian prior, the Dirichlet process prior, is a prior over distributions, rather than parameters (Blackwell and MacQueen, 1973).[8] The data generating process is now that there are an infinite number of clusters, a finite number of which appear in our particular dataset.

Both nonparametric and penalty-based approaches are applied to the full dataset and attempt to correct the greediness of statistical models with a penalty that nudges the model to use fewer clusters. Other approaches to determining the number of clusters assess how well additional clusters assist in predicting documents that have been set aside from training (Wallach et al., 2009). Adding additional clusters will always

---

[7]We can prove directly that the objective function for k-means is nondecreasing. Suppose there is an optimal clustering of a document collection with K clusters. Now suppose that we add one cluster and want to find a new solution with $K + 1$ clusters. So long as there are distinct documents within each cluster, the objective function will improve. To see the objective function improve, take the observation that fits its cluster worst (and therefore contributes the most to the objective function) and move it to the new cluster. If the partition is perfect, in the sense that each document is identical within each clustering, then a new cluster component will not affect the objective function. While this may not be an optimal solution, moving one document either improves the clustering objective function or leaves it the same, so any optimal partition must make the objective function better.

[8]The Dirichlet process prior (DPP) has two components: a base measure, G_0 and a concentration parameter ξ. The concentration parameter exercises substantial influence over the number of clusters that are formed from the model (Wallach et al., 2010). Indeed, as the number of observations goes to infinity, the expected number of clusters from the DPP is $\xi \log(1 + \frac{N}{\xi})$ (Wallach et al., 2010). Further, the DPP assumes a particular process for cluster assignment that results in a "rich get richer" dynamic: a few clusters will have many documents assigned to it and many clusters will only have a few documents. Other nonparametric priors, like the Pitman-Yor prior, generalize the DPP and relax some features of the data-generating process. But the Pitman-Yor prior retains similar features, such as a few clusters receiving a large number of documents (Pitman and Yor, 1981). And still other nonparametric priors, such as the Uniform process prior (Wallach et al., 2010), provide a different data generating process, but still make consequential modeling assumptions.

improve in sample fit, but too many clusters will result in overfitting—capturing more noise than signal—and decreasing performance.

Shortcomings of Quantitative Approaches to Choosing the Number of Clusters

A shortcoming of quantitative approaches to model selection is that they are a blunt tool for selecting a final model and there can be only a weak relationship between the output from quantitative approaches to model selection and the most useful model for discovery. As we discussed at the beginning of this chapter, without a specific research question, there is no one "right" way to organize documents into categories. The objective function for the clustering methods attempts to summarize how "well" the clustering fits the data according to the model or distance metric. This objective function can provide a useful organization of the texts, but it can be difficult to select between the model fits merely using a statistic. The problem is even more difficult, though, because there is only a weak relationship between the partitions automatic methods select and the partitions most useful for substantive research. Chang et al. (2009) show that, for a particular set of documents, there is a negative relationship between methods that receive a positive score from humans and the methods' scores from automated evaluation methods. This is further exacerbated by the simplification of the text representation. Our preprocessing steps discard substantial information when we represent texts in a document-term matrix.

The general goal—to find a useful clustering—is underspecified because we are unsure about how to directly model "interesting." It is generally impossible to define what we will find useful beforehand, even if we know what clustering is illuminating after the fact. The result is that merely using statistical procedures to discover categories will necessarily miss interesting organizations and will be insufficient to determine the number of categories.

We suggest researchers try out a wide variety of cluster sizes to explore a range of organizations of the text. Often, analysts will have an idea of what clustering granularity they are most interested in. For example, a researcher analyzing a newspaper dataset for one research question might want to identify broad categories like "Sports," "Foreign Affairs," and "Weather," but for another research question might require more specific subcategories like "Soccer," "Football," "Baseball," "International Trade," "Elections Abroad," "Weather Forecast," or "Today's Weather." The research question will drive what granularity of clustering is most interesting. Once the researcher has decided on granularity, she can turn back to the methods introduced in Section 12.4 to decide between alternative clusterings.

To give an idea of how different numbers of clusters will result in different granularities of concepts, we clustered the Lautenberg Press Releases using 40 clusters instead of four. We show the words that represent the cluster center in Table 12.7. It is clear that these smaller clusters divide the larger clusters we discussed in previous examples. For example, the chemical and transportation security cluster from Table 12.3 is now divided into cluster 36 about chemical security and cluster 23 about transportation security, providing us a more granular view of the cluster. A larger number of clusters also allows clusters to appear that may have been lost before, for example, cluster 16 reflects Senator Lautenberg's work on banning smoking in public places. In our own work, we have found that one good approach is to start with many clusters, and group the clusters together to form larger categories and concepts.

Table 12.7. 40 clusters resulting from the Lautenberg press releases.

Cluster	Top Words
1	hous, author, deadlin, system, manag, asset, new, hud, public, extend
2	epa, children, librari, test, mercuri, protect, agenc, chemic, product, health
3	s, u, compani, iran, foreign, busi, halliburton, control, airlin, sanction
4	secur, million, fund, grant, jersey, nj, homeland, port, new, dhs
5	program, educ, food, gang, train, youth, provid, job, abstin, fund
6	new, jersey, state, declar, menendez, feder, counti, disast, faa, administr
7	militari, increas, sen, famili, tricar, d, afghanistan, co, retire, fee
8	budget, new, million, cut, jersey, presid, highland, s, bush, educ
9	fire, safeti, grant, depart, firefight, colleg, campus, assist, nj, student
10	airport, grant, receiv, feder, jersey, menendez, fund, improv, announc, new
11	site, epa, ringwood, superfund, contamin, cleanup, report, resid, environment, agenc
12	presid, bush, s, senat, iraq, statement, administr, white, social, iraqi
13	rang, safeti, guard, grove, warren, air, fire, resid, communiti, account
14	senat, lautenberg, committe, monmouth, iraq, frank, commiss, fort, republican, r
15	american, women, honor, gao, iraq, news, live, mr, vaccin, propaganda
16	cigarett, tobacco, light, tar, compani, nicotin, market, smoker, low, d
17	broadband, municip, access, offer, provid, communiti, state, afford, public, prohibit
18	corp, park, armi, natur, beach, palmyra, cove, engin, dredg, munit
19	build, energi, emiss, bill, global, govern, warm, greenhous, green, feder
20	fund, new, jersey, project, menendez, transport, million, program, counti, tunnel
21	contract, presid, t, said, secretari, hud, get, jackson, select, don
22	ocean, water, state, protect, bill, pet, beach, whistleblow, legisl, nation
23	secur, port, homeland, risk, tsa, screener, rail, senat, chertoff, cap
24	safeti, airport, flight, faa, delay, truck, administr, runway, new, transport
25	judg, court, s, suprem, right, nomin, decis, senat, wigenton, attorney
26	lautenberg, press, statement, ambassador, sen, farm, issu, frank, offic, d
27	senat, lautenberg, statement, frank, r, follow, issu, unit, question, press
28	children, health, insur, care, jersey, program, new, presid, veto, bill
29	law, helmet, lautenberg, motorcycl, drink, age, legal, year, death, rider
30	tax, increas, lautenberg, relief, credit, senat, republican, elizabeth, bush, amend
31	coverag, gap, medicar, senior, drug, plan, lautenberg, prescript, republican, calcul
32	amtrak, rail, passeng, fund, lott, system, year, servic, billion, senat
33	worker, union, employe, employ, act, compens, ira, disabl, choic, free
34	gun, law, enforc, firearm, weapon, terrorist, purchas, crime, assault, tiahrt
35	project, flood, river, million, beach, control, fund, storm, raritan, bay
36	chemic, secur, law, state, administr, protect, bush, stronger, govern, provis
37	wast, regul, site, state, rail, facil, solid, railroad, jersey, board
38	elect, releas, toxic, chemic, state, bush, right, facil, know, feder
39	oil, opec, spill, price, wto, s, cartel, action, trade, product
40	victim, terror, libya, d, sen, libyan, famili, sponsor, state, bomb

12.5 The Human Side of Clustering

Clustering for discovery involves both detecting patterns in the data and interpreting those patterns in terms of some properties of the documents themselves. Chapter 11 already provided some tools that can be used to label clusters, but in this section we put the process in a broader perspective.

12.5.1 INTERPRETATION

Clustering algorithms give us a way to obtain a partition of the documents, but they don't tell us what the partition represents conceptually. To interpret the output of clustering methods, we build on suggestions from Quinn et al. (2010). The clustering algorithms provide us with a clear mapping from the features of a document to particular clusters. The goal at this stage is to translate this algorithmic rule into a substantive rule: the kind of rule that we could easily explain to manual coders. Indeed, we will argue later in this book that the best evaluation of clustering methods for many tasks will be to confirm that we can independently replicate the conceptualization from the unsupervised clustering documents using hand coding or supervised learning methods, discussed in Measurement.

Method 1: Identifying Distinctive Words

While for some models like k-means we can use model parameters like cluster centers μ to identify words that represent each cluster, there are limitations to this approach. Some methods, like Affinity Propagation (Section 12.3.4), do not have parameters on the vocabulary, and model parameters for these methods are therefore difficult to interpret. Even when the parameters are available, it is difficult to compare across clustering approaches using model parameters since they vary by method. Thankfully we can always use the techniques in Chapter 11 to identify discriminating words no matter how opaque the model parameters may be.

Method 2: Sampling Documents Assigned to Each Cluster

Following the advice of Quinn et al. (2010), the second approach that we recommend for labeling the cluster components is sampling documents assigned to each cluster component, reading those documents, and then generating labels by hand. We usually recommend reading between 10–30 of the posts assigned to each category. Our usual method is to carefully read the documents and write down a set of notes as we read. We then try to synthesize those notes into a coherent label. If no label is readily available (or we struggle to provide a label), then we have good evidence that this particular cluster (or overall partition) might not be useful for discovery purposes. Reading the documents serves two purposes. It is primarily useful for labeling the clusters, but reading texts—particularly when grouped together in a new way—can lead to new insights by itself.

12.5.2 INTERACTIVE CLUSTERING

Different clustering methods can produce similar, though distinct, clusterings when applied to the same data. Of course, we have barely scratched the surface of potential clustering methods. Other methods might specify different components of a mixture, implicitly changing the definition of similarity between the documents. Or, the different methods might use different optimization procedures to find a clustering, or even use different objective functions for defining a "good" clustering.

The potential set of models are numerous and growing quickly. Each of the new clustering methods are carefully derived, based on a clear set of assumptions, and rigorous derivations. Typically a paper introducing the method shows that the new clustering method is able to "beat" existing methods at an important task, such as information retrieval or classification. This is also an active area of research, with the number of clustering algorithms and their extensions growing rapidly.

The rigor in derivation and the growth of the field has not been met, however, with a critical examination of when to apply clustering algorithms and to what problems they should be applied. In fact, there is little guidance from the literature on how to select a clustering method for a particular problem. Theoretical guidance based on theorems is particularly lacking. There are not any (to our knowledge) generally applicable theorems that demonstrate one particular clustering method is more effective than other clustering methods for discovering useful content. The literature also lacks papers that have a more modest goal: providing guidance on when to apply clustering methods based on the observable features of the data.

When considering the clustering literature, then, there is an implicit recognition that the right methods for a task will be difficult to identify beforehand and the methods that one does end up using might be more about convenience than principle. This level of arbitrariness is a direct consequence of the vague goal of discovery—and the generally vague goal when using other unsupervised methods. The result is that we lack an objective function that is easy to write down.

Consider the goal we started this chapter with: discovering some interesting organization of the texts. Certainly we know that something is interesting once we have seen it, but in general it is impossible to know if a clustering is interesting without human intervention. This makes automated search that excludes humans altogether impossible.

A natural solution to this process is to explicitly include humans in the cluster selection process. Grimmer and King (2011), for example, argue that interesting clusterings are easy to spot once they are put in front of someone, and so they create a geography of many clusterings—essentially a map in which nearby solutions are quite similar. It was this procedure that led them to the discovery of partisan taunting using Senator Lautenberg's press releases.

Generally, there are trade-offs when applying human-in-the-loop vs. traditional clustering. Traditional methods are able to provide a single and clear clustering. Further, it is relatively easy to build more complicated models with interpretable parameters. Yet, traditional methods will necessarily limit the set of assumptions we consider when clustering the data. Human-in-the-loop methods, in contrast, enable us to explore the assumptions of clustering methods more completely than any one method could. Indeed, there will be many more clusterings considered. That said, using a human-in-the-loop method can require a great deal of work from the analyst and it is impossible to automate. In the end, the choice comes down to both researcher preference and the type of basic problem the researcher is considering.

12.6 Conclusion

In this chapter we described clustering as a way to facilitate discovery in documents by identifying potentially interesting patterns for analysts to investigate. This provides a sense of the overall process, but clustering is only one type of distillation of document contents. Constraining every document to be a member of only one cluster is a large constraint on the kind of pattern that the clustering can discover. This constraint is a blessing and a curse—clusterings are relatively simple to summarize (a document is either in or out of the cluster), but they also are limited in the kind of phenomena they can represent. In the next two chapters we talk about a series of more flexible methods for discovery: mixed membership topic models and document embeddings.

CHAPTER 13

Topic Models

Even though there are a wide array of clustering algorithms, at their core, they share a common assumption that each document belongs to one cluster. Even "soft" clustering methods operate under the assumption that there is one cluster per document while allowing for an algorithm to express uncertainty about assignments. But documents may have more than one idea contained in them, and may be evenly split between clusters or concepts. For example, political speeches may cover a variety of key themes. Newspaper articles may cover a story from a variety of perspectives. And novels are often thought to contain several themes. When documents are a mixture of distinct ideas, clustering methods will obscure this variation.

Topic models are a class of models that are closely related to clustering methods, but they make a fundamentally different assumption about the categories each document is assigned to. Rather than assign each document to only one cluster, topic models assign each document with proportional membership to all categories. That is, topic models suppose that each document is a mixture across categories—a mixed membership model. When freed in this way, topic models are able to represent much more focused concepts because no single topic needs to be representative of an entire document on its own. This specificity helps give mixed membership topic models greater human interpretability. As we will see, mixed membership models can provide important insights often unavailable in clustering algorithms.

In this chapter we describe the canonical topic model, Latent Dirichlet Allocation, and then talk about a small sample of the many extensions that have been proposed. Throughout we provide two examples of how topic models can facilitate computational discoveries.

13.1 Latent Dirichlet Allocation

The most famous topic model is *Latent Dirichlet Allocation* (LDA) (Blei, Ng, and Jordan, 2003).[1] LDA is a Bayesian hierarchical model that assumes a particular data

---

[1] Once again, there is a rich intellectual history here. In Chapter 8 we talked about Latent Semantic Indexing (LSI)—the application of Singular Value Decomposition (SVD) to a possibly weighted document term matrix. LSI was an important breakthrough for information retrieval and it remains used across several fields (Deerwester et al., 1990). The immediate predecessor to LDA was probabilistic Latent Semantic Indexing (Hofmann, 1999), which placed the purely algorithmic LSI in a probabilistic modeling framework. In Hofmann's formulation, the document-level latent parameters were not given a prior distribution, leading to

generating process for how an author produces a text and that builds on the multinomial language model we described in Chapter 6 and the multinomial mixture model of Chapter 12. We first suppose that when writing a text the author draws a mixture of topics: a set of weights that will describe how prevalent the particular topics are. Given that set of weights, the author generates the actual text. For each word the author first draws the word's topic. Then, conditional on the topic, the actual word is drawn from a topic-specific distribution. This topic-specific distribution is common across the documents and characterizes the rates at which words appear when discussing a particular topic.

Given this data generating process we can write down a specific statistical model for how the text are generated. For each document i ($i = 1, 2, \ldots, N$) we will suppose that we draw a $K \times 1$ vector of topic weights $\pi_i = (\pi_{i1}, \pi_{i2}, \ldots, \pi_{iK})$. Now suppose that we generate the words from the document in a sequence, with the mth word from a particular document ($m = 1, 2, \ldots, M_i$) called $\tilde{W}_{im}$. We will suppose that each word has a corresponding topic indicator that is a draw from a Multinomial distribution $Z_{im} \sim \text{Multinomial}(1, \pi_i)$. Then we will assume that $\tilde{W}_{im}$ is a draw from a multinomial distribution $\tilde{W}_{im} \sim \text{Multinomial}(1, \mu Z_{im})$, where μ is a $J \times K$ matrix. The kth column, $\mu_k = (\mu_{1k}, \mu_{2k}, \ldots, \mu_{Jk})$, is a $J \times 1$ vector where each μ_{jk} describes the probability of using word j when discussing topic k. This process generates an $M_i \times 1$ matrix $\tilde{W}_i$. If we sum over the columns we obtain the corresponding row in the document term matrix, $W_{i,} = \sum_{m=1}^{M_i} \tilde{W}_{i,m}$ We complete the data-generating process with priors, assuming that both π_i and μ_k are drawn from a Dirichlet distribution. While it is common to use a simple default prior for the model, other papers show that asymmetric priors can lead to more meaningful topic results (Wallach, Mimno, and McCallum, 2009). The plate diagram is shown in Figure 13.1.

For intuition about the sense in which LDA captures the topics in texts, consider a simple example about two different conversations. One conversation might involve US presidential politics. At the time of writing of this book, this might involve discussing "Donald Trump's statement" or "debate over the Russian election scandal." In contrast, we might have a conversation about gardening. And there we might discuss "insects and pesticides" and "landscape design."

The key is that there is one set of correlated vocabulary when we discuss the presidency, a second, relatively distinct, set of vocabulary when we discuss gardening. We then learn a set of topics where one would assign relatively high probabilities to "presidential" words and a second topic that would allocate relatively high probabilities to "gardening" words. Of course, some (generally common) words may receive a high weight in both topics. And both topics allocate some weight (often times a small weight) to all the words in the vocabulary. While most of the time these two topics might appear in different documents, some documents might be an equal combination of the two topics, for example a conversation about the White House's garden. The possibility of a conversation about the White House's garden highlights an important advantage of

---

the generative model being incomplete and possibly overfitting. The Latent Dirichlet Allocation model of Blei, Ng, and Jordan (2003) was introduced at the Neural Information Processing Systems Conference in 2001. Unbeknownst to the authors, the same model had been independently developed in the genetics community by Pritchard, Stephens, and Donnelly (2000). The original paper used variational inference, but another leap forward came with the introduction of a collapsed gibbs sampler (Griffiths and Steyvers, 2004). These approaches leant themselves to modular inference and so, many variants of LDA were designed. For a summary of applications of LDA, see Blei (2012) and Boyd-Graber, Hu, and Mimno (2017), which are brief and monograph-length, respectively.

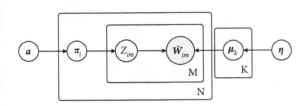

Figure 13.1. Plate diagram for the Latent Dirichlet Allocation model. Note that unlike the mixture model in Figure 12.2 there is an inner plate that indexes the individual tokens. This allows each token to have its own topic, while π is now a vector indicating the fraction of assignment the document has to each topic.

mixed-membership topic models like LDA. Under the mixed membership model, we can characterize a document well even if we have never seen another one like it, as long as we have seen its constituent components. Thus as long as there are other documents about gardening and other documents about presidential politics, the LDA model will be able to explain a lone document about the White House's garden well. This is possible because both gardening and presidential politics have specialized vocabularies. By contrast, in a single-membership model, such a lone document would likely be assigned to a cluster either about presidential politics or about gardening. Both clusters would fit the document poorly.

13.1.1 INFERENCE

As with other probabilistic models, the general strategy is to specify a data generating process and then use inference to reverse engineer what the parameters are likely to have been from the data. The complexity of the model with LDA means that inference is quite challenging, and there are three broad strategies: collapsed Gibbs sampling methods, variational approximations, and method of moments estimators. We don't have the space to discuss these in detail, but wanted to emphasize that the different approaches can actually yield quite different results.

13.1.2 EXAMPLE: DISCOVERING CREDIT CLAIMING FOR FIRE GRANTS IN CONGRESSIONAL PRESS RELEASES

In this section, we provide an example of how LDA can help to facilitate a novel discovery. We run an LDA topic model on all Senate press releases from Grimmer (2010)—72,631 press releases from over 100 senators. We removed stop words, stemmed, and removed punctuation and numbers. Using the topicmodels package in R (Grün and Hornik, 2011), we estimated a 40-topic LDA. We optimized the model using variational EM.[2]

For each topic, Table 13.1 shows the ten words with the highest probability in that topic. Immediately, we recognize familiar topics—from food and product safety (Topic 10) to immigration (Topic 16) and education (Topic 28). As Grimmer (2010) did, to use these topics, we would go through each, read representative documents, and label them with a category name.

Even this simple topic model of Congressional press releases can show how an inductive approach to research can lead researchers in new directions and help them uncover

---

[2] Parts of this section are draw from Grimmer, Roberts, and Stewart (2021).

Table 13.1. Most probable words of forty topics from Senate press releases from Grimmer (2010).

	Topic 1	Topic 2	Topic 3	Topic 4	Topic 5	Topic 6	Topic 7	Topic 8	Topic 9	Topic 10
1	secur	mikulski	court	right	letter	transport	fire	water	research	safeti
2	govern	lincoln	judg	cantwel	secretari	fund	depart	project	health	inform
3	feder	nation	senat	internet	state	project	grant	land	diseas	food
4	social	base	justic	elect	concern	airport	firefight	river	cancer	fda
5	account	pryor	nomin	vote	depart	million	program	fund	cell	requir
6	report	maryland	law	public	report	improv	fund	agricultur	medic	consum
7	contract	arkansa	attorney	nation	request	$	safeti	farm	care	protect
8	investig	said	committe	park	administr	citi	award	million	stem	product
9	taxpay	commiss	presid	access	propos	feder	assist	protect	prevent	act
10	privat	brac	leahi	communic	plan	new	equip	state	hatch	drug

	Topic 11	Topic 12	Topic 13	Topic 14	Topic 15	Topic 16	Topic 17	Topic 18	Topic 19	Topic 20
1	militari	tax	presid	veteran	nation	secur	harkin	bill	disast	trade
2	guard	health	american	murray	honor	border	iowa	senat	assist	market
3	servic	insur	bush	va	american	immigr	offic	legisl	hurrican	u.
4	nation	busi	work	care	day	homeland	school	act	emerg	industri
5	member	care	senat	affair	year	port	academi	amend	feder	product
6	famili	small	statement	health	famili	state	alaska	committe	state	china
7	defens	cost	democrat	servic	work	nation	talent	pass	obama	manufactur
8	health	famili	today	washington	world	illeg	site	hous	katrina	chambliss
9	mental	state	need	reed	histori	enforc	sen	vote	durbin	agreement
10	soldier	year	republican	island	serv	depart	high	provis	fema	isakson

	Topic 21	Topic 22	Topic 23	Topic 24	Topic 25	Topic 26	Topic 27	Topic 28	Topic 29	Topic 30
1	dakota	energi	snow	fund	new	drug	coleman	children	intellig	iraq
2	north	oil	main	$	schumer	medicar	minnesota	educ	nuclear	war
3	johnson	fuel	collin	million	clinton	senior	colorado	school	nation	troop
4	dorgan	price	lautenberg	budget	york	prescript	salazar	student	unit	iraqi
5	idaho	gas	coast	program	develop	medicaid	nelson	program	state	forc
6	south	renew	jersey	year	busi	montana	sen	colleg	terrorist	presid
7	said	increas	new	billion	scienc	plan	allard	state	world	militari
8	conrad	nation	state	cut	econom	program	beef	child	secur	secur
9	craig	product	olympia	presid	research	burn	robert	provid	foreign	american
10	contact	reduc	menendez	increas	technolog	baucus	said	help	weapon	polit

	Topic 31	Topic 32	Topic 33	Topic 34	Topic 35	Topic 36	Topic 37	Topic 38	Topic 39	Topic 40
1	law	worker	million	one	hous	loan	health	lugar	nevada	texa
2	enforc	employ	defens	peopl	domenici	hear	fund	bayh	kerri	sen
3	crime	job	system	go	new	committe	$	indiana	de	alexand
4	program	work	air	can	mexico	bank	center	u.	reid	tennesse
5	shelbi	wage	develop	us	communiti	financi	communiti	unit	ensign	cornyn
6	state	employe	militari	time	bingaman	rate	rural	state	los	hutchison
7	justic	labor	fund	know	program	chairman	program	intern	john	graham
8	email	kennedi	forc	say	develop	feingold	servic	darfur	la	frist
9	fund	year	$	just	levin	mortgag	counti	govern	el	senat
10	polic	minimum	technolog	think	$	home	provid	brownback	las	press

unexpected, but substantively important, political dynamics. Consider Topic 7, with most probable words such as "fire," "depart," and "grant." Using a topic model called the "Expressed Agenda Model" to this same set of press releases, Grimmer (2010) discovered this same category of press releases about fire departments, often referring to announcements of grants related to fire departments. No conceptualization of Congressional speech had ever proposed this as a relevant category of speech, but Grimmer was able to validate this category as referring to a real program called the Assistance to Firefighters Grant Program (AFGP), and that classification of press releases into this category was surprisingly accurate. Grimmer (2010) found that approximately 2% of press releases related to this grant program.

The topic model reveals a new and interesting group of press releases, but the next question is—why were there so many fire department press releases issued by senators around the country? After replicating the finding in House press releases, Grimmer, Westwood, and Messing (2014) decided to learn more about the origins of fire department grant press releases. Their first finding only increased the intrigue: the AFGP was designed to be impervious to Congressional influence, with grants awarded on a competitive basis. If members of Congress had no influence over the grants, why were they claiming credit for them? To find out how, Grimmer, Westwood, and Messing (2014) interviewed agency officials. One official unraveled the mystery. She explained that the agency alerted Congressional officials about the grants before the official agency announcement, creating an opportunity for elected officials to receive credit for the grants. And Grimmer, Westwood, and Messing (2014) confirmed this pattern in the aggregate using their press release data and information about the timing of AFGP announcements.

This led to a new and deeper question: if legislators couldn't influence the allocation of the grants how could they claim credit for the allocation of funds? Grimmer, Westwood, and Messing (2014) discovered legislators use *implicature* to receive credit: they imply that they are responsible for the grant, without ever literally claiming credit for the spending. Time and again in the fire department press releases legislators "announce" new money to the district and speak in broad terms about how they would keep fighting for funding like this. This is in contrast to credit claiming for expenditures legislators are directly responsible for, where they explain that they were able to "secure" funding for the district directly. Finally, Grimmer, Westwood, and Messing (2014) show that this is an effective strategy with constituents. In an experiment they showed that when legislators imply they deserved credit they received credit, but when they explained their actual contribution, constituents were reluctant to reward the elected officials.

This example shows the power of being explicitly inductive in our work. Rather than expecting their hypotheses to be present beforehand, Grimmer, Westwood, and Messing (2014) assembled evidence inductively, learning about the phenomenon—implicature—under study. Where appropriate, they applied more deductive approaches—such as an experiment to assess the effect of implicature.

13.2 Interpreting the Output of Topic Models

Similarly to clustering methods, LDA is an extremely powerful tool for suggesting new organizations of documents. And just like clustering methods, LDA can be strongly dependent upon arbitrary tuning parameters and the choice of inference method. But this variation can be useful. Recall that when using LDA for discovery we are primarily

Table 13.2. Titles of five randomly selected press releases with over 0.20 of Topic 7 related to fire grants.

	Topic 7 Example Titles
1	Shelby Announces over $102,000 for Fulton Volunteer Fire Department in Clarke County
2	Schumer Announces Four Finger Lakes Region Fire Departments Will Receive Over $280,000 In Federal Fire Grants
3	Senators Stabenow, Levin Announce a 23 Million Grant for Lansing to Help Emergency Personal Communicate During a Crisis
4	Poland Receives Firefighting Grant Through Sen. Dewine Bill
5	Pickrell Rural Fire Department Receives $123,840 from FEMA for a New Firefighting Vehicle

interested in learning new ways of seeing our documents. Even if there is variability across runs of the algorithm, so long as it provides a single useful way to look at the data, the model has been useful.

In order to understand the organizations the model suggests, we can adapt methods we used to label and interpret the output of clustering models to label the topics. In the next part we describe several ways to compare the output of topic models and to assess their performance as measurement models. When making that assessment, our goal is to assess their ability to credibly organize documents according to a particular organization. We can, however, make slight modifications to the procedures we used to validate the output of clustering methods to interpret the output of topic models. There are two primary methods that we recommend: careful reading of exemplar texts and quantitative procedures for identifying words that distinguish particular topics.

When labeling the output from clustering methods, one approach we recommend is to closely read a random sample of texts assigned to a cluster. We make a similar recommendation with topic models, though we have to adopt a slight modification because documents have partial membership in all categories. One approach is to select documents that have a large share assigned to a particular category. Specifically, we select a small subset of the documents with the highest proportion of the document assigned to the particular category under consideration. We can then read those documents to assess their common facets and to interrogate whether a particular organization makes sense. We can also sample documents such that documents with a higher share allocated to a category are more likely to be selected. For example, we might set the probability of selecting any one document as $\hat{\pi}_{ik} = \frac{\pi_{ik}}{\sum_{\ell=1}^{N} \pi_{\ell k}}$. This has the advantage of ensuring we select a variety of documents, but has the disadvantage of potentially selecting documents with little relationship to the category we are attempting to understand.

For example, Table 13.2 show the titles of five randomly selected press releases with over 0.20 loading on Topic 7, the fire department grant. Each of these five gives us a sense of the nature of Topic 7, and some ideas of how the members of Congress are using implicature to claim credit for the grants themselves.

Just like with clustering methods, we can identify words that are indicative of a particular topic, as we did in Table 13.1. The most straightforward method for obtaining these words is to select the highest probability words in each topic. While this is certainly useful, selecting the top words can obscure the distinctive features of a particular topic.

This is because there may be some words that have a high probability across topics because they are common. We explain in Section 13.5 below how to use methods for identifying separating words.

Another similarity that topic models have with clustering methods is that determining the number of topics to include in the model can be a vexing challenge. It is impossible to determine the number of topics without knowing more about the specific application of the topic model in mind. This is because topic models of differing granularity can lead us to different sorts of insights.

13.3 Incorporating Structure into LDA

Topic models build on a basic hierarchy within the data. At the top of the hierarchy there is a population-level Dirichlet distribution that characterizes the distribution of topics for the documents in the corpus. Every document's mixture of topics is drawn from this same distribution. Then, conditional on the document's mixture of topics, topic labels for each word are drawn. These topic labels are used to determine which topic-specific multinomial distribution is used to draw the actual word.

Part of what makes these approaches particularly appealing for discovery is that they require relatively little information from the analyst up front about the collection. However, social scientists often have considerably more information about their documents that they encode as metadata, document-level variables, which describe additional information about the document such as its author, venue, or date of publication. A common pattern in social science research is that researchers want to explore the way the *prevalence* of a topic varies with the metadata. For example, Catalinac (2016*b*) examines how the content of Japanese party manifestos change over time, and DiMaggio, Nag, and Blei (2013) examine how different newspapers over time frame government funding for the arts. Grimmer (2010) argues that senators adopt a presentational style that informs the topics they emphasize in their press releases. To measure this presentational style, Grimmer (2010) builds new information about a document's author into the topic model. In a different model, Quinn et al. (2010) examine the prevalence of topics in Senate debates. They argue that there is a temporal dependence across topics. They build a model that incorporates time, supposing that the topics in the US Senate evolve smoothly, with the prior day's topic informing the next day's topic distribution.

Alternatively, we might suppose that characteristics about who is speaking could inform the *content* of the topic. For example, in the United States we might expect that Republicans and Democrats would share vocabulary, but might discuss the same issue—such as tax policy—differently (Monroe, Colaresi, and Quinn, 2008; Gentzkow, Shapiro, and Taddy, 2019). Of course, incorporating information to examine how texts with different metadata discuss the same topic requires addressing a challenging conceptual issue: are texts that differ in their metadata discussing *different versions of the same* topic or are they discussing fundamentally *different* topics. This is challenging, because there is no bright-line difference between two people discussing the same topic with different information and two people discussing different topics. To navigate these issues, researchers need to exercise caution when including covariates to examine differences in topic discussion.

Incorporating metadata information into the topic model estimation itself can serve multiple distinct purposes. In the context of mixed-membership topic models, Mimno and McCallum (2008) introduce a useful distinction between *upstream* covariate models and *downstream* covariate models. Each has a different goal, with *upstream* covariates serving to model a particular structure in order to improve our topics' inter-pretability and estimate an association with topics. *Downstream* covariate models are specifically designed to generate topics that are predictive of the covariate.

13.3.1 STRUCTURE WITH UPSTREAM, KNOWN PREVALENCE COVARIATES

In upstream prevalence covariate topic models, we replace the global prior (α) of LDA for the document-topic proportions (π_i) with a document-specific prior formed as a function of document-level covariates (X_i). The "upstream" name comes from the plate diagram, where the covariates are in an area of the graph such that following the flow of the arrows downstream leads to the document-topic proportions. In practice this means that upstream covariate models allow for information to be shared, but unlike the downstream covariate models we will talk about below, the topics are not trying to explain the covariates.

Some of the earliest extensions to the original LDA model were upstream covariate models, including organizing documents by author (Rosen-Zvi et al., 2004) or time (Blei and Lafferty, 2006). This general approach also characterized the early approaches in social science (Quinn et al., 2010; Grimmer, 2010). Further extensions have generalized these specific types of covariates to more arbitrary covariates (Mimno and McCallum, 2008; Roberts et al., 2013).

Upstream covariates primarily help to fit topic models when the documents are short. Short documents are particularly vexing for topic models, because they rely upon the correlation between words to estimate topics. Long documents give the opportu-nity to observe the correlation between lots of different words—when we are expressing ideas many different ways, we tend to use different but related words to articulate our thoughts. In short documents, though, we do not have the opportunity to observe those correlations. And as a result, there is a risk that two documents about ostensibly similar topics could be viewed as very distinct.

Upstream covariate models help solve this problem by enabling the model to "borrow strength" from documents that have similar covariates through the prior. These covari-ates can therefore act as a bridge to link documents that use similar words that perhaps would be grouped together if individuals were forced to write longer documents. As individual document lengths tend toward infinity though, the data overwhelms the prior and the estimate of the topics for a given document is driven only by the words it contains. Of course, as documents become extremely long, it becomes more appealing to break them up into smaller chunks so that individual co-occurences become more meaningful. Topic models that induce a hierarchical structure like upstream covariate models can then be used to aggregate back to the true quantity of interest.

13.3.2 STRUCTURE WITH UPSTREAM, KNOWN CONTENT COVARIATES

Covariates can also be used to shape the topical *content* of the model. These models allow the topic-specific distribution of words to vary by time (Blei and Lafferty, 2006), geography (Eisenstein et al., 2010), ideological affiliation (Ahmed and Xing, 2010), or an arbitrary categorical covariate (Eisenstein et al., 2010; Roberts et al., 2013). Using a content covariate model essentially creates multiple versions of each topic, one for each level of the content covariate. These are constrained either by sparsity in the deviations between the different versions of the topic (Eisenstein et al., 2010; Roberts et al., 2014) or through a smoothness assumption such as continuity through time (Blei and Lafferty,

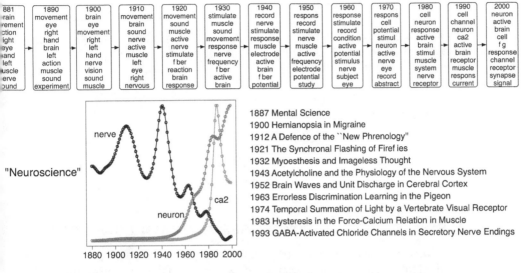

Figure 13.2. This figure from Blei and Lafferty (2006) shows one of a set of topics learned from articles in the journal *Science*. The figure traces the change in the topical content of the neuroscience topic over time.

2006). Evolution in time is demonstrated in Figure 13.2, which reprints an example from Blei and Lafferty (2006)'s study of the journal *Science*. The figure shows the neuroscience topic evolving from having most probable words like brain, movement, and action to having most probable words neuron, brain, and synapse. This provides a powerful insight into how the scholarly discourse about neuroscience evolved over time.

Topical content models can be powerful when we want to understand the differences in language use between different subpopulations who are talking about the same thing but using slightly different words. For example, Republicans might use the phrase "death tax" while Democrats use the phrase "estate tax," even though they are referencing the same set of issues. Even when the differences in language use are not the primary quantity of interest, these models can be helpful for marginalizing out a difference that is not the main quantity of interest. For example, Lucas et al. (2015) show that content covariates can be useful when working with multilingual text collections. Their idea is to machine translate to a common language and then use a content covariate indicating the language to marginalize out idiosyncracies in translation.

However, it is worth emphasizing that content covariates produce a much more substantial change to the model than prevalence covariates. This change can pose the risk that topics become incomparable with each other. For example, in Blei and Lafferty (2006)'s study of the journal *Science*, the researchers do not specify ex ante that they want to study neuroscience; the topic is discovered from the data. However, the topic fit in 2000 is very different from the topic as fit in 1881. What connects these topics is the continuity from decade to decade. In this case, the topic has evolved in a way that makes sense, but the analyst must be careful that the variations on a single topic introduced by the model don't become incomparable.[3] Sometimes this problem will be quite

---

[3] In the case of this particular model, the degree to which topics can evolve is strongly influenced by the variance parameter on the random walk over time. When the variance parameter is too large, topics will evolve into unrelated topics.

Figure 13.3. A plate diagram for a downstream covariate model. The parameters θ control the distribution of the labeled outcome y_i, which is predicted using the token-level topic indicators z.

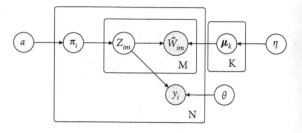

obvious, but whether two different variations of a topic are the same topic conceptually is a thorny question that does not have an obvious resolution.

13.3.3 STRUCTURE WITH DOWNSTREAM, KNOWN COVARIATES

In a downstream covariate model (see Figure 13.3), the covariate is generated from the individual token latent variable placing it downstream of the topic proportions. This forces the topics to explain both the words *and* the covariate value for a given document. These models thus serve two distinct purposes, which are fundamentally different from upstream covariate models: maximizing predictive performance and projecting words and covariates into a common space.

To motivate the predictive performance case, imagine that we want to predict the number of stars that a movie reviewer gives to a movie (y_i) on the basis of a representation of the text of the review ($W_{i,}$). The hope, for example in the original LDA paper (Blei, Ng, and Jordan, 2003), was that topics from the LDA model would be good features for use in a classifier. In practice, they often were not. While the topics learned by LDA (π_i) were good predictors of the words actually used, they weren't necessarily good predictors of our outcome of interest y_i. This is the problem Mcauliffe and Blei (2008) addressed by introducing Supervised LDA (sLDA). Their insight was that by placing the variable we want to predict, y_i downstream of the topics, the topics are forced to explain both $W_{i,}$ and y_i. For a new document we can use the observed words to infer π_i and then use π_i to predict the outcome y_i.[4] Thus including the downstream covariate helps ensure that the topics will be good predictors, an idea that will recur in Chapter 26.

In the case of sLDA we typically have a low-dimensional variable y that we ultimately want to predict and the high-dimensional words W. We can also have a high-dimensional y that we want to project into a common space with the words. A common use case is where y are votes in a political institution and $W_{i,}$ is the representation of text from political actors. For example, we might consider bills before Congress and their votes (Gerrish and Blei, 2012; Kim, Londregan, and Ratkovic, 2018) or Supreme Court opinions and votes (Lauderdale and Clark, 2014). These models project both the votes and the text into a common space, which can be an effective way to make use of data from multiple sources, both of which we believe inform the underlying measure.

---

[4]In practice we are actually using a function of the token-level variables Z because in practice it performs better. When π_i is predicting y_i it can become too disconnected from the words themselves (Mcauliffe and Blei, 2008).

13.3.4 ADDITIONAL SOURCES OF STRUCTURE

We have focused above on document-level covariate information, but there are other ways to incorporate substantive knowledge into discovery models. When information is available about the topics such that they are sparse (Wang and Blei, 2009; Williamson et al., 2010), have a hierarchical structure (Li and McCallum, 2006; Paisley et al., 2015), contain certain preferred connections between words (Andrzejewski, Zhu, and Craven, 2009), or are based on particular keywords (Magnusson et al., 2018; Eshima, Imai, and Sasaki, 2020), we can integrate this into our model. We can also use interactive human feedback as a source of information when it is available (Vikram and Dasgupta, 2016). Hu et al. (2014) introduce an approach to interactive topic model where an analyst is presented with an organization of the text and can provide feedback with the model being quickly refit on the fly.

An alternative approach seeks to use a second layer of modeling in order to group like-minded texts together. For example, Grimmer (2013a) introduces a model where senators are clustered according to their attention to topics, and Blaydes, Grimmer, and McQueen (2018) cluster topics based on their linguistic similarity. When applied to topic prevalence, this approach can be helpful to both identify substantively interesting groups and to borrow strength from across similar documents. When applied to topics, this approach can help mitigate some of the concerns with specifying the number of topics, enabling the simultaneous measurement of granular and coarse topics. We say that the covariates are discovered here, because the clustering procedure is equivalent to stratifying on a particular set of covariates, but with the covariates inferred during the estimation process.

13.4 Structural Topic Models

The previous section discussed many ways in which structure can be added to topic models, yet for many years there were few general purpose implementations that were accessible to practitioners. The Structural Topic Model (STM, Roberts, Stewart, and Airoldi, 2016) offers a way to incorporate quite general upstream metadata that can affect both topic prevalence and content.[5] To introduce the STM, suppose that for each unit i we have a set of P covariates X_i^p that will be used to explain the topic prevalence and a separate set of P' covariates X_i^c that explains topical content. With this set of covariates we are able to specify the revised data generating process. Suppose the documents are generated according to the following hierarchical model:

$$\gamma_k \sim \text{Normal}_P(0, \sigma^2 I_P)$$
$$\pi_i \sim \text{LogisticNormal}_{K-1}(\Gamma'(X_i^p)', \Sigma)$$

---

[5]STM is a generalization and combination of three prior models. Blei and Lafferty (2007) introduced the correlated topic model, which introduced the logistic normal prior as an alternative to the Dirichlet, which allowed a wider range of topic correlations. Mimno and McCallum (2008) introduced a quick general infrastructure for prevalence covariates using a parameterization of the Dirichlet prior on the document loadings. Eisenstein, Ahmed, and Xing (2011) introduced a general way to include content covariates through sparse deviations due to topics, covariates and their interactions. Several improvements in estimation were also essential to making computation feasible and effective (Khan and Bouchard, 2009; Arora et al., 2013; Wang and Blei, 2013). The STM model was introduced in a non-archival paper in Roberts et al. (2013), and the first application was published in Roberts et al. (2014). Roberts, Stewart, and Airoldi (2016) describe the model in full for a statistical audience. Key to the applied use of the model is the implementation in R, stm (Roberts, Stewart, and Tingley, 2019), which, despite the publication date, was released in 2014.

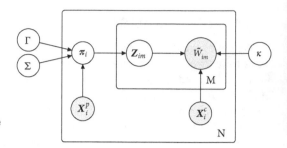

Figure 13.4. The plate diagram for the
Structural Topic Model.

$$Z_{im} \sim \text{Multinomial}_K(\pi_i)$$

$$\tilde{W}_{im} \sim \text{Multinomial}_J(\mu_c Z_{im})$$

$$\mu_{ckj} = \frac{\exp(\kappa_j^{(0)} + \kappa_{kj}^{(t)} + \kappa_{X^c j}^{(c)} + \kappa_{X^c kj}^{(\text{int})})}{\sum_j \exp(\kappa_j^{(0)} + \kappa_{kj}^{(t)} + \kappa_{X^c j}^{(c)} + \kappa_{X^c kj}^{(\text{int})})},$$

where Γ is a $P \times (K-1)$ is a matrix of coefficients for the topic prevalence model and $\{\kappa_{..}^{(t)}, \kappa_{..}^{(c)}, \kappa_{..}^{(\text{int})}\}$ describe a set of rate deviations for topics, covariates, topic-covariate interactions (respectively) from the overall distribution of the vocabulary within the corpus denoted by $\kappa^{(0)}$, and $W_i = \sum_{m=1}^{M_i} \tilde{W}_{im}$. The key idea is that each κ incorporates how the use of a word varies across a set of covariates, how the use of a feature varies with the prevalence of a topic, and how the two interact for a particular topic. This provides a flexible method for measuring the presence/absence of a topic.

STM, then, enables researchers to encode the ways topic prevalence and content varies across documents based on the document's characteristics, or metadata. Figure 13.4 provides the plate diagram. The topic prevalence covariates inform our estimate of the prominence of topics in documents, while the topic content covariates alter how the topics are discussed. In practice, most uses of STM don't use the content covariates, and so the topics are treated much as they are in LDA.

There are several reasons that including covariates can be helpful for the discovery process. Roberts, Stewart, and Airoldi (2016) show that including covariates helps STM identify more substantively interesting topics that are also more stable when there are few documents or a limited vocabulary. Figure 13.4 helps clarify the technical reason why STM can improve the topics that are discovered and the measured prevalence of those topics in documents. The prior on the document's topics enables the model to borrow information across documents to improve the estimation of topic prevalence. Without including covariates the model aggregates all the documents together into one prior, borrowing equal information across documents. Including covariates, however, enables the model to borrow information from documents with similar values of the covariates. Heuristically, this helps the model identify better topics, particularly when the included covariates explain linguistic differences.

While covariates are quite likely to be useful when using topic model for discovery, they are not a panacea for issues that might remain. As Figure 13.4 shows, when we include covariates in our model we are far removed from the text of topic models. And in modeling procedures, as we move away from the text, there is less that the covariates will be able to do to improve upon the model fit, because the borrowing of strength will matter less relative to the information in the data.

It is also possible to do a straightforward two-step approximation of the STM model. If researchers are solely interested in using topic models to describe substantive variation, they can first run an LDA model. Then, using the output from that model, they can regress the topic prevalence π_i on the document's covariates X_i. In the limit of document length and number of documents, this will provide the same differences as STM, but may sacrifice some added advantages from borrowing information.

13.4.1 EXAMPLE: DISCOVERING THE COMPONENTS OF RADICAL DISCOURSE

Karell and Freedman (2019) use the Structural Topic Model to discover themes of radical discourse that are common across radical organizations. They examine a corpus of over 23,000 pages of magazines, newspapers, speeches, and pamphlets written by radical groups in Afghanistan, Iran, and Pakistan in the second part of the twentieth century, looking to discover common rhetorical themes across these groups. Their data ranges from 1979 to 2001, covering 22 different radical groups.

While the purpose of Karell and Freedman (2019)'s study is to engage in inductive discovery of new themes, it is not free of existing theory. Instead of purely inductive, they describe their approach as "computational abductive analysis," drawing on the qualitative method of abductive analysis (Tavory and Timmermans, 2014). In contrast with grounded theory, abductive analysis generates theory based on surprising evidence that contrasts with existing theories (Timmermans and Tavory, 2012). Therefore, before analyzing their data, Karell and Freedman (2019) summarized what they viewed as current conception of radical rhetoric—"we surmised that radical discourse is commonly understood as directed outward: radicals attack powerful individuals, organizations, ideas, and ways of life in their society, but outside of their immediate community and network of supporters."

After translating their documents to English, the authors then use STM to discover topics and themes within the documents, being careful to identify any topics that diverged from previous conceptions of radical rhetoric. They then use the most probable words in each topic and most representative documents to label each of the eight topics provided by the output of the model. Karell and Freedman (2019) then identify five of the eight topics that reflect current conceptions of radical rhetoric, which they call externally oriented radicalism, or "Radicalism of Subversion."

But within their topical analysis, they also discover that two of the other topics—which they label "Local & Education Markets" and "Religious Code"—are not inwardly facing, but externally facing. Reading these documents closely, they group these topics into a larger concept that they call "Radicalism of Reversion," or efforts to change the internal workings of the group. Reading about religious and social movements elsewhere, they recognize this idea as useful in explaining a wide range of behavior of groups even outside of their study. Thus, they conclude that this could be a potentially new and useful concept for studying the rhetorics of radical groups globally.

13.5 Labeling Topic Models

Labeling topic models is ultimately quite similar to labeling clusters as discussed in Chapter 12—it is ultimately a human activity that includes a combination of careful reading and automated heuristics. However, there is always interest in more automated approaches to labeling topic models, if only to provide an initial view for discovery purposes. We think of these techniques as existing along a continuum anchored by two

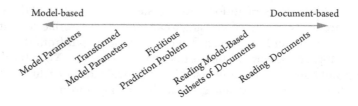

Figure 13.5. A spectrum of labeling methods that range from model-based to document-based.

extremes (Figure 13.5): model-based approaches, which use the parameters of the topic model itself, and document-based approaches that involve reading documents selected completely at random and using those readings to inform the labels.

Model-based approaches are usually easier to use and more "automatic" but typically leverage strong assumptions in the model, which may not reflect the real-world text well. Document-based approaches involve reading the original documents, which make them more difficult and costly to employ; however, by avoiding dependence on the model, these approaches are often central to understanding what the topic model is doing.

On the far left of Figure 13.5 is the most straightforward strategy for interpreting what the topics mean—directly using model parameters. The parameters μ tell us the probability of each word type given that the token is generated by a given topic. Directly reading off the most likely words can be effective, but it will tend to favor words that are very common overall, not just common in the cluster. Language is often filled with words that are extremely common, but not very discriminating in terms of meaning. Topic models have to represent these words but they co-occur with everything and are thus often spread across the topics somewhat evenly.

One way of dealing with this problem is to remove the frequent and uninformative words at the outset of the modeling, as we discussed back in Chapter 5. But even when we remove stop words from a preset list, there are often corpus-specific words that are highly frequent but relatively uninformative.

As an alternative, we can transform the model parameters to try to create a more informative summary. Roberts, Stewart, and Tingley (2019) propose one metric based on the earlier work of Bischof and Airoldi (2012) and Airoldi and Bischof (2016) called FREX. FREX captures both the **Fr**equency and **Ex**clusivity of the words associated with a given topic by using the weighted harmonic mean between the frequency of a word within a cluster as well as exclusivity to the cluster (both functions of the parameters under the model). By penalizing words that are frequent but not exclusive to the cluster, we get a better picture of what the clusters are about and what separates them even though the underlying model has not changed.

Ultimately the best approach is to label using many different approaches and use the combination of different words to get the best sense of the topic. This can be combined with words generated through a fictitious prediction problem approach (Chapter 11). Regardless, it is important to carefully read the documents.

13.6 Conclusion

In this chapter we covered topic models, a generalization of the clustering models from Chapter 12. In clustering, every document has to be represented by a single cluster, and thus a single distribution over words. In topic models, every document has a mixed membership representation, which means that each document can have a completely unique distribution over words, but one that is constrained to be a weighted combination of the topics. We also discussed how the canonical LDA model can be generalized with covariate information that allows for information to be shared effectively across documents and topics.

Of course, the approaches we describe aren't the only way to model topical information in documents. Topic models represent documents as a weighted combination of topics, but there are also approaches that use nonnegative—but otherwise unconstrained—weights (Lee and Seung, 2001), multiple membership, where any of a series of topics can be turned on or off (Griffiths and Ghahramani, 2011), and topics represented as paths down a tree (Paisley et al., 2015). The models we have considered also mostly have a relatively simple additive structure to the way that topics generate words. A limitation of this kind of model is that the model is unable to predict or adequately explain a document that is more extreme than the individual topics.[6] In practice this means that while a document can be represented by multiple topics, the topics cannot interact to produce a more precise prediction given by their overlap. If we have a model of scholarly disciplines and we represent a document as a mixture of the "humanities" and "computer science," we cannot get a higher probability of the phrase "digital humanities" than either of the original topics would give alone.

This concern can be avoided by foregoing the latent additive model structure to allow for interactions of topics to take on their own unique meanings (Salakhutdinov and Hinton, 2009; Larochelle and Lauly, 2012; Paul and Dredze, 2012; Gan et al., 2015; Ranganath et al., 2015). These models are much more flexible than any of the topic models we have discussed here and consequently can achieve much higher predictive accuracy on held-out text. However, this flexibility also makes them correspondingly more difficult to interpret. To continue our example above, consider examining the "computer science" topic from an LDA model using the words that are most probable under that topic. Under the model, these words will always have high probability for any document with a large "computer science" component. Under the multiplicative latent variable models, the high probability words are contingent on the interaction between all the topics present in a document. This is a fantastic amount of expressive power, but also makes it very difficult to contemplate how one would easily evaluate all those interactions.

This potential trade-off of flexibility and interpretability is particularly relevant in models for discovery. We can always add more complexity—for example, modeling word order or allowing interactions between topics—but we need to ensure that we can still easily recognize the discovery or it won't be that useful to us. Topic models seem to be popular in the social sciences in large part because they strike the balance well. They are more complex than clustering models, but the simple additive structure and the proportional membership representation help keep interpretation tractable.

In the next chapter we consider the final set of methods for discovery—document embeddings. These methods focus on projecting documents into an unconstrained but very low-dimensional space and are often helpful for visualization.

---

[6] Any convex combination lies on the interior of the convex hull. This means the document representation in a model like LDA cannot predict a word distribution that is sharper than the individual topics.

CHAPTER 14

Low-Dimensional Document Embeddings

We can use text as data methods to facilitate discovery by distilling the contents of texts and then using that distillation to learn about a way to organize documents. Thus far we have considered two forms of organization: partitions where documents are assigned to one cluster or admixtures where documents are assigned proportional membership in a set of topics. In this chapter we consider a third approach—low-dimensional document embedding (also sometimes called scaling). These methods place each document within a low-dimensional space (usually only one to three dimensions), which makes them well suited to visualization.

Like many of the other methods that we consider in Discovery, there is an inherent ambiguity in the application of the methods that comes from the goal being underspecified. Broadly speaking, our goal is to approximate the high-dimensional complexity of language with a low-dimensional embedding that captures the salient features of language. Unfortunately that leaves ambiguous what it means to capture the content of language well and thus how we might adjudicate across different solutions.

Scaling is notable relative to other methods in that the dimensionality of the latent representation is customarily much lower than for clustering or topic models. We consider two canonical workhorse approaches to scaling: Principal Component Analysis and Classical Multidimensional Scaling. We then conclude both the chapter and the Discovery part with a brief discussion of other approaches to discovery.

14.1 Principal Component Analysis

The goal in Principal Component Analysis (PCA) is to discover a small set of underlying latent features—the principal components—that we will use to approximate the higher-dimensional data. PCA is a common method of analyzing all kinds of data, not just text.

For simplicity, we will consider a representation of the documents closely related to the bag of words approach—the centered bag of words. We take the original bag of words and we subtract the average number of times each word appears in each column. Thus a value of 2 for word j in document i now indicates that the word is used two additional times than the average rate of use across all documents. To keep notation simple for this section we will refer to the centered vector for each document as $W_i = (W_{i1}, W_{i2}, \ldots, W_{iJ})$. Given a matrix W of these centered vectors, we will attempt to approximate each document with a set of K principal components ($k = 1, \ldots, K$). Each principal component is a $J \times 1$ vector $\mu_k = (\mu_{k1}, \mu_{k2}, \ldots, \mu_{kJ})$ that provides information on the rate of use for each word associated with that component. For each observation i we will suppose that there are K *scores* on the principal components. We will call the $K \times 1$ vector of scores for the ith observation $\boldsymbol{\pi}_i = (\pi_{i1}, \pi_{i2}, \ldots, \pi_{iK})$. Using the scores and the principal components, we will write each observation $\boldsymbol{W}_{i,}$ as,

$$\boldsymbol{W}_{i,} = \underbrace{\pi_{i1}\boldsymbol{\mu}_1 + \pi_{i2}\boldsymbol{\mu}_2 + \ldots + \pi_{iK}\boldsymbol{\mu}_K}_{\hat{\boldsymbol{W}}_{i,}} + \overbrace{\boldsymbol{\epsilon}_i}^{\text{error}}, \tag{14.1.1}$$

where the $J \times 1$ vector $\boldsymbol{\epsilon}_i = (\epsilon_{i1}, \epsilon_{i2}, \ldots, \epsilon_{iJ})$ is an error term and $\hat{\boldsymbol{W}}_{i,}$ is the approximation of $\boldsymbol{W}_{i,}$. Notice that the scores $\boldsymbol{\pi}$ stretch, shrink, or flip the principal components in order to approximate the particular observation. Because K is smaller than J, there will necessarily be some error in this approximation.

The goal in estimation is to choose $\boldsymbol{\pi}$ and $\boldsymbol{\mu}$ to minimize the magnitude of the error. That is, we will choose $\boldsymbol{\pi}$ and $\boldsymbol{\mu}$ to minimize

$$f(\boldsymbol{\pi}, \boldsymbol{\mu}) = \frac{1}{N} \sum_{i=1}^{N} \boldsymbol{\epsilon}_i' \boldsymbol{\epsilon}_i$$

$$= \frac{1}{N} \sum_{i=1}^{N} \left(\boldsymbol{W}_{i,} - \sum_{k=1}^{K} \pi_{ik}\boldsymbol{\mu}_k\right)' \left(\boldsymbol{W}_{i,} - \sum_{k=1}^{K} \pi_{ik}\boldsymbol{\mu}_k\right). \tag{14.1.2}$$

The optimal solution to minimize the magnitude of the error in Equation 14.1.2 is to use the K eigenvectors associated with the largest K eigenvalues of $\boldsymbol{W}'\boldsymbol{W}$ (the empirical variance-covariance matrix) as the K principal components. Further, the score for the ith observation on the kth principal component is $\pi_{ik} = \boldsymbol{\mu}_k' \boldsymbol{W}_{i,}$. For intuition about why the eigenvectors associated with the largest eigenvalues are selected, consider the goal: to explain as much of the variation of the document-term matrix as possible using the small set of principal components. While we avoid appealing too much to linear algebra intuition, those who are familiar with diagonalization results might note that we can better approximate a matrix by first selecting the components of the approximation that are associated with the largest eigenvalues. Therefore, choosing the eigenvectors associated with the largest eigenvalues first enables us to approximate the variance-covariance matrix as well as possible. Alternatively, deriving principal components shows that minimizing the magnitude of the error is equivalent to maximizing the variance of the scores. This is done by choosing the eigenvectors with the largest eigenvalues.

Once we have estimated the principal components and how the documents load on each principal component, we have a distillation of the documents that minimizes the error in the approximation. For purposes of discovery, however, we still need to interpret the output: label the principal components and the scores, and explain what underlying latent concepts the principal components capture. As in cluster analysis methods, we will use both automated and manual methods to understand the principal components and the scores.

14.1.1 AUTOMATED METHODS FOR LABELING PRINCIPAL COMPONENTS

The most direct way to interpret the low-dimensional representation from principal components is to examine the values in each $\boldsymbol{\mu}_k$ that are especially positive or negative. Specifically, we can choose say the ten words with the highest values in $\boldsymbol{\mu}_k$ and the ten words with the most negative values. These words are informative, because they tell us the words that, if present in a document, will lead it to have a particularly negative or positive score on that principal component, π_{ik}. This is because $\pi_{ik} = W'_{i,}\mu_k$, so the entries in μ_k that are particularly large will be particularly influential in determining where a document falls on the spectrum.

Beyond analyzing the principal components directly, we can attempt to predict where documents fall on a spectrum using other information. To do this, we can regress a document's score against other metadata for the document—including characteristics of the author or the document. This approach is particularly useful when using principal component analysis (and related methods) to measure the ideology of authors or their texts. For example, if we believe that a particular principal component measures ideology we might regress the score of authors against a well-validated measure of ideology. In the US context this often involves regressing scores from texts against DW-Nominate scores, the low-dimensional measures of ideological behavior in the US Congress derived from roll call votes (Tausanovitch and Warshaw, 2017). We do encourage one point of caution: low correlations can emerge even if two latent concepts are related. This is because measurement error can be present, dampening the correlations.

14.1.2 MANUAL METHODS FOR LABELING PRINCIPAL COMPONENTS

In addition to the quantitative approaches to labeling documents, we can use the output from principal component models to structure a close reading of the texts and then label the components. To do this, we recommend sampling documents at similar points in the spectrum. Specifically, we might read a sample of documents from the far ends of the spectrum in order to gain a sense of what those documents have in common. Alternatively, rather than deterministically select documents, we can sample documents along the spectrum, weighting documents closer to the endpoints more to ensure that we can gain a sense of why documents are grouped together at particular locations.

Once documents have been read closely, we can then label the ends of the spectrum and get a sense of how the documents vary moving across the spectrum. Reading the documents also provides us with important insights that can be used in refining the conceptualization that we learn from the data.

14.1.3 PRINCIPAL COMPONENT ANALYSIS OF SENATE PRESS RELEASES

We apply PCA to a collection of Senate press releases from Grimmer (2010), covering all the Senate press releases issued in 2005. To analyze the collection of texts, we create a single count vector for all 100 senators who served in 2005. Call document W_i, the 2796×1 normalized count vector of terms for all the press releases from senator i.

We calculate the principal components and the scores for each senator. Figure 14.1 provides two views of the principal components. The left-hand plot orders senators' scores on the first principal component and colors the senators light-gray if Republican and black if Democratic. The left-hand plot shows that there does not appear to be a natural partisan ordering to the observations—in fact there is a great deal of overlap between the two parties. This does not, however, imply that the PCA was worthless. The right-hand plot shows that the first principal component captured a fundamental feature of legislators' communication strategy that Grimmer (2013b) identifies: the

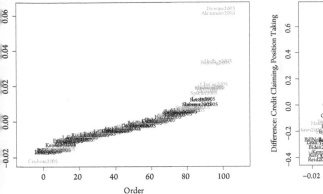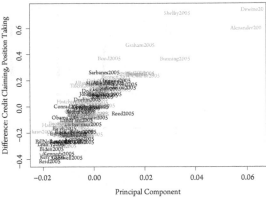

Figure 14.1. PCA applied to the 2005 US Senate press releases.

trade-off between position taking and credit claiming. So, the PCA captures systematic behavioral differences across legislators, but not in a way that might have been easy to anticipate beforehand.

That the PCA is capturing the trade-off between position taking and credit claiming can also be seen from the words with the highest and lowest values on the first principal component. Words with the highest values are depart, grant, program, fund, firefight, million, and award—all words associated with credit claiming. Words with the lowest values are american, court, judg, time, congress, justic, and iraq—all words we might expect to be associated with policy making or position taking.

14.1.4 CHOOSING THE NUMBER OF PRINCIPAL COMPONENTS

So far we have assumed that we know the number of principal components to include in the model. But, of course, one of the most important modeling decisions is determining the number of principal components to include in the model. And just as with clustering methods, we are unable to directly optimize the number of principal components using the model applied to the data. This is because principal component models are greedy: as more principal components are added to the approximation, the better the approximation becomes. Given this greedy behavior, evaluating the model using in-sample fit will yield a trivial solution—that we get the best in-sample approximation when we include as many principal components as entries in the vocabulary. This is not useful for discovery: we already know the number of unique words in our data.

The greedy property of PCA models means that we will have to use other approaches to select the number of components. Numerically, the error that remains in the model is equal to the sum of the excluded eigenvalues. This implies that we can use the size of the eigenvalues to guide our model selection. To see why, consider Figure 14.2. In it, we present data that are ostensibly five-dimensional, but only two dimensions have variance, while the remaining three dimensions are merely small amounts of noise. We can see this in the top left plot with the dimensions where points are clumped together. The top right plot shows that applying PCA we get eigenvalues with two large initial values, while the remaining three are small. And finally, the bottom plot shows the variance that each dimension explains. The first two included eigenvalues explain almost all of the variance, while the remaining three eigenvalues explain little,

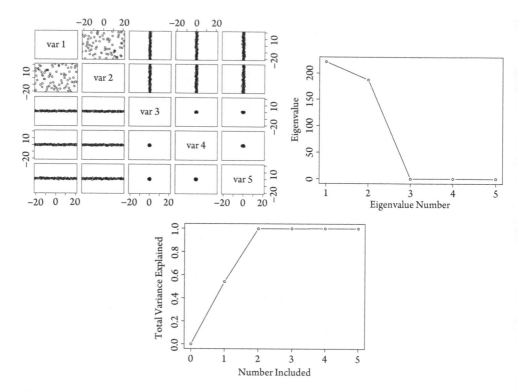

Figure 14.2. Example of using PCA to determine the number of components.

suggesting that our approximation is almost as good whether those dimensions are included or not.

Intuition from the right-hand plot in Figure 14.2 leads to the usual recommendation when selecting the number of components when performing a PCA: to look for the "elbow" in the right-hand plot of Figure 14.2. The elbow is the place where the percent explained variance bends, or where including more components does not lead to an increase in the explained variance.

Figure 14.2 is a stylized example and we caution that the strong conclusion that comes from the plot may not hold when deploying PCA to the example of interest. In actual applications the variance explained plot will almost never look so clear. Therefore, the percent variance explained will be useful, but will not provide the clear guidance that this example suggests.

A different approach includes more dimensions so long as they provide new explanatory power. To label the dimensions we can examine a number of features, including how different documents load on different parts of the principal component. This more qualitative examination is also essential so we can develop substantive interpretations of the principal components.

The key when selecting the number of dimensions for a PCA is to remember the limitations of quantitative approaches to model selection. The quantitative measures of model fit for PCA measure how much variance each additional dimension explains. It cannot tell you the "true" number of dimensions in the data, because the right number depends on your tolerance for error. In settings where simplicity is more important than extra error, we might be willing to use a smaller number of components. But in other settings accuracy will be of paramount importance, so the number of components to include will need to be larger. And in still other settings we use PCA as an input to make predictions. In those cases we can use the clear objective function to determine the number of included components. Outside of the setting, though, the number of components to include will depend on the goals of our analysis.

14.2 Classical Multidimensional Scaling

As with PCA, the goal of Classical Multidimensional Scaling (MDS) is to find a low-dimensional approximation for a collection of documents. And we will see that with some specific assumptions, MDS will provide the same answer as PCA. To get this same representation, MDS focuses on preserving the distances between texts with a lower-dimensional representation. To derive Classical MDS, suppose that we have a collection of N documents. Suppose further that we construct an $N \times N$ distance matrix $\mathbf{Q}$ where entry $q_{ii'}$ represents the Euclidean distance between documents i and i' (which we define in Chapter 7: The Vector Space Model and Similarity Metrics). The goal of MDS is to find a set of $N \times K$ vectors, $\boldsymbol{\pi}$, that approximates the distances as closely as possible. That is, we look for a lower-dimensional representation of document i, $\boldsymbol{\pi}_i$, and document i', $\boldsymbol{\pi}_{i'}$ such that we approximate the distances between i and i' as closely as possible.

To make this approximation Classical MDS searches for $\boldsymbol{\pi}$ to minimize the following objective function, which compares the distance between the observations in the distance matrix $q_{ii'}$ to the distance between observations in the latent space:

$$ f(\mathbf{Q}, \boldsymbol{\mu}) = \sqrt{ \sum_{i=1}^{N} \sum_{i' < i} \left(q_{ii'} - \sqrt{ \sum_{k=1}^{K} (\pi_{ik} - \pi_{i'k})^2 } \right)^2 } . $$

As in PCA, optimization of MDS reduces to approximating the distance matrix with eigenvectors. To do this, we double center the distance matrix by subtracting off the row means and the column means and then divide by -2. This provides the $N \times N$ matrix $\mathbf{WW'}$. We then approximate this matrix with the first K eigenvectors. The embedding for each observation $\hat{\mathbf{W}}_i = \left(\sqrt{\lambda_1}\pi_{i1}, \sqrt{\lambda_2}\pi_{i2}, \ldots, \sqrt{\lambda_k}\pi_{ik} \right)$, where λ_k refers to the eigenvalue of the kth eigenvector. See Hastie, Tibshirani, and Friedman (2013) for a full derivation.

The low-dimensional embeddings from Classical MDS are useful for discovering underlying structure in a document collection. When applying MDS, however, it useful to remember that the low-dimensional structure is strongly dependent upon the distance metric used. This is not surprising—after all, MDS is attempting to approximate the distances with fewer variables. But it is important to remember that altering the definition of close using different distance metrics will cause different structures to be found. Further, methods like MDS and PCA are only going to preserve the relative positions of documents. The derivation of PCA makes this clear, because it preserves the correlation structure in the data. And MDS only preserves the distance between objects. This implies that methods like PCA and MDS are only able to provide relative information about locations in low-dimensional space.

14.2.1 EXTENSIONS OF CLASSICAL MDS

Classical MDS is a powerful method that is useful for identifying the low-dimensional structure for a dataset. Classical MDS's objective function assesses the quality of any low-dimensional representation of the text by comparing the distances between observations in the low-dimensional space to the distances between documents in the original distance matrix. This comparison is reasonable, but it prioritizes embeddings that do a better job of approximating larger distances between documents rather than smaller distances. This could be an important goal; however, it is often the case that researchers are most concerned with accurately representing the documents in a neighborhood around a particular observation. And more error might be tolerated as documents are further away from each other.

There are several modifications to the Classical MDS objective function that ensure that a scaling of the documents prioritizes the closest distances. The most straightforward is Sammon MDS. Sammon MDS normalizes the Classical MDS distance function by normalizing by the distance between two documents. That is, the Sammon MDS objective function is:

$$f(\boldsymbol{Q}, \boldsymbol{\pi}) = \frac{1}{\sum_{i=1}^{N} \sum_{i' < i} q_{ii'}} \sum_{i=1}^{N} \sum_{i' < i} \frac{\left(q_{ii'} - \sqrt{\sum_{k=1}^{K} (\pi_{ik} - \pi_{i'k})^2}\right)^2}{q_{ii'}}.$$

When two documents are close, or $q_{ii'}$ is small, differences between the distance matrix distance and the embedded distance will be magnified. But for documents at a larger distance discrepancies between $q_{ii'}$ and the embedded distance will matter less. Altering the objective function does increase the difficulty of optimization. Rather than straightforward application of linear algebra, obtaining the embedding for a Sammon MDS requires a gradient descent algorithm.

There are several other modifications we could make to scale our observations. For example, we could use landmark MDS to embed a set of representative points and then embed the remaining documents around those points (Platt, 2005). Other methods seek a manifold—or more complicated geometric structure that is locally Euclidean in order to uncover a potentially complicated latent structure (Roweis and Saul, 2000).

14.2.2 APPLYING CLASSICAL MDS TO SENATE PRESS RELEASES

For the purposes of discovery, MDS and PCA have the same goal: finding a latent representation of the texts that provides insights into the documents. In Section 14.1.4 we saw how applying PCA to the collection of Senate press releases reveals how senators trade off between claiming credit for money in their district and articulating positions on salient issues.

The left-hand plot in Figure 14.3 compares the embeddings from MDS, where the distance between senators' aggregated press releases is calculated using Euclidean distance and PCA. This plot shows that the embeddings are exactly equal: measuring distance between documents using Euclidean distance and then applying Classical MDS is equivalent to applying PCA to the document collection. The next plot shows how different distance metrics and representations of the texts lead to different embeddings. In the right-hand plot we measure distance as $1 -$ cosine similarity between the

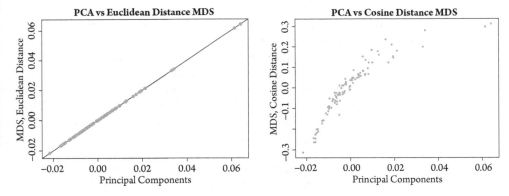

Figure 14.3. Comparing MDS and PCA on Senate press releases. Left: Classical MDS is equivalent to PCA. Right: PCA compared to cosine distance MDS.

documents. This shows that Classical MDS provides a different, though still similar, embedding of the observations.

14.3 Conclusion

In this chapter we covered techniques for projecting documents into unconstrained, low-dimensional spaces. This is often helpful for visualizing data because plots can only reasonably capture two or at most three dimensions (e.g., using color). These methods can also be helpful when we believe there are one or two very strong dimensions that explain most of the data, as ideology does for vote counts.

This also brings us to the end of Discovery, a task that we generally believe needs to be talked about more. We covered four major approaches: discriminating words, clustering, topic models, and document embeddings. All of these approaches are ways to help encourage analysts to read and see the texts in a new light—ultimately it isn't the algorithm doing the discovering, it is the researchers.

We also want to highlight that this is only a small sample of the different approaches that can be taken to discovery. Other fields have approaches to computationally driven discovery, and a fruitful approach is often borrowing the approaches of those fields.

For example, we can leverage the insights of the rich literature on social network analysis by representing word co-occurences as a weighted undirected network where each word is a node and each edge represents its co-occurence within a unit of text (Carley, 1990, 1997a,b). For example, Rule, Cointet, and Bearman (2015) leverage a community detection algorithm and numerous approaches to network visualization in order to study the evolution of discourse in US State of the Union addresses from 1790 to 2014. These community detection algorithms are closely related to the clustering algorithms described in Chapter 12, but here they are applied to the vocabulary, creating groupings of terms rather than groupings of documents.

We also don't have to restrict ourselves to using techniques from other fields to pursue the same ends. Sometimes an alternative framework can fundamentally alter our quantity of interest. Bail (2016) studies how advocacy organizations capture public attention, drawing again on the network analysis perspective. Bail (2016) hypothesizes that organizations that can create cultural bridges by connecting typically disparate themes can more easily connect with new audiences. Using a dataset of advocacy organizations for issues around autism spectrum disorder, he creates a network where each advocacy organization is a node and the weighted edges between them indicate overlapping use of nouns and noun phrases. He then measures cultural bridges using a metric called *betweenness centrality*. An organization with high betweenness centrality has a large number of shortest paths between organizations going through it. He finds that organizations that engage in substantial cultural bridging get two and a half times as many comments from new social media users. It is not only the particular method, but also the quantity of interest and the broader analytic approach that are defined by the network perspective. If we are going to make new discoveries it makes sense to continue pushing the boundaries of the ways we approach the data.

Having discovered our conceptualization of interest, we move on to the task of Measurement, which is the subject of the next part of the book. There we will discuss how to use supervised learning to measure properties of interest in documents. In the last chapter of Measurement, Chapter 21, we return to discuss the implications of using the techniques in this part of the book for the purposes of measurement.

PART IV

Measurement

In *Designing Social Inquiry*, King, Keohane, and Verba (1994) write, "if we are to understand the rapidly changing social world, we will need to include information that cannot be easily quantified as well as that which can" (p. 5). Text analysis is exciting because it greatly expands the range of phenomena that can be tractably quantified. This opportunity has contributed to the rapidly expanding evidence base of social science in the digital age (King, 2009; Lazer et al., 2009; Salganik, 2018). By transforming documents into data, text analysis allows us to create new measurements that may be closer to our theoretical quantities of interest than traditional datasets.[1]

Much of late twentieth-century social science was built around a relatively small number of large, centrally maintained datasets such as the General Social Survey, the American National Election Study, Militarized Interstate Disputes, and the Panel Study on Income Dynamics. The use of existing data is powerful because it lowers the cost of research by allowing scholars to piggyback off preexisting work. However, this convenience comes at a price; datasets had to be sufficiently broad that they could answer a wide range of questions, and collected variables must stand in for a lot of distinct concepts. Whether or not a variable is a good fit for a study often goes uninterrogated for lack of better options. By enshrining a particular conceptualization of empirical phenomena, popular large datasets can come to shape the nature of the questions that are posed.

By contrast, text as data methods have allowed an era of custom measurement to flourish, where scholars can easily generate enormous quantitative datasets specifically designed for their own projects. Stylistically, these new measurement strategies

---

[1] Parts of this introduction are drawn from Grimmer, Roberts, and Stewart (2021).

sit somewhere between quantitative and qualitative tradition. They provide us with systematic, quantifiable summaries of empirical phenomena, but they require qualitative interpretation and considerable care in application.

The advantage of having a few focal data sources is in validation. Large research teams and hundreds of scholars using the data ensure that the data and measures are carefully checked and validated. The democratization of measurement is powerful, but it thrusts more responsibility into the hands of the individual analysts who must now focus more extensively on validation.

In this part, we move from Discovery, where the goal is to generate a conceptualization of the world, to Measurement, where we want to measure that conceptualization. Because text analysis is often used to measure something that hasn't been studied before, it is often sufficiently interesting to simply count things. Being able to quantify the frequency of a characteristic or event can be a powerful first step in understanding it.

In **Chapter 15: Principles of Measurement** we describe some of the unique considerations in making this move from discovery to measurement. **Chapter 16: Word Counting** starts with the simplest measurement strategy: counting individually chosen words. This chapter includes popular dictionary-based approaches which use pregenerated collections of words and attaches weights to them to measure particular concepts. We also explore a natural generalization of this approach, supervised scaling, where the dictionaries of words are implicitly generated from the texts themselves.

There is a long tradition of leveraging human expertise to place documents into a pre-determined set of categories. This is often called "coding" the documents and the humans that label them are called "coders."[2] Once a sample of documents has been coded by humans, we can use machine learning to automate the coding process. **Chapter 17: An Overview of Supervised Classification** provides an introductory overview and default recipe to the three steps in this process: coding, classifying, and validating. The chapters that follow (**Chapter 18: Coding a Training Set, Chapter 19: Classifying Documents with Supervised Learning, Chapter 20: Checking Performance**) cover each one of the steps in more depth. **Chapter 21: Repurposing Discovery Methods** revisits the techniques discussed in Discovery and describes the implications of applying them to measurement.

---

[2] In some literatures the process would be called annotations (and done by annotators). While this avoids the confusion with coding in the sense of programming, we decided to stick with the wording that we have seen more frequently in social science.

CHAPTER 15

Principles of Measurement

In his treatise on social measurement, sociologist Otis Dudley Duncan observed,

> Measurement is one of many human achievements and practices that grew up and came to be taken for granted before anyone thought to ask how and why they work. (Duncan, 1984, p. 119)

An advantage of text as data methods being relatively new is that they have brought a renewed attention to the assumptions that go into measurement and to the importance of careful validation.

We start with the goal. The goal in measurement is to instantiate some concept within our hypothesis or theory in order to facilitate quantification.[1] From our point of view, no measurement can be completely divorced from a theoretical understanding of the thing being observed. To measure something is to invoke a series of testable and untestable assumptions about how observable data is translated to a theoretical concept. Measurement is the vital link that bridges our conceptual argument and the data we have available as evidence.

Consistent with our key principles outlined in Chapter 2, there is no single approach to measurement that is going to perform best across all settings. However, we think of most measurement as involving the following steps for the researcher,

1. *Define* the conceptualization we want to measure.
2. *Locate* a source of data that contains implications of the identified concept.
3. *Generate* a way to translate data into a latent representation.
4. *Label* the representation and connect to the identified concept.
5. *Validate* the resulting measure.

In Discovery, we described methods for helping *define* the concepts we want to measure by sparking a creative idea for new research questions or theory. In Chapter 4, we covered how to *locate* sources of text data. In this part, we turn to steps 3–5 and

---

[1] A natural baseline is provided by Stevens (1946), which defines measurement as the assignment of numeric values to objects according to some set of rules. Sociologist Otis Dudley Duncan memorably describes the Stevens definition as incomplete in the way that "playing the piano is striking the keys of the instrument according to some pattern" is (Duncan, 1984, p. 126) because Stevens does not include the idea that measurement is explicitly about assigning values to express the degree of a quality that an object has. We follow him in this more purpose-driven view of measurement but ultimately endorse a slightly broader definition that includes classification.

the development of measures that will test the observable implications of that theory. Regardless of whether our goal is description, causal inference, or prediction, we will need some means of systematically measuring phenomena from a complex world.

Measurement inevitably involves compression: in measuring something we are choosing to throw away the majority of the information about a *specific* object, in order to focus on a *generalizable* property of that object. This process of compression is formalized with a function that maps between a document and our latent representation that we will use for measurement. The next several chapters will cover both the methods we use to arrive at that function and the way in which we integrate the latent representation into our broader research process.

15.1 From Concept to Measurement

Discovery is a process of proposing an understanding of the world, unsettling that understanding with data, and then revising until we see the world in a different way. Ultimately this iterative process settles down and that is when the process of measurement begins. In practice, the discovery and measurement tasks are not always cleanly separated, often because the discovery portion is not talked about at all. By separating these two distinct stages, we can approach each with appropriate techniques and design new methods that are best suited to each task. Even though we see discovery and measurement as separate, we imagine that in most broad research programs there will be iteration back and forth between these two stages as the research question evolves.

There is no universally best method for measuring a concept and so we cannot offer a 'one size fits all' approach. Instead, we describe a wide variety of approaches, each of which leverages information from the analyst in a different way.

15.2 What Makes a Good Measurement

The role of a good measurement is to achieve a simplification of real-world phenomena that allows the analyst to accurately describe a process or test the observable implications of a theory. Because no measurement can reflect the world in all its complexity, the properties of a good measurement are intrinsically linked to the particular problem that the analyst is trying to solve.

While computer scientists and industrial data scientists have primarily focused their text analysis efforts on applications in information retrieval and prediction, social scientists and digital humanities scholars have almost exclusively focused on texts as a mechanism for measurement. Texts have been used to measure things as diverse as culture (Bail, 2014b), political agendas (Grimmer, 2010), support for violent jihad (Nielsen, 2017), and international events (Schrodt, 2012). It is not surprising that social scientists have focused on applications in measurement as there is a long history in the social sciences of both manual content analysis (Krippendorff, 2012; Neuendorf, 2016) and measurement more broadly (Stevens, 1946; Thurstone, 1954). In fact, the first computer assisted content analysis (that we are aware of) was Sebeok and Zeps (1958), which analyzed folktales. Even subtle differences of focus are important. As we will go into later, a model that is able to predict which emails are spam will not necessarily do a good job of measuring the proportion of your email that is spam. To return again to the haystack metaphor, some people want to find the strand of hay and others want to characterize the haystack. Measurement also places heavy demands on the analyst to define what the measurement is and justify its role in the research process.

It will be helpful to begin with a statement of the properties we aspire to in our measures. These five characteristics constitute a demanding set of criteria that may not be fully satisfied in any one paper or project.

15.2.1 PRINCIPLE 1: MEASURES SHOULD HAVE CLEAR GOALS

A measurement is a reduction of the original source material. There is no universally right or wrong piece of information to preserve about the original source, and as such a measure should have a clearly stated goal about what it is trying to capture about the world. This implies that the measure has clear *scope and purpose*, which helps ensure that it is used properly in the initial analysis and reduces the likelihood that it will be inadvertently misused by future scholars. Where possible, this statement should be sufficiently simple that it is clearly understandable by nonexperts in the field.

15.2.2 PRINCIPLE 2: SOURCE MATERIAL SHOULD ALWAYS BE IDENTIFIED AND IDEALLY MADE PUBLIC

Texts have varying meaning that is sensitive to attributes of the context in which it was produced. In order to clearly communicate the meaning of the measurement, the source of the original material should always be clearly stated. Although it may not always be possible, making the source texts publicly available both facilitates future work and allows for independent validation of the measure.

15.2.3 PRINCIPLE 3: THE CODING PROCESS SHOULD BE EXPLAINABLE AND REPRODUCIBLE

In order to be used as a scientific measurement, the researcher needs to understand how the measure is constructed. While this may take many different forms, in principle the reader should have available sufficient instructions so that, given the raw input documents, the resulting measure can be reconstructed. In the case of human annotators this generally involves releasing a comprehensive codebook that defines clear procedures for workers implementing the coding system. For computer-assisted tasks this involves a complete description of the model or software used to produce the labeling. The "explainable" characteristic requires that these materials be understood by the broadest possible audience. In our view, a measurement cannot properly be a part of science if we don't know how it was generated. While perhaps not obviously controversial, this rejects the use of many off-the-shelf black-box measurement strategies.

15.2.4 PRINCIPLE 4: THE MEASURE SHOULD BE VALIDATED

The accuracy of the measurement strategy should be validated on data other than what was used to develop it. Measures should also be chosen such that they are understandable to a broad audience. There is always a conceptual gap between the method by which a phenomenon is actually measured and the intended concept. However, this gap should be as small as possible. Validation is the process of establishing to readers and the researchers themselves that the measurement maps well to the theoretical concept that it purports to measure.

15.2.5 PRINCIPLE 5: LIMITATIONS SHOULD BE EXPLORED, DOCUMENTED AND COMMUNICATED TO THE AUDIENCE

Some degree of measurement error is inevitable—but the consequences of measurement error are closely tied to how we intend to use the measure in our research. Thus, it is crucial that analysts identify and disclose when the measure performs well and when it doesn't. This allows readers and users of our measures to calibrate their expectations appropriately. For example some measures discriminate well along the entire range of their possible values, while others perform best only at the extremes or in the middle. Measures may also perform with different error rates across groups, which has important implications for fairness (Jacobs and Wallach, 2021). Defining the scope conditions of our measure helps to ensure that it is used and interpreted correctly.[2]

There is a considerable literature on the theory of measurement in both the natural and social sciences. By contrast to many of these fields, text as data is in its infancy. While in this chapter we draw on insights from philosophy of science, psychometrics, and other traditions of measurement, there are many unique challenges of measurement when applying quantitative text analysis. The great insights of these earlier traditions were not generated in a vacuum; but were instead the rationalization and codification of the best procedures generated through trial and error in the early development of the field (Duncan, 1984). A full theory of measurement is beyond the scope of this work, but we offer the best guidance we have from the results of our own process of trial and error.

15.3 Balancing Discovery and Measurement with Sample Splits

It is difficult to do the work of articulating the conceptualization and measurement at the same time. Humans are human after all, and we might worry about allowing our biases or theoretical expectations to creep into our measurement or interpretation. Concerns about this kind of subjective measurement error are why interviewers will sometimes be sent in blind to key expectations about a subject or coders will not see the outcomes when doing the coding. If we want to create a measure of some property in the text, we want to minimize the degree to which our measurement is affected by something outside the text.

In describing methods to avoid this kind of measurement error, King, Keohane, and Verba (1994) counsel,

> Our advice in these circumstances is, first, to try to use judgments made for entirely different purposes by *other researchers*. This element of arbitrariness in qualitative or quantitative measurement guarantees that the measure will not be influenced by your hypotheses, which presumably were not formed until later.... If you are the first person to use a set of variables, it is helpful to let *other informed people* code your variables without knowing your theory of the relationship you wish to evaluate.

(King, Keohane, and Verba, 1994, p. 156)

---

[2] For a useful template for how to document the purpose and limitations of a predictive model (including those used for measurement), see Mitchell et al. (2019).

Often the measures we want to use in text analysis are not already available, so it is useful to separate the coding from other outcomes or covariates. One way to address this problem is by a train-test split, developing the measure on a sample of the data, the "training data," but reporting the results from the measure in the "test data."

By developing the measure in the training set and then applying the measure in the test set, we can protect ourselves from certain kinds of overfitting. Sample splits will also play a central role in our discussion of causal inference, but they are helpful here for validating our measurements.

CHAPTER 16

Word Counting

Most of this book's section on measurement will focus on labeling texts into known categories. Chapter 18 describes different approaches for annotating texts, or how to place texts into categories based on a codebook. Chapter 19 describes how to then use this annotated set of documents as training data to develop a model that will automatically place documents into the categories. In this framework, the statistical model uses the training data to learn the mapping provided between W, the representation of the text, and y, the categories of the text.

Before describing the process of supervised learning, however, we consider a group of simpler methods where the human annotates the words within the texts, rather than the documents themselves. Instead of placing groups of texts into known categories and then using a model to learn how these categories relate to the features, researchers directly write down the mapping function using a set of human-generated rules. The most fundamental of the human-generated rules are keyword- or dictionary-based methods. Underlying these methods is the assumption that when the human-generated rules are applied to a set of documents, they will produce a label at the text level that accurately reflects the category of the text. In this chapter, we will first discuss these methods, then discuss validations and potential pitfalls.

16.1 Keyword Counting

The simplest version of the dictionary approach is counting instances of a particular word or phrase. Sometimes this kind of basic counting can provide evidence about the evolution of a particular concept or idea.

Keyword counting has the advantage that it is clear and easy to communicate. Imagine that we have a collection of newspaper articles and we want to measure interest in US presidential politics. We could count the number of articles that use the word `president` at least once. However, it isn't clear that counting the word `president` for example is a precise measure of discourse about presidential politics; companies, other countries, universities, and organizations of all sorts have presidents. We could instead opt for a slightly more complicated option and count instances of the phrase `White House`. This has the advantage of producing fewer false positives (although there are, of course, other houses that are white), but many articles about presidential politics may not contain the phrase `White House`. While counting words is straightforward mechanically, it is difficult to accurately represent complex latent concepts in

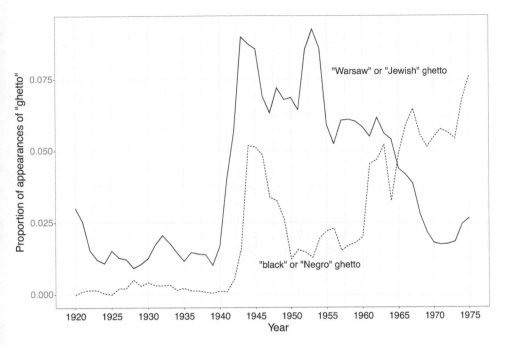

Figure 16.1. Graph 1 from Duneier (2016) depicting the proportion of the uses of the word ghetto in context of words signalling one of two uses. Data derived from Google Ngrams.

practice. Yet, when the counted words are carefully considered and the results validated with careful reading, keyword counting can be extraordinarily effective.

In his book *Ghetto: The Invention of a Place, the History of an Idea*, Duneier (2016) traces the word ghetto from its origin in sixteenth century Venice, through the Nazi ghettos in Europe and to its present day connection with the segregation of African Americans in the US. While most of Duneier (2016)'s award-winning book is a detailed historical account, he presents a single graph, reproduced in Figure 16.1, which demonstrates the way that the association with Nazi ghettos rose and then was subsequently overtaken by the connection with African American residential segregation. Figure 16.1 uses Google Ngrams to search over 800,000 books for four phrases which exemplified the two meanings of the word "ghetto." The phrases Warsaw Ghetto and Jewish Ghetto rose quickly beginning in 1940 as news of the Nazi's ghettoization of the Jews in Europe spread. This use was followed quickly by Black Ghetto and Negro Ghetto, which were the most common phrases for referencing areas of residential segregation of African Americans, primarily in northern US cities.

Duneier argues that this changing association of the idea of the ghetto is not an accident. In 1945, two African American sociologists, Horace R. Cayton and St. Clair Drake, published *Black Metropolis* and invoked the idea of the Black Ghetto in order to draw attention to the coercive housing policies driving segregation of Black people in Chicago and other US cities. Cayton and Drake drew on the association of the word ghetto with the Nazi oppression of the Jews to highlight the hypocrisy of America's treatment of its Black population. This helped to highlight the moral imperative for America to be conscious of the racial oppression in its own cities at a time when it was fighting a different type of racial oppression abroad. In his book, Duneier (2016) describes the surge in the Black press' reference to Black Ghetto during the early 1940s, reading and quoting from many of the individual books that make up the trend line in the graph.

The timing of this change, provides evidence that the term ghetto came to be associated with parts of American cities primarily as a result of the Nazi use of the term. Duneier (2016) emphasizes that restrictive covenants driving the residential segregation of the Black population in US cities began in 1928. Yet, he argues, we don't see the rise of the term "Black ghetto" until much later, following the precipitous rise in reference to the Jewish ghetto in Nazi-controlled parts of Europe. Duneier (2016) further substantiates this point by digging into how these ideas were evoked, writing,

> Drake and Cayton regarded the ghetto as a metaphor for both segregation and Caucasian purity in the Nazi era, and it was in this sense that the use of the word was particular to the historical moment. Referring to those middle-class blacks who try to move out, Drake and Cayton wrote, "They have slowly filtered southward within the Black Belt. Always, however, they hit the invisible *barbed-wire* fence of restrictive covenants" [emphasis mine]. Barbed wire was a symbol of Nazi ghettos rather than something invented in sixteenth-century Venice.
>
> (Duneier, 2016, pp. 71-72)

In other words, Duneier argues not only that the association of the word ghetto changed—something readily apparent from the graph—but also that the introduction of ghetto as a term to describe Black residential segregation was linked to the Nazi adoption of the word.

Duneier's book is a powerful example of how simple quantitative analysis can provide a useful complement to detailed and nuanced historical sociology. Duneier (2016) chooses a very simple numerical representation of the text—a count of four simple phrases—but by using that representation in concert with extensive reading of the underlying sources, he is able to make an argument more compelling than either evidence source alone is. Duneier (2016)'s use of the additional evidence is essential to the credibility of the argument. When used alone, keyword counts can ultimately be less compelling. The total uses of the word ghetto far outnumber the uses in the four bigrams that are tracked in Figure 16.1. There are also limits to using the Google Ngrams corpus to make inferences about the popularity of a phrase over time, as pointed out by Pechenick, Danforth, and Dodds (2015), due to the changing composition of sources that make up the database. But in the context of a richer qualitative analysis, a simple graph like that in Figure 16.1 provides not only a powerful visual demonstration of the point, but also helps to amplify the extensive manual analysis.

16.2 Dictionary Methods

Dictionaries are a generalization of keyword counting—they use a weighted average of the rate at which keywords appear in a text to classify documents into categories or to measure the extent to which documents belong to particular categories.[1] For example, suppose the goal is to measure the *tone* in newspaper articles (for example, Eshbaugh-Soha 2010): whether articles convey information positively or negatively. Dictionary methods use a list of words with attached tone scores and the relative rate words occur to measure a document's tone. A *dictionary* to measure tone is a list of words that are either dichotomously classified as positive or negative or contain more continuous measures

---

[1] Part of this section on dictionary methods is drawn from Grimmer and Stewart (2013).

of their content. Formally, each word j will have associated score μ_j. For the simplest measures, $\mu_j = -1$ if the word is associated with a negative tone and $\mu_j = 1$ if associated with a positive tone. If $M_i = \sum_{j=1}^{J} W_{ij}$ words are used in document i, then dictionary methods can measure the tone, π_i, for any document as,

$$\pi_i = \sum_{j=1}^{J} \frac{\mu_j W_{ij}}{M_i}.$$

Scholars often use π_i as an approximately continuous measure of document tone, but it also can be used to classify documents into tone categories if a decision rule is assumed along with the dictionary method. Perhaps the simplest coding rule would assign all documents with $\pi_i > 0$ to a positive tone category and $\pi_i < 0$ to a negative tone.

Tone is just one type of analysis a dictionary method can perform. The general idea of dictionaries makes them relatively easy and cheap to apply across a variety of problems: first, identify a set of words that separate categories and then measure how often those words occur in texts (for some examples that use dictionaries to measure a variety of concepts, see Kellstedt 2000; Burden and Sanberg 2003; Laver and Garry 2000; Young and Soroka 2012). Here, researchers can either create their own dictionary through their own expertise, or find an existing dictionary. There are a variety of widely used off-the-shelf dictionaries that provide keywords for different categories (for example, Bradley and Lang 1999; Hart 2000; Pennebaker, Francis, and Booth 2001; Turney and Littman 2003).

If scholars do not have an existing dictionary, but have documents already coded into categories, dictionaries can be produced using existing methods that we described in Chapter 11. Monroe, Colaresi, and Quinn (2008) describe a variety of methods that measure how well words separate already identified categories of interest (see also Taddy (2013) and Diermeier et al. (2012)). Any one of these methods could be used to produce dictionary-like scores of words, which could then be applied in other contexts to classify documents.

16.3 Limitations and Validations of Dictionary Methods

For dictionary methods to work well, the scores attached to words must closely align with how the words are used in a particular context. If a dictionary is developed for a specific application, then this assumption should be easy to justify (though Barberá et al. (2021) find that even task-specific dictionaries may underperform supervised learning). But when dictionaries are created in one substantive area and then applied to another, serious errors can occur. Perhaps the clearest example of this is shown in Loughran and McDonald (2011). Loughran and McDonald (2011) critique the increasingly common use of off-the-shelf dictionaries to measure the tone of statutorily required corporate earnings reports in the accounting literature. They point out that many words that have a negative connotation in other contexts, like `tax`, `cost`, `crude` (oil), or `cancer`, may have a positive connotation in earnings reports. For example, a healthcare company may mention `cancer` often and oil companies are likely to discuss `crude` extensively. And words that are not identified as negative in off-the-shelf dictionaries may have quite negative connotation in earnings reports (`unanticipated`, for example).

Dictionaries, therefore, should be used with substantial caution, and certainly coupled with explicit validation. When applying dictionaries, scholars should directly establish that word lists created in other contexts are applicable to their setting, or create a domain-specific dictionary. Researchers should also be aware that the dictionaries they come up with may not accord with the way that words are used within the documents, and therefore they must pay close attention to the application and the context. In either instance, scholars must validate their results. For example, researchers should produce hand labels for a sample of the documents the dictionary is being used to classify. Then they should compare the aggregate measure produced by the dictionary to the hand-labeled validation set.

Importantly, validation of dictionaries should be conducted in different data than that for which the dictionary was created. If, after validation, the researchers decide to change the dictionary, they cannot then validate the dictionary again in the same data. Doing so would risk overfitting, where the researchers select words for the dictionary based on what they see in the validation set, a mapping that may not generalize. To ensure accuracy, validation of the revised dictionary must be conducted on a new set of fresh data.

In practice, measures from dictionaries are rarely validated. Rather, standard practice in using dictionaries is to assume the measures created from a dictionary are correct and then apply them to the problem. The consequence of domain specificity and lack of validation is that many analyses based on dictionaries are built on shaky foundations. The problem is that dictionaries do not necessarily produce a measure with any particular properties. Even granted that we have selected the correct features to weight, the fundamental question is whether variations produced in the weights constitute underlying differences in the quantity being measured or whether they are just introducing noise. Therefore, with these methods, we think case-specific validation is paramount.

16.3.1   MOVING BEYOND DICTIONARIES: WORDSCORES

The Wordscores algorithm, by Laver, Benoit, and Garry (2003), represents a true breakthrough in the use of text as data in political science. One of the first articles to use large scale text analysis in the social sciences, Laver, Benoit, and Garry (2003) introduce a method for placing actors in an ideological space, using their written words. Rather than rely on manual coding or dictionary methods that are difficult to validate, Laver, Benoit, and Garry (2003) introduced a fully automated method for scaling political actors based on exemplar texts, *wordscores*. In their words, they sought to develop a "procedure for designing an English language dictionary ... for extracting information on substantive policy positions from political texts" without assuming relationships between words and categories outright (Laver, Benoit, and Garry, 2003, p. 626). We explain this method as a way of bridging word counting and dictionaries with supervised learning, which will be our focus in the next three chapters.

The goal of *Wordscores* is to find a measure of ideology for a given text document, a supervised version of what we described in Chapter 14. To do so, it uses a set of exemplar texts to define an ideological space and then scores documents based on features that distinguish the exemplar texts. The first step is the selection of *reference* texts that define the political positions in the space. In the simplest example, we may select two texts to define the liberal and conservative ends of the spectrum. If we wanted to scale US senators based on their speeches, for example, we may define as a reference text all the speeches from a very liberal senator, like Ron Wyden (D-OR) or Barbara Boxer (D-CA), and a very conservative senator, like Tom Coburn (R-OK) or Jim DeMint (R-OK). The reference (training) texts are then used to generate a *score* for each word. The score measures the relative rate each word is used in the reference texts. This creates a measure of how well the word separates liberal and conservative members—one measure of whether a word is *liberal* or *conservative*. The word scores are then used to scale the remaining texts. Laver, Benoit, and Garry (2003) call these the *virgin* texts, but in supervised learning we would call these texts the *test set*. To scale the documents using the word scores, first Laver, Benoit, and Garry (2003) calculate the relative rate at which words are used in each of the test documents. The position of the texts is then determined by taking the weighted average of the word scores of the words in a text, where the weights are given by the rate at which the words are used.

Wordscores is rich and generalizable to multiple dimensions and to include several reference texts. But facets of wordscores constrain the method and make it difficult to recommend for general use (see Lowe (2008) for an extended critique). By defining "liberal" and "conservative" using *only* reference texts that are indicative of the extremes, Laver, Benoit, and Garry (2003) conflate ideological language with stylistic differences across authors and impose the ideological dominance assumption on the texts. The result is that every use of wordscores will depend strongly on the reference texts that are used, in part because of stylistic differences across authors and in part because the reference texts will discuss non-ideological content. Careful preprocessing of texts, to remove words that are likely only stylistic, can mitigate part of this problem. Beauchamp (2011), for instance, shows that results are significantly improved by removing technical language, which coincides more with party power than with ideology.

16.4 Conclusion

In the chapter, we covered the simplest form of supervision—word counting. We discussed the use of dictionaries for measurement, where humans place words into categories and then use combinations of these words to scale or categorize documents. We then covered an extension of this—the Wordscores algorithm, which generates a dictionary based on "exemplar" documents that define two extremes. While these approaches are simple and straightforward, they also have several drawbacks in terms of accuracy. In the next chapter, we discuss supervised learning, which addresses many of the drawbacks of dictionary approaches by inserting human supervision at the document rather than at the word level. Unfortunately, this also requires a substantial increase in effort and time, an effort, however, we believe is often worth the investment.

CHAPTER 17

An Overview of Supervised Classification

This chapter provides a default recipe for automating measurement using supervised classification. Supervised classification uses a set of documents labeled into categories to create a statistical model (sometimes called a "classifier") that relates the words in the documents to the labels, and applies that model to obtain comparable labels for otherwise unlabeled documents. We provide an overview of the whole process of supervised classification—from labeling a training set, to training a model, to validating results. In the subsequent three chapters, we dive more deeply into each of these three components.

In supervised classification, the goal is to create a mapping between the features within the document set and more general categories and concepts that have been defined by the researcher. So far, we have considered two important scenarios for defining a mapping function: the case where the analyst selects and counts one particular word as a proxy for the measure of interest and a second where the mapping function is explicitly defined by the researcher by a dictionary. With supervised classification, we learn the mapping function from the data by training an algorithm to predict the category of interest from the text using a sample of coded documents. We define a model such that our prediction $\hat{y}_i$ for document i is generated by a function $f_\mu(W_i,)$, where $W_i,$ is the document representation and μ are the parameters of the model. We then learn the parameters of the model by observing random samples of the input W and the output y (called training samples). This essentially turns the measurement problem into a *prediction task*, leveraging statistical models to predict the label that the analyst would have assigned herself. This approach is quite general and has the advantage that once the parameters of the model are learned, classifying additional documents is essentially costless.

In this approach, the human is responsible for providing three sources of information: labels for the training documents, the representation of the input, and the class of model to learn. Having the labels typically implies that the analyst has already developed a coding scheme and a mapping function that lives in her head. We assume for now that the analyst selects the sample of training documents at random and assigns the labels y with perfect accuracy to the selected documents.

The second step is the feature representation of the input. This is an important and underappreciated part of the process. The representation chosen should match the type of task that the analyst is engaged in. A recurring theme throughout this section is that the features we use to predict the label y are substantially more important than the class of models. This point often gets lost in the literature, where authors are trying to provide advice that is generic to any type of mapping function that the analyst might encounter. However, *we will happily choose better features over better models every time.* For expository purposes, we use the vector of term counts W_i, as our representation, but we could easily have chosen a representation based on word embeddings, phrases, or a wide variety of other features extracted from the text.

The third and final step is choosing a class of models to learn. There are a dizzying array of choices; but all the different options provide different ways of sharing information. If we make no assumptions about how features map to the output, we can only classify documents that are exactly like a sample we observed in the training set. Different classes of models define how the learned function maps from the input representation to the label. We can choose relatively simple models that are often easy to interpret and require relatively little data to train, but may not be flexible enough to predict human labels. More complex models are hungrier for data and may be relatively opaque to the analyst, but can often handle complex prediction problems.

17.1 Example: Discursive Governance

To provide an overview of supervised classification, we draw on an example from Gillion (2016)'s analysis of political officials' discourse about race in America. While political strategists have argued that political officials should deracialize their discourse around policy in order to appeal to the broadest set of voters, Gillion (2016) argues that the role of race in rhetoric has implications outside of elections and the policymaking process. Gillion (2016) argues that discussing race has important implications for what he calls "discursive governance," a process by which rhetoric impacts not only elections and policy directly, but also how the public and policymakers set the agenda, design, discuss, implement, and evaluate policies. Not discussing race, he maintains, reduces the salience of racial inequality in the eyes of voters and leaves important information about policies' impact on this inequality out of the policymaking process.

As part of his evidence base, Gillion (2016) measures discussion of race in an impressive collection of statements made by the president and members of Congress – including "presidential debates, campaign fundraising speeches, farewell speeches, inaugural addresses, speeches to the nation, weekly radio addresses, news conferences, State of the Union addresses, other speeches to Congress, local speeches (e.g., graduation addresses and town hall speeches), signing statements, and addresses to foreign legislatures as well as to the United Nations (UN) General Assembly" (p. 33). He also includes all floor speeches from the House of Representatives, all documents in the *Congressional Record*, and all volumes of the *Public Papers of the Presidents*. To divide these texts into statements, Gillion (2016) uses the paragraph as the unit of analysis, ending in total with 912,466 paragraphs from presidents (1955–2012) and 2.3 million paragraphs from members of Congress (104th–112th Congress).

Next, Gillion (2016) sets out to measure "race-related discourse" in the documents, which he defines as "political dialogue or rhetoric expressed by politicians that primarily relates to an underrepresented racial or ethnic minority group or explicitly uses terms that carry a racial connotation" (p. 33). Clearly, the number of documents collected by Gillion (2016) is too large for human coders to code manually. But, as he notes, dictionaries are insufficient as well. Paragraphs that fit this definition of race-related may not actually use the word "race," even if they discuss racial issues. Other words, like "busing" may only be race-related in certain contexts.

Instead, Gillion (2016) decides to use human coding combined with supervised machine learning to code each paragraph into race-related or not race-related. Here, we follow the development of Gillion (2016)'s measurement through three steps: 1) creating a training set, 2) classifying documents with supervised learning, and 3) checking performance.

17.2   Create a Training Set

The first step in supervised classification is to create a training set, which we consider extensively in Chapter 18. Human annotators label a subset of the documents into the categories defined by the researcher. In Gillion (2016), two annotators read 12,300 paragraphs from the larger sample and indicate whether they were race-related or not race-related based on the specific definition that Gillion (2016) put forward.

Two primary considerations have to been taken when creating a training set. First, how well the supervised classifier can generalize patterns from the training set to the test set will depend on how the documents in the training set are sampled from the larger set. An unrepresentative training set could create a classifier that is biased when generalized to new documents. Using a random sample of documents for the training set is the simplest assurance that the training documents represent the rest of the sample. Gillion (2016) goes farther to ensure representation, by creating a stratified random sample of documents to make sure that they are representative of time period. In some cases, random sampling is not possible; we discuss those issues more in Chapter 18.

The second consideration is the accuracy of the human coders themselves. Even the simplest categorization scheme can be interpreted differently by different human coders. Clear communication of the categories is important, both for future work and to ensure accuracy of the training set before it is applied more broadly. As we discuss at length in Chapter 18, we recommend having at least two human annotators code the documents, and then follow this by assessing the intercoder reliability, or the proportion of documents that both coders put in the same category. Gillion (2016) reports an intercoder agreement rate between his two annotators at 97% (p. 164). When annotators disagreed, he made the final determination himself.

17.3   Classify Documents with Supervised Learning

The next step in supervised classification is to choose a classifier to learn the mapping between the features and the categories labeled in the training set. This involves first choosing how the features are represented, something we discussed in the Part 2: Representation. We suggest choosing a representation in part using the domain expertise, carefully considering the types of features that will likely be most informative of the categories. Many classifiers also incorporate a feature selection component, which will remove features that the classifier finds irrelevant. Gillion (2016) uses a bag of words approach to represent the documents, removing punctuation, numbers, white spaces, and stop words (p. 164).

The next step is to choose the model to learn the mapping. There are many models to choose from, some of which we detail in Chapter 19. Moreover, models can be combined in *ensembles* of classifiers, where researchers use many different models to "vote" on the final label of each document. This is the approach that Gillion (2016) uses to code documents into race-related and not race-related.

17.4 Check Performance

The last step of supervised classification is to check the performance of the classifier. Here the researcher should hold out a set of the training data—excluding this set from the model fitting described in (2)—to use for validation. After fitting the model, the researcher then applies the model to this held-out set of data and compares how well the model performs on the human labels.

There are a few considerations in this validation step, which we detail in Chapter 20. First, to prevent overfitting to one particular set of validation data, researchers often use cross-validation, splitting the training data, fitting the model, and assessing accuracy many different times and then averaging the performance metric. This is the approach that Gillion (2016) takes, reporting an accuracy of 0.77 in the presidential set of documents and 0.66 in the Congressional set of documents.[1]

The other consideration is the performance metric itself. While accuracy—the total number correctly classified divided by the total number in the validation set—is a natural measure of performance, high accuracy can mask bad performance, particularly if the categories in the data are quite skewed. We detail other performance metrics, including precision and recall, that can give the analyst more information about performance in Chapter 20.

17.5 Using the Measure

Once Gillion has checked performance, he is ready to move on to applying his classifier to the test set. By applying the classifier to all statements within his dataset, Gillion (2016) can use the new measure to understand how the frequency of presidential statements related to race has changed across different administrations and how statements made by members of Congress related to race are related to geography.

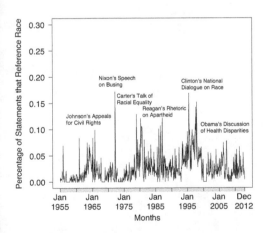
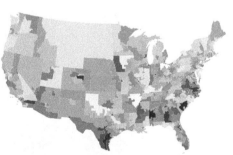

Figure 17.1. Figures 2.1 and 2.3 from Gillion (2016). The left panel shows the proportion of presidential statements related to race over time. The right panel shows the geography of representatives that make statements about race on the House floor; darker areas indicate more frequent statements.

---

[1] To improve the final accuracy above this, Gillion (2016) then did another round of hand coding guided by the classifier (165,166).

In Figure 17.1, we reproduce two figures from Gillion (2016) based on the supervised measurement. The left panel shows the proportion of presidential statements related to race over time. Surprisingly, race-related statements are quite low for President Obama in comparison to other presidents, and Gillion (2016) argues that Obama may have felt pressure to minimize discussion of race because of his identity as a Black president. The right panel shows the geography of discussions of race among statements made by members of Congress. Gillion (2016) notes that most of these discussions are centered in the Southeastern United States.

As we will discuss in the following chapters, once we have applied the classifier to our test set, we will have to think carefully about how to use it in subsequent analyses. The measures we have created with our classifiers contain measurement error, either through errors in the human coding or through errors in the classifier. Ideally, we will find ways to pass this measurement error onto the final analysis, as well as investigate whether or not this error is systematic in ways that might affect our analysis.

17.6 Conclusion

In this chapter, we provided an overview of the process of supervised classification. Drawing on measurement of race-related discourse in Gillion (2016), we provided a bird's eye view of how the researcher can create custom measurements leveraging a training set created by human coders—first by coding a training set, then by classifying documents with a supervised classifier, and last by evaluating the performance of the measure. In the next three chapters, we dive into each of these three steps in detail.

CHAPTER 18

Coding a Training Set

Human coding has long been used to organize and quantify texts. Once a researcher has defined categories, human coding is the process of putting these documents into these categories manually. While human coding predates modern approaches to statistical text analysis, it is still extremely useful on its own for small datasets and coding of complex concepts. Learning to write an excellent codebook and train coders is also important in the context of automated methods as manual coding often forms the basis of training and validation sets for statistical classifiers.

Human coding provides a mapping function from the text to the categories of interest, one that the humans produce based on their interpretation of the text. This mapping function is the combination of the codebook, training given to the coders, and their internal thought processes when assigning codes. In comparison to statistical classification, humans can use their substantive and background knowledge to fill in gaps in the coding scheme using the context in the text. Even though human coding by itself is much slower than automated classification, the process of human coding can also be useful for clarifying the categories of interest and how they are communicated.

While manually placing documents into categories might seem at first to be a relatively straightforward task, human coding can be quite complex.[1] Ambiguities in language, limited attention of coders, and nuanced concepts make the reliable classification of documents difficult—even for expert coders (Grimmer and Stewart, 2013). Unfortunately, teams of expert coders are few and far between, and the modal manual content analysis project in the social sciences is, as Schrodt (2006) colorfully put it describing the collection of events data, "legions of bored students flipping through copies of *The New York Times*" (p. 2). Complications arise because of the deeply contextual nature of language that makes it difficult to specify an entire codebook ex ante. For this reason, we recommend an explicit exploratory/discovery phase in which a preliminary and concise codebook is written to guide coders, who then apply the codebook to an initial set of documents. When using the codebook—particularly at first—coders are likely to identify ambiguities in the coding scheme or overlooked categories. This subsequently leads to a revision of the codebook. Only after coders apply the coding scheme to documents without noticing substantial ambiguities is a "final" scheme ready to be applied to a separate set of documents used for analysis. This ensures that ambiguities

---

[1] Part of this section is drawn from Grimmer and Stewart (2013).

have been sufficiently addressed without risk of overfitting to the document set used to develop the codebook.

In this chapter, we first cover the basics of developing a codebook, selecting coders, and coding a training set. We then also consider other sources of labeled data, including crowd sourcing and supervision with found data. Manual coding is a very important topic, but we cannot give a full treatment of it in this book. Fortunately, manual content analysis is a richly developed field and there are whole books on how to write a good codebook and train coders. We particularly recommend Krippendorff (2012), Neuendorf (2016), and Riffe et al. (2019) for more detailed treatments of the coding process along with practical advice. Barberá et al. (2021) provide an excellent article-length treatment of the whole supervised learning process.

18.1   Characteristics of a Good Training Set

The goal of human coding is to provide a reliable human mapping from the texts of interest to the categories the researcher is interested in. In Part 3: Discovery, we discovered the concepts we want to measure; in coding a training set, we want to *operationalize* these concepts. Many complications arise when creating this mapping, as we will detail more below. Neuendorf (2016, Chapter 1) nicely lays out the following characteristics of a good human coded dataset or training set:

- **Objectivity-Intersubjectivity**: The measurement of the categories is objective, in that the understanding of the categories is not specific to a particular person. Even if it cannot be objective, Neuendorf (2016) argues that at least it should have intersubjectivity, or a shared understanding between researchers.
- **An A Priori Design**: As we have discussed in Part 3: Discovery, defining and redefining categories is an important part of the research process. In the process of human coding, categories may need to be further refined. However, the final training set should be based on a final codebook and coded on fresh data.
- **Reliability**: The mapping of texts to categories should be reliable, in that different human coders should produce the same mapping when working independently.
- **Validity**: The measure should reflect the concept or category of interest. The category label we assign to the measure should reflect what we are indeed measuring.
- **Generalizability**: To create a training set, we will typically code only a sample of a much larger set of data. The mapping we produce with hand coding should be generalizable to the entire dataset and the final population the researcher is interested in.
- **Replicability**: The measure should be able to be replicated in the same data, and ideally different data and different contexts as well.

18.2   Hand Coding

With these goals in mind, we first consider the case where the researcher creates a training set using hand coding. Depending on the categories the researcher intends to measure and the size of the sample set aside for hand coding, the process of hand coding can be very straightforward to a process that takes weeks, months, or even years

(Baumgartner, Jones, and MacLeod, 1998). Regardless, there are a few basic steps and decisions necessary to create a human coded dataset:

18.2.1   1: DECIDE ON A CODEBOOK

The codebook is the instruction manual for the coders to place documents into categories. If the categories have been created by the researcher, she will have to write her own codebook. The codebook not only defines the categories of interest, but also must communicate them effectively in order to ensure reliability, validity, and replicability. This may mean providing example texts for each category and describing edge cases.[2] Flowcharts can also be used to help the coders understand hierarchy of the categories or deal with cases where there are many categories (Krippendorff, 2012, p. 135).

If the researcher would rather not create a custom codebook from scratch, many codebooks exist that could coincide with the goal of the research project. The advantage of adapting an existing codebook is that it has often been refined through multiple rounds of testing. For example, the Comparative Manifestos Project (https://manifesto-project.wzb.eu/) provides several versions of codebooks for categorizing the policy preferences of election manifestos.

18.2.2   2: SELECT CODERS

In order to ensure intersubjectivity, reliability, and replicability, one of the principles of human coding is that coders other than the researcher label the data (Krippendorff, 2012, p. 131). Using a separate set of coders is a test of whether the researcher can effectively communicate the categories to other people.[3]

The next question is how many coders to use to label the data. Best practice is for the researcher to select at least two for creating the training data. This allows the researcher to assess the level of agreement between the coders as a measure of reliability, which we discuss in more detail below. The total number of coders the researcher should select will depend on how precise the coders are in labeling the data. With trained coders with a lot of experience in the research area, researchers may be able to use only two coders total. With a less trained or less attentive labor pool where coders may be more imprecise, many evaluations of each data point may be necessary to reliably label the data. Barberá et al. (2021) provide an excellent overview and characterization of these trade-offs in selecting the number of coders.

18.2.3   3: SELECT DOCUMENTS TO CODE

Next, the researcher must select which and how many documents to code. For generalizability and best performance of the classifier, the training set should be representative of the larger dataset that the researcher intends to code and also of the population about which the researcher intends to draw inference. One straightforward way to ensure this is to draw a simple random sample of the larger set for the training set.

The number of documents that should be used in the training set will depend on the number of categories and the reliability of the coders. The higher the number of categories and the lower the reliability of the coders, the higher the number of documents

---

[2] See Neuendorf (2016) Chapter 5 for the trade-offs of providing example texts.

[3] We acknowledge that this may not always be possible due to funding considerations or poor access to coders with sufficient expertise to perform the coding.

the researcher will need to create a reliable classifier downstream (Barberá et al., 2021). Downstream validation of the classifier can help reveal whether a sufficient number of documents has been coded to achieve the desired accuracy.

18.2.4   4: MANAGE CODERS

For best performance, researchers should train coders before asking them to label the training set. This involves having the coders carefully read the codebook and ask any questions. It often also involves asking the coders to label a sample of texts and evaluating whether they have understood the instructions, or whether the instructions need to be revised.

Once coders have been trained and the codebook has been finalized, the coders should label the data without any contact with each other, or with resources outside of the codebook itself (Krippendorff, 2012, p. 131). This ensures that the training data produced can be evaluated for reliability. The final training data should be produced after the last revision of the codebook.

18.2.5   5: CHECK RELIABILITY

The last step in creating a human coded training set is checking for intercoder reliability.[4] This involves comparing the labels on the same documents between coders. Several different measures can be used to compare labels; two widely used metrics are Cohen's *kappa* (Landis and Koch, 1977) and Krippendorff's *alpha* (Krippendorff, 2012). We refer the reader to Chapter 6 of Neuendorf (2016) for an excellent overview of the metrics and pitfalls of assessing reliability.

18.2.6   MANAGING DRIFT

Researchers should be aware of two types of "drift" that might occur when human coding. First, the coders themselves may change the way that they assign labels to categories as the process of coding wears on. This could be due to anything from fatigue with coding to new insights gained during the process of coding (Neuendorf, 2016, Chapter 6). For this type of drift, it might be useful for the researcher to assess reliability at multiple points in the coding process.

Human coding can also be affected by data drift—where a content stream is evolving over time, which can create new ambiguities for the codebook. For example, new categories might evolve, collapse, or merge with others as the data changes over time. If the codebook is changed based on the drift, it could be that the newer data is labeled differently than the old data. In this situation, one final coding round can help assess the final reliability of the new codebook (Krippendorff, 2012, 218).

18.2.7   EXAMPLE: MAKING THE NEWS

In *Making the News*, Amber Boydstun considers the important question of what types of policy issues receive the most news coverage and why. Boydstun (2013) argues that the media do not act purely as watchdogs—patrolling all issue areas—or as alarm systems—only responding to sudden events. She instead puts forward an alarm/patrol hybrid model of news generation, one where the media are monitoring many issue

---

[4]Note that intercoder reliability does not guarantee accuracy, because coders could have similar errors (Barberá et al., 2021). However, without access to "true" labels, true accuracy is difficult to assess.

areas, but sink disproportionate resources into a few when they become "hot." To measure attention to policy issues in news, she collects a dataset of 31,034 articles from *The New York Times* and places them into policy issue areas. Because she is most interested in understanding policy areas that receive the most news attention, she limits her analysis to front page stories.

Boydstun (2013) relies on an existing codebook—the Policy Agendas Project—to label each of the front page *New York Times* articles in her dataset. In order to adapt the codebook to *The New York Times* corpus, she annotated the codebook to provide more explicit instructions to the coders. The codebook consists of many categories—27 major topic categories and 225 subtopics within these 27 major categories.

Boydstun (2013) trained the coders on a sample of articles, requiring the coders to obtain high reliability in this sample before coding the rest of the data. In order to ensure reliability over time, Boydstun (2013) ensured that coders labeled duplicate texts throughout the coding process. Boydstun (2013) reports both Krippendorff's alpha and Cohen's kappa and has made her codebook available online.

Boydstun (2013)'s hand coding of front page *New York Times* articles allows her to study attention to the different policy issues over time. She finds that issue coverage is highly skewed toward international affairs and often driven by events. For example, Figure 18.1 from Boydstun (2013, Chapter 4) shows that the attacks on the World Trade Center in September of 2001 drastically shifted media coverage on the front page of *The New York Times* to defense, crowding out issue coverage of other policy areas.

18.3 Crowdsourcing

In the last ten years, the introduction of online labor markets such as Mechanical Turk has radically altered the landscape of recruitment for annotators, survey respondents, and participants in experiments (Snow et al., 2008; Kittur, Chi, and Suh, 2008; Buhrmester, Kwang, and Gosling, 2011; Berinsky, Huber, and Lenz, 2012; Budak, Goel, and Rao, 2016; Benoit et al., 2016). Labor markets provide access to untrained or lightly trained workers at scales that would be unfathomable in a typical university setting. For tasks that can be easily explained, are relatively straightforward, and can be quickly completed, online labor markets can be a valuable way to collect document annotations.

It is tempting to think about these online labor markets as infinitely large pools of workers but they are (at least at the time of writing) actually much smaller than it might otherwise seem. For example, Amazon's Mechnical Turk is the most popular online labor market for academic research. A recent study estimates that there are less than two hundred thousand unique workers, with about two to five thousand active at any given time (Difallah, Filatova, and Ipeirotis, 2018). These workers tend to have skewed demographic and political characteristics relative to the population as a whole, although certainly not as skewed as the population of students in university settings (Huff and Tingley, 2015).

Differences between crowdsourcing and human coders. There are three big differences between working with a small team of human coders and a huge crowd. First, in the crowd setting fixed costs have to be lower, so intensive training is less feasible. In practical terms this limits the kind of work that can be done by crowd-workers to comparatively simple tasks that don't require expert background. The advantages of low fixed costs lead to the second big difference—it is more feasible to quickly scale up crowd workers to enable high throughput coding. In a university or industry setting,

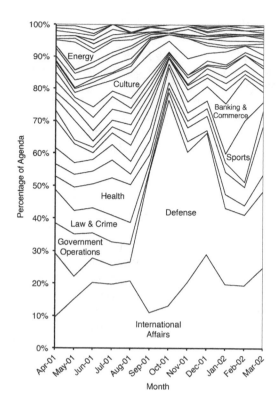

Figure 18.1. Discussion of defense in front page news articles in *The New York Times* increased substantially after September 11, 2001. Figure 4.8 from Boydstun (2013).

hiring new workers takes time, but with crowdsourcing thousands of annotations can be collected for a simple task in just a few hours. The third major difference, is that we have to fully embrace the inevitability of error in annotations. We can conceivably train a small team of annotators until error rates are tolerably low, but in crowdsourcing we have to come up with ways to reconcile conflicting labels. Thankfully this is an old problem which has seen renewed interest in recent years as a result of online labor markets (Dawid and Skene, 1979; Sheng, Provost, and Ipeirotis, 2008; Zhang et al., 2014; Benoit et al., 2016; Barberá et al., 2021). We return to these methods in Chapter 20 on validation.

Some would add a fourth major difference, that crowdsourcing is cheaper. It is certainly true that crowdsourced annotations *can* be obtained cheaper on Mechanical Turk than from undergraduate annotators, but it is questionable whether or not they should be. Because the workers are independent contractors, they often end up being paid effectively below local minimum wage. We note that while for the purposes of statistical text analysis it can be helpful to think of the crowd as a certain type of "algorithm," the workers are very much humans and so ethical considerations about appropriate compensation apply (Fort, Adda, and Cohen, 2011; Mason and Suri, 2012; Shank, 2016).

Changing the Task. In practice, the key to using crowdsourcing has generally been to find the optimal way to divide the coding task into small "bite-sized" chunks. Now that online labor markets have been around for over a decade, researchers have

Please tell us how dark or light the color below appears.   Please tell us how dark or light the color below appears.

Very dark Somewhat dark Neutral Somewhat light Very light   Very dark Somewhat dark Neutral Somewhat light Very light
  ○   ○   ○   ○   ○   ○   ○   ○   ○   ○

(a) Absolute scale (65 on a 100-pt. scale)   (b) Absolute scale (70 on a 100-pt. scale)

Which of the two shades of gray below do you think is darker?

○   ○

(c) Comparison (65 and 70 on a 100-pt. scale)

Figure 18.2. A figure from Carlson and Montgomery (2017) explaining how pairwise comparison tasks can be more tractable than absolute scale tasks. Task C is going to be much more consistent than either task A or B.

started to creatively develop new tasks that can more easily be discretized. Carlson and Montgomery (2017) introduce an approach to placing documents on a scale by collecting thousands of responses to quick pairwise comparison tasks.

The core insight is beautifully illustrated by an example from Carlson and Montgomery (2017), which is depicted in Figure 18.2. For many tasks, such as assessing how dark or light a color is, it is quite difficult to assign an absolute scale without some kind of reference point. However, it is very tractable to make a reliable assessment of a comparison between two values. These pairwise comparisons can in turn be used to recover an underlying latent dimension—an idea that has been around in psychometrics since at least Thurstone (1927), and, arguably, traces back to the 1800s.

In Carlson and Montgomery (2017), they collect many such pairwise judgments by recruiting crowd workers through Amazon's Mechanical Turk platform. They show that the system is highly reliable and compares favorably to other approaches. Remarkably, coders seem to need considerably less training to make a pairwise judgment than to accurately assign an absolute scale. The need to make pairwise comparisons causes the number of evaluations needed to scale with the number of texts squared, so this general approach works best with a moderate number of documents (the largest case is less than 2,000 documents).

It is worth emphasizing that the task in Carlson and Montgomery (2017) is not fully supervised in the sense that at no point is any unit labeled with its actual "true" value. Rather we use indirect feedback about the latent dimension (e.g., which gray is darker) to provide insight on the intended measurement. This leaves these styles of measurement as a bit of a middle ground between supervised categorization approaches and unsupervised approaches, and it is worth careful investigation that the continuous dimension that is learned has the intended outcome.

18.4 Supervision with Found Data

The last strategy we describe for building a training set is "supervision with found data," which involves using found data in order to determine the categories and label the documents. This approach uses existing categories produced by individuals outside of the research team as the training set. For example, in Richard Nielsen's book *Deadly Clerics: Blocked Ambition and the Paths to Jihad*, he explores the questions of why some Muslim clerics start to express support for violent jihad (Nielsen, 2017). To do this, he collects a census of Muslim clerics on the web and the texts they produced and builds a measure of support for violent jihad, what he calls a "Jihad Score."

Using human coding to produce the score is difficult, however. Nielsen set out to produce a measure of radicalization at the cleric level, and the average cleric in Nielsen's sample wrote 523 documents. This makes human evaluation of even a small random sample of clerics for jihadist ideology very time consuming. To sidestep this laborious process of human coding, Nielsen instead turns to a ready sample of documents chosen by jihadists themselves and posted on web forums, "The Jihadist's Bookbag," as representative of jihad. The bookbag has an added advantage of being curated by jihadists with the purpose of being an introduction to jihadist ideology, and therefore Nielsen does not have to impose his own definition of violent jihad on the texts. Nielsen pairs this collection with a curated sample of documents from known non-jihadist clerics. This labeled set of data then provides the training set for the classifier used to produce the final score.

Supervision with found data can be a low-cost approach to produce a training set. It also can have the advantage of having codes produced by true experts; in Nielsen's case, jihadists themselves. The complication is that this procedure can bias your measures in unpredictable directions for at least two reasons. First, the labels haven't been assigned by the analyst and thus come from an unknown process. The analyst needs to ensure that the contents of those documents are reflective of the categories they wish to code. Even granted that the codes for the found data are as the analyst would have assigned them, the second concern is that the documents were nonrandomly selected, and thus the estimated probabilities of words given the latent category are unlikely to be accurate. This is particularly true in practice, as supervision with found data often arises by choosing extreme cases in one direction or the other where language patterns might be quite distinct.

Nielsen (2017) is aware of these issues and provides eight distinct validations designed to establish the validity of his scores, which we will review in Chapter 20. Much as other assumptions, such as the bag-of-words or generative models of text, are wrong, the "supervision with found data" isn't a random sample, but it may work well in practice. However, it demands careful validation.

18.5 Conclusion

In this chapter, we discussed different approaches to creating a training dataset using human coding. We reviewed characteristics of good training sets and the process through which a human coded training set can be produced. Last, we discussed the benefits and drawbacks of crowdsourcing training data and supervision with found data—identifying existing data coded for other reasons than the research task. In the next chapter, we turn to using this training data to classify documents with supervised learning.

CHAPTER 19

Classifying Documents with Supervised Learning

Supervised learning uses statistical models to approximate the mapping between the examples in the training data and the labels assigned to them. These mappings can then be applied to predict category assignments in the larger set of unlabeled data. Supervised learning thus amplifies the human effort put into the training set to enable an approximation of the human mapping that can then be applied to a much larger set of data.

While many statistical classifiers are quite complex, readers can use the familiar intuition of linear regression to understand the basic process by which the labels of the training data (y) are fitted to the features extracted from the training texts (W). Each statistical classifier will approximate y with some function of W, just as in linear regression y is approximated with $X\beta$. The classifier will then choose the parameters of the model β by optimizing a *loss function*. In the case of linear regression, the loss function is $\sum_{i=1}^{N}(y_i - X_i\beta)^2$; each statistical classifier will have its own version of the loss function.

This leaves us with the question of how to represent the documents in the training set. We covered various recipes of extracting features in Part 2: Representation. As we will discuss in detail below, these features can then be transformed, multiplied together, or layered to create more complex features. The high dimensional nature of text data combined with higher order interactions of features can make the feature space very large. *Regularization*, or automatically reducing the complexity of the model, becomes important in order to make fitting the model tractable and prevent overfitting.

Once we have fit a classifier, we will have to evaluate its performance. Importantly, we should evaluate performance on data other than the data used to fit the model. Therefore, it is standard practice to leave out some training data when fitting a classifier in order to use it to evaluate performance later. We will cover more details of evaluating model performance in Chapter 20.

To provide some intuition, we will start with a careful walk through a baseline model, Naive Bayes (Maron and Kuhns, 1960), and some of its extensions. The model is important both because it performs reasonably well on its own and it forms the foundation of other more complicated models. We then turn to describe broader classes of machine learning methods that can be used for classification and prediction.

19.1 Naive Bayes

Suppose we wanted to build a model that could place each document D_i into mutually exclusive and exhaustive categories using the document-feature matrix W as input. Let $y_i \in \{1 \ldots K\}$ be the document's category label. It will be convenient to reexpress the information in y_i as π_i, a K length vector where element $\pi_{ik} = 1$ if document i is in category k (i.e., $y_i = k$) and $\pi_{ik} = 0$ otherwise. We are interested in the probability that an unseen document is in category k given that we observe document D_i. Using Bayes rule, we can write this probability as:

$$p(\pi_{ik} = 1 | D_i) = \frac{p(\pi_{ik} = 1, D_i)}{p(D_i)} \tag{19.1.1}$$

$$= \frac{p(\pi_{ik} = 1)p(D_i | \pi_{ik} = 1)}{p(D_i)}. \tag{19.1.2}$$

The denominator is going to be constant across all categories, so we can simply drop it and normalize at the end of the process. This leads to a formula whose components each have a clear meaning,

$$\underbrace{p(\pi_{ik} = 1 | D_i)}_{\text{prediction}} \propto \underbrace{p(\pi_{ik} = 1)}_{\text{prevalence of class k}} \overbrace{p(D_i | \pi_{ik} = 1)}^{\text{category-specific language model}}. \tag{19.1.3}$$

We can estimate $p(\pi_{ik} = 1)$, which we will denote with the parameter α_k, from the data. Assuming we have a random sample of documents as a training set, we can calculate the proportion that fall into each class:

$$\hat{\alpha}_k = \frac{\sum_i^N I(y_i = k)}{N}, \tag{19.1.4}$$

where $I()$ is the indicator function taking on the value 1 when its argument is true and 0 otherwise.

To this point, we have been agnostic about the form of the category-specific language model. Unfortunately, the document D_i is complicated to model without any assumptions. To handle this we will switch to the document-feature matrix representation W_i, and make the eponymous "naive" assumption. We will assume that each token in the document is drawn independently conditional on the class. This allows us to write

$$W_i, | \pi_{ik} = 1 \sim \text{Multinomial}(\overbrace{\sum_j W_{ij}}^{\text{Number of tokens}}, \underbrace{\mu_k}_{\text{word probabilities for class k}}) \tag{19.1.5}$$

$$p(W_i, | \pi_{ik} = 1) \propto \prod_{j=1}^{J} \mu_{kj}^{W_{ij}}, \tag{19.1.6}$$

where μ_k is the vector of probabilities that indicate the probability of drawing each word in class k. The Naive Bayes idea is quite general and if we had features of a different sort (for example, continuous), we could have factorized in a different way.

This naive assumption of independence conditional on the document class is almost certainly wrong, but it gets us to a set of parameters that we can more easily estimate.

$$\hat{\mu}_{kj} = \frac{\overbrace{\sum_{i}^{N} \pi_{ik} W_{ij}}^{\text{Count of feature } j \text{ in documents of class } k}}{\underbrace{\sum_{i} \sum_{j} \pi_{ik} W_{ij}}_{\text{Count of features in documents of class } k}} \tag{19.1.7}$$

We can think of estimating the parameters for class k by collecting all of the training documents assigned to class k together and calculating the frequency with which each word is used.

This does create a problem with words that are sufficiently rare that they never appear under a given class. This causes our estimate of the probability of their occurrence to be 0, which means that the given class is completely ruled out if it occurs. We want to avoid this problem, and so we add a small constant c for each word,

$$\hat{\mu}_{kj} = \frac{c + \sum_{i}^{N} \pi_{ik} W_{ij}}{Jc + \sum_{i} \sum_{j} \pi_{ik} W_{ij}}. \tag{19.1.8}$$

When $c = 1$, this is like adding a new document for each class that contains one of every word in the vocabulary. This is the same idea as Laplace smoothing, which we discussed back in Chapter 6 on the multinomial language model.

Putting this all together, the Naive Bayes algorithm can be given as:

$$p(\pi_{ik} = 1 \mid W_{i,}) \propto \alpha_k \prod_{j=1}^{J} \mu_{kj}^{W_{ij}}. \tag{19.1.9}$$

If we want to make the best prediction for a given class, we often rewrite it using the arg max notation to indicate that we want the most probable category,

$$\hat{y}_i = \text{arg max}_k \left[\hat{\alpha}_k \prod_{j=1}^{J} \hat{\mu}_{kj}^{W_{ij}} \right] \tag{19.1.10}$$

$$= \text{arg max}_k \left[\log(\hat{\alpha}_k) + \sum_{j}^{J} W_{ij} \log(\hat{\mu}_{kj}) \right], \tag{19.1.11}$$

where taking the log improves numerical stability but preserves the maximum.

Intuitively, Naive Bayes uses the training documents to form a prototype document for each class. When choosing a class, the algorithm weighs the similarity of the new document to each prototype, correcting for the rarity of the class. The Naive Bayes classifier is an attractive model to study because it is comparatively simple, performs well and contains several of the elements that will exist in additional methods we will describe below. Before moving on to a broader list of machine learning classifiers, we make a few remarks about the Naive Bayes method.

19.1.1 THE ASSUMPTIONS IN NAIVE BAYES ARE ALMOST CERTAINLY WRONG

Our derivation of Naive Bayes started with Bayes rule, and in order to simplify the document likelihood, $p(D_i|\pi_{ik} = 1)$, we made the strong assumption that it could be represented as a class-conditional set of independent multinomial draws. There is a whole series of Naive Bayes methods with different conditional distributions that all assume some form of independence. In general, we believe that all of these assumptions are wrong in real language. Importantly though, the assumption of being wrong does not necessarily keep the method from being useful or accurate. A particularly dangerous trap in automated content analysis is dismissing methods out of hand, or even spending time to change them, because the assumptions are wrong without our assessing the effect of those assumptions.

Why then do we make these assumptions and what effect do they have on our classifier? The advantage of the assumption is that it reduces the number of parameters we need to fit the model down to just $(J − 1)K + (K − 1)$. This means that the model is more limited in its ability to fit the data—for example, it is unable to capture interactions between words—but it is also takes relatively little data to fit the model well. The independence assumption does tend to make the Naive Bayes model overconfident in its predictions. What the independence assumption tells the model is that each additional word count is a new piece of information separate from all the previous pieces. In fact, we typically believe that words are "bursty"—once a particular word has been used in a text, it is more likely to be used in it again—and so the model acts as though it has more information than it really does. This overconfidence leads to a situation where the model often chooses the correct category, but predicted probabilities derived from $\hat{\pi}_i$ are poorly calibrated. Poor calibration in turn implies that averaging over a group of predictions provides a poor estimate of the total proportion in a given class. Thus when we want to estimate the proportion of documents in class k, these estimates might lead us astray (a problem we return to below).

19.1.2 NAIVE BAYES IS A GENERATIVE MODEL

In estimating the Naive Bayes classifier our goal was to estimate the probability a document was in a particular class given the contents of the document, $p(\pi_{ik} = 1|D_i)$. Yet, in the process, we introduced and maximized a joint distribution describing how the model was generated: $p(\pi_{ik} = 1, D_i) = p(D_i|\pi_{ik} = 1)p(\pi_{ik} = 1)$. In fact, we can think of this as a mixture model of the type we discussed in Part 3: Discovery, where some of the components are labeled in advance by the analyst.

One attractive part of generative model is that they provide us a way to build, adapt, and interpret algorithms. For example, when introducing the algorithm above, we discussed adding a small constant c to deal with the problem of estimating zero probability of seeing some words. We can interpret this process as adding a Bayesian prior where the pseudo-document arises as a consequence of the prior distribution. Similarly, we can address concerns about burstiness in the words by adopting a more complicated counterpart to the multinomial, the Dirichlet compound multinomial (Elkan, 2006). Generative models make great building blocks for more complex models, as we already saw with the mixture of multinomials giving rise to Latent Dirichlet Allocation and eventually the Structural Topic Model.

However, for classification tasks, there is something a bit odd about generative models. If our interest is in learning $p(y_i|D_i)$, why should we be trying to learn $p(D_i|y_i)$ at all? Can't we just directly maximize $p(y_i|D_i)$ to learn a function mapping from the input to the outcome label without making assumptions about the inputs? In fact, we can, and this gives rise to discriminative models, many of which we talk about in the next section. In these models we only condition on the features we use to represent the documents, and so we don't need to generate a model for them. This will be familiar to many social and data scientists from regression, where we assume no generative model for the features X_i we use to predict y_i.

The discriminative analog of the Naive Bayes model is multinomial logistic regression (sometimes called logistic regression or the softmax classifier in computer science). The model can be given as:

$$p(\pi_{ik} = 1 | W_{i,}) \propto \exp(W_{i,}\mu). \tag{19.1.12}$$

Ng and Jordan (2002) show theoretically and empirically that while logistic regression has higher asymptotic accuracy, Naive Bayes approaches its asymptotic accuracy faster. In other words, for small training samples we should expect Naive Bayes to provide better performance than logistic regression if the assumptions approximately hold. This makes intuitive sense. The additional assumptions we make to arrive at Naive Bayes provide us with some leverage on the problem, but if we have enough data we can eventually learn all the parameters we need to. This same idea, asymptotic efficiency, is one of the key motivations behind Multinomial Inverse Regression (Chapter 11), which also assumes a multinomial generative model (Taddy, 2013).

Discriminative models are also useful members of our toolkit because we don't require separate implementations for different types of covariates. In order to add additional information to Naive Bayes, for example the number of upvotes on a social media post, we would need to alter the model in order to specify a generative process for the upvotes. In logistic regression, we can simply add the variable in along with the word counts. While there is a price of convenience, writing down a model of the input variables does confer other benefits, such as making it easier to deal with missing data in the inputs.

Generative and discriminative models don't always exist in a clear dichotomy. A model might specify a generative process for some variables but not for others. Part of Naive Bayes's success on small datasets is almost certainly attributable to the generative structure, but it also explains why one seldom sees Naive Bayes in production-level systems containing millions of training examples.

19.1.3 NAIVE BAYES IS A LINEAR CLASSIFIER

A common thread in the models that we explore in this section is that they can be expressed as models that are linear in some set of features. This means that the classification decision can be expressed as:

$$\hat{y}_i = f\left(\mu_0 + \sum_{j=1}^{J} \mu_j W_{ij}\right), \tag{19.1.13}$$

where the function $f()$ converts the linear combination of the features to the output space of the prediction and the μ here need not correspond to the way μ was defined above.

In fact, we can see that the logged form of the Naive Bayes classifier from Equation 19.1.11 can be arranged to match the form of Equation 19.1.13:

$$\hat{y}_i = \underbrace{\arg\ \max_k}_{f()} \left[\underbrace{\log(\hat{\alpha}_k)}_{\tilde{\mu}_0} + \sum_j^J W_{ij} \underbrace{\log(\hat{\mu}_{kj})}_{\tilde{\mu}_j} \right] \tag{19.1.14}$$

$$= f\left(\tilde{\mu}_0 + \sum_{j=1}^J \tilde{\mu}_j W_{ij} \right). \tag{19.1.15}$$

Linear classifiers are quite fast to train and fit and much less prone to overfitting than some of their more sophisticated alternatives in machine learning. However, they cannot capture meaningful interactions between the features. This works well in settings where the features that we provide to the algorithm are meaningful and useful on their own. In the next section we will consider a broader set of options that can build better features at the cost of demanding more data.

19.2 Machine Learning

Naive Bayes is one of the simplest machine learning models, but there are a host of other options. Here we consider a number of ways to model the conditional density, or how y_i relates to $W_{i,}$. These methods are general to all kinds of prediction problems with arbitrary inputs and essentially arbitrary outputs.

Essentially all machine learning classifiers can be seen as an example of the following optimization problem (inspired by the excellent review article by Mullainathan and Spiess 2017).

$$\arg\ \min_\mu \sum_{i=1}^N \overbrace{L(\underbrace{f(W_{i,}, \mu)}_{\text{function of } W_{i,}}, y_i)}^{\text{training loss}} + \underbrace{R(\mu, \lambda)}_{\text{regularization}} \tag{19.2.1}$$

In words, we minimize the error in our training set—as determined by the loss function $L(\cdot)$—by choosing μ that defines a function $f(\cdot)$ subject to a complexity restriction $R(\cdot)$ whose strength is determined by λ. This might seem overwhelming at first, but let's start with simple ordinary least squares model. Here the loss function is the sum of squared errors, the function is a linear predictor, and there is no regularizer, such that,

$$L(f(W_{i,}, \mu), y_i) = (y_i - f(W_{i,}, \mu))^2 \tag{19.2.2}$$

$$f(W_{i,}, \mu) = W_{i,}\mu \tag{19.2.3}$$

$$R(\mu, \lambda) = 0 \tag{19.2.4}$$

$$\arg\ \min_{\mu} \sum_{i=1}^{N} (y_i - W_{i,}\mu)^2. \tag{19.2.5}$$

This model will be familiar to many social scientists. An attractive part of the model is the relatively simplicity. We can think of the model prediction $\hat{y}_i = W_{i,}\mu = \sum_j W_{ij}\mu_j$ as summing over the features for document i with a different weight, μ_j, for each feature W_{ij}.

We can use different loss functions to accommodate different kinds of outcomes that we might want to predict. Where linear regression is the baseline model for a continuous outcome, the *softmax classifier* is the baseline model for a multi-category outcome. The name derives from the use of the softmax function, which takes a set of real-valued continuous outcomes a and maps them to a set of values on the simplex using the function. Here we will use k to denote category k for 1 to K total categories.

$$\sigma(a)_k = \frac{\exp(a_k)}{\sum_{k'=1}^{K} \exp(a'_k)}.$$

The full model can be written as:

$$L(f(W_{i,}, \mu), y_i) = -y_i \log(f(W_{i,}, \mu)) \tag{19.2.6}$$

$$f(W_{i,}, \mu) = \frac{\exp(W_{i,}\mu_k)}{\sum_{k'=1}^{K} \exp(W_{i,}\mu_{k'})} \tag{19.2.7}$$

$$R(\mu, \lambda) = 0 \tag{19.2.8}$$

$$\arg\ \min_{\mu_k} \sum_{i=1}^{N} -y_i \log\left(\frac{\exp(W_{i,}\mu_k)}{\sum_{k'=1}^{K} \exp(W_{i,}\mu_{k'})}\right). \tag{19.2.9}$$

This model yields a simple linear classifier that gives predictions for each category that are always nonzero and sum to 1 across all categories.

Although we will consider substantially more complicated classes of function $f(\cdot)$ in the models below, we will find that they can often be represented as a linear function on some transformed feature set. In fact, one way to frame these more complex models is by noting that they are searching for the right transformation of the features to make the linear model perform well. In the next two sections, we consider two different approaches to transforming the features—fixed basis functions and adaptive basis functions. Table 19.1 provides some examples of each of these types of models, some of which may be familiar to the reader.

19.2.1   FIXED BASIS FUNCTIONS

Fixed basis function models are the closest to the basic ordinary least squares model that we will consider here. The linear predictor $f(W_i, \mu) = W_{i,}\mu$ implies that the prediction is linear and additive in the predictor variables $W_{i,}$. However, the model can represent nonlinear and interactive functions by including nonlinear transformations of the original covariates that we will denote $h(W_{i,})$. We now have the linear predictor

Table 19.1. Some examples of fixed basis function and adaptive basis function models, adapted from Mullainathan and Spiess (2017) Table 2.

	Loss Function	Regularization
Fixed Basis Function Models		
Regression	$(y_i - W_{i,}\boldsymbol{\mu})^2$	None
Lasso	$(y_i - W_{i,}\boldsymbol{\mu})^2$	$\sum_{j=1}^{J} |\mu_j|$
Ridge	$(y_i - W_{i,}\boldsymbol{\mu})^2$	$\sum_{j=1}^{J} \mu_j^2$
Support Vector Machines	$\max(0, y_i(W_{i,}\boldsymbol{\mu}))$	$\sum_{j=1}^{J} \mu_j^2$
Adaptive Basis Function Models		
Classification and Regression Trees	varies	depth, nodes, information gain at splits
Boosting	linear combination of classifiers	learning rate, number of iterations
Neural Networks	cross-entropy/mean squared error	number of layers, neurons, iterations

$f(W_{i,}, \boldsymbol{\mu}) = h(W_{i,})\boldsymbol{\mu}$ that is linear in the parameters, but nonlinear in the original predictors!

Many social scientists will likely be familiar with the idea of adding polynomials or interactions as a type of fixed basis function. For example, we could define the nonlinear transformation on each predictor as $h(W_{ij}) = (W_{ij}, W_{ij}^2, W_{ij}^3 \ldots W_{ij}^b)$ up to the bth polynomial. We could also include interactions such that $h(W_{i,})$ would return a vector of every pairwise interaction $W_{ij}W_{ij'}$. This transformation is a basis function expansion of the original predictors. As it turns out, any continuous function can be represented as a linear function on some set of basis functions. This implies that if we only have the right basis functions, we can use a simple linear model to capture any continuous function. The trick is specifying the "right basis functions."

Fixed basis function models are those that commit to a set of basis functions prior to estimation and optimize the weights $\boldsymbol{\mu}$. We can think of two types of basis functions: global and local. The coefficient of a global basis function, such as any of the polynomials discussed above, is affected by data over the entire range of W. An alternative is a local basis function, which models the data within a particular local region of W. Different basis functions are appropriate for modeling certain types of functions. For example, splines are adept at modeling smooth functions while wavelets can handle sharp discontinuities.

Even relatively simple representations of text such as document-feature matrices are high-dimensional. When we start adding basis functions, the dimensionality can explode quickly and we can reach a point where the number of created features exceeds the number of documents. In this setting, we will no longer be able to estimate the parameters $\boldsymbol{\mu}$ without some additional kind of constraint. We can add a regularizer $R(\boldsymbol{\mu}, \lambda)$, which expresses a preference for simpler functions.

Different kinds of regularizers yield different kinds of results. The Ridge regularizer $\|\boldsymbol{\mu}\|_2^2$ shrinks the parameters smoothly toward zero. By contrast the Lasso regularizer $\|\boldsymbol{\mu}\|_1$ induces sparsity, which sets many of the parameters in $\boldsymbol{\mu}$ exactly to zero. We saw examples of this latter strategy in Chapter 11 on finding separating words. Sparse regularization arose in that context because it helps in settings where we believe that most features are essentially uninformative about the quantity we are trying to estimate but we don't know which. For example, in predicting the sentiment of a product review, the vast majority of the words might be describing the product itself but carry relatively little information on whether or not the view of the product is positive or negative.

If the parameters are truly sparse, then using a sparsity promoting penalty in the high-dimensional case is uncontroversial. However, in social science and language more broadly we might believe that the world is full of small but generally nonzero effects; that is, we believe the parameter vector is *dense*, not sparse. Hastie, Tibshirani, and Friedman (2013) introduce the "bet on sparsity" principle, which is the advice that analysts "use a procedure that does well in sparse problems, since no procedure does well in dense problems." Regardless of one's philosophical position, sparsity is an important part of the regularization toolkit.

Fixed basis function models with regularization cover an enormous range of machine learning methods and could have a book's worth of material all on their own. The models give us great control over the complexity of the function we learn. These models will function best when the features carry a lot of independent information about the outcome; they will also tend to perform better than alternatives when data is limited. We consider alternatives when we don't have good features below.

19.2.2   ADAPTIVE BASIS FUNCTIONS

When features are informative about the category of interest, supervised learning is relatively easy. The biggest challenge is dealing with high dimensionality, a problem which can be addressed with regularization. The trouble is that for complicated categories, simple features, such as those based on word counts, might be insufficient to learn simple classifiers. When possible, we might engage in "feature engineering," the construction of specific features that help us make our classification problem easier. We saw examples of this earlier in Part 2: Representation.

The recent trend in machine learning has been to replace manual feature engineering with methods that adaptively learn the most predictive features from the data themselves. This requires substantially more data and is less efficient than a correctly specified fixed basis function model, but it can be extremely effective at learning classifiers in a host of other situations with less human effort in feature engineering. To see this idea in action, let's consider the idea of a neural network.

Recall the softmax classifier shown earlier. Here our prediction for y_i was given by $\sigma(W_{i,}\mu) = \frac{\exp(W_{i,}\mu_j)}{\sum_{j'=1}^{K} \exp(W_{i,}\mu_{j'})}$. Perhaps the categories that we want to predict aren't well approximated by a simple function of the $W_{i,}$. There could potentially be an alternative set of features, $\tilde{W}_{i,}$, with $\tilde{W}_{i,} = (\tilde{W}_{i1}, \tilde{W}_{i2}, \ldots, \tilde{W}_{iJ})$, which is some unknown function of the features W_i. It might be the case that $\sigma(\tilde{W}_{i,}\mu_{\tilde{W}_{i,}})$ more accurately assigns documents to categories than working with the features on their own. We can learn each of these features as a function of all the $W_{i,}$ and a separate weights matrix $\mu_{\tilde{W}_{i,}}$ such that $\tilde{W}_{ij} = f(W_{i,}\mu_W)$. Several functions have been considered in the literature— a currently popular function is the Rectified Linear Unit (ReLu), which has the form $\tilde{W}_{ij} = \max(0, \mu_{W_{ij}} W_{i,})$. In words, this means that each of the new features $\tilde{W}_{ij}$ is either the linear combination of all $W_{i,}$ using the vector of weights $\mu_{W_{ij}}$, or 0, whichever is larger. This set of features $\tilde{W}_i$, is called a "hidden layer" because it is a set of features that we don't get to observe.

Like the fixed basis functions discussed in the prior section, the hidden layer $\tilde{W}_i$, allows the model to express more complicated, nonlinear, and interactive functions of the original features W_i. However, unlike the fixed basis functions that we had to specify in advance, we can learn them here inductively from the data. As part of constructing the model, we control the number of hidden features $\tilde{W}_i$, in the hidden layer. The number of these hidden features, often called the "breadth" of the layer, determines how flexible the model is at representing functions of W_i,.

The "deep learning" revolution came when computing power and data became available to learn more than just a single hidden layer. Researchers realized that by stacking layers on top of each other, they could build even more powerful classifiers that had better generalization performance. Thus, one set of hidden features predicts the next layer of hidden features, and so on and so on. Empirically, researchers have found that by decreasing the breadth of the network (the number of hidden features in each layer) while increasing the depth (number of layers stacked on top of each other), the hidden features learn progressively more abstract concepts that generalize well.

Much of the current work in machine learning is oriented around these kinds of deep neural networks. The success of these methods has changed the focus of the field from various kinds of feature engineering to developing more complex network architectures. We have provided only a brief summary here because this is a fast moving field and descriptions of particular techniques for machine learning are covered in many existing books. For getting started with deep neural networks we recommend Goodfellow, Bengio, and Courville (2016). Chang and Masterson (2020) provide an introduction to recurrent neural network models commonly used on text that is aimed at social scientists. Hvitfeldt and Silge (2021) provide a practical introduction to estimating these models in R.

19.2.3 QUANTIFICATION

A different way to improve the results is to change the quantity of interest. For many social science applications the quantity of interest is only the proportion of documents in a category and not the individual classifications. For example, recall that King, Pan and Roberts needed to group censored and uncensored blog posts into topical categories in order to explore the motivation for Chinese censorship. They weren't interested in whether any particular post was in one category or another, but rather in what share of censored and uncensored posts fell into each category. Hopkins and King (2010) show that if the focus is on estimating the proportion of documents in each of K categories, $p(\boldsymbol{\pi}) = p(\pi_1, \pi_2, \ldots, \pi_K)$, rather than individual document classifications, it is possible to achieve substantial improvements in accuracy by directly targeting that objective and bypassing the individual document classifications altogether. They call their strategy ReadMe after the software implementing it.

Hopkins and King (2010) begin with a particular recipe for representing texts: indicators of whether each word occurs in a document (rather than counts as we have typically been assuming). They then note that, if no additional assumptions are made about the independence of words, there are 2^J possible documents under this representation. We can define a probability distribution over the 2^J possible documents and call this $p(W)$, the document distribution conditional on category as $p(W|\boldsymbol{\pi})$ (a $2^J \times K$ matrix), and the quantity of interest, the probability distribution over classes, as $p(\boldsymbol{\pi})$, a K-length vector denoting the proportion of documents in each class. Again, without any assumptions other than the process used to represent the texts, we can write the data generating process for the texts as,

$$p(W) = p(W|\pi)p(\pi). \tag{19.2.10}$$

Hopkins and King (2010)'s insight (building on insights from King and Lu 2008) is that if $p(W)$ and $p(W|\pi)$ are known, then the problem reduces to simple matrix algebra. $p(W)$ can be estimated from the test set, but the high dimensionality of $p(W|\pi)$ implies that it cannot be estimated without additional assumptions. King and Lu (2008) and Hopkins and King (2010) propose using the training set and matrix smoothing algorithms to compute $p(W|\pi)$ and then solve for $p(\pi)$. This ensures that the dependence across a large number of features is maintained, while also estimating a model useful for classification. Notice, Equation 19.2.10 looks very similar to the Naive Bayes model, but ReadMe avoids the Naive Bayes independence assumptions. Later work by Jerzak, King, and Strezhnev (2019) has considered alternate models for $p(W|\pi)$.

The move to proportions in Hopkins and King (2010) pays dividends for inference, but comes at the cost of losing individual document classifications. It weakens the assumptions necessary for the training data. Rather than requiring a random sample the data need only share the distribution of features conditional on the category—$p(W|\pi)$ (a more plausible assumption for documents that have not yet been written). It also helps correct the bias that occurs when using an individual classifier with a large number of categories. For example, if five documents each have a 0.2 probability of being in category k, an individual classifier would place them all in a different category, whereas ReadMe could contribute these estimates to the proportion of document in category k.

The ReadMe algorithm is less practical for users who have few documents or want to assess their results in relation to an external covariate. For example, we cannot use ReadMe to assess how sentiment varies by individual. In the case where we have many documents for each value of the covariate, we can run ReadMe on each individual strata, but with continuous covariates or those with many strata, we would need to use individual classification.

19.2.4   CONCLUDING THOUGHTS ON SUPERVISED LEARNING WITH RANDOM SAMPLES

Beyond the complexity of the various algorithms we introduced here, there is a core idea. A perfectly reasonable strategy for measurement is to define a set of categories, have humans annotate a random subset of documents using those categories, and then train a machine learning algorithm to predict those categories. As long as the machine learning algorithm predicts accurately in the kind of documents you want to measure, it doesn't much matter what it is. For those looking to read more about the many options for machine learning techniques that can be applied to text we recommend: Bishop (2006), Eisenstein (2019), Murphy (2021), and Aggarwal (2018).

19.3   Example: Estimating Jihad Scores

In this section, we return to Richard Nielsen's book *Deadly Clerics: Blocked Ambition and the Paths to Jihad* for an example of supervised classification in action. Nielsen (2017) explores the questions of why some Muslim clerics start to express support for violent jihad. He argues that a major driver of a turn toward an ideology that supports violence is blocked ambition—circumstances where the cleric is shut out of prominent government jobs, effectively thwarting his goals.

To build evidence on this question, he collects the first census of Muslim clerics on the web and the writings that clerics place online, including their articles, books, sermons, and fatwas (legal rulings in Islam). These texts capture their *expressed ideology*, which are the object of focus here. He then creates a measure of their support for violent jihad using supervised learning.

Nielsen (2017) aggregates all the texts for a particular cleric together. For a training set, Nielsen (2017) uses what we call "supervision with found data," or existing labels, combining "The Jihadist's Bookbag," a collection of documents designed to provide an introduction to jihadist ideology, with a curated set of documents from non-jihadist texts.

Nielsen (2017) uses this training set and the Naive Bayes (NB) model we explained in depth to estimate the probability that any cleric's writings would be classified into The Jihadist's Bookbag versus the curated set of texts written by clerics who do not support violent jihad. Instead of using this probability directly, he uses the output of the model to calculate a "Jihad Score" that is a continuous measure of the support for violent jihad. Under the NB model assumptions, the score for document i is calculated as the log-odds of document i being in the jihad class assuming equal prior odds for jihad and not (Beauchamp, 2011; Perry and Benoit, 2017). The score for document i is

$$\text{Jihad Score}_i = \frac{1}{\sum_j W_{ij}} \sum_j W_{ij} \underbrace{\log\left(\frac{\mu_{j1}}{\mu_{j0}}\right)}_{\text{word score}}, \tag{19.3.1}$$

where $\mu_{j\cdot}$ indicates the probability of seeing word j given the document is from either a jihadist (μ_{j1}) or not (μ_{j0}). When the probability of seeing the observed word is higher in a jihadist document, the score contribution for that word will be positive; when the probability of seeing the observed word is higher in a non-jihadist document, the score contribution will be lower. Thus the log-ratio of probabilities acts like a weight for each word, which is then simply summed up over all words in each cleric's writing. These weights can be examined as in Figure 19.1.

Nielsen (2017) uses the training set to estimate the probabilities of seeing each word in each category of text. With these key parameters estimated, he forms the scores for each cleric in his dataset and validates them in a number of different ways, which we describe in Chapter 20. With this validated measure of expressed ideology in hand, he provides support for his main hypothesis that blocked ambition is a significant cause of clerics' turning to support violence.

Rather than use the NB model to classify clerics into binary categories of jihadist and not jihadist, Nielsen (2017)'s approach is what we call *predictability as measurement*. This is a common approach in low-dimensional embedding methods where humans would have a difficult time creating a gold-standard judgment of the exact continuous value to assign to some underlying trait. This is also closely related to the fictitious prediction problem that we outlined in Chapter 11, where we use a *prediction* task to measure the *intensity* of some dimension.

Of course in the case of Nielsen (2017), the prediction isn't fictitious at all: it would actually be useful to classify clerics into jihadist and not. While Nielsen (2017)

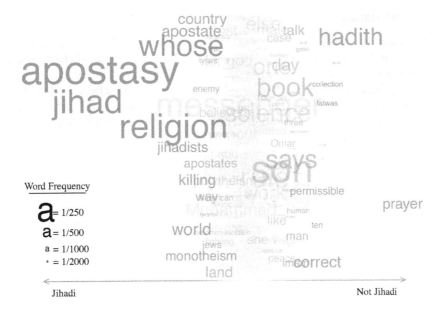

Figure 19.1. Plot of the weights on each word in Nielsen (2017)'s Jihad Score with English translations. Figure 5.2 from Nielsen (2017).

is generally careful to treat the jihad scores as an indicator of how likely it is that the individual supports violent jihad, he does at times seem to suggest that this also measures intensity of support. Others are more direct in making the claim that the prediction of a class provides a measurement of intensity along a dimension such as ideology (Beauchamp, 2011) and polarization (Gentzkow, Shapiro, and Taddy, 2019). In these tasks the predictability of the outcome is a surrogate function for the underlying dimension of interest.

One interesting and understudied complication of using supervised learning for measurement is how to incorporate the uncertainty of the measure into subsequent analyses.[1] Because the measurements are the result of a classifier, there will inevitably be some level of error and thus uncertainty about the true measurement. If we fail to account for this uncertainty it will, at the very least, cause us to have an inaccurate sense of our uncertainty. If the errors are systematically related to the other variables in the analysis, this could further introduce omitted variable bias (Fong and Tyler, 2020). Nielsen (2017) uses a block bootstrap approach to evaluating uncertainty about the cleric scores, resampling with replacement the words for each cleric and then recalculating the score to calculate the uncertainty (Benoit, Laver, and Mikhaylov, 2009). Fong and Tyler (2020) propose an alternative general method of moments approach to incorporating measurements from machine learning in downstream analyses.

---

[1]Note that this is also a problem for hand coding, where error in human annotation is often ignored in analyses downstream.

19.4 Conclusion

In this chapter, we reviewed different models for supervised learning. First, we covered the Naive Bayes model in detail, to build intuition for statistical classifiers. Then, using the intuition of linear regression, we reviewed classes of machine learning models, covering both fixed basis function and adaptive basis function models. Last, we showed how a variant of Naive Bayes has been applied using Nielsen (2017)'s measure of cleric ideology. In the next chapters, we move on to discuss validation, in our last step of supervised learning.

CHAPTER 20

Checking Performance

In this chapter, we outline some approaches for validating measurements. Measurement is a compression of data into categories or a value on a continuous line—one particular operationalization of a concept. Through the process of validation, we ensure that our compression reflects the concept that we intend to study and that we have correctly understood what we compressed and what information we discarded. We use validation to ensure that our measure performs well in data other than that which we used to train our model.

There are myriad validation techniques and no single clear organizing framework. However, there is one underlying principle that unites the various options: vulnerability to being proven wrong. By repeatedly exposing our measures to tests that they are only likely to pass if they are working correctly, we start to build a base of evidence that can be convincing both to ourselves and our readers.

No amount of validation can completely assure us that we are correct, and different settings will call for different levels of certainty, and thus different levels of validation. In all circumstances, though, we emphasize trying to build in an evaluation loop— a process of validating and subsequently updating the measure at regular intervals throughout the research process and after deployment (for ongoing measurements). This provides us a regular, external check on our model. As reflected in the principles laid out in this book, we do not believe any text model is self-justifying and thus we should avoid blindly using any method without validating it.

What does it mean to validate? Essentially, validations shows that the measure captures the phenomenon we are interested in studying. In measurement we are implicitly invoking an assumption of concept homogeneity (Goertz, 2008; Teune and Przeworski, 1970; Gerring and Thomas, 2005), which states that two observations assigned the same value of the measurement are equivalent with respect to the conceptual dimension the measure is seeking to recover. We are attempting to evaluate both that the conceptual dimension captures our theoretical measure of interest and that the observations are correctly placed on the conceptual dimension.

20.1 Validation with Gold-Standard Data

We start by setting out the infrastructure for the simplest case. We assume that we are in the canonical setting for supervised learning that contains four components: a set of categories that are mutually exclusive and exhaustive, a set of documents with

Table 20.1. Example format of a confusion matrix.

	C_1	C_2	C_3	C_4	Machine
C_1	N_{11}	N_{12}	N_{13}	N_{14}	$N_{1,}$
C_2	N_{21}	N_{22}	N_{23}	N_{24}	$N_{2,}$
C_3	N_{31}	N_{32}	N_{33}	N_{34}	$N_{3,}$
C_4	N_{41}	N_{42}	N_{43}	N_{44}	$N_{4,}$
Human	$N_{,1}$	$N_{,2}$	$N_{,3}$	$N_{,4}$	N

gold-standard labels for those categories that are randomly sampled from the population of interest, a set of unlabeled documents we wish to measure, and a statistical classifier to obtain a mapping function that extrapolates from the gold-standard labels to unlabeled documents. By gold-standard we mean that the labels are correctly coded and perfectly reflect the concept of interest. We can evaluate the accuracy of the classifier using the gold-standard labels.

20.1.1 VALIDATION SET

Remember that we want to validate the classifier with data other than that which we used to fit the model. This means we should not use all of our gold-standard labeled data to fit the model. Instead, we should leave some data out, in what we call a *validation set*, so we can test the performance of the model in this held-out data.

We divide our gold-standard documents into a train and validation set. The training documents can be used to obtain a mapping function and we can evaluate accuracy on the validation set. Because the validation set contains labeled data, we can directly compare the labels in the validation set to those that we predicted for it. We can make this comparison using a *confusion matrix*: a $K \times K$ cross-tabulation where the rows describe predictions and the columns characterize the gold-standard codes. Each cell describes the number of documents that received the classification from the respective row and column. In the simplified setting where the model produces a predicted class for a new document and no other information (e.g. a predicted probability), the confusion matrix provides a straightforward summary of the typically most relevant performance information.

For example, N_{12} describes the number of documents an automated method coded as a 1 that the gold-standard labeled a 2. In general, if the on-diagonal elements of Table 20.1 are large, then the method is performing well.

Directly using confusion matrices to evaluate model performance can be difficult—so it is standard to summarize the matrices. The three most prominent summaries used are: (1) *Accuracy*—the proportion of correctly classified documents, (2) *Precision* for category k–the number of documents correctly classified into category k, divided by the total number of documents classified as category k, and (3) *Recall* for category k—the number of correctly classified category k documents divided by the number of gold-standard documents in category k.

$$\text{Accuracy} = \frac{N_{11} + N_{22} + N_{33} + N_{44}}{N}; \ \text{Precision}_k = \frac{N_{kk}}{\sum_{k'=1}^{K} N_{kk'}}; \ \text{Recall}_k = \frac{N_{kk}}{\sum_{k'=1}^{K} N_{k'k}}$$

Which metric to use for performance will depend on the quantity of interest. Sometimes, there are specific considerations in the application that make precision more important than recall, for example. Consider the spam filter for your email—in this case it is more costly to put an important message in the spam folder than for a piece of spam to filter into the inbox. The spam filter should therefore prioritize precision of classifying spam (making sure spam is really indeed spam), over recall (putting all spam into the spam box).

By contrast, many tasks in the social sciences are trying to "characterize the haystack" and measure the proportion of documents in a given category for a given stratum (such as a time period or author) with approximately equal weight given to different errors. In these cases, accuracy, precision, and recall at the document level are less important than the bias in the estimate of the proportion. For each specific research task, researchers should consider carefully the most relevant metrics of model performance.

20.1.2 CROSS-VALIDATION

Validation is an iterative procedure where we fit the model, check its accuracy, and then tune or change the model and refit it, checking accuracy again.[1] If we only use one validation set in these settings, our procedure will likely overfit to that particular validation set. In order to address this, we can use *cross-validation* (Efron and Gong, 1983; Hastie, Tibshirani, and Friedman, 2013). In V-fold cross-validation, the training set is randomly partitioned into V ($v = 1 \ldots, V$) groups. The model's performance is assessed on each of the groups, ensuring all predictions are made on data out of sample. For each group v, the model is trained on the $V - 1$ other groups, then applied to the Vth group to assess performance. V-fold cross-validation then creates V measures of performance, which can be averaged to evaluate any given model. Cross-validation is useful—it avoids overfitting by focusing on out-of-sample prediction and selects the best model for the underlying data from a set of candidate models (this is known as the Oracle property) (van der Vaart, Dudoit, and van der Laan, 2006).[2]

While cross-validation is a useful method of approximating out-of-sample fit, this only provides an accurate estimate of the prediction error of interest if the gold-standard documents are a random sample from the population of interest. If, for example, the goal is to categorize internet news posts today from a training set of news posts from 1993, we are unlikely to accurately estimate our error. While this example may seem far-fetched, many articles attempt to build systems that will classify documents that have not yet been written. In cases where there is conceptual drift or some other change in the data generating process, we will no longer have an accurate estimate of the error, even if we have achieved good cross-validated performance.

20.1.3 THE IMPORTANCE OF GOLD-STANDARD DATA

The above examples assume that we have gold-standard data that is completely accurate, but in reality this can be difficult to do. Human coding is often thought about as the gold standard, but creating a human coded training set can be challenging because of misinterpretation, complicated categories, or lack of coder training. As we discussed

---

[1] Parts of this section are drawn from Grimmer, Roberts, and Stewart (2021).

[2] These properties only apply when all steps (including selection of relevant predictors) are handled within the training set of the cross-validation and not within the full labelled data. See Section 7.10.2 of (Hastie, Tibshirani, and Friedman, 2013) for more information on the proper application of cross-validation.

in Chapter 18, validating the human coded training dataset by assessing intercoder reliability is an important first step before validating the classifier, which relies on the assumption that the labels are correct.

20.1.4 ONGOING EVALUATIONS

In many large projects, data is designed to be continually collected over a long period of time. In these settings we strongly recommend building habitual evaluation of classifier performance into the maintenance of the system. Changes over even relatively short periods of time can dramatically change performance. Consider a classifier designed to assess sentiment on Twitter. Not only is language rapidly evolving, but so is the population of people using the platforms. These kinds of changes are not accounted for in the original accuracy estimate.

20.2 Validation without Gold-Standard Data

When we are less certain that we can rely on the training set as a reservoir of gold-standard data that we can use for validation, checking performance is more difficult. We might lack gold-standard data for any number of reasons—known errors in human coding, reliance on found data for the training set, or use of dictionary methods instead of supervised learning for classification. In these cases, we view lacking gold standard data as shifting the burden of human effort from the initial stages of labeling documents to the later stage of validation. And even when we believe that our training set is close to gold standard, the evaluations below can still be useful for evaluating the behavior of the classifier. Here we present some approaches to validation without gold-standard data. However, we note that these are neither mutually exclusive, nor exhaustive, and generally should be tailored to each application.

20.2.1 SURROGATE LABELS

While we may not have gold-standard data, we still may be able to collect surrogate labels, which are a close enough approximation to let us know that we are on the right track. In the psychometric literature this often falls under the broader category of *convergent validity*, establishing that our measure accords with other relevant measures (Adcock and Collier, 2001). For example, if we were trying to categorize news articles by subject, we could compare them to the section they appeared in in the newspaper, or a tag given to them in an online database. While they are approximate, we should expect our labels and these external labels to have some correspondence.

Approximate labels can be an important part of the validation process, but they aren't gold-standard data. We highlight two ways in which they could potentially lead us astray. This isn't a reason to not use these methods, but rather to be cautious about what they can and can't tell us.

First, approximate labels have a tendency to tell us only about the most extreme cases. This is part of the broader point that we should be cautious of measures that are difficult or for which it is impossible to obtain an exact gold standard. This can lead to circumstances where we fail to notice that our measures lack a discriminating power that they would appear to have on their face. Goertz (2008) identifies a concern in measurement more generally that he calls the "the gray zone," a range of intermediate points along a scale that are not really distinguished from each other. He gives an example using the Polity scale for democracy, which ranges from -10 to $+10$. He notes that if you take only the most extreme values (-10 and $+10$), which account for 23% of the data, and replace all other values with random uniform draws, you get a measure that correlates at .5 with the measure of interest. The concern here is that we can easily trick ourselves into believing that we have a measure that discriminates well along an entire dimension but really just picks up a coarse distinction between two extremes.

The second concern is that surrogate labels are often nonrandomly selected and thus not representative of the population of interest. This might be because the surrogate labels are found data, or because we are interested in evaluating the accuracy of a fairly rare category that would require an inordinately large number of randomly sampled documents to efficiently evaluate. Thankfully there are evaluation designs developed specifically for this purpose (King and Lowe, 2003).

20.2.2   PARTIAL CATEGORY REPLICATION

One of the challenges with validation can be that the number of categories is too large to validate or achieve high performance for all categories. However, even in settings with 100 or more categories it is often the case that only a subset of categories (or an aggregation of categories) is relevant to the quantity of interest. In these settings, it is possible to write a codebook for only the subset of categories of interest (grouping the rest into another category) and perform standard supervised learning and validation. Grimmer (2013a) uses this approach to establish that the supervised method ReadMe is able to capture aggregate categories of interest about legislative credit claiming.

20.2.3   NONEXPERT HUMAN EVALUATION

It is often helpful to have nonexpert human evaluations. For example, we could take a sample of the text that the classifier placed in one category, and introduce an intruder from another category. Then we could ask human evaluators to find the text that doesn't fit. Or, we could ask nonexpert humans to evaluate *semantic validity* by asking human coders to produce labels based on the most distinctive words representing that category and compare their labels to our own. We provided overviews of some of the relevant experimental designs in Part 3: Discovery, including the cluster quality evaluations of (Grimmer and King, 2011) and the intruder detection tasks of (Chang et al., 2009). Pairwise comparisons and ranking tasks are another useful way of soliciting evaluations (Lowe and Benoit, 2013; Carlson and Montgomery, 2017).

20.2.4   CORRESPONDENCE TO EXTERNAL INFORMATION

Accurate measures should have particular relationships to external information. When these relationships can be anticipated and specified beforehand, we can evaluate *hypothesis validity*. For example, we might expect swings in Congressional speech on the House floor should be predictable based on major news events (Quinn et al., 2010) or that committee chairs in the Senate talk more about the issues related to their committee (Grimmer, 2013b).

The key to hypothesis validity is carefully choosing the hypotheses so that a failure to see the observed relationship is extremely unlikely except when the measure is performing poorly. This often creates a bit of a paradox where researchers show that their new measures have some expected relationships and then in their key finding show an unexpected relationship.

20.3 Example: Validating Jihad Scores

To give a sense of what validation might look like in the absence of gold-standard data, we describe the validation process for the development of the jihad scale in Nielsen (2017), the context for which we described in Chapter 18. Nielsen (2017, Ch. 5) uses an eight-part validation to assess different assumptions and performance qualities of his measure. This is a particularly difficult case, as part of the motivation for his scaling exercise was the difficulty in obtaining gold-standard data. Importantly, many of the validations are paired with close readings of samples of the texts.

Validation 1: Representativeness of the labeled documents. Recall that Nielsen (2017) uses a "supervision with found data" strategy in which the scale is pinned down by two extremes: a set of documents from known jihadists called The Jihadist's Bookbag. These documents are a form of "found data"; they were not annotated for this purpose and they aren't a set of documents we are trying to classify. As a result, it is important to think about whether or not they are representative of the definition of jihad that Nielsen lays out in the book. There is theoretical justification for this set of texts—jihadists themselves have constructed this set—but Nielsen needs to verify that the contents comport with his description of jihad and how the scholarly community has come to define this term.

To ensure that the documents in The Jihadist's Bookbag are indeed a reflection of what he intends to measure, Nielsen (2017) runs an LDA topic model with $K = 5$ topics to describe the training data. In the book he presents the top five words for each topic (using FREX scores), and titles of three documents per topic that have the highest proportions of the given topic. He then further groups the authors of these documents into clusters based on their use of different topics to show patterns of particular jihadist authors. He concludes through these assessments and reading of the material that these documents are accurate reflections of his conception of jihadist ideology.

Validation 2: Sensitivity to alternate dataset. To ensure that his findings were not driven by the particular set of labeled documents he chose, Nielsen (2017) generated a new scaling using documents in the online jihadist library "Pulpit of Monotheism and Jihad." He originally did not choose this dataset because it was too ideologically broad. Still he shows it produces qualitatively similar findings to his scores.

Validation 3: Assessing the word weights. Scaling models of this sort has the distinct advantage that the way a document is scored is fairly transparent. Nielsen (2017) examined the word weights to see that they seemed on their face reasonable. He also visualized the translated results (Figure 19.1). This helps to assure us that the classifier is doing something reasonable while also communicating more information to the reader about what words are indicative of jihad.

Validation 4: Comparison of the resulting scores for known individuals. Nielsen (2017) reports on some baseline checks on the nature of the scores. He shows the distribution of scores and indicates where key figures are placed on the score continuum (Figure 20.1). He couples this with descriptions of why these clerics are reasonably placed along the scale. He also investigates all the clerics at the most extreme end of the scale and confirms that they are in fact extreme jihadists.

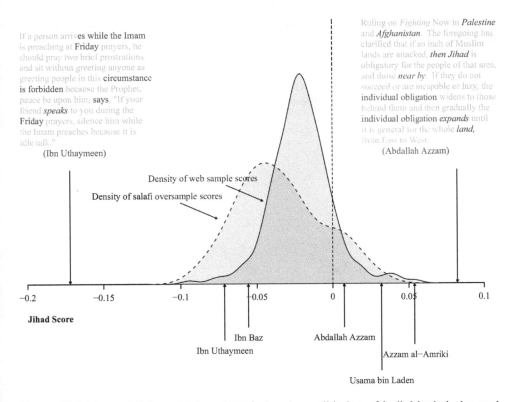

Figure 20.1. Figure 5.3 from Nielsen (2017) showing validation of individual clerics and translated excerpts from their writing.

Validation 5–8: Checks against external sources. If the jihad scores are accurate, we might expect that they align with other sources of expert knowledge. Nielsen (2017) assesses four sources of such knowledge: (5) biographies of clerics (which may identify them as jihadists), (6) a list of supporters of al-Qaeda generated by Ayman al-Zawahiri, the current leader of al-Qaeda, (7) a set of three jihadist websites listing both fellow jihadists and clerics whom they explicitly reject, and (8) assessments by counter-terrorism specialists appearing in McCants, Brachman, and Felter (2006). In each case he demonstrates that his jihad scores are predictive of the classifications in these lists, and, in the case of errors, carefully explains the nature of the error and why it is unlikely to be problematic for the validity of the final scores.

These validations are all quite specific to the particular case, but they run the gamut of establishing that the training data in fact reflects the concept of interest and that the scores predict known jihadist clerics and are consistent with lists of jihadist clerics. Of course, there are always more validations that one can do, but this assessment is quite extensive—the validation section takes up 20 pages in the book (pp. 114–130, appendix pp. 204–209) and includes six figures and two tables. Because the scores are core to the book's argument, this careful validation is warranted.

20.4 Conclusion

In this chapter, we discussed validation of supervised classification. Ideally, with gold-standard training data, we can leave out a part of the training set as a validation set, which we can use to evaluate the accuracy of our model. We discussed various measures of performance (accuracy, precision, and recall), and we introduced cross-validation.

In addition, we discussed approaches to validation when gold-standard data is unavailable. Using Nielsen (2017) as an example, we showed how using surrogate labels, checking word weights for semantic validity, and close reading can also provide tests of performance of our measure.

CHAPTER 21

Repurposing Discovery Methods

In Part 3: Discovery, we covered a number of techniques for discovery: single-membership clustering models, mixed-membership topic models, and low-dimensional embedding strategies. We introduced these techniques in the discovery part of this book because they require little human input up front and therefore are useful when the researcher is still exploring the corpus and the concepts that will make up the research question. However, these techniques can also be used for the purpose of measurement. In this chapter, we provide an overview of how we approach measurement with unsupervised methods, and how this approach differs from the way that we use these methods for the purpose of discovery.

In the use of text as data in the social sciences, including in our own work, the role of discovery and measurement has frequently been blurred. In this chapter, we advocate for separating measurement and discovery by conducting the two tasks on different sets of data. For example, as discussed in Chapter 12, Grimmer and King (2011) discover their conceptualization of how legislators communicate in press releases using a small corpus from a single senator. They then use a measurement strategy on a different corpus to confirm their finding. We have found that splitting the data into two distinct samples to first develop then apply a measurement resolves some of the concerns about using unsupervised methods for measurement.

We first start with a discussion of what types of concepts unsupervised methods will typically be more equipped to measure. Then, we describe a workflow for using unsupervised measures for measurement. Last, we address some of the concerns we have frequently heard about using unsupervised methods for measurement. We conclude by relating unsupervised measures to "found" data.

21.1 Unsupervised Methods Tend to Measure Subject Better Than Subtleties

Unsupervised models such as clustering, topic models, and embeddings all work by compression. What makes the topics learned by these models interpretable to humans is that they are trying to squeeze high-dimensional information through a low-dimensional channel. For example, a standard topic model needs to represent all J individual words that appear in a document using only K topics. Because J is generally much larger than K, the model puts words that frequently co-occur in the same topic because there are only a small number of topics to work with.

The need to explain all the observed words in a document using the K topics tends to favor words that are frequent. Language in general is quite noun-heavy (particularly after stop words are removed). This tends to weight topic models toward picking up subject matter rather than, for example, sentiment. This is where topic models get their name. We haven't made any explicit decision in the model that forces it to pick up subject matter; it is the interaction of the way language is used combined with a modeling approach that weights more heavily frequent words that produces this result.

Unsupervised methods more generally will be more likely to work well if the goal of measurement is to pick up the primary subjects of the text rather than style, tone, or some other more subtle property of the text. These methods will always be most sensitive to what is prominent in the text. If we hope to measure something more subtle with unsupervised methods, the best approach is to change the contents of the document-feature matrix to change the type of latent feature that will be discovered. For example, using part-of-speech tagging, we could discard everything except the adjectives and adverbs in a set of texts if we wanted to push the model more toward sentiment. But in general, if an analyst has a specific quantity that she wants to extract and if that quantity is not contributing to a large portion of the preprocessed text, the use of unsupervised methods can be an incredibly frustrating experience because they might be too coarse to pick this quantity up.

Another implication of this, consistent with our agnostic view, is that what the unsupervised method is returning is not any true latent structure within the text, but a parsimonious compression of that text. For example, a topic in a topic model is just a distribution over words that is reasonably effective at reconstructing the bag of words representation for the document. Any meaning that we infer from that is justified by our validation more than by the result of the model itself.

21.2 Example: Scaling via Differential Word Rates

In this section, we provide an example of when unsupervised methods can work for measurement and under which conditions they fail.[1] We consider using an unsupervised scaling method that uses a corpus of text to estimate a political spectrum. First Monroe and Maeda (2004), then later Slapin and Proksch (2008), introduce statistical models of text based on *item response theory* (IRT) to automatically estimate the spatial location of political parties. Politicians are assumed to reside in a low-dimensional political space, which is represented by the parameter θ_i for politician i. A politician's (or party's) position in this space is assumed to affect the rate at which words are used in texts. Using this assumption and text data, unsupervised scaling methods can then be used to measure the underlying positions of political actors.

Slapin and Proksch (2008) develop their method, Wordfish, as a Poisson-IRT model. Specifically, Slapin and Proksch (2008) assume that each word j from individual i, W_{ij}, is drawn from a Poisson distribution with rate λ_{ij}, $W_{ij} \sim \text{Poisson}(\lambda_{ij})$. λ_{ij} is modeled as a function of individual i's loquaciousness (α_i), the frequency with which word j is used (ψ_j), the extent to which a word discriminates between the underlying ideological space (μ_j) and the politician's underlying position (π_i),

$$\lambda_{ij} = \exp(\alpha_i + \psi_j + \mu_j \pi_i).$$

---

[1] This section is a reproduction of Sections 7.2 and 7.3 of Grimmer and Stewart (2013).

To use this unsupervised method to estimate underlying positions, however, we need an *ideological dominance assumption*—that the primary distinguishing feature of the language of the political actors is ideology. When the assumption holds, the model will reliably capture ideological differences in the use of language. But the models will fail when these ideological differences are dwarfed by other types of variation in the text. For example, nonideological differences across actors may be about their focus on policy or pork (Grimmer, 2013*b*), the style in which the essays were written, or the tone of the statements. Because the model does not include supervision explicitly, it is difficult to guarantee that the output of the model will pick up the ideological locations of political actors, and therefore the model requires careful validation.

When the ideological dominance assumption fits the data, the model can reliably retrieve valid ideological dimensions from political texts. Take, for example, the left-hand plot of Figure 21.1. This replicates a plot in Figure 1 of Slapin and Proksch (2008), who apply the Wordfish algorithm to German party platforms. As Slapin and Proksch (2008) show, the estimates in the left-hand plot separate the German parties and replicate expert assessments of German party movement over time.

But when ideological dominance assumption fails to fit the data, Wordfish fails to retrieve underlying policy dimensions. The right-hand plot applies the Wordfish algorithm to Senate press release data introduced in Grimmer (2010). The bottom, right-hand plot in Figure 21.1 is a density of the Democrat (black line) and Republican (gray lines) positions from the Wordfish algorithm. The model clearly fails to separate Democrat and Republican senators—a necessity for any valid scaling of political ideology in the now polarized Senate.

The Wordfish scaling is meaningful substantively, but it does not correspond to standard policy space. The top plot shows that the Wordfish algorithm reproduces the spectrum Grimmer (2013*b*) identified using the expressed agenda model—how senators balance position taking and credit claiming in press releases. This plot presents the scaling from Grimmer (2013*b*) against the scaling from Wordfish on the horizontal axis, and the black line is a lowess curve (Cleveland, 1979). The relationship between the two measures is extremely strong—correlating at 0.86, clear evidence that Wordfish has identified this interesting—though nonideological—spectrum in the Senate press releases.

This illustrates when unsupervised methods are likely to recover the measure of interest—when the concept of interest coincides with the subject matter that is highly frequent in the text. For Wordfish, when political actors are engaging in heavily ideological speech—as in German party platforms—unsupervised methods appear able to retrieve reliable position estimates. But when political actors can avoid ideological speech—as in Senate press releases—scaling methods retrieve some other, nonideological scaling. Therefore when applying unsupervised measures for measurement, careful validation is needed to confirm that the intended space has been identified.

21.3   A Workflow for Repurposing Unsupervised Methods for Measurement

In this section, we provide an overview of the ideal process for using unsupervised methods for measurement. Here we assume that the researcher already has in mind a measure that she wishes to estimate from the corpus. For purposes of example, we suppose the researcher would like to estimate the proportion of a newspaper corpus that is about the environment and chooses to use a topic model to make this estimation.

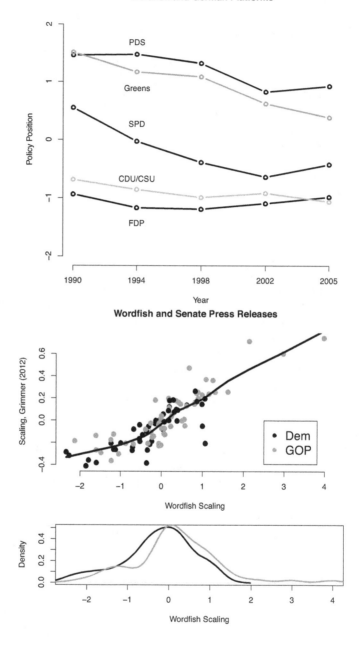

Figure 21.1. Performance varies across contexts with the Wordfish algorithm. Figure 7 from Grimmer and Stewart (2013).

21.3.1 1: SPLIT THE DATA

The first step in using an unsupervised method for measurement is splitting the dataset into a training and test set. Splitting the data allows the researcher to explore different approaches to measurement without worrying about overfitting to the particular dataset or selecting a measure based on the results it produces rather than on the quality of the measure itself. Splitting the dataset also provides an opportunity for the researcher to test the generalizability of the measure, ensuring that it will perform well in data outside of that which the measure was created with.

How much data to include in the training set versus the test set will depend on the concept the researcher intends to measure and the amount of data the researcher has on hand to study it. On the one hand, the researcher needs sufficient data in the training set to be able to develop a reliable measure and be confident that it will generalize to other datasets. On the other hand, the researcher will need sufficient data in the test set to be able to make precise final measurements.

21.3.2 2: FIT THE MODEL

Once the data has been split into a training and test set, the researcher can then fit the unsupervised model on the training data. The split sample allows the researcher to explore several different models to find the measure that fits with the concept she intends to measure. She might, for example, fit many different topic models with different numbers of topics to find the model that most cleanly produces a topic related to the environment. Or, she might try different starting values, stopping rules, or hyperparameters to explore different fits of the model. In this process, she is searching for the model that creates a measure that best captures the concept she is interested in.

Fitting and refitting the model in the training data does not invalidate the final measure the researcher produces. And, as we discuss in greater detail below, even if the model does not produce the same result every time it is run, does not mean that the measures are not useful. For example, say the topic related to the environment only appeared in one of the many topic models that the researcher fit. This does not mean that documents related to the environment do not appear in the corpus or that the topic model that produces the environment topic is wrong. It just means that only one of the topic models produces parameters to estimate the proportion of the corpus related to the environment. The researcher should pick the model for measurement that best aligns with her concept of interest.

21.3.3 3: VALIDATE THE MODEL

Once the researcher has selected a model, she must validate the measure. Here, we describe a few different approaches to validating unsupervised models used for measurement. Some of these approaches overlap with those we discussed in Chapter 20, while some are specific to repurposing discovery models for measurement.

Hand Coding

Hand coding is the most straightforward approach to validating an unsupervised method used for measurement. Even when unsupervised methods produce many different topics or clusters, validation can be performed on the primary concepts of interest, if not the whole model. The researcher in our example might ask research assistants to hand code a sample of documents from her corpus into two categories: 1) about the environment and 2) not about the environment. If she hand coded a random sample of documents, she could compare the proportion of the hand coded documents about the environment to the estimate the topic model produces of the proportion of documents about the environment. She could also compare the topic loading in documents coded as about the environment to those that were not coded as about the environment.

One of the difficulties of using hand coding to validate unsupervised methods is that unsupervised methods often produce continuous instead of categorical measures. In these cases, such as unsupervised scaling and topic models, we may want to coarsen the output of the unsupervised method in order to validate. For example, in a topic model of newspaper articles, an analyst may be able to confirm that an article is substantially about the "environment," but not that the environment accounts for .18 of the tokens in the document. In this case, we could coarsen the continuous topic proportion to make the comparison to the human coded validation set.

Hand coding and nonexpert evaluation can also be used to understand the meaning of the uncovered measures and label them. For example, human coders could be used to label topics based on their most probable words or the most representative documents. We discussed some approaches to using evaluators to ensure semantic validity in Chapter 20 as well as in Part 3: Discovery.

Surrogate Labels

As we described in Chapter 20 for supervised classification, surrogate labels could also be used for validation. When hand coding is not an option, researchers can look for labels for the documents that were produced for a different purpose and compare them to the output of the model. For example, the output of a topic model on newspaper articles could be compared to keyword tags given to the articles in a newspaper database. While surrogate labels can be quite useful in the absence of hand coding, we refer readers back to Chapter 20 for some pitfalls to avoid when using surrogate labels for validation.

Hypothesis Validity

If measures are working well, they should have particular relationships with other external variables. As we discussed in Chapter 20, if we can specify relationships that we should see in advance, we can use these as a validation of the measure. For example, if we were interested in creating a measure of news about the flu, we should expect this news to rise in the winter and fall in the summer. If we did not see this relationship, we might doubt that our measure was actually picking up the correct topic. The key here is specifying relationships that the absence of would indicate failure of the measure.

Catalinac (2016a), whose work we discussed extensively in Chapter 1, uses a Latent Dirichlet Allocation topic model to estimate the topics in candidate manifestos in Japan. To validate the model, she engages in extensive tests of hypothesis validity. For example, she shows that topics about agriculture and forestry are more prevalent in manifestos in rural rather than urban areas, but that topics about tourism and industry are more prevalent for candidates running for office in urban areas (Catalinac, 2016a, p. 97).

Model-Based Assessments

One of the most straightforward assessments, but perhaps the least revealing, is model-based assessments. Here we assess the fit of the model based either on the criterion it was originally designed to optimize or some related external criterion. Because we are interested in the models only instrumentally for what they can tell us about the world and not as ends unto themselves, the model-based assessments are not as revealing as the other approaches. Still, they are often the easiest validations to compute and thus can be useful supplements, if certainly not replacements, for other modes of validation.

For generative models of text, the most straightforward model-based evaluation is the held-out log-likelihood, which assesses the fit of the model in a sample not used in training the model. This provides an indication of the ability of the compressed latent variable to reproduce the observed data that was used in the generative model (e.g., the word counts).

Unfortunately, due to the nature of latent variable models, even calculating the held-out log-likelihood exactly can be intractable (Wallach et al., 2009). For a given test document i we want to calculate $p(W_i | W_{\text{train}}) = \int_{\pi_i, \mu} p(W_i, \pi_i, \mu | W_{\text{train}}) d\pi_i d\mu$, but the integral is intractable. For the topic model case, Wallach et al. (2009) offer an overview and comparison of existing approximation techniques. These methods are only really interpretable comparatively. Foulds and Smyth (2014) show an approach for directly estimating relative performance between models using annealing paths. Optimizing held-out likelihood maximizes the performance of the model on a task that we are not actively engaged in: predicting term count vectors for documents. It protects us from a certain kind of overfitting, but does not ensure that we have captured anything about the underlying meaning of the documents.

21.3.4 4: FIT TO THE TEST DATA AND REVALIDATE

Once the researcher has finished validation, the final step in using unsupervised methods for measurement is fitting to the test data and then revalidating. Here, we want to use the fitted model we developed on the training data and apply it to the test data. Importantly, this does not mean rerunning the same model with different data. It means using the parameters estimated with the training data to produce output for the test data. Using this output, we can then perform the analyses we are interested in for our research task.

Extensive validation in the training data should provide some assurance that the model will fit well in the test data, particularly if the training data was randomly sampled from the larger set. However, there is always the chance that the model fit on the training data produces measures in the test data that do not reflect the concepts the researcher wants to measure. Therefore, we recommend doing a second validation in the test data in order to ensure that the final measure reflects the concept of interest.

21.4 Concerns in Repurposing Unsupervised Methods for Measurement

While discovery is mostly concerned with how to spark a good idea, measurement requires making a specific claim about what the mapping function is capturing and how it approximates some theoretical concept. When these methods are turned to the measurement task, we reasonably have additional concerns. Below we address a number of concerns expressed about using unsupervised methods for measurement and give a general reply. Thankfully, all the concerns have a common response consistent with our agnostic perspective: the value of the measurement is justified not by the model itself, but by our validation of the result as a useful social scientific measure of some quantity. These are tools that can lead to useful measurements in practice, but also may not. To help keep the ideas tractable, we discuss the concerns in the case of mixed-membership topic models; however, the concerns are more general.

21.4.1 CONCERN 1: THE METHOD ALWAYS RETURNS A RESULT

This concern is often phrased as the objection: "if this model always yields clusters/topics/scales (even when the data is random), how can this be a valid measurement strategy?" As with many other statistical models, we first assume the model and then find the parameters that best fit the data. In the same way that a linear regression will always return a line, the latent variable models will always return some structure in the data. This is why validation is such an important part of the research process. It is not the results of the model that let us know that we have measured something, it is the process of labeling and validating.

The objection does correctly identify that latent variable models tend to be poor tools for asserting the existence of a particular underlying structure—even in purely synthetic data where we know such structure to exist. Running a cluster model with $K = 5$ provides only minimal evidence that there are five clusters in the data. Rather, what the method produces is the best five-cluster approximation to whatever structure does exist. This guarantees neither that there is an underlying cluster structure, nor anything about the number of clusters. In general, we don't even think there is a "true" underlying structure in real-world data, merely things that are more and less useful for particular goals.

21.4.2 CONCERN 2: OPAQUE DIFFERENCES IN ESTIMATION STRATEGIES

For any one model there are several different approaches to estimating the best fitting parameters. Although the details of estimation are largely beyond the scope of this book, we want to emphasize that these differences can be particularly salient in certain applications.

To make this concrete, consider the vanilla Latent Dirichlet Allocation model. This is a Bayesian model where the goal in estimation is to approximate the posterior distribution. There are three broad approaches to inference for this model: collapsed Gibbs sampling (Griffiths and Steyvers, 2004; Yao, Mimno, and McCallum, 2009), variational inference (Blei, Ng, and Jordan, 2003) and spectral methods (Arora et al., 2013). These methods all have benefits and drawbacks. Unfortunately these differences can be important for certain problems and quantities of interest (Asuncion et al., 2009; Boyd-Graber, Mimno, and Newman, 2014). For example, using a single pass of a collapsed Gibbs sampler will tend to yield topics that appear sparse; that is, each document expresses only a small number of topics and each topic has support on only a small number of words. By contrast, the variational approximation to the same posterior distribution will typically be dense, placing nonnegligible mass on many topics within documents and words within topics. This makes inference about how "focused" a set of documents is on a small set of topics fraught with issues that might not be apparent to a casual user.

In practice, we recommend that authors always indicate the approach to estimation in addition to the particular software implementation they used.

21.4.3 CONCERN 3: SENSITIVITY TO UNINTUITIVE HYPERPARAMETERS

We have already discussed the selection of K, probably the most obvious parameter that one manually sets in using topic models. However, there are a number of other hyperparameters that we set explicitly or implicitly that can substantially affect performance (Wallach, Mimno, and McCallum, 2009; Wallach et al., 2010). Ultimately these choices are difficult because practioners may have few intuitions about how to set them optimally. We find the best strategy when forced to set them manually is to consider many different options and choose based on substantive fit.

21.4.4 CONCERN 4: INSTABILITY IN RESULTS

The final concern is also at the heart of the other concerns: the instability of latent variable models, especially relative to other common statistical models in the social sciences like linear regression. Essentially all the methods described above lead to non-convex (and thus not easily solvable) optimization problems. In practice, results are sensitive to the initial starting values, and each time the model is run, we can get a different result. The different results arise because the model is finding locally optimal solutions instead of a globally optimal solution.

This is understandably unsettling to practitioners who are concerned about whether their results are accurate. A number of articles have explored the problem in some depth. For example. Roberts, Stewart, and Tingley (2016) explain the issue, provide strategies for exploring different solutions, and offer different initialization strategies (see also Chuang et al. 2015, which provides additional visualization approaches).

The instability issue isn't a simple problem of computational reproducibility (being able to generate the same results from the same data). The analyst can set the random number generator seed in order to ensure that results are consistent across computers.[2] Roberts, Stewart, and Tingley (2016) go further and propose an initialization strategy that relies on a deterministic and (under certain conditions) globally consistent estimator developed by Arora et al. (2013).[3] This approach does not guarantee we will find the globally best solution in any one case, but it does perform well empirically and offers asymptotic guarantees. Even when we can find stable initialization strategies, the models are often relatively sensitive to seemingly minor changes such as preprocessing or changes in the underlying data (Denny and Spirling, 2018; Wilkerson and Casas, 2017). This instability in turn makes the distinction between globally and locally optimal solutions less relevant. Because small perturbations of the data can cause a local optimum to potentially become global, the distinction of one that is higher than the others is arguably less relevant—they simply measure different things, which may at different times provide the best fit to the data you have. We still believe that

---

[2] In practice, even this can be difficult due to different versions of the software and different levels of numerical precision on different machines. However, these are engineering problems that can be addressed by virtual environments that exactly reproduce the environment where the analysis was originally run.

[3] See also the careful numerical analysis and initialization strategy of Lancichinetti et al. (2015).

having a locally optimal solution is important though, because it lets us know that, given what we are measuring and the data we have, this measurement is the best fit to the data.

Denny and Spirling (2018) eloquently articulate the core concern in their paper on the impact of text preprocessing steps for unsupervised methods:

> To underline our philosophical point here, note that the issue is not simply that dishonest researchers might cynically pick a specification they like and run with it, to the detriment of scientific inquiry. The more subtle problem is that well-meaning scholars would have *no idea of the truth value* of their findings. A particular feature of unsupervised models of text is that *there are typically many possible specifications, and many plausible "stories" about politics that can be fit to them, and validated, after estimation.* Fundamentally then, a lack of attention to preprocessing produces a potentially virulent set of "forking paths" (in the sense of Gelman and Loken, 2014) along which researchers interpret their results and then suggest further cuts, tests and validation checks *without realizing that they would have updated had they preprocessed their documents differently* [emphasis ours]   (Denny and Spirling, 2018, p. 187)

This concern is held more broadly by a number of social scientists who are skeptical of the ability of discovery methods to be used for measurement. The authors ultimately suggest that in the absence of strong theory, we would like to see that our results are robust to different preprocessing decisions and ideally we would average over different alternatives. Wilkerson and Casas (2017) make a similar appeal for robustness across different parameter values more broadly.

21.4.5 RETHINKING STABILITY

Unsupervised methods don't have direct information about the quantity that the analyst wants to measure. When we have an objective, easily evaluable criterion for performance, these discussions are more straightforward: we simply search over the space of possible solutions and find the one that performs best on that criterion. What is remarkable about discovery methods is that they offer a workable *surrogate* criterion to an unspecified measurement objective. Sometimes this works to measure the concept of interest and sometimes it doesn't.

The key to the critiques of Denny and Spirling (2018) and Wilkerson and Casas (2017) is a presumption of a stable, underlying target that these methods are trying to measure. Under this worldview, every different model solution is a different approximation to some underlying truth in the document. In that case, it absolutely makes sense to pursue a result that is robust to different variations of the model.

We argue instead that every respecification of the model is capturing something different about the documents. We shouldn't confuse instability in the *measurement of a fixed concept* with differences in the *choice of concept we are measuring*. While there are differences in what we can measure from a set of documents, a properly validated measurement is constrained by the actual content of the documents.

If this seems counterintuitive, we offer the simple assertion: most scholars would find it absurd if someone claimed there was only one right way to read a text. But this is what a stable, underlying target measurement implies in this context. This stability seems natural when compared to many other quantitative activities, like estimating a well-defined estimand using an experiment or regression analysis. But that presumption of stability is not there in the more comparable qualitative manual content analysis tradition. Consider two different teams of qualitative scholars approaching the same set of documents—they would come up with different coding schemes. We wouldn't dismiss the findings of either team because they chose to employ different methods and answer potentially different questions. We should judge the content analysis enterprise not by whether multiple methods come to the same solution, but by what the resulting measure tells us about the world.

21.5 Conclusion

In his book, *Bit by Bit: Social Research in the Digital Age*, Matt Salganik highlights the possibilities for researchers of repurposing data collected for another purpose such as administrative or industry applications. This data, Salganik notes, poses challenges because while it was designed for a particular purpose, that purpose was *not* research, and this difference in goals leads to a difference in properties.

We find it helpful to think of the results of unsupervised learning as measurement designed for another purpose. Since this measurement may conflict with the researchers' goals there is always some gap between what the user wants the measurement to be and what it is. However, that isn't a reason to abandon the enterprise entirely. Just as repurposing data can be extremely useful, repurposing discovery methods for measurement can be extremely valuable.

Salganik offers useful advice that translates nicely to our context,

> I always recommend that you try to understand as much as possible about the people and the process that created your data. Second, when you are repurposing data, it is often extremely helpful to imagine the ideal dataset for your problem and then compare that ideal dataset with the one you are using. If you didn't collect your data yourself, there are likely to be important differences between what you want and what you have. Noticing these differences will help clarify what you can and cannot learn form the data you have, and it might suggest new data that you should collect. (Salganik, 2018, p. 16)

With measures developed from unsupervised approaches, it is helpful to understand something about the objective that the model is optimizing (the "process" that created your data) and to consider carefully the differences between the data you would like to have in an ideal world and the data you have in the real world.

This chapter also concludes Part 4: Measurement. In this part, we have provided an overview of a wide variety of different techniques for creating measures from text data. We started with dictionary approaches for measurement, then provided an overview of supervised learning, including coding a training set, fitting a classifier, and validating a measure. Last, we described how to repurpose discovery methods for measurement.

While creating a human coded training set, training a classifier, and validating it using gold-standard data is perhaps the most robust method of designing measures for text data, this approach requires resources and particular forms of data that are not always available to researchers. We suggested several alternatives, from dictionary methods, to supervision with found data, to repurposing discovery methods that can be effective substitutes when supervised learning is not practical.

All of these methods, however, including supervised classification, require extensive validation.

Once measures have been developed, we can start asking broader questions, including those relating measures to each other or to other metadata, or creating experiments where the measures we have created act as treatments or outcomes. We move on to this next task in the next part: Inference. There we discuss in more detail using similar methods that we described in measurement for prediction, and using and developing measures for the purpose of causal inference.

PART V

Inference

While measurement gives us the tools to describe an observed population, there are additional challenges that come with trying to make inference about an unobserved population. That population could be unobserved for many reasons: it might be more difficult to measure, it might be realized in the future or it might be counterfactual. A central challenge of these kinds of inference problems is that they aren't always obvious ahead of time. Clarity about the assumptions needed for inference requires clarity about the precise goal of the analysis (Lundberg, Johnson, and Stewart, 2021).

Remarkably, the knowledge about how to make credible inferences about different domains, the future, and counterfactual settings has exploded over the last few decades. In these next few chapters we connect this burgeoning literature with the text as data literature, paying particular attention to the specific challenges of making causal inferences with text. **Chapter 22: Principles of Inference** follows our general pattern of first setting principles for the task at hand. In this chapter we pay particular attention to the similarities and differences between prediction and causal inference.

In 2009, Google used the terms people searched for to predict the flu rates reported by the Center for Disease Control before that data was available (Ginsberg et al., 2009). This same idea has been applied to Twitter data using language in tweets to predict outcomes as diverse as heart disease mortality (Eichstaedt et al., 2015) and political opinion polls (O'Connor et al., 2010; Beauchamp, 2017). This is a process called "nowcasting" (Choi and Varian, 2012)—predicting the present state of the world in a way that accords with another measurement that is, could be, or will be collected. In **Chapter 23: Prediction** we tackle this and a variety of other prediction tasks.

We then turn to the task of making causal inferences, which involves making inferences about counterfactual populations under some intervention. **Chapter 24: Causal Inference** lays out the basics of causal inference as well as some of the features that arise with text in particular. Then across a trio of chapters, we consider each role that text can play in a causal inference framework: **Chapter 25: Text as Outcome, Chapter 26: Text as Treatment**, and **Chapter 27: Text as Confounder**.

CHAPTER 22

Principles of Inference

In this section of the book we consider *inferential* tasks. We narrowly define inference to mean instances where we use a sample to estimate a quantity found in a well-defined (but possibly counterfactual) population. By contrast, in both discovery and measurement we focused on finding a useful function of the high-dimensional data that captures a concept of interest in the sample of documents we have. With inference, we will need stronger assumptions in order to make inferences to a broader population.[1]

22.1 Prediction

One task is *prediction*: what value of the outcome do we expect for a unit or units out of a distinct population of units? We will see that the prediction task appears superficially similar to the supervised learning tasks that we have considered earlier in the book. But there is a key difference: previously we had assumed that we could randomly sample from the population of interest, because we had already observed all units. This is powerful, because in expectation it implies that the relationships in the sample will reflect the relationships in the population.

Prediction to a new population implies that we can't draw a random sample from the population of interest, *yet*. The most common prediction task is forecasting: using the information that is available now to predict what the outcome will look like in the future. But, of course, we can't draw a random sample from the future. Therefore, prediction requires an additional assumption: the relationship between the outcome and features in the past continues into the future. Before we make a prediction, this assumption is unverifiable. Yes, we can creatively approximate the assumption using our data, but we will never be able to test the assumption until we observe the actual units. This is different from the supervised learning tasks that we described in the measurement chapter. If we observe all the data, then we can take a random sample of our units to build our classifiers. The random sample justifies the assumption that the relationship found in our training set is, on average, the same as that found in the test set.

In other words, forecasting methods require that prior predictive performance be indicative of future success. In social science data this is a strong assumption—particularly when we are forecasting events that occur rarely and with underlying processes that may change rapidly. Consider, for example, a popular forecasting task:

---

[1] Parts of this chapter are drawn from Grimmer, Roberts, and Stewart (2021).

predicting presidential elections. Building on a 30-year old political science literature, a large number of forecasters followed Nate Silver's meteoric rise to make probabilistic predictions about presidential elections. It is now commonplace to see forecasters argue about the probability with which a particular candidate will win the election, in some cases months ahead of the election.

The statistical models of election prediction all rely on the same basic insight: public opinion polls about presidential vote choice are predictive of election results. Using data from prior elections, forecasters model the relationship between opinion polls and the prior election results. They then use the relationship found in prior elections and apply it to polling data from the current election to predict the result of the upcoming election. The strong assumption is that the relationship between the polls and outcomes found in prior elections will also be found in the current election. This assumption is unverifiable, though we do get to observe the accuracy of the predictions after the result of the election. But the accuracy of forecasts in prior elections is no guarantee that they will be accurate in subsequent elections.

Making accurate predictions requires identifying features that are simultaneously predictive of the outcome of interest, available when the prediction is made, and are likely to have the same relationship with the outcomes that are out of the population. To go back to the election forecast, a large literature in American politics has noted that the economic conditions of the country are related to incumbent presidents' reelection chances. And yet, forecasters were uncertain about how to handle the economic downturn in 2020 due to the COVID-19-related shutdowns. While an economic downturn usually portends disaster for the incumbent party, there was no guarantee this would be the case in the 2020 election. We might have guessed that the public would excuse President Trump for the downturn. After all, some component of the economic contraction was on purpose—with businesses closing to stop the spread of COVID-19. Or, we might have guessed the opposite: the public would blame Trump for mishandling the government's response to coronavirus and likely prolonging the economic downturn that was the result of the pandemic. The inherent uncertainty about how the economy and voting will be linked in the future means that at the time there was no data available to directly test whether the relationship between the economy and incumbent performance in 2020 would be similar to what it was in prior elections.

22.2 Causal Inference

A separate inferential task is *causal inference*: how do outcomes differ if we intervene in the world? The applications of causal inference are wide ranging: from assessing the effect of taking a drug, to the effect of implementation of a policy in a country, to the effect of an advertisement on the purchasing decisions of consumers. The key to a causal statement is that scholars ask how the outcome would have been different *if only* the intervention had changed.

At first glance, we might think that causal inference is just another prediction problem. After all, the response of a unit to an intervention is just another example of "predicting" a response outside of our data. Conflating prediction and causal inference, however, has caused confusion in the computational social science literature and represents a serious obstacle to progress on computational questions. To help avoid this confusion we highlight four major differences between prediction and causal inference. We document how they differ on: (1) the role of identification and estimation, (2) the primary goals, (3) the validation of the models, and (4) the role of features.

22.2.1 CAUSAL INFERENCE PLACES IDENTIFICATION FIRST

For both prediction and causal inference we draw a distinction between two components of the process: identification and estimation. Heuristically, we will say that parameters are identified if datasets map uniquely to a set of parameter values. Identification is about what we can possibly learn from our observed datasets with infinite data. In prediction, an identification assumption might be that the data that we have in hand are useful for the out-of-sample data. For causal inference, the identification assumption is that there are no background "confounding" factors that are also associated with treatment assignment—that is, that the observed association represents the unobserved counterfactual population of interest.

Estimation is about how we actually characterize the properties of our observed dataset. Estimation assumptions might be about functional forms used for estimation or the way particular statistical models are fit. For example, when making a prediction we might make use of standard models—such as linear regression—or regularized versions of these models—such as Lasso or Ridge regression. Estimation assumptions are about the ability of a given estimator to characterize the data well.

Both identification and estimation are important, but scholars of causal inference have tended to focus on identification as a first priority. This is because identification assumptions are often unverifiable from the data. And without identification, no estimation routine could possibly reliably estimate the correct parameters. In contrast, scholars of prediction often put estimation first. This is because with prediction we will eventually get to see whether we were correct—and consequently, predictions will often be made even if the identification assumptions are violated.

A major difference between causal inference and prediction is that scholars attempting to make causal inferences will explicitly construct research designs to make the identification assumptions more likely. For example, scholars will explicitly design randomized experiments—the gold standard for causal inference because they identify causal effects under weaker assumptions. In observational causal inference studies, scholars will seek variation that enables them to use research designs to limit potential confounding under relatively weak identification assumptions.

This is not to say that design and identification issues are unimportant when making predictions. We have to ensure that we are using the relevant data to make predictions. So, for example, we might ask in the context of election prediction whether data from the 1932 US election is useful for forecasting the results of the 2020 US election (probably not). But determining which data to include or exclude amounts to making identification assumptions about predictions.

22.2.2 PREDICTION IS ABOUT OUTCOMES THAT WILL HAPPEN, CAUSAL INFERENCE IS ABOUT OUTCOMES FROM INTERVENTIONS

Prediction and causal inference have fundamentally different goals. The entire enterprise of prediction is focused on estimating the outcome for a unit outside of the population used to make the forecast. In contrast, causal inferences are focused on estimating how an intervention affects an outcome. These two tasks are conceptually distinct and performing well at one task does not imply that you're well equipped to perform the other.

When making a prediction the entire focus of our efforts is developing an estimate of some out-of-sample value, using the information that we have in the sample. While having a theory of how the data was generated or how the outcome relates to the features might help build a more accurate model, no theoretical explanation is needed for the inclusion of features. A feature is useful if it helps us to build a better future estimate (although we often need careful assumptions to be confident in our evaluations of accuracy). And as a result, models that are good at prediction can be inappropriate to apply to other settings. As we explain below, even a very accurate predictive model will often suggest misleading explanations and provides little insight into why things happen. This disconnect occurs because these "what if" or "why" questions are themselves causal, even when about the future.

When we make a causal inference we have a fundamentally different focus. Causal inferences are focused *only* on estimating the effect of an intervention. By an intervention, we mean some feature of the world that could plausibly be changed. A causal effect occurs when changing only that intervention results in a different outcome for a unit. Of course, we can never observe this counterfactual state of the world. So, the entire goal of causal inference will be to design studies and estimate models that make the comparisons that we observe plausible estimates of the counterfactual state of the world where *only* the intervention changes. This means that we have to be much more selective when choosing features.

22.2.3 PREDICTION AND CAUSAL INFERENCE REQUIRE DIFFERENT VALIDATIONS

Predictions and causal inferences also differ in the information available to evaluate our models. When we make a prediction, we eventually see the true answer. When we estimate a causal effect we never see what would have happened in the counterfactual world where our intervention of interest was changed. As a result, we can never directly validate our estimated causal effects—either for a group or at the individual level. Holland (1986) calls this the fundamental problem of causal inference. This difference in information implies that different standards are used when assessing predictions and causal inferences.

With the actual results in hand we can directly compare our predictions to the truth, comparing how well the predicted values of the outcome align with the true values of the outcome. While this is straightforward, different comparisons yield information about different properties of the forecast. For example, we might be interested in computing a forecast's accuracy: the proportion of the time it guessed correctly. Or, we might be interested in assessing whether a forecast is calibrated: does the predicted probability of an event occurring correspond with the true probability of the event occurring.

In contrast, we are never able to see the actual counterfactual outcomes and as a result evaluating actual causal inferences is necessarily more indirect. One common approach to evaluating causal inferences rests on assessing identification conditions: the assumptions used to ensure that any confounding in the data does not make it impossible to credibly estimate the causal effects of interest. Another approach to validation is to use a *sensitivity* analysis. In sensitivity analysis we make assumptions about plausible confounding and then assess how big that confounding would have to be to affect a finding. And in other settings we use different estimation strategies to show that our findings are not robust to particular assumptions when estimating effects.

The differences between prediction and causal inference suggests that the most common evaluation technique in computer science—the shared task—is much less useful for causal inference. Incredible progress has been made on shared predictive tasks in computer science. In these tasks research teams demonstrate new predictive models work well by showing that these methods outperform prior methods applied to the same dataset.

Shared tasks are less useful for causal inference because analysts necessarily have to generate the entire dataset to know the true answer. And as a result, the confounding that is found in these applications may not reflect the nature of confounding in the real world. This implies that causal inference shared tasks necessarily are assuming that particular kinds of confounding occur in real applications. If other kinds of confounding are actually more prevalent, relying on a shared task approach to evaluating causal methods could lead to the selection of less effective methods. We might select causal inference methods that perform well on the shared task, but poorly when applied to real-world tasks. Further, shared tasks necessarily prioritize estimation strategies, rather than identification conditions—which will necessarily be held constant within any shared task.

We do not want to take this position too far—simulated datasets can be very useful for assessing new causal inference methods. In fact, it is necessary (but not sufficient) for causal inference methods to retrieve the correct estimates when applied to data generated using the methods' assumptions. What's more, simulated datasets can help characterize how the method performs as small perturbations are made to the identification conditions. Yet, these tasks cannot serve as a stand-in for more careful and application-specific analysis of the identification assumptions used for a causal inference method in a particular setting.

22.2.4 PREDICTION AND CAUSAL INFERENCE USE FEATURES DIFFERENTLY

Features in prediction and causal inference serve fundamentally different roles. In prediction, the features are merely tools used to make a prediction for units outside of the sample. We merely want to find information available in our dataset that is likely to have the same relationship with the outcome in our prediction set. For example, it is quite common to use lagged values to predict the future. Of course, we may not know why the previous values of an outcome relate strongly to the future values— or where those previous values come from—but nevertheless they are still useful for prediction.

In causal inference, however, we take a fundamentally different view of features. In causal inference we differentiate between *treatments* and *covariates*. Treatments will represent the intervention we are assessing the effect of. Covariates will be used to enable the more accurate, unbiased, and precise estimation of causal effects. This leads to dramatically different advice when considering what information to include in our models. In prediction we seek out whatever covariates we can use to predict the outcome well, are available when we make our prediction, and will likely have a stable relationship with the dependent variable. In causal inference we have to be attentive to where the covariates fall in the causal process. For example, we can only include covariates that are *pre-treatment*: they are not a causal consequence of the intervention of interest (Montgomery, Nyhan, and Torres, 2018). And even among pre-treatment covariates, we want to avoid other variables that could induce bias. This includes *colliders* or variables with a particular dependence structure that results in making bias worse, not better (Elwert and Winship, 2014).

22.3 Comparing Prediction and Causal Inference

Both prediction and causal inference are about imputing values that are missing. But with prediction, we will eventually observe the true missing value. In causal inference, however, we will never see the true, counterfactual, value. Despite the seeming clarity of this distinction, the differences between prediction and causal inference can be subtle and require careful delineation.

Suppose, for example, we are hired to assess the effectiveness of an internet advertising campaign. We can imagine a request from the company to predict who will buy its product. To make this assessment we would likely use a host of demographic, socioeconomic, and proprietary data to predict who is going to buy the product. We can then imagine a separate question: does our ad campaign induce individuals to buy our product? This is a causal question. It asks how the behavior of an individual who sees an advertisement differs from individuals who are not shown the advertisement—a question about counterfactual states of the world.

The company may ask us to answer more subtle questions that blend together causal inference and prediction. For example, the company might ask: will this individual buy the product if we show them the advertisement? At face value, this is a prediction question. This is because it merely asks us to assess whether an individual (with a set of characteristics) will buy a product given that we also serve them with an advertisement. We might answer that there is a high probability of purchase even if the advertisement has little to no effect on the individual. In contrast, we can ask: who is most responsive to the advertisement? This is a well defined causal inference question that focuses on estimating conditional average treatment effects and identifying strata of individuals where the advertisement is found to be very effective.

The distinction between causal inference and prediction does not mean that the tools from prediction are unhelpful when performing causal inferences. For example, a growing literature uses machine learning methods to estimate conditional average treatment effects: how the effect of a particular intervention differs across characteristics of individuals. These conditional average treatment effects ask a related question: on average, what is the effect for individuals with a particular set of characteristics? This is distinct from the analogous prediction question: what is likely to happen for individuals with a particular set of characteristics?

22.4 Partial and General Equilibrium in Prediction and Causal Inference

As a separate matter, we might ask about how causal effects differ when the treatment is applied to just one individual and when the treatment is applied to a group. This is the difference between what is often called partial and general equilibrium.

As an example, consider the social media site Twitter's decision to allow users to create posts that are 280 characters long, double the previous constraint of 140 characters. Because they were curious about the effect of this change, Twitter first ran an experiment: randomly giving the ability to use more than 140 characters to a small set of accounts. Of course this randomization ensured that the accounts able to write 280 characters were not systematically different from the accounts that weren't. But this doesn't mean that the experiment was informative about what would happen if the policy was rolled out generally.

This is because the small set of users had access to an ability on the site that other users didn't. And as a result, users who could write longer tweets tended to write a series of high engagement tweets that highlighted their ability to write longer tweets than other users.

This is a 'partial' effect in the sense that it depends on only a subset of users having access to the tweet. Once all users have 280 characters, the "general equilbrium" effect will take hold and the novelty of composing longer tweets is gone and we would expect that effect to go away (Jaidka, Zhou, and Lelkes, 2019).

The differences between partial and general equilibrium are essential for understanding how to interpret the results of a study, because they speak directly to what will happen if a policy from a small experiment is implemented generally. There are abundant analogous examples that explain why. Job training may be useful for workers to gain a competitive advantage, but if all workers have the same job training then that advantage goes away and we might find that the job training doesn't increase wages. Similarly, college degrees can be valuable both for the information that is acquired in school and because it can offer a signal about someone's ability to work effectively. But if everyone attends to college, that signaling value of college goes away.

Partial and general equilibrium issues highlight some of the limits of randomized control trials (RCTs). RCTs have revolutionized work across the social sciences and are often touted as the gold standard for causal inference. We certainly see value in RCTs and we have all used them in our research. But there are serious limitations to RCTs for some of the most important causal questions that we might ask.

RCTs are almost exclusively designed to estimate partial equilibrium effects, but many of our most interesting social science (and policy) questions are general equilibrium questions. Consider, for example, an RCT that is designed to estimate the effect of a campaign message on vote choice during an election (Kalla and Broockman, 2018). Our randomized trial could be to compare a message from a campaign to no message at all. We can then compare the vote choice across conditions, providing us with evidence on the marginal effect of a single message. Suppose we found a null effect, with no difference between receiving a message and not. This is an interesting finding that suggests that this particular message given all other aspects of the campaign is not particularly effective. But it is a logical error to conclude that campaign messages in general are not effective. This is because we might expect that there would be a substantially different reaction to a campaign that stopped messaging altogether. And we cannot reach a conclusion, therefore, about the overall effect of campaigns on the vote choice of citizens.

There is a parallel set of concerns that comes when making predictions. When we make predictions based on historical data, we are making the strong assumption that the relationship between the outcome and features in the past apply in the out-of-sample data. This could be wrong if the world changes—in particular, if our forecast alters how individuals behave. This is a problem that social media companies regularly face. The company might ask, for example, if a potential political advertiser will run campaign ads that adhere to campaign regulations. Even if this forecast method is accurate for the past data, strategic nefarious actors might attempt to game the new prediction method to hide their future intentions. This strategic response results in the forecast method no longer being particularly predictive. This idea is an example of the Lucas Critique from macroeconomics (Lucas, 1976). The key idea is that strategic actors know the past response and then will alter their behavior in anticipation of that response.

22.5 Conclusion

Inference is the ultimate goal of many research projects. But like the other stages of research that we have described in this book, understanding the specific inferential task of interest is essential for determining how to make the appropriate inferences. Computer scientists have emphasized prediction, while social scientists have allocated much more attention to causal inference.

It is clear that both prediction and causal inference are essential components of the research process. It is also essential that researchers are clear about which inferential task they are undertaking. This is because prediction and causal inference require different assumptions and come with different validations. In the next chapter we characterize those assumptions and validations for prediction.

CHAPTER 23

Prediction

Understanding how to use text for *measurement* can help us operationalize *concepts of interest*. In this chapter, we will use a similar set of approaches for a very different task—prediction. Predicting what will happen to a person, an economy, an institution, or a country can inform policy decisions, make us money, and deepen our understanding of the social world. One of the primary businesses on the internet and drivers of technical development in machine learning is optimizing the choice of advertisements on web pages by predicting when users will click. Predicting stock market prices is a primary task of investors and economic forecasters. Anticipating spelling errors or the next word in a text message is now a default software task on most phones, computers, and search engines. Instead of using the text to measure a concept within it, in this chapter we will consider using the text to tell us something about the future.

Text contains a wide range of information about people, businesses, and governments that is not captured in structured data and can also be extremely useful for prediction. For example, no spammer would explicitly mark emails as "spam," but email clients are able to use the text of messages to classify whether the message should go to the spam folder or the inbox. Text is also useful in social forecasting—researchers are using the text of legal proceedings to predict decisions (Aletras et al., 2016), the text of tweets to predict box office returns on movies (Asur and Huberman, 2010), and the text of newspaper articles to predict the onset of conflict (Mueller and Rauh, 2017).

While machine learning algorithms in computer science and industry have been developed with a near-exclusive eye toward prediction, social scientists and digital humanities scholars have been more hesitant to make prediction a central goal of their research, and instead often focus on making descriptive or causal inferences. However, as social science has encountered a deluge of new types of data available in real time, prediction may begin to take on increasing importance (Hofman, Sharma, and Watts, 2017). Predictive models may even play an increasingly important role in clarifying the utility of particular types of social science theories by adjudicating which have the ability to explain events in advance (Cranmer and Desmarais, 2017). Like any powerful technique, predictive methods can also be misused, particularly when the task is poorly defined, a topic we return to throughout the chapter.

We begin the chapter by introducing the basic task of prediction and clarifying how it is and is not similar to measurement. We discuss some general principles about prediction that we return to throughout the chapter. Then, we will turn to four different types of predictive tasks—*source prediction*, which detects the identity or attributes of the source of a text; *linguistic prediction*, which generates text; *social prediction*, which forecasts economic, political, or sociological events; and *nowcasting*, which predicts ongoing events that cannot be measured quickly enough through other means.

23.1 The Basic Task of Prediction

The standard prediction task has three components: data, a model, and an evaluation metric. To fix ideas, consider the task of predicting election polls in the United States using data from Twitter. Polls are often limited by how expensive they are to field. In the context of a presidential election that might mean that polls are not run in states that aren't expected to be highly contested. However, there are many reasons, both academic and commercial, that we might be interested in being able to predict how a particular presidential candidate would poll in a given state in a given week.

The basic task is to predict an outcome y_i—in this case a poll—where i indicates that the prediction is made for a particular unit (such as a state poll or national poll).[1] We denote our prediction for y_i as $\hat{y}_i$.

Unit i is associated with a set of text and non-text features that may be useful for prediction and that are available before the prediction needs to be made. We refer to non-text features associated with a unit as X_i, which is a vector of P variables for unit i that we have available to predict y_i. In the case of polls, this could be economic indicators from the state, or other non-text entities. We will refer to text predictors of y_i as W_i. In the case we are considering, we want to predict polls with tweets, so W_i, would describe the text of the tweets.

First, we need some data that is *labeled*, meaning that we have some data where we know both the predictors X_i and W_i, as well as the y_i that serves as the target for prediction. In the polling example, this would be a set of actual polls conducted along with tweets from the week and locality of interest. This labeled data will be divided into a *training* and *test* set—as in Chapter 19, this allows some data to be used to actually fit the model while leaving a separate set available to evaluate performance.

The second component is the model. We can think of selecting the model (as we did in Chapter 19) as selecting a *loss function* $L(\cdot)$ that quantifies the difference between the predicted outcome and the actual outcome within the labeled data. The model will try to find the parameters that minimize $L(\cdot)$. For example, consider the linear regression that minimizes the sum of squared errors in the training set I, such that

$$\hat{\mu} = \texttt{arg min}_{\mu} \sum_{i \in I} (y_i - W_{i,}\mu)^2 \tag{23.1.1}$$

to obtain coefficients $\hat{\mu}$.

We would then be able to use the estimated $\hat{\mu}$ in the future when we don't know y_i to obtain a prediction $\hat{y}_i$ based on computing $W_{i,}\hat{\mu}$ using the $W_{i,}$ that we observed at the time. Thus, in our example, we use weeks where we do have polls available to learn how to predict the poll results for weeks where don't have polls. Linear regression is

---

[1] Often this y_i will include additional indices which specify other aspects of the prediction. For example, we might want to predict y_i at time $t + 1$ or in geography g. In this case, the task could be to predict $y_{i,g,t+1}$. For now, we will keep things general to application and denote our quantity we are interested in predicting as y_i.

a simple predictive model and we should get improved performance using any of the more complex machine learning methods discussed in the measurement chapter.

The third component of the prediction task is the evaluation metric. Clearly, we would like our prediction model to always produce exactly the right answer, but in practice, it is important to have a way to evaluate performance that reflects the goals of the analyst. The best approach to evaluating performance will typically be tied to the reason for the prediction task in the first place. For example, political scientists might want to use tweets to predict what the polls would have been retroactively, because they are trying to study the effects of negative campaigning and they want to fill in polls for all candidates in weeks where they didn't happen. Political consultants, on the other hand, might only care about predicting support for their specific candidate and only for the current week. These are very different tasks that require different evaluation strategies.

Generally the evaluation metric is some form of the *generalization error*—the prediction error when applying the model to unseen data from the population of interest. If we have a random sample from the population of interest, we can approximate this quantity using an expectation over a held-out sample O such that

$$\text{Error}_{\text{out}} = E_{i \in O}[L(y_i, f(\hat{\mu}, W_i,))|I].$$

This can be estimated either using a true hold-out set or through a cross-validation procedure as described in Chapter 20. We discuss complications of this simple recipe in the principles section below.

23.2   Similarities and Differences between Prediction and Measurement

Up until now, we have described a problem almost identical to the supervised learning problem described in Part 3: Measurement, where y_i is the category of interest and W_i, are the words within the document that we use to predict that category. It is also very close to the setup of the problem in causal inference that we will discuss in the next chapter, where y_i is the outcome of interest, t_i is the "treatment" of interest—a variable that encodes the level of an intervention a unit receives—and X_i are potential confounders—variables correlated with both the treatment and the outcome. In all cases, we could use a variety of models to estimate the relationship between y_i and the predictors. In each case, we also advocate for some type of split sample approach for model validation.

While all three seem similar on the outside, prediction is closer to the supervised learning problem described in the measurement chapter than it is to causal inference. Supervised learning is one specific example of prediction—we are trying to predict how hand coders would label a document given the words within the document W and their covariates X. We describe estimating misclassification error in the same way that we describe estimating prediction error here and suggest similarly that analysts use held-out samples to characterize this error. The only difference in what this chapter will tackle in comparison to the supervised learning problem discussed in measurement is that we are interested in predicting a range of y_is much broader than just the label of a particular document, including the outcome of Supreme Court decisions, the future of the stock market, or even the contents of future documents.

Predicting unobserved values of y_i in a completely different (and often future) dataset comes with more considerations than the more focused task of labeling concepts within documents. Unlike documents, where we often have a fixed corpus before beginning the task of measurement, prediction invariably deals with the complication of time—we are trying to predict what will happen in the future or fill in unobserved values between intermittent measurements. This means that our labeled data will not always reflect the data that we are trying to predict, which could generate drift over time. In particular, the individuals we are studying or the context that they exist in might change their behavior and strategies so that our predictions are no longer useful. We return to this point throughout the chapter to highlight the ways in which prediction might be more difficult than the task of measurement we described in the previous chapter.

23.3 Five Principles of Prediction

In real-world prediction problems there are many complications to the basic recipe we have outlined above. This leads in part to a series of principles about prediction that have helped guide our own analyses.

23.3.1 PREDICTIVE FEATURES DO NOT HAVE TO CAUSE THE OUTCOME

A prediction task does not require that predictors cause the outcome. How we arrive at the prediction matters less than the accuracy of the prediction. For example, say that we want to predict swimsuit sales. We find that social media mentions of ice cream are a good predictor of swimsuit sales. Of course, social media mentions of ice cream do not cause swimsuit sales, but the two might be correlated because they are both caused by a combination of hotter weather and summer vacation. However, social media mentions of ice cream could still be used in a predictive model of swimsuit sales if the data improved overall predictive power.

Of course, causal factors may be useful for prediction, and including them in a model may increase the accuracy of the predictions. Including information on the weather, weekends, or vacations—all of which likely affect swimsuit sales—may indeed help in a model predicting swimsuit sales. Including such features can be particularly important to the stability of predictions over time and space. But in some cases even causal factors may not be very predictive of the outcome—if the causal effect is minimal in magnitude, even if it is significantly different from zero, it will not necessarily improve the accuracy of the prediction (Lo et al., 2015).

Not only do the predictors not have to cause the outcome, the predictors in a predictive analysis can even be the result the outcome. In an example that we'll cover in more detail at the end of this chapter, nowcasting often uses data that is the *result* of y_i to predict y_i. For example, the incidence of flu in any given area is difficult to observe, and data from flu cases often lags several weeks because it first has to be collected by health officials. However, one result of an increased incidence of the flu is that people in the area search for flu remedies on Google. Researchers have used this search data to predict flu incidence data, even though flu incidence itself causes the search, not the other way around (Ginsberg et al., 2009).

23.3.2 CROSS-VALIDATION IS NOT ALWAYS A GOOD MEASURE OF PREDICTIVE POWER

In Chapter 20, we described how we can evaluate a model's predictive performance by holding out a subset of the data and estimating the error rate on the held-out data.

We noted that if the test data is a random sample of the population of interest, then estimating the generalization error on the test data would be a good estimate of its performance of the ultimate task. However, often when we want to make predictions, we want to predict points of data that have yet to occur. If the data we train the model on is historical data, it is not typically a random sample of the points we are hoping to predict—future data. If the held-out historical data differs systematically from the future data that we are interested in using for prediction, then in general, cross-validation will not accurately estimate the error rate.

Let's go back to the example of social media mentions of ice cream predicting swimsuit sales. We might use data from the past two summers to estimate when swimsuit sales will peak based on social media mentions of ice cream. And we might have sold our model to a swimsuit store, who is using it to predict demand this summer. But perhaps in the meantime, the social media platform we are using changed their algorithm to downweight ice cream in the news feed in order to promote the health of their users. Because users aren't reading about ice cream, they might not be sharing as much about ice cream. This would increase our error of predicting swimsuit sales because the relationship between social media mentions of ice cream and swimsuit sales has changed.

The best case for using cross-validation to estimate the error rate for a prediction problem will be when the future is like a random sample of past data, in other words when we have information about the future in past data. Forecasting and predictive models that are based on historical data rely on the similarity between the past and the future. Of course, the problem is the future can change quickly—the relationship between a good predictor and an outcome can be broken in the future time period. Take a trivial example—mentions of "Obama" on social media in 2008 might have predicted whether or not the Democratic presidential candidate won the election, but this relationship is unlikely to have been as powerful in 2016 when Obama was not a presidential candidate. Such cases of drift over time in the relationship between the predictors and outcomes will complicate our efforts to tune accurate models.

Importantly for social science research and application, successful predictions can ironically create drift in the relationship between the predictors and outcomes, undermining an analyst's predictions by making these predictions. Say that it becomes well known that the words within financial reports of companies predict their future stock market value. If the prediction becomes widely known, either the companies or the investors may change their behavior. Companies might omit or find words that substitute for those that predict negative stock changes. Investors may change the way they sell and buy these stocks. The change in behavior might undermine the prediction, as the relationship between financial reports and the stock market will have changed *because* of the predictions. In these cases, cross-validation in the historical data is unlikely to be a good measure of the error rate.

While cross-validation might be an accurate and low cost way in many cases to measure the predictive power of a prediction, in the end what really matters is how well the prediction holds up in the real world. Making predictions and then subsequently checking them based on real time data is the best measure of accuracy. In some predictive cases such as spam or clicks, when data on outcomes comes quickly, measuring accuracy in real time is more feasible. In other cases, such as predicting war or elections, an analyst making real-time predictions must wait a long time between observations of outcomes, and it therefore might be infeasible to tune a model based only on real-time predictions.

23.3.3 IT'S NOT ALWAYS BETTER TO BE MORE ACCURATE
ON AVERAGE

As we stated in the beginning of this chapter, we want to make our predictions as accurate as possible. But what does accuracy actually mean? Take a simple example where we are hoping to predict whether an email is spam, $y_i \in \{0, 1\}$. One way we could approach the problem is to try to optimize average accuracy, or the proportion of time our prediction was correct, $\sum_{i=1}^{N} \frac{I(y_i = \hat{y}_i)}{N}$.

But accuracy is not always the best metric to use when evaluating a predictive model. To see why, let's return to the example of spam. Say in a random sample of your email, you have two spam emails and 998 emails that are not spam. Then the model would do quite well if we predicted that none of your emails were spam; we would have accuracy $998/1000 = .998$, or be right 99.8% of the time. But in doing so, we would never predict spam—the point of the model in the first place. This is what is often known as the *accuracy paradox*—higher accuracy does not always mean a better model.

One way to mitigate the accuracy paradox is to use what is called an F1 score. The F1 score takes into account both *recall*—how many of the actual class were predicted to be of that class—and *precision*—how many of the predicted class were of the actual class. To see this more clearly, consider the confusion matrix below for a binary classifier.

		Actual Class	
		Positive	Negative
Predicted Class	Positive	True Positive	False Positive
	Negative	False Negative	True Negative

Across the columns is the actual class, across the rows is the predicted class. Remember that recall is the number of True Positives divided by the number of True Positives and False Negatives, in other words, how many of the actual class positives were predicted to be positive. Precision is the number of True Positives divided by the number of True Positives and False Positives. In other words, how many of the predicted positives were actually positive.

$$\text{Recall} = \frac{\text{True Positives}}{\text{True Positives} + \text{False Negatives}}$$

$$\text{Precision} = \frac{\text{True Positives}}{\text{True Positives} + \text{False Positives}}$$

The F1 score is one way to trade off precision and recall by multiplying them together. In other words, if either recall and precision get too low, the F1 score will also get low, since it reflects the product rather than the sum of recall and precision.

$$F1 = 2 \times \frac{\text{Recall} \times \text{Precision}}{\text{Recall} + \text{Precision}}$$

But still, F1 might not accurately reflect the costs and benefits of precision and recall to the analyst. For example, we might think that it is much more costly to label an email incorrectly as spam rather than label a spam email as not spam and turn out to be wrong.

In other words, there may be times when we care more about the *precision* of the classi-fier (how many of the predicted spam were indeed spam), than the *recall* of the classifier (how many of the true spam were identified as spam). There may be other times when we care more about recall than precision, for example, when diagnosing a rare disease. If we can quantify this cost, by specifying C, the number of times recall is more important than precision, then we can update the F1 score to reflect this cost, using:

$$F_C = (1 + C^2) \times \frac{\text{Recall} \times \text{Precision}}{\text{Recall} + (C^2 \times \text{Precision})}.$$

Overall accuracy will also not always reflect accuracy within subgroups. Analysts should also take into consideration the types of units for which they tend to make accu-rate predictions versus those where predictions tend to be inaccurate. This has come up frequently in the literature on predicting gender and race from images, as it has been shown that facial recognition algorithms are more accurate for white males than for darker-skinned females (Buolamwini and Gebru, 2018). Such differences in accuracy across subgroups could create serious racial and gender bias in use of the algorithm in downstream applications.

23.3.4 THERE CAN BE PRACTICAL VALUE IN INTERPRETING MODELS FOR PREDICTION

While in the first principle we noted that how you arrive at a prediction is much less important than in causal inference, we present a caveat here that there can be prac-tical advantages of being able to explain predictions. In areas where predictions have consequences, for example, in foreign policy or medicine, decision makers may view with skepticism algorithms that take in a set of inputs and opaquely produce a forecast. Those affected by predictions, say in credit scoring or in the context of legal artificial intelligence, may demand to know why they received a particular prediction, what the European Union has called a 'right to explanation' (Goodman and Flaxman, 2017).

We note that the point we are making – that there are *practical* advantages to mak-ing predictions interpretable – is a very different point than those made in the debate around algorithmic transparency, which deals with whether or not it is *ethical* to make consequential decisions based on opaque algorithmic functioning. While we think this debate is an important one to have, our argument here is that for analysts making pre-dictions, explanations of algorithms are of practical value, even if not required by ethics, as the public, decision makers, and experts often view predictions with skepticism until they understand their essential components.

23.3.5 IT CAN BE DIFFICULT TO APPLY PREDICTION TO POLICYMAKING

Policymakers are increasingly using predictive machine learning models to make policy decisions, ranging from policing (Perry, 2013), to education (Williamson, 2016), to immigration (Bansak et al., 2018), to food inspection.[2] While supervised machine learning is a powerful tool that can leverage enormous amount of data in making predictions, it is not without policy pitfalls. The challenges of using predictions in

---

[2] "Food Inspection Forecasting," City of Chicago, URL: https://chicago.github.io/food-inspections-evaluation/

policymaking have been popularly covered by O'Neil (2016), but also by scholars in computer science and economics (Athey, 2017).

First, using a predictive model in order to implement a policy should not be confused with evaluating the impact of that policy. Athey (2017) makes this point with the example of using a predictive model to estimate the buildings that should be targeted for inspection—predicting which buildings are likely to fail a building inspection could be useful if it reveals buildings that are falling in disrepair. However, it does not mean that inspecting these buildings would have the largest impact on building safety. It could be that the buildings most likely to fail the inspection are also those most difficult to repair. In this case, targeting buildings that will both fail the inspection and be easy to repair might be a more cost-effective strategy, but would not be revealed by the predictive algorithm.

Second, implementing a policy based on predictive modeling changes the incentives of actors involved in a way that could undermine the model itself. This could lead individuals affected by the policy to put enormous resources into something that would affect their prediction, but may not actually lead to better outcomes. (See O'Neil (2016) for a discussion of how the college rating system leads colleges to invest in policies that may not be better for students.) It could also undermine the algorithm itself; for example, if owners know their building will have a low chance of being inspected, this could incentivize them to skip updating the building (Athey, 2017).

Further complicating efforts to introduce prediction in policymaking is the possibility that data collection can be a result of the policies put in place, which can feed into and undermine the model. Lum and Isaac (2016) describe "feedback loops" that result from predictive policing, where predictive models inform police to patrol a particular area. Because police are more likely to be in those areas, more arrests might be made in those areas. This data is fed back into the model, reconfirming the prediction that police should be in those areas. While steps can be taken to mitigate these feedback loops under certain conditions (Ensign et al., 2018), naive implementation of predictive models for policy could run into any of the pitfalls discussed in this section.

Prediction tools are powerful and can be used in ways unintended by the researcher. For example, Chancellor et al. (2019) consider the ethical considerations of creating tools to predict the mental health status of users from their social media posts. While these tools can identify and provide resources to people in need of them, they also bring up concerns about privacy and could be used by parties without good intentions (for example, advertisers or harassers). Outside of the issue of consent, which we discussed in Chapter 3, researchers should spend time considering whether the benefits of the predictive tools they intend to create outweigh the potential harms, and use their knowledge of the context above and beyond consultation with the Institutional Review Board to decide whether to pursue the research and also whether to make their tools publicly available.

In sum, what we hope to convey through the principles outlined here is that prediction is far from a straightforward exercise. Trying to predict outcomes that may not be represented by the training data can undermine the usefulness of cross-validation. Accuracy, which may at first seem like a obvious evaluation of a prediction, may not be the ideal metric to evaluate predictive performance. And applying predictions to policy may not only require validation, but also may have unintended consequences. We make reference to these principles as we examine examples of predictions based on text in the following sections.

23.4 Using Text as Data for Prediction: Examples

With these important principles in mind, we review examples of using text for prediction. Since we have already covered many of the models used for prediction in Chapter 19, here we focus on illustrating the blurry line between the prediction and measurement contexts. We separate out prediction using text as data into four categories (which are neither exclusive nor exhaustive): Source Prediction—predicting the person or the characteristics of the person who wrote the text; Linguistic Prediction—forecasting what a person would say or will say next; Social Forecasting—using text as an input to predict societal phenomena, such as war, the passage of laws, or what the market will do next; and Nowcasting—using text to measure social phenomena occurring now, such as to measure the incidence of flu, unemployment, or consumer confidence.

23.4.1 SOURCE PREDICTION

Our social world is full of text—news, emails, letters, books, social media, and articles written by a wide variety of people and many with unknown source or origin. One of the primary ways in which text is used for prediction is to understand the source or the characteristics of the source of some text. While this does not involve prediction into the future, we consider this a prediction problem because the analyst is hoping to estimate information outside of the text (the source) with the information contained in the text.

Source prediction has already been brought up in several different contexts in this book. In Chapter 3, we discussed Mosteller and Wallace (1963), who used the text of the Federalist Papers that had known authors to predict who wrote the Federalist Papers with unknown authorship. Using filler words, the authors predicted that the papers with unknown authorship were written by Madison. Airoldi, Fienberg, and Skinner (2007) later used similar techniques to determine authorship of President Ronald Reagan's radio addresses.

Fraud prediction is an example of source prediction, where the algorithm tries to predict whether an email, for example, was sent to a large number of people with the intent of deceiving or making money. Source prediction is often used to detect bad actors on the internet, including malicious websites (Ma et al., 2009), bots (Ferrara et al., 2016), fake reviewers (Li et al., 2014) and online propagandists (King, Pan, and Roberts, 2017).

These same techniques can also be applied to learn about the characteristics of the author, even if it doesn't reveal the author's identity. Texts are used to predict the author's personality (Tausczik and Pennebaker, 2010; Pennebaker and Graybeal, 2001) and whether the author is telling the truth (Mihalcea and Strapparava, 2009), or to predict the popularity of the author's text (Yano, Cohen, and Smith, 2009). Text has more recently been used to try to predict the author's underlying level of depression (De Choudhury et al., 2013; Resnik, Garron, and Resnik, 2013).

We illustrate source prediction in this chapter, drawing inspiration from a blogpost written by David Robinson.[3] Robinson's post, which was written during the US presidential campaign in 2016, shows that data obtained from Twitter about then candidate

---

[3] Robinson, David. "Text analysis of Trump's tweets confirms he writes only the (angrier) Android half." *Variance Explained*. http://varianceexplained.org/r/trump-tweets/

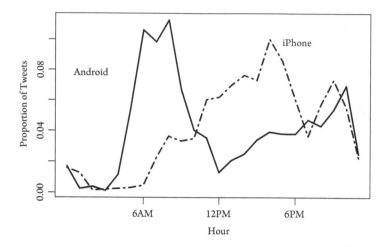

Figure 23.1. Proportion of Trump's tweets from Android vs. iPhone by hour. Recreated from http://varianceexplained.org/r/trump-tweets/.

Donald Trump's tweets could distinguish between whether Donald Trump himself was tweeting or Donald Trump's staff was tweeting. The secret was that Donald Trump tended to tweet from an Android device, while his staff tweeted from an iPhone device. Tweets from the Android device tended to come in the early hours of the morning or late at night, consistent with Trump's schedule, while tweets from the iPhone device tended to come in the middle of the day, consistent with his staff's schedule; see Figure 23.1. Robinson's post goes on to show systematic differences between the text of the tweets on the iPhone versus the text of the tweets on the Android, including that those from the Android tend to be more negative in tone.

Sometime in 2017, President Trump began tweeting from an iPhone, instead of from an Android device. While previously Trump and his staff could be distinguished, now they could not be. But we could use what we learned from the campaign Twitter account to try to predict which tweets came from Trump and which tweets came from his staff based on the content of the message.[4] This is a classic case of source prediction, as we can use information about known source from before to predict source in the future.

To illustrate, we took a dataset of 1,390 tweets from Trump's campaign provided by Robinson to train a model that predicts tweets from Android versus tweets from iPhone using only the words within the tweet. Many different classifiers could be fit; for illustration, we fit a Naive Bayes classifier we discussed in detail in Chapter 19 using the word within the tweets of the text as features. With the final model, we achieved a precision of 0.82 and recall of 0.75 (estimated with cross-validation), indicating good model performance on the historical data. In Table 23.1 we show the top 20 words most predictive of an Android tweet in the historical data and an iPhone tweet in the historical data. Trump's tweets are associated with words like `win`, `hillary`, and `crooked`. Staff tweets are associated with links, thank yous, and hashtags like #makeamericagreatagain and #trump2016.

---

[4]Others have also done this exercise; McGill, Andrew. "A bot that can tell when it's really Donald Trump who's tweeting." *The Atlantic*. March 28, 2017. URL: https://www.theatlantic.com/politics/archive/2017/03 /a-bot-that-detects-when-donald-trump-is-tweeting/521127/ and the Twitter handle TrumporNot.

Table 23.1. Words most predictive of iPhone and Android tweets in historical data.

	iPhone	Android
1	...	”
2	thank	:
3	#trump2016	@realdonaldtrump
4	,	hillary
5	#makeamericagreatagain	crooked
6	amp	trump
7	&	cruz
8	;	.
9	!	ted
10	join	-
11	great	win
12	tax	clinton
13	new	bernie
14	democrats	@cnn
15	america	bad
16	%	job
17	soon	said
18	news	media
19	/	get
20	today	people

We then collected 471 tweets from Trump's feed.[5] We used the model we created, we predicted which of the 471 tweets came from Trump versus his staff. As we discussed in the principles at the beginning of this chapter, even though we achieve satisfactory precision and recall in the historical data, we will not necessarily achieve high precision and recall in current data. The topics that both Trump and his staff tweeted about had changed, both because there were different current events and due to the shifting strategy of the Trump team as it moved from campaigning to governance. While we have no way of knowing for certain whether or not our model was indeed good at predicting which tweets were written by Trump and which by his staff, here we do some validation to see if the model produces results that are consistent with what we knew about Trump's Twitter behavior.

First, we look at tweets that were predicted to be highly likely to be written by Trump's staff versus Trump himself. Table 23.2 shows the five tweets most likely to come from Trump's staff and the most likely to have come from Trump. The algorithm predicts that the staff authored announcements about events or new reports, whereas Trump authored tweets about ISIS, votes in the House, and news coverage. Reading these, they conform to our expectations given the type of phone.

---

[5] These were the 471 most recent tweets on February 16, 2018 when data was collected.

Table 23.2. Tweets predicted to be authored by Trump's staff versus Trump.

Predicted Staff Tweets	Predicted Trump Tweets
When Americans are free to thrive, innovate, & prosper, there is no challenge too great, no task too large, & no go... https://t.co/FaGl53u1Db	I was recently asked if Crooked Hillary Clinton is going to run in 2020? My answer was, "I hope so!"
This week, the Senate can join the House & take a strong stand for the Middle Class families who are the backbone o... https://t.co/ILfhlLOkSE	'Trump Rally: Stocks put 2017 in the record books' https://t.co/0foQGaFjMh
Biggest Tax Bill and Tax Cuts in history just passed in the Senate. Now these great Republicans will be going for f... https://t.co/5hPQSNDZV3	Report: 'ANTI-TRUMP FBI AGENT LED CLINTON EMAIL PROBE' Now it all starts to make sense!
House Democrats want a SHUTDOWN for the holidays in order to distract from the very popular, just passed, Tax Cuts.... https://t.co/NRQRR8w3pp	Bernie Sanders supporters have every right to be apoplectic of the complete theft of the Dem primary by Crooked Hillary!
Nobody knows for sure that the Republicans & Democrats will be able to reach a deal on DACA by February 8, but ever... https://t.co/2qBHLtCo1u	... Based on that, the Military has hit ISIS "much harder" over the last two days. They will pay a big price for every attack on us!

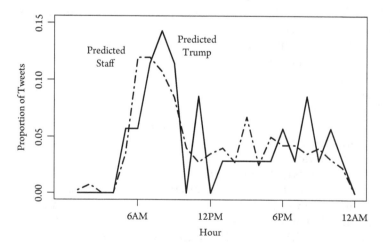

Figure 23.2. Proportion of tweets predicted to be from Trump versus predicted to be from staff by hour during February 2018.

Second, we look at the hourly timing of tweets predicted to be written by Trump's staff versus tweets predicted to be written by Trump. Figure 23.2 shows the proportion of tweets sent each hour of those predicted to be written by Trump versus predicted to be written by his staff. Surprisingly, we see the hours of predicted Trump and staff tweets converge, shown in Figure 23.1. The pattern of tweeting diverges from our expectation in the historical data. Is this because Trump's staff schedule has changed, or is the model predicting incorrectly based off of the text? Without the true labels for tweets during this period, we might not ever know. However, the model gives us an overall guess as to the continued social media behavior of the president, even after his tweets cannot be separately identified.

23.4.2 LINGUISTIC PREDICTION

The second category of text prediction we consider is linguistic prediction—using text data to predict subsequent text data. Can we predict what someone will say next or what someone meant to say? This category is more difficult than source prediction because the space of possible outcomes is typically much higher. We do not just want to predict whether Trump or his staff wrote a tweet, we'd like to predict the next tweet, the next word within a tweet, or the way that a particular tweet would be translated.

Linguistic prediction appears in many practical applications that people use every day. Autocorrect is one form of prediction—predicting which words you mistyped and which you would like to change. Autocomplete in search, text messaging, and email predicts what you plan to write even before you write it. Each of these forms of linguistic prediction can be customized to the individual by using what the individual has written or searched for before to improve prediction of what that individual intended to say subsequently.

Question answering is another type of linguistic prediction where the algorithm guesses what will be the most useful answer to a question posed by the user. Usually, instead of generating text from scratch, the computer searches a database of possible answers to find one or a list of results it predicts to be most relevant, then returns these answers to the user. This type of question answering is one example of a larger class of information retrieval tasks where the algorithm tries to retrieve information it predicts to be relevant to the user. Famous question answering programs include IBM's Watson and Apple's Siri.

Machine translation is another type of linguistic prediction where the algorithm predicts how the same text would be expressed in a different language. The most straightforward way to do machine translation is to take each word within a sentence and translate it directly to the target language by looking each word up in a dictionary and replacing it with the translated word, a process called *direct translation* (Jursfsky and Martin, 2009, Chapter 25). However, since the structures of languages vary extensively, direct word-by-word translation typically lacks fluency and can be completely uninterpretable.

While there are deterministic algorithms specific to two languages that can make direct translation more fluent, statistical approaches to machine translation have proven more successful. The basic idea of many statistical approaches to machine translation is that there is a trade-off between the fidelity of the translation and the fluency of the translation. Thus, machine translations often jointly optimize a metric of translation quality between languages and the level of fluency of the final result (Jursfsky and Martin, 2009, Chapter 25).

Machine learning is increasingly the approach of choice for doing machine translation. One approach is to take texts each with several expert translations and learn models that most closely produce the expert translation from the source text (Koehn, Och, and Marcu, 2003). More recently, researchers have begun to use back-translation more extensively, where the text is translated from Language A to Language B, and then back to Language A (Sennrich, Haddow, and Birch, 2016). The model then attempts to minimize the difference between the original version of the text and the back-translated version of the text.

23.4.3 SOCIAL FORECASTING

So far we've covered predicting the source of text and automatically generating text. But analysts using natural language processing have also aspired to more lofty goals—predicting what will happen in society using the information encoded in text. In this section, we discuss just a few examples of this type of prediction, which we call *social forecasting*.

One financially lucrative area for text prediction is using language to predict markets. Features extracted from business news, message boards, Twitter, and company websites have been used to predict how well the stock market will fare, from the S&P 500 to the Taiwan stock exchange (for a review, see Nassirtoussi et al. (2014)). Others have set out to more specifically predict company success by using 10-K reports from companies (Kogan et al., 2009) or news stories that specifically mention a particular company (Tetlock, Saar-Tsechansky, and Macskassy, 2008). Relatedly, researchers have used social media to predict sales performance (Liu et al., 2007), box office returns (Asur and Huberman, 2010), and consumer confidence (O'Connor et al., 2010).

In the political realm, researchers have used text to predict political outcomes. Aletras et al. (2016) use the facts described in European human rights court cases to predict the decisions of these cases. Reilly, Richey, and Taylor (2012) identify trends in Google searches for the name and topic of ballot measures to determine which ballot measures in local elections are likely to be subject to "roll-off," or be measures where people abstain from voting on them even though they voted for other measures or candidates on the ballot. Nay (2017) forecasts the probability that bills proposed to Congress will eventually become law, leveraging the text of the bill as data for the prediction.

Using text for prediction also has significant potential for providing forecasts that augment the public good. Tkachenko, Jarvis, and Procter (2017) use Flickr tags related to nature to predict where floods are likely to happen in the future. Kang et al. (2013) use features from Yelp reviews to flag restaurants that are likely to have lower hygiene scores, which they suggest could be used to more efficiently audit restaurants to ensure public safety.

We now take a closer look at social forecasting by reviewing in detail Beauchamp (2017), who uses Twitter data to predict state-level polling in the United States, and, by extension, election outcomes at the state level. Beauchamp (2017) is interested in predicting state-level polls not just in the future, but also in interpolating historical polls, predicting polls for states that conduct very few, and identifying sharp changes in opinion at the local level. Usefully, Beauchamp (2017) lays out four "lessons" of doing prediction with social media that guide the development of his approach:

- **Statistics**: Prediction requires statistical measures of success, and therefore Beauchamp (2017) points out that there has to be enough reference data to effectively validate it using statistical approaches.

- **Benchmarks**: The success of the prediction has to be evaluated based on a benchmark. This means the prediction should be compared to the best alternative approach, rather than to naive or random predictions.
- **Training**: Instead of relying on proxies (candidate mentions to predict polling, etc.), the model should be trained on data with true values of the dependent variables (e.g., historical polls).
- **Out of Sample**: Beauchamp (2017) emphasizes that the test data should be truly out of sample, and ideally forward in time.

With these lessons in mind, Beauchamp (2017) collects data from the Twitter API that contains one or more of a set of political keywords. In total, his collection is 120 million tweets, in the two months before the 2012 presidential election. He extracts the geography of these tweets using geo-tagging and the free text description of location in the user's profile. He represents these tweets by the top 10,000 unigrams in the text, and aggregates these to the state-day level.

Beauchamp (2017) then combines this text data with 1,200 state-level polls, where he extracts the proportion of support for Obama as the outcome of interest. For training, he focuses only on states that had at least 15 polls during the range of the Twitter data described above. This leaves him to estimate the model on only 24 out of 50 states. Beauchamp (2017) fits three standard models—an elastic net, support vector machine, and random forest. He also fits an additional model—an ensemble approach that allows for the inclusion of time trends and fixed effects.

Beauchamp (2017) uses three out-of-sample tests of his model. First, he considers how the model with just the text of the tweets predicts election day results for the 24 states within his sample compared to the polls themselves. Here, he finds that the text model does almost as well as polls. Second, he compares how the text model predicts election results in the states *other* than the 24 states he used to train the model. This test is truly out of sample, and extrapolating to other states. In this test, he finds surprisingly good accuracy, despite the fact that there are very few state-level polls.

In his last test, he considers how his model of text with the inclusion of time trends and fixed effects compares to polling when forecasting the next day's polls recursively across the whole period. Here, he finds that the text adds predictive power above and beyond the polling baseline in identifying short-term changes in polling and interpolating between polls.

Beauchamp (2017) then looks to see what types of features are most predictive of support for Obama versus support for Romney. Interestingly, mentions of the candidates themselves are not among the most predictive features in the models. Instead, surprising features predict changes in support for Obama; for example, https, which Beauchamp interprets as links to external information, predicts increased support for Obama, and rt, or retweets, predicts support for Romney.

The Beauchamp (2017) example highlights several important elements of social forecasting. First, we need repeated measures of a phenomenon in order to predict it. This means it will be difficult to use approaches to social forecasting for infrequently occurring events. Even election outcomes, one of the outcomes Beauchamp (2017) is interested in predicting, occur infrequently, and therefore he must use polls as proxies to train the model. Second, out-of-sample data is the only way to ensure that our model is performing well. Because the relationship between social media and outcomes like polls and elections is constantly changing, we can only ensure we have found something useful if our model truly predicts for geographies and time periods outside of that which we have trained it on. Finally, Beauchamp (2017) makes the important point that our measures have to be better at predicting than current approaches in order to be useful. It is easy for Beauchamp (2017) to show that his predictions outperform random predictions, but only some of his models are better at predicting than current approaches of using polls.

23.4.4 NOWCASTING

Projecting social forecasts long into the future can be difficult when the forecasts are impacted by factors whose relationships change quickly with time. Typically, the bigger the time gap between the data used for the prediction and the predicted behavior, the more likely it is that prediction accuracy will be low. In some cases, such as predicting civil conflict (Mueller and Rauh, 2017), predictions are likely to be inaccurate because they are made one or two years in advance and the causes of such phenomena are complicated and dynamic. In other cases, such as predicting roll-off ballots or stock volatility, predictions are made one to two days before an event, allowing analysts to use more recent information to make the prediction.

Nowcasting is one specific type of social forecasting that takes the time between the prediction and predicted event to zero; it "predicts" events that are happening at the same time as the prediction is being made. While at first glance this may seem to have little practical value, events that are happening in the present are often difficult to measure and official data on such events are unlikely to appear for days or even months after the event actually occurs. Nowcasting is the process of using alternate data to predict measures of the present that will only be released in the future.

Text data are extremely useful for nowcasting because text from social media and news provides a constant stream of data about the world that often reflects underlying phenomena. Social media data have been used to nowcast consumer confidence and unemployment (O'Connor et al., 2010; Askitas and Zimmermann, 2009), as they often reflect individuals' perceptions of their own livelihood and of the economy. Nowcasting also frequently employs Google search data—the content and frequency of user searches on Google—to predict the level of economic activity, such as sales of merchandise, houses, and cars (Choi and Varian, 2012).

Scholars have been working on using social media for nowcasting in order to try to address major events that require a quick response. Some work has tried to monitor and gather data on ongoing events such as hurricanes (Preis et al., 2013), food poisoning (Nsoesie, Kluberg, and Brownstein, 2014), and the fallout of migrations after natural or man-made disasters (Bengtsson et al., 2011).

Perhaps most famously, nowcasting has been used as a real-time measure of flu activity. Ginsberg et al. (2009) created "Google Flu Trends"—a collaboration between Google and the US Center for Disease Control and Prevention—that used user search data to predict the number of flu-related physician visits in the United States. Ginsberg and colleagues used historical user flu data to find 45 searches that were most highly correlated with flu-related doctor visits. They then used data on the prevalence of these 45 searches to predict future flu-related doctor visits.

While the initial Google Flu Trends (GFT) algorithm was very predictive of flu-related doctor's visits and was available in the US and other countries as a reference after 2008,[6] the accuracy of the algorithm decreased substantially with time. In 2009,

---

[6]Moisse, Katie. "'Google Flu Trends' Found to Be Nearly on Par with CDC Surveillance Data." *Scientific American*. May 17, 2010. https://www.scientificamerican.com/article/google-flu-trends-on-par-with-cdc-data/

researchers discovered that GFT did not do well at predicting the outbreak of swine flu (Cook et al., 2011). By 2013, GFT's estimates of flu levels were nearly double of actual flu rates (Butler, 2013). Other researchers showed that the utility of GFT's predictions were weak—using past flu data to predict current flu data performed almost equally as well, suggesting there were few practical advantages of the algorithm (Goel et al., 2010).

Why was GFT not more successful in leveraging search results to predict the flu over the long term? One of the main reasons is that a model trained to nowcast in 2008 needs to be constantly updated to also be accurate in 2009, or 2013. Media coverage of the outbreak of swine flu in 2009 created a very different type of public interest in flu, which could have changed the patterns of search results (Cook et al., 2011; Butler, 2013). Further, Google is constantly updating its search algorithms, which impacts user search behavior and search results (Lazer et al., 2014). With so much data to use for prediction—GFT started with 50 million words and phrases that people search on—and so little data to leverage as the outcome of the prediction, GFT could find search terms that were only coincidentally related to flu season (Lazer et al., 2014). As we discussed more generally in the principles of this chapter, the drift of the relationship between online searches and flu may overwhelm the ability to predict flu without constant supervision and tweaking to the algorithm.[7]

23.5 Conclusion

Text data provides us with new opportunities to predict source characteristics, future text, social outcomes, and current measurements. Because the world is producing text in near realtime, leveraging this information can provide us with a more accurate picture of what tomorrow will look like.

Still, prediction is a difficult problem. In linguistic prediction, while it may be relatively straightforward to use a spell checker to predict what someone meant to write or predict a list of endings to a search string, predicting a conversation or other more complex textual interaction is still very difficult. In societal forecasting, prediction of an outcome that will occur days, months, or years after the prediction inputs is likely to be less accurate than predictions that occur more proximate to the data. And in nowcasting, the constant drift between the predictors and outcome can render previously quite accurate models inaccurate. We emphasize in the last part of the chapter that continuous validation with real-time data will be the most accurate measure of a model's accuracy, and more accurate than cross-validation.

In this chapter, we also highlighted the potential pitfalls of using prediction. We talked about how variables that cause the outcome are not necessarily always the most predictive. We discussed how causal inference might not always be good measure of predictive power and how accuracy might need to take into account the costs of misclassification. We also discussed the potential pitfalls of using prediction in policymaking. In particular, the impact of the use of prediction in policymaking should be evaluated separately from the prediction itself, taking into account potential feedback loops, changes in strategy of participants, and propensity for discrimination.

---

[7] Some have argued that perhaps other types of real-time text data such as data from Twitter would be better able to predict flu trends than search data (Broniatowski, Paul, and Dredze, 2013). Still, these data are likely to suffer from the same drift problems as search trends (Lazer et al., 2014).

In the next chapter, we move on to causal inference. Whereas with prediction we focus on what *will* happen, in causal inference, the inferential problem is predicting what *would* have happened. This lends less flexibility in the types of information we can include within the model, but can have more straightforward policy implications. Understanding how the task of prediction differs from other social scientific tasks is essential to understanding how to best leverage text data for each particular problem, and we highlight the differences between causal inference and prediction in the following chapter.

CHAPTER 24

Causal Inference

Over the last two decades, computer scientists and statisticians have made great strides in producing and developing methods to analyze natural language. The goal of many of these models has been to predict an outcome, which we covered in the last chapter. For example, predictive models have been developed to identify spam, predict advertisements that a user of a website might click on, or serve relevant links to a user through search. These models use a labeled set of data to learn a relationship between the predictors and the outcome in order to make decisions.

While prediction is useful for serving specific content to individuals on a web interface, social scientists are often interested in asking questions that inform social policies—to make decisions that inform policymakers. For example, social scientists might be interested in understanding how a change in campaign strategy—"going negative" in campaign advertisements, for example—might affect overall support for a candidate. Or they might be interested in how misinformation on social media affects public perceptions of election fairness. These questions do not focus on predicting the future accurately—what *will* happen—instead, they are focused on estimating what *would* have happened under a different version of the world.

Because methods to analyze natural language were typically not designed for causal inference, when social scientists began adapting these methods to the study social phenomena, they first applied these techniques for descriptive purposes of discovery and measurement, tasks that we have described in previous chapters. For example, in sociology and psychology, these methods were used to track the ways in which the US government discussed arts and culture (DiMaggio, Nag, and Blei, 2013) and how language reflects personality and social interaction (Schwartz et al., 2013). In political science, text methods were used to measure deliberation in the Federal Reserve (Bailey and Schonhardt-Bailey, 2008), study the ideology of the author of a text (Slapin and Proksch, 2008; Benoit and Laver, 2003; Lowe, 2008), and assess the sentiment of social media posts (Hopkins and King, 2010).

Some of the initial work in the social sciences that used text as data for discovery and measurement explicitly incorporated metadata into the measurement model to explore variation in measurement between various subsets of data. For example, the Expressed Agenda Model of Grimmer (2010) explicitly models information about the author of a group of posts into a topic model, estimating how the amount an issue is talked about varies by each individual author. Grimmer (2013*b*) extends this model to explore how members of the US Congress focus on different issues when talking with their constituents depending on their characteristics, such as the competitiveness of their district. Quinn et al. (2010) create a dynamic topic model that is able to measure how topics change over time and use it to study changes to discussions in the US Senate over a seven year period. These models developed in conjunction with a large literature in computer science that explored using metadata in conjunction with text in measurement models, for example, Mimno and McCallum (2008) and Eisenstein, Ahmed, and Xing (2011).

The ability to include metadata into the measurement model inspired further research that explored how text as data methods could be used in conjunction with causal inference. If metadata could be included into a measurement model of text, then could an indicator of the treatment and control condition in an experiment also be included to estimate the impact of treatment on a text outcome? Roberts et al. (2014) and Roberts, Stewart, and Airoldi (2016) explore a general model which we reviewed in Chapter 13, the Structural Topic Model, for including metadata into text and show how the model can be used to estimate treatment effects in an experiment where text is the outcome. Gill and Hall (2015) show how permutation tests can be used to test the impact of a randomized treatment on a text outcome. These papers took the first steps toward defining the problem and addressing the challenge of using experiments in conjunction with unstructured text.

In this chapter, we take the next step toward explicitly defining the research processes and assumptions necessary to make causal inferences where text is a measure of the treatment, outcome, or confounding variables within a causal inference design. We build off of previous work that defines the problem of making causal inferences with text to explicitly outline the opportunities of using text in causal analyses, along with challenges of making causal inferences with high-dimensional data like text.

We begin this chapter by providing a brief overview of causal inference and again reviewing the differences between prediction, measurement, and causal inference. We then introduce five guiding principles of using text data with causal inference and return to these in detail throughout the remainder of the chapter. Then we outline the basic problem of causal inference and the challenges that text data poses for causal inference, and propose solutions to these problems. Chapters 25 and 26 provide several examples of using text in experiments as an outcome and as a treatment. We also explore conditioning on text in observational studies in Chapter 27. Our chapter draws extensively not only on the previous work on using text data in conjunction with experiments in the social sciences, but also on companion papers, Egami et al. (2018), Fong and Grimmer (2021), and Roberts, Stewart, and Nielsen (2020).

24.1 Introduction to Causal Inference

We begin this chapter with a basic introduction to causal inference. The goal of causal inference is to identify the effect of a treatment variable t_i on an outcome variable y_i. This framework is general enough to apply to many different causal processes in social science—from the effect of negative ads deployed during a campaign on a candidate's vote share, to the effect of partisan news consumption on the political views of a research participant. t can take on one of a few different states; in other words, there are different treatments, and we want to estimate the difference in outcomes y between units treated with different treatments. For an excellent introduction to causal inference that we draw on here, see Morgan and Winship (2015).

We begin with the simplest example and say t_i only takes on two states—treatment and control. We observe—either experimentally or observationally—two groups of individuals, one that received the treatment and one that received the control. The concept that drives the framework for understanding causal inference is that no matter whether a unit received treatment or control, each observation has two *potential outcomes*, or potential values of the outcome variable y_i: what would have happened if it had received treatment and what would have happened if it had received control. Typically, we denote these potential outcomes $y_i(1)$ and $y_i(0)$, or the outcome had individual i received treatment ($t_i = 1$), or the outcome had individual i received control ($t_i = 0$).

The goal of causal inference is to describe the differences between potential outcomes—how the outcome of unit i under treatment will differ from the outcome under control. For any individual, the causal effect of treatment t_i is the difference between the potential outcomes under the different states of t, $y_i(1) - y_i(0)$. However, each individual can only receive one treatment. Therefore, we only observe one of $y_i(1)$ and $y_i(0)$. The outcome that we observe is commonly known as the *factual* and the outcome we do not observe is commonly known as the *counterfactual*. The *fundamental problem of causal inference* is that we only observe the factual and not the counterfactual (Holland, 1986). Therefore, we cannot observe the individual causal effects directly.

Even so, we do observe two groups of individuals, one set that received treatment and one set that received control. Under some circumstances, we can use these two groups to understand the causal effect. First, we change the quantity of interest to the *average causal effect* $\bar{y}^T - \bar{y}^C$, where $\bar{y}^T = \frac{1}{N} \sum_{i=1}^{N} y_i(1)$ and $\bar{y}^C = \frac{1}{N} \sum_{i=1}^{N} y_i(0)$. We cannot estimate either $\bar{y}^T$ or $\bar{y}^C$ directly because we do not observe $y_i(1)$ or $y_i(0)$ for all i. However, we can decompose the average causal effect $\bar{y}^T - \bar{y}^C$ into components that reflect the data that we have. Say that p_T is the proportion of our sample in the treated group, T collects all the treated units, and C collects all the control units; then:

$$\bar{y}^T - \bar{y}^C = p_T \underbrace{(\bar{y}^T_{i \in T} - \bar{y}^C_{i \in T})}_{\text{Avg. Effect on Treated}} + (1 - p_T) \underbrace{(\bar{y}^T_{i \in C} - \bar{y}^C_{i \in C})}_{\text{Avg. Effect on Control}}$$

$$= \underbrace{p_T \bar{y}^T_{i \in T} - (1 - p_T) \bar{y}^C_{i \in C}}_{\text{observed terms}} + \underbrace{(1 - p_T) \bar{y}^T_{i \in C} - p_T \bar{y}^C_{i \in T}}_{\text{unobserved}}$$

We do observe $\bar{y}^T_{i \in T}$, or the mean outcome of treatment on the treated group, and $\bar{y}^C_{i \in C}$, or the mean outcome of control on the control group. We do not observe $\bar{y}^C_{i \in T}$ or $\bar{y}^T_{i \in C}$, or the counterfactuals for each of these groups.

This decomposition reveals what we can do with the data that we have to estimate the data that we don't have. If we wanted to estimate $\bar{y}^T - \bar{y}^C$ with our observable data, $\bar{y}^T_{i \in T} - \bar{y}^C_{i \in C}$, this will work only if $\bar{y}^T_{i \in T} = \bar{y}^T_{i \in C}$ and $\bar{y}^C_{i \in T} = \bar{y}^C_{i \in C}$. In other words, if we can substitute the observed outcomes of the treatment group under the treatment state for the missing outcomes of the control group under the treatment state, and vice versa for the control state, then we will be able to estimate the average causal effect without the missing potential outcomes.

When will $\bar{y}^T_{i \in T} = \bar{y}^T_{i \in C}$ and $\bar{y}^C_{i \in T} = \bar{y}^C_{i \in C}$? This will happen only when the potential outcomes are not related to whether or not an individual got assigned to treatment, i.e., when $\bar{y}^T_{i \in C}$ is not somehow systematically different because it applies to the control group than $\bar{y}^T_{i \in T}$. What can go wrong? First, the notation itself as we have presented it relies on the idea that there are two potential outcomes for each unit (one under each treatment status). The *stable unit treatment value assumption* (SUTVA) formalizes this assumption by stating that when we observe the outcome under a given treatment status, it reflects the counterfactual for that unit with that treatment status. For example, SUTVA rules out interference between units—the treatment of one unit does not affect the response of another unit. It also assumes that the treatment is consistent across units—one group is not receiving a different type of treatment than another. If SUTVA does not hold, then the outcomes of one group may reflect the treatments of the other, which means we cannot estimate the average causal effect in the usual way. Say, for example, we are interested in the effect of seeing a news story on support for a political candidate. We share the news story with a treated group on social media, but not the control group. But then the treated group shares the news story so that members of the control group also see it. The control group is no longer a good counterfactual for the treated group, as it no longer reflects what would have happened to the treated group if it had not seen the story.

Second, the assignment mechanism may be *confounded*. That is, the association between the treatment and the outcome may reflect not just the causal effect, but also some non-causal association. If the control group is different from the treated group in a way that is related to the potential outcomes, then the outcomes of the control group under the control assignment cannot be used as estimates for the outcomes of the treatment group under the control assignment. To be able to estimate the average causal effect with observed data, we need *ignorability*, or the potential outcomes need to be independent of the treatment assignment: $(y_i(1), y_i(0)) \perp\!\!\!\perp t_i$. Say, for example, that the researcher allows people to opt in to receiving news stories and therefore people who are interested in politics select into the treatment. The treated group and the control group are no longer comparable (the treated group was more political from the outset), and treatment (deciding to receive news stories) is related to the potential outcomes.

One particularly powerful way that scientists deal with confounding is randomization of treatment assignment. If the treatment and control group were assigned based on a random number generator, then on average across experiments the treatment group will be similar to the control group, and the outcomes of one can be substituted for the potential outcomes of the other. Under randomization, it is unlikely that the treatment group and control group will differ in a systematic way that will be related to the outcome. Randomization ensures that treatment assignment is independent of potential outcomes, as units cannot select into treatment.

If the conditions of SUTVA and ignorability are met, the parameters in a simple linear regression correspond to the average treatment effect.[1] Regression of the *y* on *t* results in the equation:

$$y_i = \beta_0 + \beta_1 t_i + \epsilon_i.$$

From this regression, the components of the average treatment effect are:

$$\bar{y}_{i \in T}^T = E[y_i | t_i = 1] = \beta_0 + \beta_1 + E[\epsilon_i | t_i = 1]$$
$$\bar{y}_{i \in C}^C = E[y_i | t_i = 0] = \beta_0 + E[\epsilon_i | t_i = 0].$$

---

[1] Importantly, this is a special case setting where we are controlling for no additional covariates and the treatment is binary. Thus, the regression is effectively calculating a difference in means.

$\bar{y}^T_{i \in T} - \bar{y}^C_{i \in C}$ will only equal the treatment effect β_1 when the errors are uncorrelated with treatment status, which is another way of saying that the treatment assignment is uncorrelated with the potential outcomes. Researchers using experiments for causal inference will often use regression to estimate the average causal effect.

24.2 Similarities and Differences between Prediction and Measurement, and Causal Inference

Despite all the conceptual work we have done so far to describe the purpose of causal inference, we have ended at a simple linear regression, quite similar to the approach we have described in the measurement chapter and in the prediction chapter. Indeed, in the supervised learning problem described in the measurement and predictions chapters, we also began with a simple linear regression where y_i is the category or prediction of interest, and W_i are the words within the document that we use to predict that category or outcome.

In causal inference, we are interested in what *would* have happened or would have been different had one or a set of independent variables changed. The difference between what *would* have happened—the counterfactual—and what did happen—the outcome—is the causal estimand of interest, which we want to estimate without bias. Unlike with prediction, we often do not care so much about whether or not our model accurately predicts the outcome because we observe the outcome; instead, we want to predict the *potential outcome*, or our best guess of what *would* have happened had one or a set of the independent variables been different.

The differences between the tasks of causal inference and prediction have important implications for what we do with the data in each case. Indeed, we believe that much confusion about causal inference and prediction stems from their conflation with each other. In prediction, as we discussed in the last chapter, we are much less interested in what goes *into* the model, as long as the predicted outcome of the model is accurate. In prediction, we are comfortable introducing bias to the coefficients in the model, as long as it improves our predictive power. Not so in causal inference, where we have to be very careful about the role in the causal process for each variable that enters the model so to make sure we are estimating what would have happened, importantly by avoiding post-treatment bias and accounting for potential confounding.

Similarly, while we suggest a split sample approach for validation in both causal inference and prediction, the split sample is used differently in each case. In prediction, we use the split sample to estimate the error rate and tune the model. That is, we revisit the model to retune it until we have minimized the generalization error in the test data. Not so in causal inference, where the split sample is used for identification and to ensure that we are correctly characterizing the uncertainty around the treatment effect or the coefficient of interest. Because we think the distinction between prediction and causal inference is so important, we will return to this theme throughout the chapter.

24.3 Key Principles of Causal Inference with Text

24.3.1 THE CORE PROBLEMS OF CAUSAL INFERENCE REMAIN, EVEN WHEN WORKING WITH TEXT

Nothing about using text data absolves us from the core challenges with causal inference. Even with new data like text, we run into the fundamental problem of causal inference: that we cannot observe what would have happened under a different treatment condition for an individual observation (Holland, 1986). In order to accurately estimate the counterfactual—the value of some outcome if the state of the world had been different—we require the same basic ingredients as any good causal inference. We need to have a good design, be attentive to the sample we are working with, and be cautious when relying on the selection on observables assumption. Confounding, reverse causality and dependence between observations are just as plausible in cases where we have text data as those where we do not and we need to be vigilant about these and other threats to inference.

24.3.2 OUR CONCEPTUALIZATION OF THE TREATMENT AND OUTCOME REMAINS A CRITICAL COMPONENT OF CAUSAL INFERENCE WITH TEXT

In the discovery chapter, we illustrated how the analyst could discover new concepts from text data by exploring different representations of text. In the measurement chapter, we described how researchers can use supervised machine learning to measure a given concept in the text at scale. In this chapter, we show how we can leverage these concepts to make causal inferences. However, unlike in the previous chapters, we now have to be particularly careful about how we arrived at our conceptualization—particularly whether we used information about treatment and control in developing our conceptualization. We will emphasize two major risks when developing and discovering concepts in a causal inference framework. The first risk should feel familiar—we are concerned that we will overfit the text. That is, one risk is that we will develop a categorization scheme that captures non-systematic facets of the text, essentially uncovering ephemeral noise in the documents. When this happens with measurement or discovery the risk is that we allocate attention to categories that are exceedingly rare and unlikely to appear in other samples. Overfitting in causal inference is even more pernicious, because it can lead us to infer interventions had a systematic effect when they didn't.

The second risk is a problem we call the Fundamental Problem of Causal Inference with Latent Variables (FPCILV) (Egami et al., 2018). FPCILV occurs when the analyst creates dependence between units by developing the mapping function with reference to the outcome of treatment in the experiment. If the mapping function is developed with the same data as is used in the final analysis, then the estimated potential outcome of one unit will depend on the treatment status of other units because the mapping function depends on the other units. This dependence violates SUTVA, one of the necessary conditions for causal inference. We explain overfitting and FPCILV in more detail later in this chapter.

24.3.3 THE CHALLENGES OF MAKING CAUSAL INFERENCES WITH TEXT UNDERSCORE THE NEED FOR SEQUENTIAL SCIENCE

Social science is the process of creating generalizable knowledge that explains or predicts societal patterns. The best causal inferences, or explanations, in social science emerge from a close relationship between theory and careful empirical evidence. This interaction is sequential—theory is updated as we learn from experiments and the experiments that we run are guided by theory. Because this interaction is sequential, the acquisition of evidence is never completely done and no one experiment is completely pivotal. Replication of experiments in different time periods or in different populations expands our evidence base from which we can draw more accurate theories. These theories in turn suggest the next experiments.

Because of the interplay between experiments and theory, many have suggested that before an experiment has been conducted, all of the parameters within the experiment should be laid out, including the variables the experiment will study, how those variables are measured, and the ultimate tests that the experiment should report (Humphreys, Sanchez de la Sierra, and Van der Windt, 2013). In the words of this book, the mapping function must be specified before the experiment is conducted. The intuition behind this recommendation is that if an experiment is truly testing a theory known beforehand, that the experiment should not change after it has been started and that reporting results outside of the preconceived research design may undermine the analysis. Many have suggested that researchers pre-register their experiments before conducting them, creating a *pre-analysis plan* (PAP) that ties the researchers hands so that they cannot change the data collection and analysis until after the experiment is run.

While such inflexibility in the analysis of data can be very useful in particular contexts, as we will describe below, it relies on a great deal of certainty about the about the variables we're likely to use, how those variables are measured, and the properties of the data we're examining. It relies on the experiment running smoothly, without unanticipated hiccups. Of course, it is rarely the case we have all that information in hand before running an experiment or that unexpected events during implementation change the research design. This is especially true when dealing with high-dimensional data like text, where researchers may not be able to foresee the topics and sentiments that will be expressed by the subjects. The difficulties in anticipating how the experiment will run can lead to awkward applications of the PAP and the creation of institutions that diminish their effectiveness. For example, it is now common that PAPs are amended to incorporate new data or are altered after experiences with partner organizations. And because it is impossible to anticipate all the issues with a PAP, researchers are trying to develop standard operating procedures when confronted with deviations. Once we are able to alter a bit, we open the door to many of the same abuses that PAPs, at their best, are able to defend against.

Instead of relying on perfect foresight to predict potential deviations in research design, we advocate for conducting the interplay between theory and experimentation *within each experiment*. That is, our research designs encourage users to randomly divide texts and other data into a training and a test set. While this split is familiar in machine learning and used throughout the book, we use it here for different reasons. First, if we already have a mapping function in hand, we can use the training set to rule out any deviations from our anticipated data collection efforts. We can validate that what we intended to measure is actually measured. Once we have done that, we can then write down a well-defined PAP and analyze the test data. Second, when we do not know the mapping function beforehand, we can use the training data to discover it, exploring our data to ensure that we uncover a coding scheme that is useful to our dataset. With that coding scheme in hand, we can define a clear set of rules that are easily applied to test data, without unexpected hiccups. The use of sample splitting, as we will show in this chapter, ensures that we avoid issues of FPCILV, limits our opportunity to overfit, and helps us to constrain researcher degrees of freedom credibly. We argue that it is less wasteful than conducting a pre-analysis plan before collecting any data, as it allows researchers to define the most useful measures for the data, discover unanticipated patterns, and take into account the actual implementation of the experiment, while still ensuring that final inferences made from the data are credible.

Central to the discussion of these last two principles is the mapping function—how we discover it and when we fix it to make causal inference. As a result, we start this chapter by reviewing this function—why we need it, how we discover it, and what properties we would like it to have.

24.4 The Mapping Function

The central task of Part 3: Discovery and Part 4: Measurement was to create a mapping from the text to some lower-dimensional summary of the text. This mapping function, which Egami et al. (2018) call g, is fundamental to using text as data because it reduces the complex and high-dimensional nature of text into a low-dimensional distillation of the essence of the text that is central to our research question. This mapping allows us to then conduct subsequent analyses where we relate our measure to other variables.

So far in this book, we've seen the mapping function take many forms. Catalinac (2016a) used a Latent Dirichlet Allocation topic model to create a mapping from election manifestos in Japan to a measure of attention of candidates to foreign policy. Gillion (2016) measures race-related discourse in politics with a supervised classifier that takes as input presidential and Congressional speeches. And Nielsen (2017) uses texts written by Muslim clerics to create a mapping function using a scale based on the Naive Bayes classifier to create a measure of cleric support for jihad. These mapping functions are all quite diverse—we have seen the development of mapping functions using tools ranging from hand coding, to dictionary methods, supervised methods, unsupervised methods, and scaling methods. The measures created by these functions have at times been continuous and at other times categorical. But in each case, the function results in a simplification of the text into a measure of interest.

We stress that while creating measures from text inherently requires a mapping from the text to a simplification of the text, various forms of a mapping function appear in almost every research study, including those that do not use text. For example, when we use an index to measure the extent to which a country is a democracy, like the Polity Index, we are collapsing a great deal of information about the institutions in a country onto one number—"Polity." While it would be difficult to use the concept of democracy in a quantitative analysis without reducing its dimensionality somewhat, we should always seek to understand how much our measures actually reflect the concepts that we are interested in studying.

In our agnostic approach to text analysis, we have emphasized that there is no one right organization of a given set of texts; rather, the distillation we create of the texts must be specific to the goal of the researcher. The mapping function we produce is not a model of how the individuals produced the text in our corpus, as much as a tool to produce a measure of interest, which is driven by the research question. Because of this agnostic approach, in Part 3: Discovery, we encouraged researchers to explore their data, investigating new organizations of the text by applying different mapping functions that would lead them to new ideas and subsequently new concepts and measures. In Part 4: Measurement, we encouraged researchers to refine their measures in an iterative process, iteratively developing codebooks for hand coding and classifiers for supervised learning in order to best capture the concept they want to measure. In both of these parts, we have emphasized the importance of extensive validation of the ultimate measure.

While we have advocated throughout the book for exploring and learning mappings from text to the concept of interest, the process of developing a mapping function can create complications for making causal inference. In this section, we follow Egami et al. (2018) to first introduce the mapping function into the casual inference notation above. Like Egami et al. (2018), we call the mapping function g. We then describe the problems with discovering g and estimating a causal effect using g in the same analysis. Last, we introduce a workflow that includes a sample splitting procedure in order to address this problem.

24.4.1 CAUSAL INFERENCE WITH g

As we discussed in Section 24.1, we make several important assumptions in order to identify the average treatment effect. First, we make a Stable Unit Treatment Value Assumption (SUTVA), which requires that each unit's potential outcomes are not affected by another unit's treatment status. Second, we assume ignorability, that each unit's potential outcomes are independent of treatment assignment. And last, we assume positivity—that all units have at least some probability of receiving treatment. We will call the set of possible values of treatment $\mathcal{T}$.

Assumption 1 (SUTVA) *For all individuals i, $y_i(t) = y_i(t_i)$.*

Assumption 2 (Ignorability) $y_i(t) \perp\!\!\!\perp t_i$ *for $t \in \mathcal{T}$.*

Assumption 3 (Positivity) $Pr(t_i = t) > 0$ *for $t \in \mathcal{T}$.*

In order to explain the challenges that discovering g creates for causal inference, we introduce g into the causal inference notation. In order to consider both outcomes and treatments that are text, we consider two different applications: 1) where the treatment is binary and the text measures the outcome variable, which we call "text as outcome" and 2) where the treatment is the text and the outcome variable is a scalar, which we call "text as treatment." In the first case, the outcome y_i is multidimensional, and in the second case, the treatment t_i is multidimensional. We cover particular examples of each of these cases in more detail in Chapters 25 and 26.

Assume for now that in each case—text as treatment and text as outcome—the mapping function g is known. That is, we have already decided upon a compression of the text that we will use for our analysis. We call this compression of the text π_i $(i = 1, \ldots, N)$, which is the value of π for unit i. This compression takes on values in the space $\mathcal{P}$. The compression could be any representation of text we have discussed so far in this book—it could represent the categories of hand coded documents, the topic proportions for a document from a topic model, or a scale produced by a dictionary or supervised learning algorithm. In the case of text as outcome, g maps y to $\mathcal{P}$, $g : \mathcal{Y} \to \mathcal{P}_y$, and $g(y_i) = \pi_i$. In the case of text as treatment, g maps t to R, $g : \mathcal{T} \to \mathcal{P}_t$, and $g(t_i) = \pi_i$. For conceptual ease, we will typically consider $\mathcal{P}$ as a set of K binary feature vectors in the text as treatment case (Fong and Grimmer, 2016; Egami et al., 2018; Fong and Grimmer, 2021).

Using g, we can rewrite the average treatment effect we defined in Section 24.1, but this time include g. Consider first the text as outcome case with a binary treatment, where the outcome is mapped by g into one of K categories. We can then redefine the potential outcomes as $g(y_i(1)) = \pi_i(1)$ under treatment and $g(y_i(0)) = \pi_i(0)$ under control, where $\pi_i(1)$ is a vector of K categories that the outcome would have under treatment. We define $\pi_{ik}(1)$ as the potential outcome for the k category under treatment. The average treatment effect can then be rewritten as:

$$\text{ATE}_k = E[g(\boldsymbol{y}_i(1))_k - g(\boldsymbol{y}_i(0))_k] \tag{24.4.1}$$
$$= E[\pi_{ik}(1) - \pi_{ik}(0)].$$

24.4.2 IDENTIFICATION AND OVERFITTING

In the previous section, we were imagining that g has already been created by the researcher. However, throughout much of this book, we have not only described the process of discovering and creating g, but also encouraged exploration and iteration on g. In the context of causal inference, however, discovering g and estimating it in the same analysis can be problematic. Egami et al. (2018) describe two main problems with the discovery of g while estimating causal effects: identification—what Egami et al. (2018) call the "Fundamental Problem of Causal Inference with Latent Variables" (FPCILV)—and overfitting.

Fundamental Problem of Causal Inference with Latent Variables

For SUTVA (Assumption 1) to hold, the potential outcomes of each unit should not depend on the treatment status of other units. However, when we use the data to discover a g, the mapping function g depends on the text of all units. In a topic model, for example, we use similarities between the documents to find groups of words that tend to appear together within texts. In a supervised learning method, the algorithm uses all of the text to learn the differences between documents with different labels. Even in hand coding, we develop a coding scheme based on the differences we see within the documents.

What this means is that had the texts been different, we most likely would have discovered a different mapping function. By extension, the π_i for each document then also depends on the text of all other units. In the text as outcome case, this means that the potential outcomes of each unit $\pi_i(1) = g(\boldsymbol{y}_i(1))$ and $\pi_i(0) = g(\boldsymbol{y}_i(0))$ are affected by the treatment assignments of other units because they depend on g. In the text as treatment case, this means that the treatments themselves affect each other through the mapping function. In both cases, this creates a fundamental problem for casual inference because the potential outcomes cannot be defined without reference to other units. A more technical account of the problem is available in Egami et al. (2018).

Overfitting

Discovering g and estimating a casual effect in the same analysis can also result in *overfitting*, where the researcher discovers relationships that might not generalize. Overfitting can be a problem in any research design, but because text is so high dimensional it is more acute with text, where there are many possible gs that could be discovered. Take the case of text as outcome, where the researcher wants to measure the effect of the treatment on the sentiment of a text. Imagine that completely by chance a disproportionate number of treated texts used the word sunny. The researcher might not have included that word in an a priori dictionary of positive sentiment, but while searching for g's might get excited that it was related to treatment and therefore select it as a measure, a form of fishing (Simmons, Nelson, and Simonsohn, 2011). Or the researcher might include it in the dictionary because of its meaning, even if she were unaware of its relationship to the outcome. In either case, the finding would not generalize outside of the dataset because sunny was related to the treatment by chance, not systematically. When there are many features, as there are with text data, at least some of them will be related to the treatment by chance, making it particularly important for researchers to guard against overfitting.

24.5   Workflows for Making Causal Inferences with Text

In this section, we introduce different approaches for making causal inferences with text that address the two concerns articulated above—the FPCILV and overfitting. In each of the approaches below, the important feature is separating out discovering g from estimating the casual effect.

24.5.1   DEFINE g BEFORE LOOKING AT THE DOCUMENTS

The simplest approach to splitting the discovery of g from estimation of the causal effect is to define g beforehand. For example, as we discussed in Chapter 16, researchers could use an existing dictionary as g. Or, as we discussed in Chapter 18, researchers could use an existing codebook instead of defining their own. In each of these cases, we could directly estimate the causal effect in either the text as outcome or text as treatment example.

However, we have also noted drawbacks to this approach throughout this book. In Chapter 16, we described how off-the-shelf dictionaries developed on one corpus may not generalize well to another, as in Loughran and McDonald (2011). This applies to off the shelf codebooks as well. Take the example of Boydstun (2013), who used the existing Policy Agendas Codebook to code newspaper articles as we described in Chapter 18. Even with an existing codebook, she updated and annotated the codebook so it could be accurately applied to her documents. Without updating, her labels for the newspaper articles would have ultimately been less accurate.

Indeed, using existing off-the-shelf measures sacrifices much of what we see as the promise of text as data. The discoveries and measurements we have described throughout this book all came from exploring and refining concepts. By specifying g beforehand in every analysis, we would miss important findings and discoveries. Even when we have an idea of what concept we wanted to measure beforehand, operationalizing that measure with a g before looking at the data might lead us to an unsatisfactory proxy of the true concept of interest.

24.5.2   USE A TRAIN/TEST SPLIT

An alternative approach is to split the sample into two sets—one to discover and refine g, and another to estimate the causal effect. This approach is proposed by Fong and Grimmer (2016) and Egami et al. (2018). The sample split addresses the problem of FPCILV because the potential outcomes are defined in the test set—in the test set, g does not depend on the treatment status of any unit. It also addresses the problem of overfitting by ensuring that any relationship discovered in the training set generalizes to the test set. This has the advantage that we can use the training set to explore and refine g knowing that we will be able to guard against overfitting by estimating the final ATE in our test set.

The workflow is as follows:

1. **Split the sample.** After running the experiment, the researcher first splits the sample into two pieces, one for discovery (the training set) and one to estimate the causal effect (the test set). How much data to place in the training versus the test set will depend on the trade-off between how much data is needed to discover and refine g versus how much data is needed to estimate a precise effect. Which split to choose will necessarily be application-specific, but whatever split is used, we recommend selecting the training documents at random.

    Importantly, the test set should be put somewhere where it is not touched or viewed until g has been estimated. The test set can only be used once—to estimate the casual effect. This version of the train/test split is therefore quite different from using cross-validation to train a classifier, which we discussed in Chapter 20. Cross-validation in this case would generate multiple different measures (one for each fold) and would end up violate FPCILV across the set of the measures. Instead, the procedure we are suggesting here is more similar to the train/test split we described in Chapter 21, where the test set is only used once—for the final measurement.

2. **Discover g.** After splitting the sample and removing the test set, the researcher can then begin the process of discovering and refining g. Here, we can use all of the methods described in this book to explore, discover, measure, and validate concepts that we want to use. We hope to find a measure that is useful to the research question, but also generalizable—one that we are likely to find and be able to measure in other datasets besides the training data.

3. **Validate g.** After settling on a g, we must validate it, as we described in Part 3: Discovery and Part 4: Measurement, particularly in Chapters 12, 20, and 21. Validation ensures that we are indeed measuring the concept that we claim to measure and that our accuracy is high. Validation will often require splitting the training set into pieces as well, in the process of cross-validation (Chapter 20) or validating an unsupervised method used for measurement (Chapter 21).

4. **Apply to the test set and revalidate.** Because we can only use the test set once, before opening up the test set, we have to make sure we are happy with g and that all of the aspects of g are well defined, including how we will represent the text in the test set and how we will apply the mapping function to obtain the labels. At this point, we can even write a pre-analysis plan or declare our design so that we ensure we have a plan for calculating the ATE (Gerber and Green, 2012; Humphreys, Sanchez de la Sierra, and Van der Windt, 2013; Blair et al., 2019).

    We then apply g to the test set and estimate the average causal effect. But we are not quite done yet, we need to revalidate g. If we have overfit the model in the training set or if the training set was too small or unrepresentative, g could have an entirely different interpretation in the test set. We should evaluate accuracy in the test set in order to ensure that g obtains similar levels of accuracy in the test set and that its interpretation is what we intended. If g does not fit well in the test set, unfortunately, we cannot return to the training data or change g. However, even a failed test set validation provide us with important information about how we could improve upon our measures in future experiments.

Splitting the sample presents a significant trade-off—the efficiency loss of having less data to compute the ATE. This is complicated by the fact that we do not know how much data we need in the training set—this is like having to articulate the "power we need for discovery" (Egami et al., 2018). We hope future work in this area will take up how to most effectively partition data in order to refine concepts and compute treatment effects.

24.5.3 RUN SEQUENTIAL EXPERIMENTS

The last workflow we introduce for making causal inferences with text data is running sequential experiments. In this design, the researcher uses the data from the first experiment to develop g, then discards the data from this experiment and runs a follow-up experiment where g is used to map the text to a treatment or outcome. This design is similar to running a pilot study where the data from the pilot study is used to define g. In this case the pilot not only serves to design the survey or randomized control trial, but also helps fix the analysis.

Sequential experiments provide a stronger test of the generalizability of the research finding than sample splits. Replicating results across sequential experiments not only requires g to generalize to another dataset, but also requires the casual effect to generalize to a slightly different time period and population. Whereas a random train/test split on average will reflect the same ATE, the ATE across sequential experiments might change. Sequential experiments are therefore ideal for testing generalizability, but take more resources and time to implement. A more general version of this is replication of studies across contexts and researchers, where the sequential experiment is peformed as part of a community of scientists, rather than within one particular study.

24.6 Conclusion

In this chapter, we first provided an review of the basic tenants of causal inference. We discussed similarities and differences between prediction, measurement, and casual inference and introduced some principles of using causal inference with text. We then described the problem of making causal inferences in the same dataset as discovering the mapping function g, introducing the Fundamental Problem of Causal Inference with Latent Variables (Egami et al., 2018) and the problem of overfitting. Last, we described some workflows to address this, including using an existing mapping function, splitting the data, and running sequential experiments.

Of course, these workflows work well in theory, but are more difficult to implement in practice. In the next two chapters, we provide examples of research designs to make causal inference for text as outcome (Chapter 25) and text as treatment (Chapter 26). In Chapter 27 we extend our discussion of text and causal inference to consider cases where text is a confounder in an observational study. We note throughout this discussion that the use of text data in causal inference is a new, exciting, and continously developing field. We hope to provide a foundation here for future work.

CHAPTER 25

Text as Outcome

The text as outcome setting is analytically straightforward. In particular, g provides a mapping from the text—now denoted y to emphasize it is the outcome under study—to the lower-dimensional outcome of interest, π. Assuming a particular g, we would like to estimate the average treatment effect (ATE). Using the train/test split approach that we discussed in Chapter 24, g is developed on the training documents, which we indicate by subscripting it by I. The ATE, however, is estimated on the test set O, which we indicate using subscript O. Assuming SUTVA, ignorability, and positivity (Assumptions 1–3 from Chapter 24), and notation from Egami et al. (2018), we can define the ATE as:

$$\widehat{ATE} = \frac{\sum_{i \in O} I(t_i = 1) g_I(y_i(1))}{\sum_{j \in O} I(t_j = 1)} - \frac{\sum_{i \in O} I(t_i = 0) g_I(y_i(0))}{\sum_{j \in O} I(t_j = 0)}.$$

In other words, by learning g on the training documents I, we treat it as a fixed transformation of the data in O and do estimation as we ordinarily would. Egami et al. (2018) provides an identification proof.

In this chapter, we review two examples of using text as outcome. First, we discuss a survey experiment on attitudes toward immigration conducted by Egami et al. (2018). Second, we highlight the work of Franco, Grimmer, and Lim (2018), who estimate the impact of presidential speeches on media coverage. In each case, the authors use the train/test split to discover g, then estimate the causal effect in sequence. In addition, Egami et al. (2018) use sequential experiments to iteratively refine g before finally estimating the ATE.

25.1 An Experiment on Immigration

Egami et al. (2018) study how awareness about an individual's criminal history affects attitudes toward immigration using a survey experiment. Building off of an older study by Cohen, Rust, and Steen (2004), they randomly assign the survey respondents to read two different hypothetical scenarios describing an illegal immmigrant. In both cases, the person entered the United States illegally. However, in one case the scenario describes the person as having a criminal history.

The treatment vignette was as follows:

> "A 28-year-old single man, a citizen of another country, was convicted of illegally entering the United States. Prior to this offense, he had served two previous prison sentences each more than a year. One of these previous sentences was for a violent crime and he had been deported back to his home country."

The control vignette was as follows:

> "A 28-year-old single man, a citizen of another country, was convicted of illegally entering the United States. Prior to this offense, he had never been imprisoned before."

Respondents were then asked an open-ended question asking them to describe what the US government should do in this situation.

> "Should this offender be sent to prison?" (responses: yes, no, don't know) but followed by asking, "Why or why not? Please describe in **at least two sentences** what actions if any the U.S. government should take with respect to this person and why?"

The goal of the analysis is to estimate the impact of the vignette on the writing of the respondents about what actions the US government should take. In order to estimate this, however, the authors have to develop a g function to map the text of the open-ended responses into a useable quantity of interest.

Egami et al. (2018) used a combination of train/test splits and sequential experiments to discover g and estimate the causal effect. First, they analyzed the data provided by Cohen, Rust, and Steen (2004) using the Structural Topic Model described in Chapter 13 (Roberts et al., 2014). They then replicated this experiment with several design changes in a Mechanical Turk experiment in July of 2017. Last, they re-replicated the experiment in September 2017. In each case, they used a train/test split to develop g and estimated the ATE on the test set only.

We first show the results from the final experiment that they ran. Table 25.1 shows the most probable words for each of 11 topics, the topic labels given by Egami et al. (2018), and the estimated effect size and confidence interval. As you can see, topics vary from advocating for deportation (Topics 2 and 3) to requesting more information about the case (Topic 5). Clearly, the treatment has an impact on the topics written by the respondent. Being told that the immigrant has a criminal history increases the amount the respondent writes about deportation and decreases the probability that the respondent argues that the person should be able to stay in the country.

Egami et al. (2018) find similar results in their analyses of the original Cohen, Rust, and Steen (2004) study and of the first replication of the study, even though the g used in each case is slightly different.

Table 25.1. Topics, highest probability words, and estimated effects of treatments ordered by effect size from Experiment 3 of Egami et al. (2018).

	Label	Highest Probability Words	Effect	CI
Topic 3	Deport because of money	just, send, back, countri, jail, come, prison, let, harm, money	0.032	(0.015, 0.049)
Topic 7	Punish to full extent of the law	crime, violent, person, law, convict, commit, deport, illeg, punish, offend	0.024	(0.01, 0.037)
Topic 4	Depends on the circumstances	first, countri, time, came, jail, man, think, reason, govern, put	0.012	(0, 0.026)
Topic 1	Limited punishment with help to stay in country, complaints about immigration system	legal, way, immigr, danger, peopl, allow, come, countri, can, enter	0.01	(−0.005, 0.029)
Topic 11	Repeat offender, danger to society	believ, countri, violat, offend, person, law, deport, prison, citizen, individu	−0.002	(−0.004, 0.001)
Topic 9	No prison, deportation	deport, prison, will, person, countri, man, illeg, serv, time, sentenc	−0.002	(−0.014, 0.009)
Topic 10	Should be sent back	sent, back, countri, prison, home, think, pay, origin, illeg, time	−0.003	(−0.012, 0.007)
Topic 2	Deport	deport, think, prison, crime, alreadi, imprison, illeg, sinc, serv, time	−0.003	(−0.009, 0.001)
Topic 8	Allow to stay, no prison, rehabilitate, probably another explanation	dont, crimin, think, tri, hes, offens, better, case, know, make	−0.015	(−0.028, −0.001)
Topic 6	Crime, small amount of jail time, then deportation.	enter, countri, illeg, person, jail, deport, time, proper, imprison, determin	−0.024	(−0.04, −0.003)
Topic 5	More information needed, if violent imprison	state, unit, prison, crime, immigr, illeg, take, crimin, simpli, put	−0.024	(−0.042, −0.006)

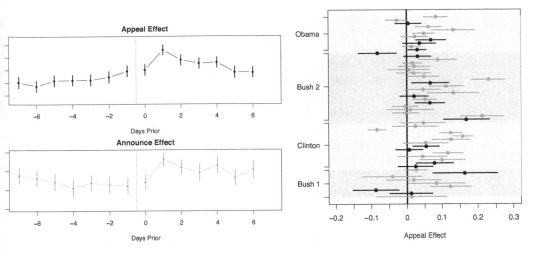

Figure 25.1. The effect of presidential public appeals on media coverage. Figure 8 from Grimmer, and Lim (2018)

25.2 The Effect of Presidential Public Appeals

In our second example on using text as a dependent variable, Franco, Grimmer, and Lim (2018) examine the effect of presidents making public appeals during prime time television on subsequent media coverage. A large literature presents mixed results about the ability of presidents to affect public opinion and how they are covered in the news. One reason for the mixed results is that prior studies use different research designs and shifting types of evidence to asses the effect of presidential appeals. To isolate the effect of the appeals, Franco, Grimmer, and Lim (2018) restrict attention to presidential public statements made during prime time television coverage. They then collect coverage of the president from the top ten newspapers in the week before and the week after the speech, along with broadcast news transcripts from the same time period. The result is a collection of nearly 160,000 stories that mention the president, collected across the president's public appeals.

Franco, Grimmer, and Lim (2018) use these data to ask about the effect presidents have on the type of coverage they receive from the media. To make this assessment Franco, Grimmer, and Lim (2018) use a Structural Topic Model to estimate a set of topics, using 10% of the news stories and transcripts as a training set and the remaining 90% as a test set. This split ensures there is enough information in the training set to discover the salient topics and enough content in the test set to infer if there is a treatment effect.

Given this topic fit, Franco, Grimmer, and Lim (2018) then identify the salient topic of each presidential public appeal. Using this identified salient topic, they then estimate the effect of the president's speech on this salient topic within the subsequent news media.

The left plot in Figure 25.1 shows the effect of the president's speech on the topic coverage in two different situations: 1) when the president makes an appeal to Congress (the black, top lines) and 2) when the president makes an announcement that conveys that some major world event happens (the gray, bottom line). Using these percentages, Franco, Grimmer, and Lim (2018) infer the effect of the speech by comparing the share of coverage in the day immediately before and after the speech was given.

The left plot shows that when presidents make public appeals they substantially increase coverage. Following an appeal to Congress, presidents receive 3.4 percentage points more coverage about the topic, compared to the rate immediately before the speech. The bottom plot shows why it can be problematic to assess the effect of presidential speech after he announces a major world event. After the president announces an event, there is a seven percentage point increase in the coverage of that topic in articles that mention the president. Of course, some of that increase is attributable to the event that occurred, rather than the president's speech, so the estimate conflates the president's speech with the additional coverage of that event in the world. Perhaps not surprisingly, we see that the increased coverage of announcements lasts longer than the appeals.

Franco, Grimmer, and Lim (2018) also provide speech-by-speech estimates of the effect of appeals on subsequent news coverage. The right plot in Figure 25.1 shows the increase in coverage on a topic for announcements (gray) and appeals (black). This figure shows that while news coverage rises more after the president makes an announcement related to a world event, again, this may be because the major news story results in additional coverage outside of the president's speech. Further, this figure shows that presidents do not appear to get better at influencing media coverage over their presidency; later speeches, which are closer to the top of the figure, are not more effective than earlier speeches, at the bottom of the figure.

25.3 Conclusion

In this chapter, we've reviewed two examples of using text as outcome. In the Egami et al. (2018) immigration experiment, we highlighted the usefulness of combining sequential experiments with the train/test split. Even when spanning experiments over 15 years, that example shows relative stability in the relationship between perceptions of criminal history and US survey respondent opinion on US government policy. Through the Franco, Grimmer, and Lim (2018) example, we showed how text as outcome can be used in an interrupted time series design to estimate the impact of presidential statements on media coverage, again using the train/test split design to discover g. In the next chapter, we move on to examples of text as treatment.

CHAPTER 26

Text as Treatment

In the last chapter, we described two examples of using text as outcome. In this chapter, we move on to a slightly more complicated form of text in causal inference—using text as treatment. To fix ideas, consider the large literature that is interested in the effect of campaign advertisements on voters' turnout decisions. We might be interested in the effect of encountering a campaign's negative advertisement—compared to an advertisement without an attack on an opponent—on an individual's probability of turnout in the election. The treatment is the text of the advertisement—denoted t_i to emphasize it is the treatment. The potential outcomes $y_i(t_i)$ reflects respondent i's decision to turn out after viewing advertisement t_i.

One way to approach estimating the impact of t_i on turnout would be to compare the impact of two different advertisements. This is the A/B testing framework familiar to many from its use in industry settings. However, typically social scientists are interested in understanding what underlying latent value of the text affects the outcome. In this setting, whether an advertisement contains a negative attack on an opponent is a latent variable—a negative attack could manifest itself in many different forms within the advertisement, but we could map these attacks to a categorical variable of either containing or not containing an attack. An alternative approach to A/B testing, which we consider in this chapter, is for the researcher to assign many different campaign advertisements to respondents, a portion of which might mention the negative attack. Here, following Egami et al. (2018), we can denote the treatment of interest $\pi_i = g(t_i)$ as the mapping between the text of the advertisement and a variable of whether or not the advertisement contains a negative attack or some other feature of interest. The Average Treatment Effect (ATE) would then be:

$$\widehat{ATE} = \frac{\sum_{i \in O} I(\pi_i = g_I(t_i) = 1) y_i(1))}{\sum_{j \in O} I(\pi_j = g_I(t_j) = 1)} - \frac{\sum_{i \in O} I(\pi_i = g_I(t_i) = 0) y_i(0))}{\sum_{j \in O} I(\pi_j = g_I(t_j) = 0)} . (26.0.1)$$

As in Chapter 25, we use g_I to indicate that g was developed within the training set and O to reflect the fact that the ATE is estimated in the test set.

With text as treatment, however, we will rarely be able to design texts so that the only relevant feature is the treatment of interest. Rather, there will often be other treatments that are present in the texts. Campaign advertisements contain more aspects that just negative attacks; they might also contain information about the candidates, emphasize the economy, vary in tone or even text format. Therefore, the treatment will be multidimensional. In the case of multidimensional treatments, using a topic model to represent the treatment is difficult because the space of topics $\mathcal{P}$ is a simplex—each π_i sums to 1. For the purposes of this chapter, we will follow Fong and Grimmer (2016) and Egami et al. (2018) to represent text as treatment as binary treatments. That is, g will be learned from a model that maps the text t to a vector of length K where each element π_{ik} is an indicator of whether unit i contains treatment k. In total, therefore, there will be 2^K possible treatment vectors.

To address those additional, unobserved treatments, Fong and Grimmer (2021) introduce a second function h that maps t_i to a vector of binary treatments that are not explicitly represented. We will represent the values of $h(t_i) = b_i$ with $b_i \in \mathcal{B}$. Even though g and h are deterministic functions of the treatments, the random assignment of the documents creates a joint distribution between the observed and unobserved treatments, which we will denote as $p(\pi_i, b_i)$.

We will make an *exclusion* restriction that supposes that the text only affects responses through the observed and unobserved treatments. Specifically, we will suppose that $y_i(t_i) = y_i(g(t_i), h(t_i), t_i) = y_i(g(t_i), h(t_i))$. Using this definition of the treatments and assuming that there is only one dichotomous treatment of interest $g(t_i) = \pi_i \in \{0, 1\}$, Fong and Grimmer (2021) define the Average Treatment Effect as

$$\text{ATE} = \sum_{b \in \mathcal{B}} \Big(E[y_i(\pi_i = 1, b_i = b)] - E[y_i(\pi_i = 0, b_i = b)] \Big) \, Pr(b_i = b).$$

In order to identify the causal effect of latent treatments in this more general setting, we need an additional assumption compared to the text as outcome setting. Whereas in the text as outcome case we could manipulate the treatment directly, in the text as treatment case we are interested in a latent treatment. In addition to the three in Chapters 24 and 25—SUTVA, Ignorability, and Positivity[1]—Fong and Grimmer (2021) characterize two sufficient assumptions that enable the identification of the ATE.

Assumption 1 (Sufficiency) *Suppose that either:*

1) *The measured and unmeasured treatments are independent. Formally,*
   $p(\pi, b) = p(\pi)p(b)$.
2) *The unmeasured treatments are unrelated to the outcome, on average*
   $E[y_i(\pi, b)] = E[y_i(\pi, b')]$ *for all* $b, b' \in \mathcal{B}$.

These two conditions are similar to assumptions that researchers commonly make when conducting observational research. The first assumption supposes that the measured treatments are independent of the unmeasured treatments. For observational research, this assumption is similar to a common assumption that the causal effect of interest is independent of unmeasured confounders. The second assumption is that the unmeasured treatments have no effect on the outcome, on average. The analogue to observational research is that a confounder is unrelated to the outcome. Fong and Grimmer (2021) and Fong and Grimmer (2016) provide an identification proof.

Assumption 1 shows that when using texts as treatments, randomization of the texts alone is insufficient to identify causal effects. In addition, we need strong assumptions

---

[1] Positivity in this case means that all treatments are possible: $f(\pi_i) > 0$ for all $\pi_i \in \text{Range } g(\cdot)$ (Egami et al., 2018)

about how our treatments of interest relate to unobserved treatments within the document. In our running example, this means that if we are interested in the effect of negative advertising on a voter's turnout decision, we must assume that other features of the advertisement—the other information provided, the topics that are discussed, or even the font that is used—are either independent of the negative information about the other candidate or have no effect on the outcome. Even when analysts have direct control over the contents of the documents, such as in vignette experiments, this can be a difficult assumption to satisfy.

Having delineated the assumptions necessary to identify casual effects in the text as treatment case, we now move on to discuss two examples of using text as treatment. For the first example, we discuss Fong and Grimmer (2021)'s application of a text as treatment design to discover the aspects of President Trump's tweets that impact survey respondents' reactions. In the second example, we highlight an application from Fong and Grimmer (2016) that discovers the features of candidate biographies that impact evaluations of these candidates by survey respondents.

26.1 An Experiment Using Trump's Tweets

In this section, we discuss the application by Fong and Grimmer (2021) of text as treatment to Twitter posts by former President Donald Trump. Not only were Donald Trump's tweets widely discussed in the media during his time as president, a large political science literature also investigates the effect of presidential speech on public opinion. Fong and Grimmer (2021) set out to discover not only the overall effect of speech, but also the aspects of the speech that have the largest impact. To do this, Fong and Grimmer (2021) use data from a 2017 YouGov survey that asks respondents to evaluate a random set of Twitter messages from President Trump, with ratings "Great," "Good," "OK," "Bad," or "Terrible."

Fong and Grimmer (2021) use the supervised Indian Buffet Process (SIBP) developed by Fong and Grimmer (2016) to discover the latent treatments from the combination of Trump's tweets and the ratings. The SIBP is a supervised topic model that seeks to identify topics related to the outcome of interest—in this case the timeliness of the response. Importantly, instead of estimating topic proportions as in LDA, SIBP identifies a binary topic vector, an indicator for whether a topic is included or not included in each document.

The authors then split the data, using one-third of the data in the training set and two-thirds of the data in the test set. The sample split allows the authors to search over a number of different models before finally settling on a measure of the treatment that they are satisfied with. Table 26.1 reproduces the table from Fong and Grimmer (2021) that summarizes the most probable words in the treatments for the model that they decided upon. Treatment 1 corresponds to aspects of tweets attacking Hillary Clinton and the media. Treatment 2 relates to strong economic performance, treatment 3 on repealing and replacing the Affordable Care Act, treatment 4 on the First Lady and the controversy over the NFL national anthem protests, and treatment 5 on the stock market and relations with North Korea.

Fong and Grimmer (2021) then use the test set to estimate the impact of the treatments on the ratings produced by the survey. To do this, they estimate the impact of each treatment on favorability among Republicans, Democrats, and Independents (Table 26.2). The results produce some surprising findings. President Trump's attacks on Clinton and the news media are negatively evaluated among all three groups. In

Table 26.1. Words most strongly associated with treatments.
Table 5 from Fong and Grimmer (2021).

Treatment 1	Treatment 2	Treatment 3	Treatment 4	Treatment 5
fake	cuts	obamacare	flotus	prime
news	strange	senators	behalf	minister
media	tax	repeal	anthem	korea
cnn	luther	healthcare	melania	north
election	stock	replace	nfl	stock
story	market	republican	flag	market
nbc	alabama	vote	prayers	china
stories	reform	republicans	bless	executive
hillary	record	senate	ready	prayers
clinton	high	north	players	order

Table 26.2. Regression of tweet favorability on latent features.
Table 6 from Fong and Grimmer (2021).

	Democrats		Independents		Republicans	
	1	2	3	4	5	6
Intercept	−76.57	−88.50	2.32	−6.33	98.52	91.73
	(1.67)	(2.16)	(1.32)	(1.71)	(1.06)	(1.38)
Treatment 1	−45.22	−33.83	−31.75	−27.27	−18.91	−15.28
	(5.18)	(5.02)	(4.03)	(3.94)	(3.27)	(3.20)
Treatment 2	10.59	8.18	10.89	9.21	16.45	15.09
	(8.91)	(8.55)	(7.02)	(6.78)	(5.63)	(5.45)
Treatment 3	−35.93	−34.42	−25.69	−24.73	−10.27	−9.41
	(4.78)	(4.58)	(3.74)	(3.61)	(3.02)	(2.92)
Treatment 4	18.14	18.98	22.66	23.41	16.89	17.37
	(8.37)	(8.02)	(6.48)	(6.25)	(5.29)	(5.11)
Treatment 5	34.11	33.32	18.84	18.32	7.84	7.39
	(7.4)	(7.09)	(5.82)	(5.62)	(4.68)	(4.52)
Pos. Sent		23.74		17.23		13.5
		(2.89)		(2.29)		(1.84)
N	752		752		752	

contrast, Trump's touting of the economy (treatments 2 and 4) are positively evaluated across all three groups.

The authors provide an extensive discussion of whether or not the assumptions necessary for text as treatment hold in their example. SUTVA might be violated if the subject is affected by tweets other than those presented to them in the study. This is plausible, given that subjects within the study are likely to have run across other tweets made by President Trump during 2017. Random assignment, however, is more plausibly met. Because YouGov designed the study, it had control over assignment of tweets to respondents.

Outside of SUTVA and randomization, Fong and Grimmer (2021) also need the two assumptions related to unmeasured treatments from Assumption 1 to hold. This assumption stipulates that there are no unmeasured aspects of the tweets that are related to the discovered treatments that also impact the outcome. Fong and Grimmer (2021) explore the possibility that this assumption might be violated in their experiment— perhaps treatments 1 and 3 have more negative sentiment than the other treatments. If respondents were reacting primarily to negative sentiment and sentiment was correlated with the treatments, this would be a violation of the assumption. Using a sentiment dictionary, Fong and Grimmer (2021) find that indeed sentiment is related to the treatments. However, including the measure of sentiment as a confounder in Table 26.2 does not change the results.

26.2 A Candidate Biography Experiment

In another example, Fong and Grimmer (2016) use a text as treatment framework to study the features of candidates' biographies that affect constituent evaluations. A large literature in political science asks how voters evaluate the characteristics of people who run for office (Canon, 1990; Popkin, 1994; Bartels, 2002; Carnes, 2012; Campbell and Cowley, 2014). For example, recent work studies the overrepresentation of lawyers in elected office (Bonica and Sen, 2017). One way scholars study how candidates' personal histories affect their electoral support is with survey experiments. In these experiments, researchers manipulate some feature of the text, hoping to identify how individuals react to a particular piece of information. For example, we might construct a biography that alters an individual's occupation. Or, we might run a conjoint study that varies several features of the candidate's background.[2]

Fong and Grimmer (2016) take a different approach to assessing the effect of candidate biographies. They use a collection of candidate biographies to discover features of candidates' backgrounds that voters find appealing. To uncover the features of candidate biographies that voters are responsive to, they acquire a collection of 1,246 Congressional candidate biographies from Wikipedia. Fong and Grimmer (2016) then anonymize the biographies—replacing names and removing other identifiable information—to ensure that the only information available to the respondent was explicitly present in the text.

A condition for this experiment to uncover latent treatments is that each vector of treatments has nonzero probability of occurring. This is equivalent to assuming that none of the treatments are *aliased*, or perfectly correlated (Hainmueller, Hopkins, and Yamamoto, 2014). Aliasing is more likely if there are only a few distinct texts that are provided to participants in our experiment. Therefore, Fong and Grimmer (2016) assign each respondent in each evaluation round a distinct candidate biography. To bolster statistical power, they ask respondents to evaluate up to four distinct candidate biographies, resulting in each respondent evaluating 2.8 biographies on average.[3] After presenting the respondents with a candidate's biography, they ask each respondent to

---

[2] Part of this section is drawn from Fong and Grimmer (2016).

[3] The multiple evaluations of candidate biographies is problematic if there is spillover across rounds of our experiment. We have little reason to believe observing one candidate biography would systematically affect the response in subsequent rounds.

Table 26.3. Top words for 10 treatments sIBP discovered.
From Fong and Grimmer (2016).

Treatment 1	Treatment 2	Treatment 3	Treatment 4	Treatment 5
appointed	fraternity	director	received	elected
school_graduated	distinguished	university	washington_university	house
governor	war_ii	received	years	democratic
worked	chapter	president	death	seat
older	air_force	master_arts	company	republican
law_firm	phi	phd	training	served
elected	reserve	policy	military	committee
grandfather	delta	public	including	appointed
office	air	master	george_washington	defeated
legal	states_air	affairs	earned_bachelors	office

Treatment 6	Treatment 7	Treatment 8	Treatment 9	Treatment 10
united_states	republican	star	law	war
military	democratic	bronze	school_law	enlisted
combat	elected	germany	law_school	united_states
rank	appointed	master_arts	juris_doctor	assigned
marine_corps	member	awarded	student	army
medal	incumbent	played	earned_juris	air
distinguished	political	yale	earned_law	states_army
air_force	father	football	law_firm	year
states_air	served	maternal	university_school	service
air	state	division	body_president	officer

rate the candidate using a *feeling thermometer*: a well-established social science scale that goes from 0 when a respondent is "cold" to a candidate to 100 when a respondent is "warm" to the candidate.

Fong and Grimmer (2016) recruited a sample of 1,886 participants using Survey Sampling International (SSI), an online survey platform. The sample is census matched to reflect US demographics on sex, age, race, and education. Using the sample there are 5,303 total observations. They assign 2,651 responses to the training set and 2,652 to the test set. They then apply the sIBP process to the training data. To apply the model, they standardize the feeling thermometer to have mean zero and standard deviation 1. They set K to a relatively low value ($K = 10$) reflecting a quantitative and qualitative search over K. They select the final model varying the parameters and evaluating the CE score.

Table 26.3 provides the top words for each of the ten treatments the sIBP discovered in the training set. Fong and Grimmer (2016) selected ten treatments using a combination of guidance from the sIBP, assessment using CE scores, and their own qualitative assessment of the models (Grimmer and Stewart, 2013). The treatments cover salient features of Congressional biographies from the time period that we analyze. For example, treatments 6 and 10 capture a candidate's military experience.

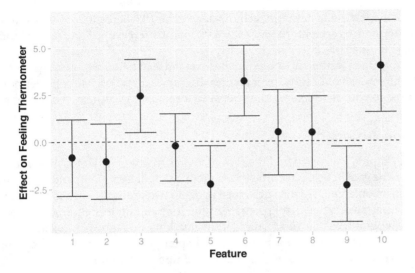

Figure 26.1. 95% confidence intervals for effects of discovered treatments. The mean value of the feeling thermometer is 62.3. Figure 2 from Fong and Grimmer (2016).

Treatments 5 and 7 are about previous political experience and treatments 3 and 9 refer to a candidate's education experience. Obviously, there are many features of a candidate's background missing here, but the treatments discovered provide a useful set of dimensions to assess how voters respond to a candidate's background.

After training the model on the training set, Fong and Grimmer (2016) apply it to the test set to infer the treatments in the biographies. They assume there are no interactions between the discovered treatments in order to estimate their effects.[4] Figure 26.1 shows the point estimate and 95-percent confidence intervals, which take into account uncertainty in inferring the treatments from the texts and the relationship between those treatments and the response.

The treatment effects reveal intuitive, though interesting, features of candidate biographies that affect respondent evaluations. For example, Figure 26.1 reveals a distaste for political and legal experience—even though a large share of Congressional candidates have previous political experience and a law degree. Treatment 5, which describes a candidate's previous political experience, causes a 2.26 point reduction in feeling thermometer evaluation (95-percent confidence interval, $[-4.26, -0.24]$). Likewise, treatment 9 shows that respondents dislike lawyers, with the presence of legal experience causing a 2.34 point reduction in feeling thermometer (95-percent confidence interval, $[-4.28, -0.29]$). The aversion to lawyers is not, however, an aversion to education. Treatment 3, a treatment that describes advanced degrees, causes a 2.43 point increase in feeling thermometer evaluations (95-percent confidence interval, $[0.49, 4.38]$).

In contrast, Figure 26.1 shows that there is a consistent bonus for military experience. This is consistent with intuition from political observers that the public supports veterans. For example, treatment 6, which describes a candidate's military record, causes

---

[4]This assumption is not necessary for the framework we propose here. Interaction effects could be modeled, but it would require us to make much stronger parametric assumptions using a method for heterogeneous treatments such as Imai and Ratkovic (2013).

a 3.21 point increase in feeling thermometer rating (95-percent confidence interval, $[1.34, 5.12]$) and treatment 10 causes a 4.00 point increase (95-percent confidence interval, $[1.53, 6.45]$).

This experiment reveals how varying the texts can lead to intuitive, though still useful insights into the effect of texts on outcomes. In our next section, we consider how text can be used to eliminate confounding between a numeric treatment and outcome.

26.3 Conclusion

In this chapter, we considered the case of text as treatments. Unlike the text as outcome case, the goal in text as treatment is to identify latent treatments and estimate their impacts on an outcome. We then described in detail two examples—uncovering the features of Trump tweets that drive partisan evaluations and understanding the aspects of candidate biographies that affect candidate evaluations. So far, we've considered text as outcome and text as treatment. In the next chapter, we turn to a third use of text in causal inference: using text to measure and condition on confounding.

CHAPTER 27

Text as Confounder

Not only can text be used as an outcome or an intervention in experiments, text can also be used to control for variables in observational analyses. Here we draw on work by Roberts, Stewart, and Nielsen (2020) to describe how text can be a confounder in causal analyses and how we can use text analysis to control for this type of confounding.[1]

Text as a confounding variable occurs frequently within social science applications. To take one example, Maliniak, Powers, and Walter (2013) provide evidence that articles written by women in International Relations are less likely to be cited than articles written by men on account of the perceived gender of the author. The authors find this relationship even when accounting for scholarly credentials, such as tenure and rank of school, and for article-level covariates such as publication venue, topic, perspective, and article age.

Is an article with a female author less likely to be cited than if it had a male author? In this case, the gender of the author is treatment and the outcome are the number of citations. However, because gender is not randomly assigned, we cannot simply take the mean difference in citations between men and women as our estimate of the causal effect of gender on citations. Most importantly, women write about different topics in International Relations than men do. The textual content of the article may be related to both treatment (perceived gender) and the outcome (citations); therefore the text of the article confounds the relationship between gender and citations. As a result, Maliniak, Powers, and Walter (2013) spend much of the paper accounting for this by using hand coded categories that describe the article content as control variables.

Text as a confounder appears surprisingly often in the analysis of social data. The content of legislative bills might confound the relationship between veto threats and repositioning in Congress. Students college admissions profiles or recommendation letters may be associated both with their race or gender and their probability of achieving admission to college. The content of international agreements might confound the relationship between trade and international cooperation.

Controlling for numeric variables is relatively straightforward—the researcher can use basic linear regression or matching to condition on the confounder. However, controlling for the content of a text is much more difficult. Researchers cannot include every unique word in the article in the match or the regression because there are probably many more words than observations. In addition, researchers do not want to completely

---

[1] Part of this chapter is drawn from Roberts, Stewart, and Nielsen (2020).

control *all of* the text—ideally they just want to adjust for the words or clusters of words that confound the treatment and the outcome.

Adjusting for confounding using a high-dimensional covariate like text poses the challenge of the "curse of dimensionality." The difficulty with conditioning on text is to figure out which aspects of the text should be included and which elements of the text should *not* be conditioned on. Oftentimes, researchers do not know offhand what aspects of the text are related both to the treatment and to the outcome. They might not know how women and men discuss topics differently in International Relations and which aspects of these differences might be related to citation counts. Therefore, in these cases researchers must *estimate* the aspects of the text that are confounding the relationship.

Mathematically, the structure of the confounding problem is as follows. As in Chapter 24, we start with a dataset of N units. Each unit i is assigned treatment t_i, which takes a value of 1 for treated units and 0 for control. Under the potential outcomes framework, the outcome variable y_i takes on the value $y_i(1)$ when unit i is treated and $y_i(0)$ when unit i is a control.

Because we are considering cases where our data is observational, t_i is not randomly assigned, and treated and control groups may not be comparable. A common practice is to match on P pre-treatment covariates for our N observations in the $N \times P$ matrix X to improve similarity in the distribution of covariates within treatment and control groups, a condition called balance. When X includes all sources of confounding, we can use matching to achieve balance ($X_i \perp\!\!\!\perp t_i$), which allows unbiased estimation of the average treatment effect on the treated.

In most matching applications, X is low dimensional, with $P \ll N$. Taking a selection on observables strategy, we assume conditional ignorability: $t_i \perp\!\!\!\perp y_i(0), y_i(1) | X_i$. Under this assumption, balancing the distribution of observed covariates X across treatment groups provides us a way to estimate the causal effect of interest. In some settings, the P variables of X under which selection on observables would hold are known to the researcher because the treatment assignment mechanism is transparent.

However, in the cases we consider where we want to condition not only on X, but also on the document term matrix W, the dimensionality of these two matrices combined, $P + J$, is very large. In this case, J, the vocabulary of the corpus, may be much larger than N, the number of observations. Further, we do not necessarily know which aspects of W are related to the treatment and outcome. We believe that some words in the text affect treatment, but are unsure which ones. If we attempt to match on all words, we will not identify any matches unless two texts have *identical* word frequencies, a possibility that becomes vanishingly small as the dimension of W grows large.

Our approach is to estimate a low-dimensional summary of the variables in W that we can use to address confounding, a g function for the confounders instead of the treatment, and the outcome as we had before. Text matching thus requires the following:

Assumption 1 (SUTVA) *For all individuals i, $y_i(t) = y_i(t_i)$.*

Assumption 2 (Conditional Ignorability) $t_i \perp\!\!\!\perp (y_i(0), y_i(1)) | g(W_i,).$

Assumption 3 (Positivity) *For all individuals i $Pr(t_i = t) > 0$ for all $t \in \mathcal{T}$.*[2]

---

[2] D'Amour et al. (2021) provide a reassessment of positivity in the high-dimensional context and show that this assumption can often fail. This is another way in which high-dimensional data are a challenge for current matching approaches.

In this section, we explore several different methods for finding the right g to adjust for confounding using text data—both regression-based and matching-based adjustments. While we focus on only a few simple approaches, we note that this is a quickly developing field. Since Roberts, Stewart, and Nielsen (2020) originally posted their paper on text matching in 2015, new developments in adjusting for text confounding quickly followed. Mozer et al. (2020) varies the representation and distance metric used to match texts to evaluate hundreds of different text matching methods. And Veitch, Wang, and Blei (2019) create a method that uses word embeddings to adjust for confounding. See Keith, Jensen, and O'Connor (2020) for a review.

Throughout the chapter we use the example from Maliniak, Powers, and Walter (2013) studying gendered citation bias in the discipline of International Relations (IR). Evidence of citation bias against female scholars in IR would be strongest if women wrote identical articles to men but were then cited less often. However, men and women tend to write about different topics within IR, use different methods, and have different epistemological commitments. Because these factors might affect citation counts, it is possible the lower citation counts of women reflect bias against certain topics and approaches, rather than against women themselves.[3] Maliniak, Powers, and Walter (2013) address this challenge using information from the TRIP Journal Article Database to control for the broad subfield of each article, the issue areas covered, the general methodology, paradigm,[4] and epistemology. In this application, we attempt to use automated methods rather than hand coding to address this confounding.[5]

With the help of JSTOR's Data For Research Program, Roberts, Stewart, and Nielsen (2020) obtain the full text of 3,201 articles in the IR literature since 1980, 333 of which are authored solely by women.[6] In what follows, we use the data collected by Roberts, Stewart, and Nielsen (2020) to explore a variety of different methods for conditioning on the text of the articles while examining the influence of gender on citations. We discuss the drawbacks and benefits to each of these methods in what follows.

27.1   Regression Adjustments for Text Confounders

The most common way of adjusting for confounding in social science data analysis is including the confounding variable in a regression. Therefore, the simplest extension to adjusting for confounding with a high-dimensional variable like text is including it in a regression, but using a shrinkage method to select the best subset of the regressors for the application at hand. As discussed in Chapter 19, penalized regression estimators such as Ridge regression and Lasso can select the covariates that are highly predictive of the outcome, shrinking or eliminating covariates that are less important. If these estimators select the relevant words to adjust for with confounding, then we could use them in adjusting for text confounders.

---

[3] Although we emphasize that devaluing of work often pursued by women is itself a serious problem, the quantity of interest to Maliniak, Powers, and Walter (2013) is whether the perceived gender of the author matters for citations. Thus the ideal comparison is the same text with two different names attached.

[4] Scholarship in International Relations is sometimes organized into "paradigms," or schools of thought about which factors are most crucial for explaining international relations. The predominant paradigms are Realism, Liberalism, and Constructivism, though others exist.

[5] The Maliniak, Powers, and Walter (2013) hand coding has an additional benefit of allowing us to validate our approach.

[6] They analyze more articles than Maliniak, Powers, and Walter (2013) because the TRIP database has coded more articles since 2013. However, they are missing data for a few articles used by Maliniak, Powers, and Walter (2013) because they are not in JSTOR's dataset.

We take this first very simple approach for conditioning on the text of the articles to estimate the impact of gender. We estimate a Lasso where we regress citations of each article on the term-document matrix of the articles and all of the other covariates that Maliniak, Powers, and Walter (2013) include within their analyses, such as article age, tenure, and journal. We also include an indicator variable for treatment: whether the article was written by only female authors. We do not include a penalty on the treatment coefficient, as this is the coefficient of interest. We use cross-validation to choose the optimal penalty on the remaining coefficients. We then include words selected by the Lasso model in a linear regression predicting citations.

The hope is that the Lasso model will select important words and covariates that are highly predictive of the outcome and therefore allows us to discard the many words that are not of interest. Figure 27.1 shows the words that are ultimately included in the model, and thus highly predictive of citations, including words related to funding like `Minerva`, words related to methodology such as `cause-effect` and `zscore`, and words related to substance such as `surgenc` and `democ`. Citations of particular authors also seem to be important in predicting citations, such as `weingast`, and `shepsl`. The model also suggests particular covariates coded by Maliniak, Powers, and Walter (2013) to be important, such as whether the article was published in the *American Political Science Review*—the primary political science venue—or whether the article has a positivist framework, both of which predict higher citations. The coefficient estimated on female authorship is negative, indicating that adjusting for the words selected by Lasso and the other confounders, female authorship has a negative relationship with citations.

Using a Lasso is a relatively straightforward way to select a set of words in a text regression, but it has some important drawbacks that are illustrative of the complexities of doing causal inference with high-dimensional confounding. The first drawback is that our ability to adjust for confounding is limited by the combination of representation of the text we have chosen (word count) and the linear model. For example, this rules out interactions between words, but it could be that when `minerva` is used with words like `democracy`, it produces a lot of citations, but when it's used with `autocracy` it has very few. The second drawback arises from the use of the Lasso regularized regression to address the high dimensionality of the potentially confounding variables. As Belloni, Chernozhukov, and Hansen (2014) explain, while the Lasso selects variables that are good predictors, it may not select the best confounders.[7] This is another case of our general point that when importing tools designed for other purposes, some care is needed to adapt them to the task of interest. Belloni, Chernozhukov, and Hansen (2014) suggest an alternative strategy that involves two different Lasso regressions—one predicting the outcome and one predicting the treatment—and then a final regression adjustment using the union of the selected variables.

An alternative approach is to work with a lower-dimensional representation of the text where such regularization is not as necessary. For example, we could use a topic model to represent each document as a combination of topics. We could then estimate the influence of gender on citations, controlling for topical content. If the topics are sufficient to capture the confounding, this strategy will be much more efficient as the

---

[7] In Lasso regressions when there are two highly correlated predictors one is likely to be zeroed out. In this case this will zero out predictors that are highly correlated with the treatment, but those could be the most important confounders! Also, the way we choose the regularization parameter λ minimizes prediction error, but this is not necessarily the same as the parameter that would minimize error on the causal effect of interest.

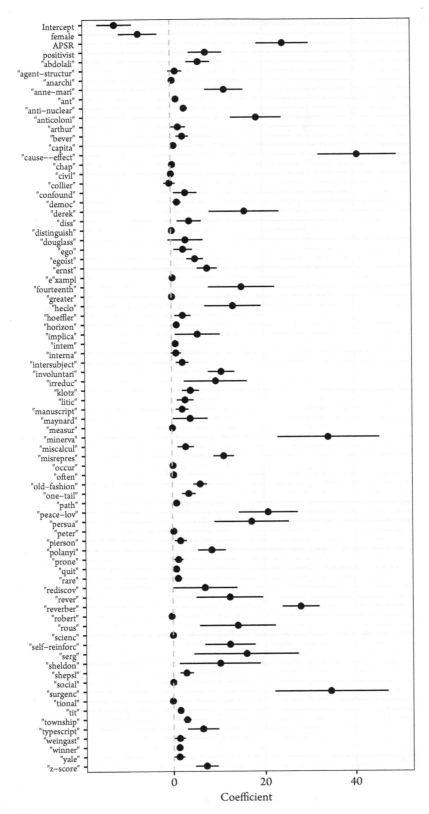

Figure 27.1. Regression of citations on gender with words and covariates selected by a Lasso model.

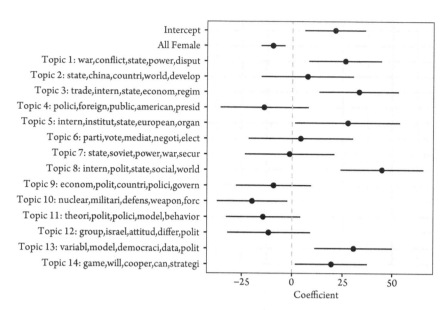

Figure 27.2. Regression of citations on gender controlling for topic proportions.

dimensionality of the topics is typically much lower than the vocabulary. The possible efficiency gains in this strategy are similar to the benefits of Naive Bayes (Chapter 19) when the assumptions hold.

Figure 27.2 shows the regression output of citations regressed on gender conditioning on the topic proportions estimated within each document. Many of the topics should be recognizable to political scientists—the authors discuss topics ranging from war to economic development to foreign policy. Topic 13, associated with quantitative models, has overall higher citation counts than topic 7, associated with the Soviet Union and the military. The female coefficient is similar to that in the Lasso, indicating that, controlling for topic, women still receive fewer citations than men.

There are many approaches one could take to controlling for lower-dimension representations of the data, and analysts would want to select the one that they thought was most important in confounding the relationship between treatment and outcome. For example, principal components analysis (PCA) or singular value decomposition (SVD) could be used in place of topics to control for clusters of words that explain variance in the documents. However, note that PCA, SVD, and even basic topic modeling approaches do not take advantage of the outcome or treatment when creating the reduction of the text. For example, the most probable words in the topics in Figure 27.2 did not contain the word `minerva` even though this word highly predicts citations. Including information about the outcome or the treatment when selecting covariates may be useful in ensuring that the model is picking up confounders.

27.2 Matching Adjustments for Text

An alternative to using a regression adjustment is to use text analysis to find matches between treated and control units that write about similar topics or use similar words. Roberts, Stewart, and Nielsen (2020) argue that the advantage of matching is that comparable units are more easily examined—matching allows users to find documents that

Table 27.1. Example of matched document pairs. The left column contains examples from all female authorial teams. Table 4 from Roberts, Stewart, and Nielsen (2020) Supplemental Materials.

Treated Document	Matched Control Document
"Democratic Synergy and Victory in War, 1816-1992." Ajin Choi. 2004. *International Studies Quarterly*. Abstract: "This study investigates the question of why democracies are more likely to win wars than non-democracies. I argue that due to the transparency of the polities, and the stability of their preferences, once determined, democracies are better able to cooperate with their partners in the conduct of wars, and thereby are more likely to win wars. In support of my argument, the main findings in this study show that, other things being equal, the larger the number of democratic partners a state has, the more likely it is to win; moreover, democratic states are more likely to have democratic partners during wars. These results are in contrast with those in current literature about the high likelihood of prevailing by democracies in wars, which emphasize, on the one hand, the superior capacity of democratic states to strengthen military capabilities and, on the other hand, to select wars in which they have a high chance of winning."	"Third-Party Interventions and the Duration of Intrastate Conflicts." Patrick M. Regan. 2002. *Journal of Conflict Resolution*. Abstract: "Recent research has begun to focus on the role of outside interventions in the duration of civil conflicts. Assuming that interventions are a form of conflict management, ex ante expectations would be that they would reduce a conflict's expected duration. Hypotheses relating the type and timing of outside interventions to the duration of civil conflicts are tested. The data incorporate 150 conflicts during the period from 1945 to 1999, 101 of which had outside interventions. Using a hazard analysis, the results suggest that third-party interventions tend to extend expected durations rather than shorten them. The only aspect of the strategy for intervening that reduces the likelihood that a conflict will end in the next month is that it be biased in favor of either the opposition or the government. In effect, neutral interventions are less effective than biased ones."
"The Present As Prologue: Europe and Theater Nuclear Modernization." Catherine McArdle Kelleher. 1981. *International Security*. Introduction: "More than a year after formal Alliance decision, controversy still surrounds NATO's plan for new long-range theater nuclear force (LRTNF) deployments. The controversy focuses both on the substance and the process involved. Proponents, in Washington as elsewhere, see the decision as an Alliance success, and the process as a model for future decision-making. The Alliance has now demonstrated it can meet new Soviet challenges; the exhaustive consultation procedures did lead to a genuinely informed NATO consensus despite the inherent political risks. Although not designed to match Soviet LRTNF capabilities, ground-launched cruise missiles (GLCMs) and Pershing IIs do provide a new element in the overall East-West military balance. And there has been due, measured common attention to the problems both of reinforcing American strategic linkage, and of pursuing opportunities for East–West limitations on LRTNF deployments."	"Counterforce: Illusion of a Panacea." Henry A. Trofimenko. 1981. *International Security*. Introduction: "In recent years, American military strength has been moving in a vicious cycle. It has been unable to get out of the impasse created by Washington's desire to outstrip the Soviet Union in strategic arms and by the practical impossibility of achieving this aim. The Soviet Union is fully resolved not to fall behind the United States, nor to permit such U.S. preponderance. Recent evidence of this strategic merry-go-round was provided by the Carter Administration's Directive No. 59, which returned U.S. strategy to the concepts of counterforce nuclear targeting. This policy concludes the long campaign in the U.S. media and academic press that was intended to frighten the Americans with a purported Soviet counterforce and "war-winning" threat."
"Locating "Authority" in the Global Political Economy." A. Claire Cutler. 1999. *International Studies Quarterly*. Abstract: "This article addresses the problematic nature of "authority" in the global political economy. Focusing on the rules governing international commercial relations, which today form part of the juridical conditions of global capitalism, the location and structure of political authority are argued to be historically specific. They have changed with the emergence of different historic blocs and as a result of consequent alterations in state-society relations. The article emphasizes the significance of private corporate power in the construction of the global political economy and hegemonic authority relations. However, the significance of private authority is obscure and little understood by students of international relations. This gives rise to analytical and normative grounds for adopting a historical materialist approach to the analysis of global authority that incorporates national, subnational, and transnational influences."	"South Korean and Taiwanese Development and the New Institutional Economics." David C. Kang. 1995. *International Organization*. Introduction: "The publication of books by both Alice Amsden and Robert Wade provide an opportune moment to reflect on the study of East Asian development. After an inital surge of interest beginning in the 1970s, the field has reached a plateau, and scholars recently have cast a wide net searching for ways to extend the field. In assessing the "state of the art" regarding economic development of the East Asian newly industrialized countries (NICs), this review will treat three themes. First, I will argue that the focus on states versus markets is becoming stale and much scholarly interest lies in the politics behind the economics. Second, I argue that political scientists have underexplored the historical origins of Korean and Taiwanese capitalism and that such attention promises to strengthen both theories and explanations of development. Third, I argue that the international system has been more important in promoting development in East Asia than accounts in the "first wave" have recognized."

the matching method would consider similar, read them, and evaluate whether these observations would be good counterfactuals for each other. Text models can fail, so, as we have stressed throughout this book, this approach allows the analyst to judge whether matched units are sufficiently similar that treatment assignment is plausibly "as-if random." This manual validation complements other formal balance checks often used in matching.

There are hundreds of matching approaches that could be used in the context of conditioning on text confounders, each with strengths and weaknesses. Roberts, Stewart, and Nielsen (2020) develop one approach, Topical Inverse Regression Matching (TIRM), that integrates two features of matching strategies they find desirable: *modeling treatment assignment* and *coarsening*. To do this they use the Structural Topic Model (STM) to jointly estimate topics—coarsening words into groups of topics—and document-level scores—to indicate how likely each document was treated. By using the treatment as a *topical content covariate* in an STM model they can estimate both the topics and the document-level scores jointly. They then match on both the estimated topics and the document-level scores.

To model treatment assignment, TIRM creates an analog to propensity score matching by estimating a projection from the model that is a sufficient reduction of the information in the word counts about the probability of treatment. Following Taddy (2013), Roberts, Stewart, and Nielsen (2020) derive a sufficient reduction of the information contained in the word counts about treatment. By estimating this document-level score in the context of a topic model, the projection represents the information about the treatment *not* carried in the topics.

To match on coarsened groups of topics, Roberts, Stewart, and Nielsen (2020) extract the topical content of the documents from the STM model. A slight complication arises because, when topic-treatment interactions are present because treatment is included as a content covariate, the same topic can have different estimated distributions of words under treatment and control. The authors ensure that topics are comparable irrespective of treatment/control differences by adding a final estimation step to the STM in which they reestimate the topic proportions of all control as though they were treated. This choice is consistent with an estimand that is a (local) average treatment effect on the *treated*. They then match on both the STM projection and the estimated topic proportions from the STM, which ensures that matches are both topically similar and have similar within-topic probabilities of treatment.

Roberts, Stewart, and Nielsen (2020) apply TIRM to Maliniak, Powers, and Walter (2013), specifying 15 topics in the STM portion of the algorithm to recover broad topics. For comparison, they also create matched samples using only the projection and only the topics. They then reestimate the models of Maliniak, Powers, and Walter (2013) using the TIRM matched sample and find that gender differences in citations are even more pronounced than those originally reported. They find an average of 6.5 fewer citations to articles written by women, when compared to as-identical-as-possible articles written by men or mixed-gender groups. Figure 27.1 comprises example matched pairs they provide of similar articles with different treatment status.

27.3 Conclusion

Text measures so many social phenomena, but is currently used rarely in analyses to make causal inferences. In this part of the book, we developed a framework for thinking about how to use text in causal inferences by spelling out the potential pitfalls researchers may run into when using text as a treatment, outcome, or control variable. We included many examples of using text in casual inference throughout the chapter to demonstrate how vast the potential is for using text to study causation in social science.

Of course, causal identification is difficult, and using text in causal analyses does not solve any of the core problems of causal inference. On the contrary, using text for causal inference may add more, not fewer, complications. We urge readers to take advantage of the large literature in this area if they have not previously studied causal inference (Morgan and Winship, 2015; Imbens and Rubin, 2015; Hernán and Robins, 2020). We suggest, in addition, that analysts take advantage of train/test splits to simulate replication within each experiment, and, as often as possible, repeat their experiments in new populations and time periods.

PART VI

Conclusion

CHAPTER 28

Conclusion

Our book is a guide to using text as data tools in the social sciences. The emerging prevalence of text as data in the social sciences coincides with a new era of abundance and opportunity for social scientists. With the ability to analyze large quantities of texts, social scientists are able to make insights at a scale that has been previously impossible. At the same time the multitude of new statistical models and computational tools makes analyzing these large new datasets easier than ever before.

In this concluding chapter we first review the core argument from our book and provide guidance on how to extend these principles. In the social sciences, data methods are best used when they are focused on social science tasks. So even though many of the methods we use when analyzing text as data have their origin in computer science, we argue that those methods need to be repurposed when applied to social sciences. And critically, the ways we evaluate those methods will be different when applied to social science problems. We also argue that text as data inferences are best made when they are done iteratively and sequentially. While social scientists have often proceeded deductively, we argue that inferences with text data are improved when we build our evidence base inductively from our datasets. And that when we work sequentially we can improve the concepts that we define, the measurements that we take, and ultimately the inferences we make from our data. Finally, we assert that when working with machine learning models we should have a baseline skepticism—agnosticism—about the true data generating process. The models that we use all have value in providing distinct summaries of the complex text data. But because of the complex relationship between how text data are represented and how language actually works, we avoid validations that rely upon us assuming that we have the correct model. Instead, we argue that validations focused on our core task of interest are essential for assessing whether the models perform well for social science tasks.

While we have focused on text, the core principles of this book apply far beyond just text as data. In fact, we view our approach to text as data as more generally applicable to many other new data sources—including images, sound, and video. Like texts, these data sources have a long history of being used in qualitative studies in the social sciences. But it has been difficult to work with these data at a large scale. New computational tools developed in computer science make working with these data sources much easier at scale. The same issues emerge, though. The tasks that computer scientists focus on when working with images, video, and sound are not the same tasks of interest for social scientists. Our framework provides a guide of how to apply these new tools to do social science inferences.

Text as data methods, and machine learning more generally, are heralded as providing major advancement for social scientists. And in many ways, we agree. The new data sources and methods enable researchers to ask and answer questions about social interactions we previously could not study at scale. These methods are not a panacea. We doubt that there even could be a silver bullet to solve social science problems. No matter how impressive new methods are, social scientists will still face daunting challenges of causal inference, prediction, and carefully defining concepts for measurement. We finish this book with a discussion of why modesty when developing new methods is essential to avoid the disappointment that comes from overpromising.

28.1 How to Use Text as Data in the Social Sciences

28.1.1 THE FOCUS ON SOCIAL SCIENCE TASKS

The rapid expansion of text as data in the social sciences builds on a large and massively successful literature from computer science, statistics, and linguistics. These methods are incredibly useful, but were targeted to solve distinct problems from those in the social sciences. For example, unsupervised text as data methods were developed for information retrieval tasks, where the primary goal is to help pick a needle out of a haystack—a task often evaluated in terms of predictive accuracy of held-out data. But social scientists want to characterize the whole haystack, not find the needle, and they are rarely interested in prediction as a metric for unsupervised texts. In fact, it turns out that models that perform better at prediction are sometimes worse at providing social scientific insights. For this reason, we organize methods around the social scientific reasons that we would apply those methods.

The tasks of social scientists follow the trajectory of research projects. At the start of research projects we engage in *discovery*, determining new conceptualizations of texts to gain insights into the underlying patterns. Given those organizations, we engage in *measurement* or assigning observations to the categories. And finally we engage in inference: either *causal inference*, where we ask what effect a specific intervention would have, or *prediction*, where we make an out-of-sample estimate given our data.

This task-based approach is useful beyond text as data work. In fact, we think that orienting work explicitly around these sorts of tasks is conducive to productive research agendas. We have found that when advising graduate students about how to approach serious research for the first time, deconstructing research into these stages can make daunting research projects much more manageable. It also helps to decompose existing projects to understand what is driving inferences.

We also want to be clear that while our book does not explicitly have a chapter on theory, we view social science theory as an integral component of the research process. Theory can suggest conceptualizations, can motivate measurement, and can aid in our interpretation of causal effects. While some have suggested that the age of big data will indicate the end of theory, we think the opposite is true. Theory is essential for interpreting the results of statistical models, and with more data we have the opportunity to aggregate up our inferences and have more stylized facts to build models.

28.1.2 ITERATIVE AND SEQUENTIAL NATURE OF THE SOCIAL SCIENCES

We have argued that we learn the most from our data when our inferences are iterative and sequential. There are basic reasons why we think this is true. Iteratively building from our data enables us to better understand how our models apply in a particular context and to tune feature representation and other model features to our particular application. Working sequentially enables researchers to accumulate evidence across studies. When we have hypotheses that are developed when performing an analysis, thinking sequentially means that we can test those hypotheses with new data and the next research design.

Beyond the benefits to the analysts, we think that the sequential approach is more honest about how research is actually performed. While it is common for scholars to write papers as if ideas are created deductively, our experience is that this is rarely the case. Rather, ideas are developed iteratively and sequentially as papers are written. Being more clear about the research process will make it more explicit how research builds on prior efforts and how future work can build on the current paper.

We also think that an iterative and sequential approach to research helps address issues of "fishing." A major concern in the use of experiments is that researchers will make decisions in their analysis in order to create the impression of a statistically significant result, when the true difference is null. One approach to address this has been pre-registration. Of course, this can be useful. But it does little to address the incentives of researchers to publish papers with significant results. In their place, we think a sequential approach to research could create incentives for researchers to replicate their findings (and have other researchers replicate their findings).

28.1.3 MODEL SKEPTICISM AND THE APPLICATION OF MACHINE LEARNING TO THE SOCIAL SCIENCES

When we work with text data, our view is that we should be skeptical that we ever have the correct model. Language is astonishingly complex, and even our representation of language requires extensive simplifying assumptions. As a result, the models we use throughout the book are obviously wrong, but some are useful. This means that the models can be useful to measure quantities of interest, suggest new conceptualizations, and even facilitate causal inferences.

But this implies that when we engage in model choice, we should not focus only on model fit statistics. This is because model fit rarely optimizes for the particular way social scientists are going to use the model. Rather, we have argued that to select the most useful models we want to engage in validations that are closely tied to how the model will be used. And this often involves placing "humans in the loop" to assess the models. Keeping humans in the loop is important not only to be sure our measures are valid and models are meaningful, but also, as we have stressed throughout the book, to use knowledge of context and substance to ensure that we are applying models and conducting research practically and ethically, constantly keeping in mind that those who wrote the texts are also humans, not just data points.

28.2 Applying Our Principles beyond Text Data

In our book we have focused on text as data, but our argument applies much more generally to other data sources. In fact, we think that as new data sources become available and as new methods are imported from other fields, it is essential that we ask how those methods will be used in political science. Thinking about how social scientists can best use these new data sources will, we think, lead to their most productive use in the social sciences.

Incredible progress has already been made across related new data. For example, increasingly scholars use machine learning techniques to make social science inferences from image data. For example, Torres (2019) examines how protestors are depicted in photographs in the press. More generally, we think scholars have long recognized the power of images for social interactions. Machine learning approaches to studying images provide the opportunity to study how groups are depicted at scale and to understand how those depictions affect the public.

Similarly, there has been incredible work studying actual political speech at scale. Of course, we think that how things are said matters. Democrats have widely praised Barack Obama's ability to deliver soaring speeches with a cadence and tone that has added life to his rhetoric. Similarly, Ronald Reagan inspired conservatives with his easygoing, sincere, and amused delivery of the most important messages. Social scientists have made important progress analyzing the role of speech in social interactions. For example, Kaufman, Kraft, and Sen (2019) have shown that how Supreme Court justices speak can predict how they rule on a case and Knox and Lucas (2021) provide a general method for decomposing the content of speech.

Even video can be used to make granular inferences on how individuals react with treatments in real time. For example, Dietrich and Sands (N.d.) use traffic cameras in New York City to measure how individuals react to randomly placed people of different identities. But there is a massive amount of video still available and huge questions to be asked about how the near constant feed of video information—on television and the internet—affects society.

Across all these examples our same basic principles hold. And in many instances, similar models can be used. In short, we think our book's utility extends far beyond text data only.

28.3   Avoiding the Cycle of Creation and Destruction in Social Science Methodology

We conclude our book with a call for humility in the creation of new methods. Too often it seems that there is a boom-to-bust cycle in social science methodology. Some new method or estimator is introduced and hailed as a breakthrough capable of solving the toughest problems. Proponents assert the method is revolutionary and researchers rush to reevaluate past empirical claims using the latest technology. But new methods, inevitably, fail to deliver on these massive and unrealistic promises. This leads to a flurry of scholars pointing out the gap between the promises of a method's proponents and what it is actually capable of delivering. The too-pessimistic conclusion from this exchange is that the new method was not really all that useful to begin with, and scholars conclude the new statistical technology really isn't all that useful for their problems. The result is that new methods are tossed to the side, when they could still be useful for some narrow tasks that they are well equipped to perform.

There is a risk that text as data could be subjected to a similar boom-and-bust cycle—even though text as data methods have largely avoided this fate thus far. We think this is due, in part, to the fact that early papers in text as data avoided over-promising on what it could deliver. Text is necessarily hard to work with and new text methods are incredibly useful. But these new methods cannot necessarily provide a unified and comprehensive approach to all text as data problems.

New statistical models in the social sciences confront a similar set of facts. New research designs and machine learning methods can certainly improve our inferences.

But no amount of computing power or "big data" can solve the fundamental challenges of social science. Researchers will still need to formulate conceptualizations and measure according to those organizations. And, of course, the fundamental problem of causal inference remains even if a dataset has many rows. While no method can eliminate these problems, new methods and approaches can improve work on each stage of the research process.

This book has been our modest contribution to explain how best to apply the exciting new text as data methods to the social sciences and improve research on the toughest problems in the social sciences.

Acknowledgments

We've been working on this book for a while. It feels like we have been one year away from finishing for about five years. Over this time we have benefited from a fantastic community of scholars working at the intersection of machine learning and social science. It would be impossible to list all of the amazing people who made this book what it is, but we are certainly going to try.

First, we thank those who have worked with us on text as data projects in the past and provided us with feedback on the book or related projects at different stages in the process, including John Ahlquist, Edo Airoldi, Anthony Anderson, Chris Bail, Pamela Ban, Kathryn Baragwanath Vogel, Nick Beauchamp, Clark Bernier, Lisa Blaydes, Dave Blei, Sarah Bouchat, Amber Boydstun, Amy Bridges, Elizabeth Bruch, Dan Butler, Amy Catalinac, Allison Chaney, Keng-Chi Chang, Scott de Marchi, Scott Desposato, Paul DiMaggio, Mitch Duneier, Naoki Egami, Jacob Eisenstein, Barbara Engelhardt, James Evans, Chris Felton, Kevin Flannagan, Annie Franco, Christian Fong, Maggie Frye, Daniel Gillion, Amarnath Gupta, Will Hobbs, Geoffrey Hoffman, Jiying Jiang, Rebecca Johnson, Megan Kang, Patrick Lam, Chloe Lim, Chris Lucas, Ben Liebman, Ian Lundberg, Alison McQueen, Kennedy Middleton, Juan Pablo Micozzi, David Mimno, Jacob Montgomery, Burt Monroe, Cambria Naslund, Laura Nelson, Rich Nielsen, Brendan O'Connor, Jennifer Pan, Gregoire Phillips, David Robinson, Pedro Rodríguez, Luke Sanford, Thomas Scherer, Cheryl Schonhardt-Bailey, Nicholas Smith, Rachel Stern, Brian Tsay, Hannah Waight, Hanna Wallach, Bertrand Wilden, Adam Wu, Xiaohan Wu, Luwei Ying, Eddie Yang, Young Yang, Leo Yang, Yin Yuan, Simone Zhang, and Yile Zhang. In several places we made use of replication data provided by other scholars and we give them our warmest gratitude for making that data available.

We particularly thank the attendees of our 2017 book conference—Naoki Egami, Christian Fong, James Fowler, Erin Hartman, Arthur Spirling, Yiqing Xu, and Teppei Yamamoto—for graciously giving us their time for two days in San Diego and providing excellent feedback that greatly improved the manuscript. We thank the Division of Social Sciences at UC San Diego for sponsoring the book conference and DeAnna Barrett for her assistance in organizing the event. Years later, three anonymous reviewers for Princeton University Press provided us with insightful comments on an early version of the manuscript that greatly shaped the ultimate direction the book moved in.

Over the last decade, we have especially benefited from our interactions at the annual Text as Data conference which started with a 2009 conference at Harvard titled New Directions in Text Analysis hosted by Peter Bol, Kevin Quinn, and Stuart Shieber. We thank the organizers of this conference throughout the years and those who have been involved in creating this community, including but not limited to Ken Benoit, Amber Boydstun, Michael Colaresi, Will Lowe, David Mimno, Kevin Quinn, Philip Resnik,

Noah Smith, Arthur Spirling, and Hanna Wallach. These conferences provided an intellectual infrastructure for sharing ideas about methods, applications, and research design. Equally important is the group of people who have built and freely distributed the software infrastructure that makes this work possible. We are profoundly grateful to Ken Benoit and the team that develops and maintains quanteda, Ingo Feinerer for building tm, and Julia Silge and David Robinson for creating tidytext as well as all the other packages that make the text as data ecosystem possible. All of these packages work only because of the tireless efforts of the developers and maintainers of the R language.

We are grateful for the students in our classes at Princeton, Stanford, Chicago, and UC San Diego as well as in numerous smaller workshops and classes run all over the world. These students have shaped the manuscript directly through feedback on the text and by pushing us through their questions to think harder and communicate more clearly. We also thank Elliott Ash and Alexandra Siegel for using the book manuscript in their own classes and providing us with feedback both from their students and from an instructor's perspective.

We thank John Wilkerson for being an advocate of text as data methods and a supporter of all of us throughout the years. His 2010 workshop, Tools for Text: Annotation Methods for Political Science Research, hosted with Phil Schrodt at University of Washington, was the first opportunity that Brandon had to teach text as data methods. Mike Alvarez deserves special kudos for suggesting the original idea for Justin and Brandon's 2013 "Text as Data" article. Finally, Matt Salganik read many drafts of various chapters of the book and always provided insightful and encouraging feedback, including just by asking, "hey, how's your book coming?"

All three of us started working on text as data in graduate school and had related material in our dissertations. We benefited from incredible advisors including: Jeff Frieden, Claudine Gay, D. Sunshine Hillygus, Elizabeth Perry, Kevin Quinn, and Beth Simmons. Dustin Tingley deserves special mention for both feedback and support as a member of Molly's and Brandon's committees, but also for collaboration on the Structural Topic Model and related projects. Through countless conversations about the application of text as data methods, Dustin is responsible for many of the insights woven throughout this book. Finally, Gary King was the chair for all three of our dissertations and has remained an indefatigable mentor in the years since we graduated. His feedback and insight has shaped our perspective probably even more than we know.

We thank our editor Meagan Levinson at Princeton University Press for providing us with many rounds of feedback on the organization and direction of the book. Special thanks to Eric Crahan at Princeton University Press as well, with whom we discussed the book in its early stages. We thank Matthew Tyler for his feedback on the book and help in making the notation consistent. Lisa McKay provided excellent assistance in editing early drafts and Bhisham Bherwani provided excellent copyediting at the very end.

For generous funding support of the work discussed within this book, we thank the National Science Foundation RIDIR program, for award numbers 1738411 and 1738288, and the Eunice Kennedy Shriver National Institute of Child Health & Human Development of the National Institutes of Health for award number P2CHD047879.

In a few places this book uses direct text from several of our papers, including Grimmer and Stewart's "Text as Data: The Promise and Pitfalls of Automatic Content Analysis Methods for Political Texts," which appeared in *Political Analysis* (2013); Fong and Grimmer's "Discovery of Treatments from Text Corpora," which appeared in *Proceedings of the 54th Annual Meeting of the Association for Computational Linguistics*

(2016); Roberts, Stewart, and Nielsen's "Adjusting for Confounding with Text Matching," which appeared in *American Journal of Political Science* (2020); and Grimmer, Roberts and Stewart's "Machine Learning for Social Science: An Agnostic Approach," which appeared in the *Annual Review of Political Science* (2021). We thank the publishers for permissions to reproduce this work. Several figures are reproduced from our work and others. We thank the publishers and the authors for allowing us to reproduce these figures.

Justin is grateful to Izzy, Eli, and Holden for providing so many fun opportunities to recharge by playing 5,000, winning team Fortnite challenges, and always being up for a game of tag. He is also thankful to his parents, Karl and Becky Grimmer, whose endless hard work made it possible for him to pursue his dreams. And most importantly, he is thankful for Terese Grimmer's relentless love, unwavering support, and profound patience that makes each day better than the last.

Molly offers a very special thanks to Rae and Theo for arriving on the scene in time to provide unending amounts of love and entertainment during the process of writing this book. To Don and Barbara Roberts and Lisa and Alan Fenning for helping take care of them (and her), so as to make finishing this book possible during the tumultuous year of 2020. Last, to David for his unconditional love and support, skillful engineering of quiet stretches of writing time for her even in the midst of chaos, and invaluable feedback and insights on so much of her work.

Brandon thanks the people who have made life outside of work joyful over the last several years: Alice, Carolina, Daniel, Luke, and Mary. Each has heard about this book in varying amounts of detail over an extended period of time during weekly walks, writing retreats, and late-night phone calls. Olga provided continual support and encouragement throughout the long process of finishing the project. Finally, he thanks his parents, Jerry and Candi, for their unwavering support and the model they set for what it means to be a kind and generous person.

Bibliography

Abello, James, Peter Broadwell, and Timothy R. Tangherlini. 2012. "Computational folkloristics." *Communications of the ACM* 55(7):60–70.

Achen, Christopher H. 2002. "Toward a new political methodology: Microfoundations and ART." *Annual Review of Political Science* 5(1):423–450.

Adair, Douglass. 1944. "The authorship of the disputed Federalist Papers." *The William and Mary Quarterly: A Magazine of Early American History* 1(2):97–122.

Adcock, Robert and David Collier. 2001. "Measurement validity: A shared standard for qualitative and quantitative research." *American Political Science Review* 95(3):529–546.

Aggarwal, Charu C. 2018. *Machine Learning for Text*. Springer.

Ahmed, Amr and Eric P. Xing. 2010. "Staying informed: Supervised and semi-supervised multi-view topical analysis of ideological perspective." In *Proceedings of the 2010 Conference on Empirical Methods in Natural Language Processing*. Cambridge, MA: Association for Computational Linguistics pp. 1140–1150.

Airoldi, Edoardo M. and Jonathan M. Bischof. 2016. "Improving and evaluating topic models and other models of text." *Journal of the American Statistical Association* 111(516):1381–1403.

Airoldi, Edoardo M., Stephen E. Fienberg, and Kiron K. Skinner. 2007. "Whose ideas? Whose words? Authorship of Ronald Reagan's radio addresses." *PS: Political Science & Politics* 40(3):501–506.

Aletras, Nikolaos, Dimitrios Tsarapatsanis, Daniel Preoţiuc-Pietro, and Vasileios Lampos. 2016. "Predicting judicial decisions of the European Court of Human Rights: a Natural Language Processing perspective." *PeerJ Computer Science* 2:e93.

Anderson, Chris. 2008. "The End of Theory: The Data Deluge Makes the Scientific Method Obsolete." *Wired* .
URL: *https://www.wired.com/2008/06/pb-theory/*

Andrzejewski, David, Xiaojin Zhu, and Mark Craven. 2009. "Incorporating domain knowledge into topic modeling via Dirichlet forest priors." In *Proceedings of the 26th Annual International Conference on Machine Learning*. ACM pp. 25–32.

Ansolabehere, Stephen and Shanto Iyengar. 1995. *Going Negative: How Political Advertisements Shrink and Polarize the Electorate*. Simon & Schuster.

Arnold, Taylor and Laura Tilton. 2017. "Basic Text Processing in R." *The Programming Historian* 6.

Aronow, Peter M. and Benjamin T. Miller. 2019. *Foundations of Agnostic Statistics*. Cambridge University Press.

Arora, Sanjeev, Rong Ge, Yonatan Halpern, David Mimno, Ankur Moitra, David Sontag, Yichen Wu, and Michael Zhu. 2013. "A practical algorithm for topic modeling with provable guarantees." In *International Conference on Machine Learning*. pp. 280–288.

Arora, Sanjeev, Yingyu Liang, and Tengyu Ma. 2017. "A simple but tough-to-beat baseline for sentence embeddings." In *5th International Conference on Learning Representations, ICLR 2017, Toulon, France, April 24-26, 2017, Conference Track Proceedings*.

Arora, Sanjeev, Yuanzhi Li, Yingyu Liang, Tengyu Ma, and Andrej Risteski. 2018. "Linear algebraic structure of word senses, with applications to polysemy." *Transactions of the Association for Computational Linguistics* 6:483–495.

Arthur, David and Sergei Vassilvitskii. 2007. "K-Means++: The advantages of careful seeding." In *Proceedings of the Eighteenth Annual ACM-SIAM Symposium on Discrete Algorithms*. SODA '07 USA: Society for Industrial and Applied Mathematics p. 1027–1035.

Askitas, Nikolaos and Klaus F Zimmermann. 2009. "Google econometrics and unemployment forecasting." *Applied Economics Quarterly* 55(2):107–120.

Asuncion, Arthur, Max Welling, Padhraic Smyth, and Yee Whye Teh. 2009. "On smoothing and inference for topic models." In *Proceedings of the Twenty-Fifth Conference on Uncertainty in Artificial Intelligence*. AUAI Press pp. 27–34.

Asur, Sitaram and Bernardo A Huberman. 2010. "Predicting the future with social media." In *Web Intelligence and Intelligent Agent Technology (WI-IAT), 2010 IEEE/WIC/ACM International Conference on*. Vol. 1 IEEE pp. 492–499.

Athey, Susan. 2017. "Beyond prediction: Using big data for policy problems." *Science* 355(6324):483–485.

Bafumi, Joseph and Michael C. Herron. 2010. "Leapfrog representation and extremism: A study of American voters and their members in Congress." *American Political Science Review* 104(3):519–542.

Bagozzi, Benjamin E. 2015. "Forecasting civil conflict with zero-inflated count models." *Civil Wars* 17(1):1–24.

Bail, Christopher. 2014*a*. *Terrified: How anti-Muslim fringe organizations became mainstream*. Princeton University Press.

Bail, Christopher A. 2012. "The fringe effect: Civil society organizations and the evolution of media discourse about Islam since the September 11th attacks." *American Sociological Review* 77(6):855–879.

Bail, Christopher A. 2014*b*. "The cultural environment: Measuring culture with big data." *Theory and Society* 43(3–4):465–482.

Bail, Christopher Andrew. 2016. "Combining natural language processing and network analysis to examine how advocacy organizations stimulate conversation on social media." *Proceedings of the National Academy of Sciences* 113(42):11823–11828.

Bailey, Andrew and Cheryl Schonhardt-Bailey. 2008. "Does deliberation matter in FOMC monetary policymaking? The Volcker Revolution of 1979." *Political Analysis* 16(4):404–427.

Baker, Collin F., Charles J. Fillmore, and John B. Lowe. 1998. "The Berkeley FrameNet project." In *36th Annual Meeting of the Association for Computational Linguistics and 17th International Conference on Computational Linguistics, Volume 1*. pp. 86–90.

Ball, Geoffrey H. 1965. "Data analysis in the social sciences: What about the details?" In *Proceedings of the November 30–December 1, 1965, Fall Joint Computer Conference, Part I*. pp. 533–559.

Bamman, David and Gregory Crane. 2009. "Discovering Multilingual Text Reuse in Literary Texts." *Perseus Digital Library*.

Bamman, David and Noah A. Smith. 2014. "Unsupervised discovery of biographical structure from text." *Transactions of the Association for Computational Linguistics* 2:363–376.

Banerjee, Arindam, Inderjit Dhillon, Joydeep Ghosh, and Suvrit Sra. 2005. "Clustering on the unit hypersphere using von Mises-Fisher distributions." *Journal of Machine Learning Research* 6:1345–1382.

Banerjee, Arindam, Srujana Merugu, Inderjit S. Dhillon, and Joydeep Ghosh. 2005. "Clustering with Bregman divergences." *Journal of Machine Learning Research* 6:1705–1749.

Bansak, Kirk, Jeremy Ferwerda, Jens Hainmueller, Andrea Dillon, Dominik Hangartner, Duncan Lawrence, and Jeremy Weinstein. 2018. "Improving refugee integration through data-driven algorithmic assignment." *Science* 359(6373):325–329.

Barberá, Pablo, Amber E. Boydstun, Suzanna Linn, Ryan McMahon, and Jonathan Nagler. 2021. "Automated Text Classification of News Articles: A Practical Guide." *Political Analysis* 29(1):19–42.

Barberá, Pablo. 2014. "Birds of the same feather tweet together: Bayesian ideal point estimation using Twitter data." *Political Analysis* 23(1):76–91.

Barberá, Pablo and Gonzalo Rivero. 2015. "Understanding the political representativeness of Twitter users." *Social Science Computer Review* 33(6):712–729.

Baroni, Marco, Georgiana Dinu, and Germán Kruszewski. 2014. "Don't count, predict! A systematic comparison of context-counting vs. context-predicting semantic vectors." In *Proceedings of the 52nd Annual Meeting of the Association for Computational Linguistics (Volume 1: Long Papers)*. pp. 238–247.

Bartels, Larry M. 2002. "The impact of candidate traits in American presidential elections." *Leaders' Personalities and the Outcomes of Democratic Elections* pp. 44–69.

Baumer, Eric P. S., David Mimno, Shion Guha, Emily Quan, and Geri K. Gay. 2017. "Comparing grounded theory and topic modeling: Extreme divergence or unlikely convergence?" *Journal of the Association for Information Science and Technology* 68(6):1397–1410.

Baumgartner, Frank R., Bryan Jones, and Michael C. MacLeod. 1998. "Lessons from the trenches: Quality, reliability, and usability in a new data source." *The Political Methodologist* 8(2):1–11.

Beauchamp, Nicholas. 2017. "Predicting and interpolating state-level polls using Twitter textual data." *American Journal of Political Science* 61(2):490–503.

Beauchamp, Nick. 2011. "Using text to scale legislatures with uninformative voting." Working Paper New York University.

Beieler, John. 2016. "Creating a real-time, reproducible event dataset." *arXiv preprint arXiv:1612.00866*.

Beieler, John, Patrick T. Brandt, Andrew Halterman, Philip A. Schrodt, and Erin M. Simpson. 2016. "Generating political event data in near real time." In *Computational Social Science*, ed. R Michael Alvarez. Cambridge University Press pp. 98–120.

Belloni, Alexandre, Victor Chernozhukov, and Christian Hansen. 2014. "High-dimensional methods and inference on structural and treatment effects." *Journal of Economic Perspectives* 28(2):29–50.

Bengio, Yoshua, Réjean Ducharme, Pascal Vincent, and Christian Jauvin. 2003. "A neural probabilistic language model." *Journal of Machine Learning Research* 3(Feb):1137–1155.

Bengtsson, Linus, Xin Lu, Anna Thorson, Richard Garfield, and Johan Von Schreeb. 2011. "Improved response to disasters and outbreaks by tracking population movements with mobile phone network data: A post-earthquake geospatial study in Haiti." *PLoS Medicine* 8(8):e1001083.

Benjamin, Ruha. 2019. *Race After Technology: Abolitionist Tools for the New Jim Code*. Wiley.

Benoit, Kenneth, Drew Conway, Benjamin E Lauderdale, Michael Laver, and Slava Mikhaylov. 2016. "Crowd-sourced text analysis: Reproducible and agile production of political data." *American Political Science Review* 110(2):278–295.

Benoit, Kenneth and Michael Laver. 2003. "Estimating Irish party policy positions using computer wordscoring: The 2002 election—A research note." *Irish Political Studies* 18(1):97–107.

Benoit, Kenneth, Kevin Munger, and Arthur Spirling. 2019. "Measuring and explaining political sophistication through textual complexity." *American Journal of Political Science* 63(2):491–508.

Benoit, Kenneth, Michael Laver, and Slava Mikhaylov. 2009. "Treating words as data with error: Uncertainty in text statements of policy positions." *American Journal of Political Science* 53(2):495–513.

Berinsky, Adam J., Gregory A. Huber, and Gabriel S. Lenz. 2012. "Evaluating online labor markets for experimental research: Amazon.com's Mechanical Turk." *Political Analysis* 20(3):351–368.

Berliner, Daniel and Aaron Erlich. 2015. "Competing for transparency: Political competition and institutional reform in Mexican states." *American Political Science Review* 109(1):110–128.

Berry, Christopher R. and Anthony Fowler. 2016. "Cardinals or clerics? Congressional committees and the distribution of pork." *American Journal of Political Science* 60(3):692–708.

Berry, David M. and Anders Fagerjord. 2017. *Digital Humanities: Knowledge and Critique in a Digital Age*. Polity Press.

Biber, Douglas. 1991. *Variation across Speech and Writing*. Cambridge University Press.

Bischof, Jonathan and Edoardo M. Airoldi. 2012. "Summarizing topical content with word frequency and exclusivity." In *Proceedings of the 29th International Conference on Machine Learning*. pp. 201–208.

Bishop, Christopher. 2006. *Pattern Recognition and Machine Learning*. Springer.

Blackwell, David and James B. MacQueen. 1973. "Ferguson distributions via Pólya urn schemes." *The Annals of Statistics* 1(2):353–355.

Blair, Graeme, Jasper Cooper, Alexander Coppock, and Macartan Humphreys. 2019. "Declaring and diagnosing research designs." *American Political Science Review* 113(3):838–859.

Blaydes, Lisa, Justin Grimmer, and Alison McQueen. 2018. "Mirrors for princes and sultans: Advice on the art of governance in the medieval Christian and Islamic worlds." *Journal of Politics* 80(4):1150–1167.

Blei, David M. 2012. "Probabilistic topic models." *Communications of the ACM* 55(4):77–84.

Blei, David M. 2014. "Build, compute, critique, repeat: Data analysis with latent variable models." *Annual Review of Statistics and Its Application* 1(1):203–232.

Blei, David M., Andrew Y. Ng, and Michael I. Jordan. 2003. "Latent Dirichlet allocation." *The Journal of Machine Learning Research* 3:993–1022.

Blei, David M. and John D. Lafferty. 2006. "Dynamic topic models." In *Proceedings of the 23rd International Conference on Machine Learning*. ACM pp. 113–120.

Blei, David M. and John D. Lafferty. 2007. "A correlated topic model of science." *The Annals of Applied Statistics* 1(1):17–35.

Bojanowski, Piotr, Edouard Grave, Armand Joulin, and Tomas Mikolov. 2017. "Enriching word vectors with subword information." *Transactions of the Association for Computational Linguistics* 5:135–146.

Bolukbasi, Tolga, Kai-Wei Chang, James Zou, Venkatesh Saligrama, and Adam Kalai. 2016. "Man is to computer programmer as woman is to homemaker? debiasing word embeddings." In *Proceedings of the 30th International Conference on Neural Information Processing Systems*. pp. 4356–4364.

Bond, Robert and Solomon Messing. 2015. "Quantifying social media's political space: Estimating ideology from publicly revealed preferences on Facebook." *American Political Science Review* 109(1):62–78.

Bonica, Adam. 2013. "Ideology and interests in the political marketplace." *American Journal of Political Science* 57(2):294–311.

Bonica, Adam and Maya Sen. 2017. "The politics of selecting the bench from the bar: The legal profession and partisan incentives to introduce ideology into judicial selection." *The Journal of Law and Economics* 60(4):559–595.

boyd, danah and Kate Crawford. 2012. "Critical questions for big data: Provocations for a cultural, technological, and scholarly phenomenon." *Information, Communication & Society* 15(5):662–679.

Boyd-Graber, Jordan, David Mimno, and David Newman. 2014. "Care and Feeding of Topic Models: Problems, Diagnostics, and Improvements." In *Handbook of Mixed Membership Models and Their Applications*, ed. Edoardo M. Airoldi, David Blei, Elena A. Erosheva, and Stephen E. Fienberg. CRC Handbooks of Modern Statistical Methods Boca Raton, Florida: CRC Press.

Boyd-Graber, Jordan, Yuening Hu, and David Mimno. 2017. "Applications of topic models." *Foundations and Trends in Information Retrieval* 11(2-3):143–296.

Boydston, Michelle D. 1991. "Press censorship and access restrictions during the Persian Gulf War: A First Amendment analysis." *Loy. LAL Rev.* 25:1073.

Boydstun, Amber E. 2013. *Making the News: Politics, the Media, and Agenda Setting*. University of Chicago Press.

Bradley, Margaret M. and Peter J. Lang. 1999. "Affective norms for English words (ANEW): Instruction manual and affective ratings." Technical report C-1, the center for research in psychophysiology.

Brandt, Patrick T., John R. Freeman, and Philip A. Schrodt. 2011. "Real time, time series forecasting of inter-and intra-state political conflict." *Conflict Management and Peace Science* 28(1):41–64.

Breiger, Ronald L., Robin Wagner-Pacifici, and John W. Mohr. 2018. "Capturing distinctions while mining text data: Toward low-tech formalization for text analysis." *Poetics* 68:104–119.

Broderick, Tamara, Brian Kulis, and Michael Jordan. 2013. "MAD-Bayes: MAP-based asymptotic derivations from Bayes." In *International Conference on Machine Learning*. pp. 226–234.

Broniatowski, David A., Michael J. Paul, and Mark Dredze. 2013. "National and local influenza surveillance through Twitter: an analysis of the 2012-2013 influenza epidemic." *PloS One* 8(12):e83672.

Brown, Tom, Benjamin Mann, Nick Ryder, Melanie Subbiah, Jared D Kaplan, Prafulla Dhariwal, Arvind Neelakantan, Pranav Shyam, Girish Sastry, Amanda Askell, Sandhini Agarwal, Ariel Herbert-Voss, Gretchen Krueger, Tom Henighan, Rewon Child, Aditya Ramesh, Daniel Ziegler, Jeffrey Wu, Clemens Winter, Chris Hesse, Mark Chen, Eric Sigler, Mateusz Litwin, Scott Gray, Benjamin Chess, Jack Clark, Christopher Berner, Sam McCandlish, Alec Radford, Ilya Sutskever, and Dario Amodei. 2020. "Language Models are Few-Shot Learners." In *Advances in Neural Information Processing Systems*, ed. H. Larochelle, M. Ranzato, R. Hadsell, M. F. Balcan, and H. Lin. Vol. 33 Curran Associates, Inc. pp. 1877–1901.

Budak, Ceren, Sharad Goel, and Justin M. Rao. 2016. "Fair and balanced? Quantifying media bias through crowdsourced content analysis." *Public Opinion Quarterly* 80(S1):250–271.

Buhrmester, Michael, Tracy Kwang, and Samuel D. Gosling. 2011. "Amazon's Mechanical Turk: A new source of inexpensive, yet high-quality, data?" *Perspectives on Psychological Science* 6(1): 3–5.

Buolamwini, Joy and Timnit Gebru. 2018. "Gender shades: Intersectional accuracy disparities in commercial gender classification." In *Conference on Fairness, Accountability and Transparency.* pp. 77–91.

Burden, Barry and Joseph Sanberg. 2003. "Budget rhetoric in presidential campaigns from 1952 to 2000." *Political Behavior* 25(2):97–118.

Burgess, Matthew, Eugenia Giraudy, Julian Katz-Samuels, Joe Walsh, Derek Willis, Lauren Haynes, and Rayid Ghani. 2016. "The legislative influence detector: Finding text reuse in state legislation." In *Proceedings of the 22nd ACM SIGKDD International Conference on Knowledge Discovery and Data Mining.* pp. 57–66.

Butler, Declan. 2013. "When Google got flu wrong." *Nature* 494(7436):155.

Caliskan, Aylin, Joanna J. Bryson, and Arvind Narayanan. 2017. "Semantics derived automatically from language corpora contain human-like biases." *Science* 356(6334):183–186.

Cameron, Charles M. 2000. *Veto Bargaining: Presidents and the Politics of Negative Power.* Cambridge University Press.

Campbell, Rosie and Philip Cowley. 2014. "What voters want: Reactions to candidate characteristics in a survey experiment." *Political Studies* 62(4):745–765.

Canes-Wrone, Brandice, David W Brady, and John F Cogan. 2002. "Out of step, out of office: Electoral accountability and House members' voting." *American Political Science Review* 96(1):127–140.

Canon, David T. 1990. *Actors, Athletes, and Astronauts: Political Amateurs in the United States Congress.* University of Chicago Press.

Caporaso, James A. 1995. "Review: Research design, falsification, and the qualitative-quantitative divide." *American Political Science Review* 89(2):457–460.

Card, Dallas, Peter Henderson, Urvashi Khandelwal, Robin Jia, Kyle Mahowald, and Dan Jurafsky. 2020. "With little power comes great responsibility." In *Proceedings of the 2020 Conference on Empirical Methods in Natural Language Processing (EMNLP).* Online: Association for Computational Linguistics pp. 9263–9274.

Carley, Kathleen M. 1990. "Content analysis." In *The Encyclopedia of Language and Linguistics.* Pergamon Press.

Carley, Kathleen M. 1997*a*. "Extracting team mental models through textual analysis." *Journal of Organizational Behavior* pp. 533–558.

Carley, Kathleen M. 1997*b*. "Network text analysis: The network position of concepts." In *Text Analysis for the Social Sciences: Methods for Drawing Statistical Inferences from Texts and Transcripts*, ed. Carl W. Roberts. Routledge pp. 79–100.

Carlson, David and Jacob M. Montgomery. 2017. "A pairwise comparison framework for fast, flexible, and reliable human coding of political texts." *American Political Science Review* 111(4):835–843.

Carnes, Nicholas. 2012. "Does the numerical underrepresentation of the working class in congress matter?" *Legislative Studies Quarterly* 37(1):5–34.

Catalinac, Amy. 2016*a*. *Electoral Reform and National Security in Japan: From Pork to Foreign Policy.* Cambridge University Press.

Catalinac, Amy. 2016*b*. "From pork to policy: The rise of programmatic campaigning in Japanese elections." *The Journal of Politics* 78(1):1–18.

Celebi, M. Emre, Hassan A. Kingravi, and Patricio A. Vela. 2013. "A comparative study of efficient initialization methods for the k-means clustering algorithm." *Expert Systems with Applications* 40(1):200–210.

Chadefaux, Thomas. 2017. "Conflict forecasting and its limits." *Data Science* 1(1-2):7–17.

Chancellor, Stevie, Michael L. Birnbaum, Eric D. Caine, Vincent M.B. Silenzio, and Munmun De Choudhury. 2019. "A taxonomy of ethical tensions in inferring mental health states from social media." In *Proceedings of the Conference on Fairness, Accountability, and Transparency*. pp. 79–88.

Chang, Charles and Michael Masterson. 2020. "Using word order in political text classification with long short-term memory models." *Political Analysis* 28(3):395–411.

Chang, Jonathan, Sean Gerrish, Chong Wang, Jordan L. Boyd-Graber, and David M. Blei. 2009. "Reading tea leaves: How humans interpret topic models." In *Advances in Neural Information Processing Systems*. pp. 288–296.

Chatman, Jennifer A. and Francis J. Flynn. 2005. "Full-cycle micro-organizational behavior research." *Organization Science* 16(4):434–447.

Chen, Jidong, Jennifer Pan, and Yiqing Xu. 2016. "Sources of authoritarian responsiveness: A field experiment in China." *American Journal of Political Science* 60(2):383–400.

Chiba, Daina and Kristian Skrede Gleditsch. 2017. "The shape of things to come? Expanding the inequality and grievance model for civil war forecasts with event data." *Journal of Peace Research* 54(2):275–297.

Choi, Hyunyoung and Hal Varian. 2012. "Predicting the present with Google Trends." *Economic Record* 88(s1):2–9.

Chuang, Jason, Christopher D. Manning, and Jeffrey Heer. 2012. "ıWithout the clutter of unimportant wordsj Descriptive keyphrases for text visualization." *ACM Transactions on Computer-Human Interaction* 19(3):1–29.

Chuang, Jason, Margaret E. Roberts, Brandon M. Stewart, Rebecca Weiss, Dustin Tingley, Justin Grimmer, and Jeffrey Heer. 2015. "TopicCheck: Interactive Alignment for Assessing Topic Model Stability." In *Proceedings of the 2015 Conference of the North American Chapter of the Association for Computational Linguistics: Human Language Technologies*. Denver, Colorado: Association for Computational Linguistics pp. 175–184.

Chung, Cindy and James W. Pennebaker. 2007. "The psychological functions of function words." *Social Communication* 1:343–359.

Citron, Daniel T. and Paul Ginsparg. 2015. "Patterns of text reuse in a scientific corpus." *Proceedings of the National Academy of Sciences* 112(1):25–30.

Cleveland, William S. 1979. "Robust locally weighted regression and scatterplots." *Journal of the American Statistical Association* 74(368):829–836.

Clinton, Joshua, Simon Jackman, and Douglas Rivers. 2004. "The statistical analysis of roll call data." *American Political Science Review* 98(02):355–370.

Cohen, Mark A., Roland T. Rust, and Sara Steen. 2004. "Measuring perceptions of appropriate prison sentences in the United States, 2000. ICPSR version. Nashville, TN: Vanderbilt University, 2000." *Ann Arbor, MI: Inter-university Consortium for Political and Social Research* .

Cook, Samantha, Corrie Conrad, Ashley L. Fowlkes, and Matthew H. Mohebbi. 2011. "Assessing Google flu trends performance in the United States during the 2009 influenza virus A (H1N1) pandemic." *PloS One* 6(8):e23610.

Corbin, Juliet and Anselm Strauss. 1990. "Grounded theory research: Procedures, canons and evaluative criteria." *Qualitative Sociology* 13(1):3–20.

Cranmer, Skyler J. and Bruce A. Desmarais. 2017. "What can we learn from predictive modeling?" *Political Analysis* 25(2):145–166.

Cunha, Evandro, Gabriel Magno, Marcos André Gonçalves, César Cambraia, and Virgilio Almeida. 2014. "He votes or she votes? Female and male discursive strategies in Twitter political hashtags." *PloS One* 9(1):e87041.

Da, Nan Z. 2019. "The computational case against computational literary studies." *Critical Inquiry* 45(3):601–639.

D'Amour, Alexander, Peng Ding, Avi Feller, Lihua Lei, and Jasjeet Sekhon. 2021. "Overlap in observational studies with high-dimensional covariates." *Journal of Econometrics* 221(2):644–654.

Danzger, M. Herbert. 1975. "Validating conflict data." *American Sociological Review* 40(5):570–584.

Dawid, Alexander Philip and Allan M. Skene. 1979. "Maximum likelihood estimation of observer error-rates using the EM algorithm." *Journal of the Royal Statistical Society: Series C (Applied Statistics)* 28(1):20–28.

De Choudhury, Munmun, Michael Gamon, Scott Counts, and Eric Horvitz. 2013. "Predicting depression via social media." *Proceedings of the International AAAI Conference on Web and Social Media* 7(1).

Deerwester, Scott, Susan T. Dumais, George W. Furnas, Thomas K. Landauer, and Richard Harshman. 1990. "Indexing by latent semantic analysis." *Journal of the American Society for Information Science* 41(6):391.

Dempster, Arthur P., Nan M. Laird, and Donald B. Rubin. 1977. "Maximum likelihood from incomplete data via the EM algorithm." *Journal of the Royal Statistical Society: Series B (Methodological)* 39(1):1–22.

Denny, Matthew J. and Arthur Spirling. 2018. "Text preprocessing for unsupervised learning: why it matters, when it misleads, and what to do about it." *Political Analysis* 26(2):168–189.

Devlin, Jacob, Ming-Wei Chang, Kenton Lee, and Kristina Toutanova. 2019. "BERT: Pre-training of deep bidirectional transformers for language understanding." In *Proceedings of the 2019 Conference of the North American Chapter of the Association for Computational Linguistics: Human Language Technologies, Volume 1 (Long and Short Papers)*. Minneapolis, Minnesota: Association for Computational Linguistics pp. 4171–4186.

Diermeier, Daniel, Jean-François Godbout, Bei Yu, and Stefan Kaufmann. 2012. "Language and ideology in Congress." *British Journal of Political Science* 42(1):31–55.

Dietrich, Bryce and Melissa Sands. N.d. "Using Public Video Feeds to Understand Intergroup Exposure." Technical report University of Iowa.

Dietrich, Bryce J., Ryan D Enos, and Maya Sen. 2019. "Emotional arousal predicts voting on the US supreme court." *Political Analysis* 27(2):237–243.

Difallah, Djellel, Elena Filatova, and Panos Ipeirotis. 2018. "Demographics and dynamics of mechanical Turk workers." In *Proceedings of the Eleventh ACM International Conference on Web Search and Data Mining*. pp. 135–143.

DiMaggio, Paul. 2015. "Adapting computational text analysis to social science (and vice versa)." *Big Data & Society* 2(2):1–5.

DiMaggio, Paul, Manish Nag, and David Blei. 2013. "Exploiting affinities between topic modeling and the sociological perspective on culture: Application to newspaper coverage of US government arts funding." *Poetics* 41(6):570–606.

Dodds, Peter Sheridan, Kameron Decker Harris, Isabel M. Kloumann, Catherine A. Bliss, and Christopher M. Danforth. 2011. "Temporal patterns of happiness and information in a global social network: Hedonometrics and Twitter." *PloS One* 6(12):e26752.

D'Orazio, Vito, Steven T. Landis, Glenn Palmer, and Philip Schrodt. 2014. "Separating the wheat from the chaff: Applications of automated document classification using support vector machines." *Political Analysis* 22(2):224–242.

Downs, Anthony. 1957. "An economic theory of political action in a democracy." *The Journal of Political Economy* pp. 135–150.

Duncan, Otis Dudley. 1984. *Notes on Social Measurement: Historical and Critical*. Russell Sage Foundation.

Duneier, Mitchell. 1999. *Sidewalk*. Macmillan.

Duneier, Mitchell. 2016. *Ghetto: The Invention of a Place, the History of an Idea*. Macmillan.

Efron, Bradley and Gail Gong. 1983. "A leisurely look at the bootstrap, the jackknife, and cross-validation." *American Statistician* 37(1):36–48.

Egami, Naoki, Christian J. Fong, Justin Grimmer, Margaret E. Roberts, and Brandon M. Stewart. 2018. "How to make causal inferences using texts." *arXiv preprint arXiv:1802.02163*.

Eichstaedt, Johannes C., Hansen Andrew Schwartz, Margaret L. Kern, Gregory Park, Darwin R. Labarthe, Raina M. Merchant, Sneha Jha, Megha Agrawal, Lukasz A. Dziurzynski, Maarten Sap, Christopher Weeg, Emily E. Larson, Lyle H. Ungar, and Martin E.P. Seligman. 2015. "Psychological language on Twitter predicts county-level heart disease mortality." *Psychological Science* 26(2):159–169.

Eisenstein, Jacob. 2019. *Introduction to Natural Language Processing*. MIT press.

Eisenstein, Jacob, Amr Ahmed, and Eric P. Xing. 2011. "Sparse additive generative models of text." In *Proceedings of the 28th International Conference on International Conference on Machine Learning*. Omnipress pp. 1041–1048.

Eisenstein, Jacob, Brendan O'Connor, Noah A. Smith, and Eric P. Xing. 2010. "A latent variable model for geographic lexical variation." In *Proceedings of the 2010 Conference on Empirical Methods in Natural Language Processing*. Association for Computational Linguistics pp. 1277–1287.

Elkan, Charles. 2006. "Clustering documents with an exponential-family approximation of the Dirichlet compound multinomial distribution." In *Proceedings of the 23rd International Conference on Machine Learning*. ACM pp. 289–296.

Elwert, Felix and Christopher Winship. 2014. "Endogenous selection bias: The problem of conditioning on a collider variable." *Annual Review of Sociology* 40:31–53.

Ensign, Danielle, Sorelle A. Friedler, Scott Neville, Carlos Scheidegger, and Suresh Venkatasubramanian. 2018. "Runaway feedback loops in predictive policing." In *Conference on Fairness, Accountability and Transparency*. pp. 160–171.

Eshbaugh-Soha, Matthew. 2010. "The tone of local presidential news coverage." *Political Communication* 27(2):121–140.

Eshima, Shusei, Kosuke Imai, and Tomoya Sasaki. 2020. "Keyword assisted topic models." *arXiv preprint arXiv:2004.05964* .

Evans, James A and Pedro Aceves. 2016. "Machine translation: Mining text for social theory." *Annual Review of Sociology* 42:21–50.

Faruqui, Manaal, Jesse Dodge, Sujay Kumar Jauhar, Chris Dyer, Eduard Hovy, and Noah A. Smith. 2015. "Retrofitting word vectors to semantic lexicons." In *Proceedings of the 2015 Conference of the North American Chapter of the Association for Computational Linguistics: Human Language Technologies*. Denver, Colorado: Association for Computational Linguistics pp. 1606–1615.

Faruqui, Manaal, Yulia Tsvetkov, Pushpendre Rastogi, and Chris Dyer. 2016. "Problems With Evaluation of Word Embeddings Using Word Similarity Tasks." In *Proceedings of the 1st Workshop on Evaluating Vector-Space Representations for NLP*. Berlin, Germany: Association for Computational Linguistics pp. 30–35.

Feinerer, Ingo, Kurt Hornik, and David Meyer. 2008. "Text mining infrastructure in R." *Journal of Statistical Software* 25(5):1–54.

Fenno, Richard F. 1978. *Home Style: House Members in Their Districts*. HarperCollins.

Ferrara, Emilio, Onur Varol, Clayton Davis, Filippo Menczer, and Alessandro Flammini. 2016. "The rise of social bots." *Communications of the ACM* 59(7):96–104.

Finkelstein, Lev, Evgeniy Gabrilovich, Yossi Matias, Ehud Rivlin, Zach Solan, Gadi Wolfman, and Eytan Ruppin. 2001. "Placing search in context: The concept revisited." In *Proceedings of the 10th International Conference on World Wide Web*. pp. 406–414.

Firth, John Rupert. 1957. *Studies in Linguistic Analysis*. Wiley-Blackwell.

Flood, Barbara J. 1999. "Historical note: The start of a stop list at Biological Abstracts." *Journal of the Association for Information Science and Technology* 50(12):1066.

Fong, Christian and Justin Grimmer. 2016. "Discovery of treatments from text corpora." In *Proceedings of the 54th Annual Meeting of the Association for Computational Linguistics (Volume 1: Long Papers)*. Vol. 1 pp. 1600–1609.

Fong, Christian and Matthew Tyler. 2020. "Machine learning predictions as regression covariates." *Political Analysis* p. 1–18.

Fong, Christian J. and Justin Grimmer. 2021. "Causal Inference with Latent Treatments." *Stanford University Mimeo* .

Forgy, Edward W. 1965. "Cluster analysis of multivariate data: Efficiency versus interpretability of classifications." *Biometrics* 21:768–769.

Fort, Karën, Gilles Adda, and K Bretonnel Cohen. 2011. "Amazon Mechanical Turk: Gold mine or coal mine?" *Computational Linguistics* 37(2):413–420.

Foulds, James and Padhraic Smyth. 2014. "Annealing paths for the evaluation of topic models." In *Proceedings of the Thirtieth Conference on Uncertainty in Artificial Intelligence*. UAI'14 Arlington, Virginia, USA: AUAI Press p. 220–229.

Fowler, Anthony and B. Pablo Montagnes. 2015. "College football, elections, and false-positive results in observational research." *Proceedings of the National Academy of Sciences* 112(45):13800–13804.

Fraley, Chris and Adrian Raftery. 2002. "Model-based clustering, discriminant analysis, and density estimation." *Journal of the American Statistical Association* 97(458):611.

Franco, Annie, Justin Grimmer, and Chloe Lim. 2018. "The limited effect of presidential appeals." Working Paper Stanford University.

Frantzi, Katerina, Sophia Ananiadou, and Hideki Mima. 2000. "Automatic recognition of multi-word terms: The C-value/NC-value method." *International Journal on Digital Libraries* 3(2):115–130.

Franzosi, Roberto. 1989. "From words to numbers: A generalized and linguistics-based coding procedure for collecting textual data." *Sociological Methodology* 19:263–298.

Franzosi, Roberto. 2004. *From Words to Numbers: Narrative, Data, and Social Science*. Cambridge University Press.

Frey, Brendan J. and Delbert Dueck. 2007. "Clustering by passing messages between data points." *Science* 315(5814):972–976.

Gan, Zhe, Changyou Chen, Ricardo Henao, David Carlson, and Lawrence Carin. 2015. "Scalable deep Poisson factor analysis for topic modeling." In *International Conference on Machine Learning*. pp. 1823–1832.

Ganitkevitch, Juri, Benjamin Van Durme, and Chris Callison-Burch. 2013. "PPDB: The paraphrase database." In *Proceedings of the 2013 Conference of the North American Chapter of the Association for Computational Linguistics: Human Language Technologies*. pp. 758–764.

Garg, Nikhil, Londa Schiebinger, Dan Jurafsky, and James Zou. 2018. "Word embeddings quantify 100 years of gender and ethnic stereotypes." *Proceedings of the National Academy of Sciences* 115(16):E3635–E3644.

Gava, Roy, Julien M. Jaquet, and Pascal Sciarini. 2021. "Legislating or rubber-stamping? Assessing parliament's influence on law-making with text reuse." *European Journal of Political Research* 60:175–198.

Gelman, Andrew, John B. Carlin, Hal S. Stern, David B. Dunson, Aki Vehtari, and Donald B. Rubin. 2013. *Bayesian Data Analysis*. CRC press.

Gentzkow, Matthew, Bryan Kelly, and Matt Taddy. 2019. "Text as data." *Journal of Economic Literature* 57(3):535–74.

Gentzkow, Matthew and Jesse M. Shapiro. 2010. "What drives media slant? Evidence from US daily newspapers." *Econometrica* 78(1):35–71.

Gentzkow, Matthew, Jesse M. Shapiro, and Matt Taddy. 2019. "Measuring group differences in high-dimensional choices: Method and application to congressional speech." *Econometrica* 87(4):1307–1340.

Gerber, Alan S. and Donald P. Green. 2012. *Field Experiments: Design, Analysis, and Interpretation*. WW Norton.

Gerring, John and Craig W. Thomas. 2005. "Comparability: A key issue in research design." *Committee on Concepts and Methods. Working Paper Series* 4:1–20.

Gerrish, Sean and David M. Blei. 2011. "Predicting legislative roll calls from text." In *Proceedings of the 28th International Conference on Machine Learning*. pp. 489–496.

Gerrish, Sean and David M. Blei. 2012. "How they vote: Issue-adjusted models of legislative behavior." In *Advances in Neural Information Processing Systems*. pp. 2753–2761.

Gill, Michael and Andrew B Hall. 2015. "How judicial identity changes the text of legal rulings." Working Paper Stanford University.

Gill, Michael and Arthur Spirling. 2015. "Estimating the severity of the WikiLeaks US diplomatic cables disclosure." *Political Analysis* 23(2):299–305.

Gillion, Daniel Q. 2016. *Governing with Words: The Political Dialogue on Race, Public Policy, and Inequality in America*. Cambridge University Press.

Gimpel, Kevin, Nathan Schneider, Brendan O'Connor, Dipanjan Das, Daniel Mills, Jacob Eisenstein, Michael Heilman, Dani Yogatama, Jeffrey Flanigan, and Noah A. Smith. 2011. "Part-of-speech tagging for Twitter: Annotation, features, and experiments." In *Proceedings of the 49th Annual Meeting of the Association for Computational Linguistics: Human Language Technologies: Short Papers - Volume 2*. HLT '11 USA: Association for Computational Linguistics p. 42–47.

Ginsberg, Jeremy, Matthew H. Mohebbi, Rajan S. Patel, Lynnette Brammer, Mark S. Smolinski, and Larry Brilliant. 2009. "Detecting influenza epidemics using search engine query data." *Nature* 457(7232):1012.

Glaser, Barney G. 2002. "Conceptualization: On theory and theorizing using grounded theory." *International Journal of Qualitative Methods* 1(2).

Glaser, Barney G. and Anselm L. Strauss. 1967. *The Discovery of Grounded Theory: Strategies for Qualitative Research*. New York: Aldine De Gruyter.

Goel, Sharad, Jake M. Hofman, Sébastien Lahaie, David M. Pennock, and Duncan J. Watts. 2010. "Predicting consumer behavior with Web search." *Proceedings of the National Academy of Sciences* 107(41):17486–17490.

Goertz, Gary. 2008. "Concepts, theories, and numbers: A checklist for constructing, evaluating, and using concepts or quantitative measures." In *The Oxford Handbook of Political Methodology*, ed. J.M. Box-Steffensmeier, H.E. Brady, and D. Collier. Oxford University Press.

Goffman, Erving. 1959. *The Presentation of Self in Everyday Life*. Doubleday.

Golder, Scott A. and Michael W. Macy. 2011. "Diurnal and seasonal mood vary with work, sleep, and daylength across diverse cultures." *Science* 333(6051):1878–1881.

Goodfellow, Ian, Yoshua Bengio, and Aaron Courville. 2016. *Deep Learning*. MIT Press.

Goodman, Bryce and Seth Flaxman. 2017. "European Union regulations on algorithmic decision-making and a "right to explanation"." *AI Magazine* 38(3):50–57.

Granato, Jim and Frank Scioli. 2004. "Puzzles, proverbs, and omega matrices: The scientific and social significance of empirical implications of theoretical models (EITM)." *Perspectives on Politics* 2(2):313–323.

Griffiths, Thomas L. and Mark Steyvers. 2004. "Finding scientific topics." *Proceedings of the National academy of Sciences* 101(suppl 1):5228–5235.

Griffiths, Thomas L. and Zoubin Ghahramani. 2011. "The Indian buffet process: An introduction and review." *Journal of Machine Learning Research* 12(Apr):1185–1224.

Grimmer, Justin. 2010. "A Bayesian hierarchical topic model for political texts: Measuring expressed agendas in Senate press releases." *Political Analysis* 18(1):1–35.

Grimmer, Justin. 2013a. "Appropriators not position takers: The distorting effects of electoral incentives on congressional representation." *American Journal of Political Science* 57(3):624–642.

Grimmer, Justin. 2013b. *Representational Style in Congress: What Legislators Say and Why It Matters*. Cambridge University Press.

Grimmer, Justin and Brandon M. Stewart. 2013. "Text as data: The promise and pitfalls of automatic content analysis methods for political texts." *Political Analysis* 21(3):267–297.

Grimmer, Justin and Gary King. 2011. "General purpose computer-assisted clustering and conceptualization." *Proceedings of the National Academy of Sciences* 108(7):2643–2650.

Grimmer, Justin, Margaret E Roberts, and Brandon M Stewart. 2021. "Machine Learning for Social Science: An Agnostic Approach." *Annual Review of Political Science* 24.

Grimmer, Justin, Sean J. Westwood, and Solomon Messing. 2014. *The Impression of Influence: Legislator Communication, Representation, and Democratic Accountability*. Princeton University Press.

Grün, Bettina and Kurt Hornik. 2011. "topicmodels: An R package for fitting topic models." *Journal of Statistical Software* 40(13):1–30.

Gueorguiev, Dimitar D. and Edmund J. Malesky. 2019. "Consultation and selective censorship in China." *The Journal of Politics* 81(4):1539–1545.

Gup, Ted. 2008. *Nation of Secrets: The Threat to Democracy and the American Way of Life*. Anchor.

Hainmueller, Jens, Daniel J. Hopkins, and Teppei Yamamoto. 2014. "Causal inference in conjoint analysis: Understanding multidimensional choices via stated preference experiments." *Political Analysis* 22(1):1–30.

Halterman, Andrew. 2017. "Mordecai: Full text geoparsing and event geocoding." *Journal of Open Source Software* 2(9):91.

Halterman, Andrew. 2019. "Geolocating political events in text." In *Proceedings of the Third Workshop on Natural Language Processing and Computational Social Science*. Minneapolis, Minnesota: Association for Computational Linguistics pp. 29–39.

Halterman, Andy. 2020. "Extracting political events from text using syntax and semantics." Technical report MIT.

Handler, Abram, Matthew Denny, Hanna Wallach, and Brendan O'Connor. 2016. "Bag of what? Simple noun phrase extraction for text analysis." In *Proceedings of the First Workshop on NLP and Computational Social Science*. Austin, Texas: Association for Computational Linguistics pp. 114–124.

Harford, Tim. 2014. "Big data: A big mistake?" *Significance* 11(5):14–19.

Hart, R.P. 2000. *Diction 5.0: The Text Analysis Program*. Thousand Oaks, CA: Sage-Scolari.

Hartigan, John A. and Manchek A. Wong. 1979. "Algorithm AS 136: A k-means clustering algorithm." *Journal of the Royal Statistical Society. Series C (Applied Statistics)* 28(1):100–108.

Hastie, Trevor, Robert Tibshirani, and Jerome Friedman. 2013. *The Elements of Statistical Learning*. Springer.

Healy, Andrew J., Neil Malhotra, and Cecilia Hyunjung Mo. 2010. "Irrelevant events affect voters' evaluations of government performance." *Proceedings of the National Academy of Sciences* 107(29):12804–12809.

Hernán, Miguel A. and James M. Robins. 2020. *Causal Inference: What If*. Chapman & Hall/CRC.

Herrera, Yoshiko M. and Devesh Kapur. 2007. "Improving data quality: Actors, incentives, and capabilities." *Political Analysis* pp. 365–386.

Hertel-Fernandez, Alexander. 2019. *State Capture: How Conservative Activists, Big Businesses, and Wealthy Donors Reshaped the American States—and the Nation*. Oxford University Press, USA.

Hertel-Fernandez, Alexander and Konstantin Kashin. 2015. "Capturing business power across the states with text reuse." In *Annual Conference of the Midwest Political Science Association, Chicago, April*. pp. 16–19.

Hinton, Geoffrey E. 1986. "Learning distributed representations of concepts." In *Proceedings of the Eighth Annual Conference of the Cognitive Science Society*. Vol. 1 Amherst, MA p. 12.

Hofman, Jake M., Amit Sharma, and Duncan J. Watts. 2017. "Prediction and explanation in social systems." *Science* 355(6324):486–488.

Hofmann, Thomas. 1999. "Probabilistic latent semantic analysis." In *Proceedings of the Fifteenth Conference on Uncertainty in Artificial Intelligence*. Morgan Kaufmann Publishers Inc. pp. 289–296.

Holland, Paul W. 1986. "Statistics and causal inference." *Journal of the American Statistical Association* 81:945–960.

Hopkins, Daniel J. and Gary King. 2010. "A method of automated nonparametric content analysis for social science." *American Journal of Political Science* 54(1):229–247.

House, Freedom. 2015. *Freedom on the Net 2015:Privatising Censorship, Eroding Privacy*. Freedom House.

Hu, Yuening, Jordan Boyd-Graber, Brianna Satinoff, and Alison Smith. 2014. "Interactive topic modeling." *Machine Learning* 95(3):423–469.

Huang, Haifeng. 2015. "Propaganda as signaling." *Comparative Politics* 47(4):419–444.

Huff, Connor and Dustin Tingley. 2015. ""Who are these people?" Evaluating the demographic characteristics and political preferences of MTurk survey respondents." *Research & Politics* 2(3):1–12.

Humphreys, Macartan, Raul Sanchez de la Sierra, and Peter Van der Windt. 2013. "Fishing, commitment, and communication: A proposal for comprehensive nonbinding research registration." *Political Analysis* 21(1):1–20.

Hvitfeldt, Emil and Julia Silge. 2021. *Supervised Machine Learning for Text Analysis in R*. CRC Press.

Imai, Kosuke and Marc Ratkovic. 2013. "Estimating treatment effect heterogeneity in randomized program evaluation." *The Annals of Applied Statistics* 7(1):443–470.

Imbens, Guido W. and Donald B. Rubin. 2015. *Causal Inference in Statistics, Social, and Biomedical Sciences*. Cambridge University Press.

Jacobs, Abigail Z. and Hanna Wallach. 2021. "Measurement and fairness." In *Proceedings of the 2021 ACM Conference on Fairness, Accountability, and Transparency.* pp. 375–385.

Jaidka, Kokil, Alvin Zhou, and Yphtach Lelkes. 2019. "Brevity is the soul of Twitter: The constraint affordance and political discussion." *Journal of Communication* 69(4):345–372.

Jansa, Joshua M., Eric R. Hansen, and Virginia H. Gray. 2019. "Copy and paste lawmaking: Legislative professionalism and policy reinvention in the states." *American Politics Research* 47(4): 739–767.

Jaros, Kyle and Jennifer Pan. 2018. "China's newsmakers: Official media coverage and political shifts in the Xi Jinping era." *The China Quarterly* 233:111–136.

Jerzak, Connor T., Gary King, and Anton Strezhnev. 2019. "An improved method of automated nonparametric content analysis for social science." Forthcoming at *Political Analysis*.

Joachims, Thorsten. 1998. "Text categorization with support vector machines: Learning with many relevant features." In *European Conference on Machine Learning*. Springer pp. 137–142.

Jockers, Matthew L. 2013. *Macroanalysis: Digital Methods and Literary History*. University of Illinois Press.

Jones, Bryan, John Wilkerson, and Frank Baumgartner. 2009. "The Policy Agendas Project." http://www.policyagendas.org.

Jursfsky, Dan and James Martin. 2009. *Speech and Natural Language Processing: An Introduction to Natural Language Processing, Computational Linguistics, and Speech Recognition*. Upper Saddle River: Prentice Hall.

Justeson, John S. and Slava M. Katz. 1995. "Technical terminology: Some linguistic properties and an algorithm for identification in text." *Natural Language Engineering* 1(1):9–27.

Kalla, Joshua L. and David E. Broockman. 2018. "The minimal persuasive effects of campaign contact in general elections: Evidence from 49 field experiments." *American Political Science Review* 112(1):148–166.

Kang, Jun Seok, Polina Kuznetsova, Michael Luca, and Yejin Choi. 2013. "Where not to eat? Improving public policy by predicting hygiene inspections using online reviews." In *Proceedings of the 2013 Conference on Empirical Methods in Natural Language Processing*. pp. 1443–1448.

Karell, Daniel and Michael Freedman. 2019. "Rhetorics of radicalism." *American Sociological Review* 84(4):726–753.

Kaufman, Aaron Russell, Peter Kraft, and Maya Sen. 2019. "Improving Supreme Court forecasting using boosted decision trees." *Political Analysis* 27(3):381–387.

Keith, Katherine, Abram Handler, Michael Pinkham, Cara Magliozzi, Joshua McDuffie, and Brendan O'Connor. 2017. "Identifying civilians killed by police with distantly supervised entity-event extraction." In *Proceedings of the 2017 Conference on Empirical Methods in Natural Language Processing*. pp. 1547–1557.

Keith, Katherine, David Jensen, and Brendan O'Connor. 2020. "Text and causal inference: A review of using text to remove confounding from causal estimates." In *Proceedings of the 58th Annual Meeting of the Association for Computational Linguistics*. Association for Computational Linguistics pp. 5332–5344.

Kellstedt, Paul. 2000. "Media framing and the dynamics of racial policy preferences." *American Journal of Political Science* 44(2):245–260.

Khan, Mohammad Emtiyaz and Guillaume Bouchard. 2009. "Variational EM algorithms for correlated topic models." Technical report University of British Columbia.

Khodak, Mikhail, Nikunj Saunshi, Yingyu Liang, Tengyu Ma, Brandon M. Stewart, and Sanjeev Arora. 2018. "A la carte embedding: Cheap but effective induction of semantic feature vectors." In *Proceedings of the 56th Annual Meeting of the Association for Computational Linguistics (Volume 1: Long Papers)*. Melbourne, Australia: Association for Computational Linguistics pp. 12–22.

Kim, In Song, John Londregan, and Marc Ratkovic. 2018. "Estimating ideal points from votes and text." *Political Analysis* 26(2):210–229.

King, G., R.O. Keohane, and S. Verba. 1994. *Designing Social Inquiry: Scientific Inference in Qualitative Research*. Princeton University Press.

King, Gary. 2009. "The changing evidence base of social science research." In *The Future of Political Science: 100 Perspectives*, ed. Gary King, Kay Schlozman, and Norman Nie. New York: Routledge Press.

King, Gary and Will Lowe. 2003. "An automated information extraction tool for international conflict data with performance as good as human coders: A rare events evaluation design." *International Organization* 57(3):617–642.

King, Gary and Ying Lu. 2008. "Verbal autopsy methods with multiple causes of death." *Statistical Science* 23(1):78–91.

King, Gary, Jennifer Pan, and Margaret E. Roberts. 2013. "How censorship in China allows government criticism but silences collective expression." *American Political Science Review* 107(2):1–18.

King, Gary, Jennifer Pan, and Margaret E. Roberts. 2014. "Reverse-engineering censorship in China: Randomized experimentation and participant observation." *Science* 345(6199):1251722–1251722.

King, Gary, Jennifer Pan, and Margaret E. Roberts. 2017. "How the Chinese government fabricates social media posts for strategic distraction, not engaged argument." *American Political Science Review* 111(3):484–501.

King, Gary, Patrick Lam, and Margaret E. Roberts. 2017. "Computer-assisted keyword and document set discovery from unstructured text." *American Journal of Political Science* 61(4):971–988.

Kiros, Ryan, Yukun Zhu, Russ R. Salakhutdinov, Richard Zemel, Raquel Urtasun, Antonio Torralba, and Sanja Fidler. 2015. "Skip-thought vectors." *Advances in Neural Information Processing Systems* 28:3294–3302.

Kittur, Aniket, Ed H. Chi, and Bongwon Suh. 2008. "Crowdsourcing user studies with Mechanical Turk." In *Proceedings of the SIGCHI Conference on Human Factors in Computing Systems*. ACM pp. 453–456.

Knox, Dean and Christopher Lucas. 2021. "A dynamic model of speech for the social sciences." *American Political Science Review* 115(2):649–666.

Koehn, Philipp, Franz Josef Och, and Daniel Marcu. 2003. "Statistical phrase-based translation." In *Proceedings of the 2003 Conference of the North American Chapter of the Association for Computational Linguistics on Human Language Technology—Volume 1*. Association for Computational Linguistics pp. 48–54.

Kogan, Shimon, Dimitry Levin, Bryan R. Routledge, Jacob S. Sagi, and Noah A. Smith. 2009. "Predicting risk from financial reports with regression." In *Proceedings of Human Language Technologies: The 2009 Annual Conference of the North American Chapter of the Association for Computational Linguistics*. Association for Computational Linguistics pp. 272–280.

Kozlowski, Austin C., Matt Taddy, and James A. Evans. 2019. "The geometry of culture: Analyzing the meanings of class through word embeddings." *American Sociological Review* 84(5):905–949.

Kraft, Peter, Hirsh Jain, and Alexander M. Rush. 2016. "An embedding model for predicting roll-call votes." In *Proceedings of the 2016 Conference on Empirical Methods in Natural Language Processing*. pp. 2066–2070.

Krehbiel, Keith. 1990. "Are congressional committees composed of preference outliers?" *American Political Science Review* 84(1):149–163.

Krehbiel, Keith. 1998. *Pivotal Politics: A Theory of US Lawmaking*. University of Chicago Press.

Krippendorff, Klaus. 2012. *Content Analysis: An Introduction to Its Methodology*. Sage.

Kulis, Brian and Michael I. Jordan. 2012. "Revisiting k-means: New algorithms via Bayesian nonparametrics." In *Proceedings of the 29th International Coference on International Conference on Machine Learning*. ICML'12 Madison, WI, USA: Omnipress p. 1131–1138.

Lampos, Vasileios and Nello Cristianini. 2010. "Tracking the flu pandemic by monitoring the social web." In *2010 2nd International Workshop on Cognitive Information Processing*. IEEE pp. 411–416.

Lampton, David M. 2015. "Xi Jinping and the National Security Commission: Policy coordination and political power." *Journal of Contemporary China* 24(95):759–777.

Lancichinetti, Andrea, M. Irmak Sirer, Jane X. Wang, Daniel Acuna, Konrad Körding, and Luís A Nunes Amaral. 2015. "High-reproducibility and high-accuracy method for automated topic classification." *Physical Review X* 5(1):011007.

Landis, J. Richard and Gary G. Koch. 1977. "An application of hierarchical kappa-type statistics in the assessment of majority agreement among multiple observers." *Biometrics* 33(2):363–374.

Larochelle, Hugo and Stanislas Lauly. 2012. "A neural autoregressive topic model." In *Advances in Neural Information Processing Systems*. pp. 2708–2716.

Lauderdale, Benjamin E. and Tom S. Clark. 2014. "Scaling politically meaningful dimensions using texts and votes." *American Journal of Political Science* 58(3):754–771.

Lauretig, Adam M. 2019. "Identification and inference in Bayesian word embeddings." In *Proceedings of the Third Workshop on NLP and Computational Social Science*.

Laver, Michael and John Garry. 2000. "Estimating policy positions from political texts." *American Journal of Political Science* 44(3):619–634.

Laver, Michael, Kenneth Benoit, and John Garry. 2003. "Extracting policy positions from political texts using words as data." *American Political Science Review* 97(2):311–331.

Lazarsfeld, Paul Felix and Neil W Henry. 1968. *Latent Structure Analysis*. Houghton Mifflin Co.

Lazer, David, Alex Sandy Pentland, Lada Adamic, Sinan Aral, Albert Laszlo Barabasi, Devon Brewer, Nicholas Christakis, Noshir Contractor, James Fowler, Myron Gutmann, Tony Jebara, Gary King, Michael Macy, Deb Roy, and Marshall Van Alstyne. 2009. "Life in the network: The coming age of computational social science." *Science* 323(5915):721.

Lazer, David, Ryan Kennedy, Gary King, and Alessandro Vespignani. 2014. "The parable of Google Flu: Traps in big data analysis." *Science* 343(6176):1203–1205.

Le, Quoc and Tomas Mikolov. 2014. "Distributed representations of sentences and documents." In *Proceedings of the 31st International Conference on Machine Learning*, ed. Eric P. Xing and Tony Jebara. Vol. 32 of *Proceedings of Machine Learning Research* Bejing, China: PMLR pp. 1188–1196.

Lee, Daniel D. and H. Sebastian Seung. 2001. "Algorithms for non-negative matrix factorization." In *Advances in Neural Information Processing Systems*. pp. 556–562.

Lee, Sophie J., Howard Liu, and Michael D Ward. 2019. "Lost in space: Geolocation in event data." *Political Science Research and Methods* 7(4):871–888.

Leskovec, Jure, Lars Backstrom, and Jon Kleinberg. 2009. "Meme-tracking and the dynamics of the news cycle." In *Proceedings of the 15th ACM SIGKDD International Conference on Knowledge Discovery and Data Mining*. pp. 497–506.

Levy, Omer and Yoav Goldberg. 2014. "Neural word embedding as implicit matrix factorization." *Advances in Neural Information Processing Systems* 27:2177–2185.

Levy, Omer, Yoav Goldberg, and Ido Dagan. 2015. "Improving distributional similarity with lessons learned from word embeddings." *Transactions of the Association for Computational Linguistics* 3:211–225.

Li, Huayi, Zhiyuan Chen, Bing Liu, Xiaokai Wei, and Jidong Shao. 2014. "Spotting fake reviews via collective positive-unlabeled learning." In *Data Mining (ICDM), 2014 IEEE International Conference on*. IEEE pp. 899–904.

Li, Wei and Andrew McCallum. 2006. "Pachinko allocation: DAG-structured mixture models of topic correlations." In *Proceedings of the 23rd International Conference on Machine learning*. ACM pp. 577–584.

Lieberman, Evan S. 2005. "Nested analysis as a mixed-method strategy for comparative research." *American Political Science Review* 99(3):435–452.

Linder, Fridolin, Bruce Desmarais, Matthew Burgess, and Eugenia Giraudy. 2020. "Text as policy: Measuring policy similarity through bill text reuse." *Policy Studies Journal* 48(2):546–574.

Liu, Yang, Xiangji Huang, Aijun An, and Xiaohui Yu. 2007. "ARSA: A sentiment-aware model for predicting sales performance using blogs." In *Proceedings of the 30th Annual International ACM SIGIR Conference on Research and Development in Information Retrieval*. ACM pp. 607–614.

Liu, Yinhan, Myle Ott, Naman Goyal, Jingfei Du, Mandar Joshi, Danqi Chen, Omer Levy, Mike Lewis, Luke Zettlemoyer, and Veselin Stoyanov. 2019. "Roberta: A robustly optimized bert pretraining approach." *arXiv preprint arXiv:1907.11692* .

Livermore, Michael A. and Daniel N. Rockmore. 2019. *Law as Data: Computation, Text, & the Future of Legal Analysis*. Santa Fe Institute Press.

Lloyd, Stuart. 1982. "Least squares quantization in PCM." *IEEE Transactions on Information Theory* 28(2):129–137.

Lo, Adeline, Herman Chernoff, Tian Zheng, and Shaw-Hwa Lo. 2015. "Why significant variables aren't automatically good predictors." *Proceedings of the National Academy of Sciences* 112(45):13892–13897.

Long, Hoyt and Richard Jean So. 2016. "Literary pattern recognition: Modernism between close reading and machine learning." *Critical Inquiry* 42(2):235–267.

Lorentzen, Peter. 2014. "China's strategic censorship." *American Journal of Political Science* 58(2):402–414.

Loughran, Tim and Bill McDonald. 2011. "When is a liability not a liability? Textual analysis, dictionaries, and 10-Ks." *The Journal of Finance* 66(1):35–65.

Lowe, Will. 2008. "Understanding wordscores." *Political Analysis* 16(4):356–371.

Lowe, Will and Kenneth Benoit. 2013. "Validating estimates of latent traits from textual data using human judgment as a benchmark." *Political Analysis* 21(3):298–313.

Lucas, Christopher, Richard A. Nielsen, Margaret E. Roberts, Brandon M. Stewart, Alex Storer, and Dustin Tingley. 2015. "Computer-assisted text analysis for comparative politics." *Political Analysis* 23(2):254–277.

Lucas, Robert E. 1976. "Econometric policy evaluation: A critique." *Carnegie-Rochester Conference Series on Public Policy* 1:19–46.

Luhn, Hans Peter. 1960. "Key word-in-context index for technical literature (kwic index)." *American Documentation* 11(4):288–295.

Lum, Kristian and William Isaac. 2016. "To predict and serve?" *Significance* 13(5):14–19.

Lundberg, Ian, Arvind Narayanan, Karen Levy, and Matthew J. Salganik. 2019. "Privacy, ethics, and data access: A case study of the Fragile Families Challenge." *Socius* 5:2378023118813023.

Lundberg, Ian, Rebecca Johnson, and Brandon M. Stewart. 2021. "What is your estimand? Defining the target quantity connects statistical evidence to theory." *American Sociological Review* 86(3):532–565.

Ma, Justin, Lawrence K. Saul, Stefan Savage, and Geoffrey M. Voelker. 2009. "Beyond blacklists: learning to detect malicious web sites from suspicious URLs." In *Proceedings of the 15th ACM SIGKDD International Conference on Knowledge Discovery and Data Mining.* ACM pp. 1245–1254.

MacKinnon, Rebecca. 2008. "Flatter world and thicker walls? Blogs, censorship and civic discourse in China." *Public Choice* 134(1-2):31–46.

MacQueen, James. 1967. "Some methods for classification and analysis of multivariate observations." *Proceedings of the Fifth Berkeley Symposium on Mathematical Statistics and Probability* 1(14):281–297.

MacRae, Duncan. 1965. "A method for identifying issues and factions from legislative votes." *American Political Science Review* 59(4):909–926.

Magnusson, Måns, Richard Öhrvall, Katarina Barrling, and David Mimno. 2018. "Voices from the far right: A text analysis of Swedish parliamentary debates." *SocArXiv* .

Malesky, Edmund, Paul Schuler, and Anh Tran. 2012. "The adverse effects of sunshine: A field experiment on legislative transparency in an authoritarian assembly." *American Political Science Review* 106(04):762–786.

Maliniak, Daniel, Ryan Powers, and Barbara F. Walter. 2013. "The gender citation gap in international relations." *International Organization* 67(04):889–922.

Manning, Christopher D., Mihai Surdeanu, John Bauer, Jenny Finkel, Steven J. Bethard, and David McClosky. 2014. "The Stanford CoreNLP Natural Language Processing Toolkit." In *Association for Computational Linguistics (ACL) System Demonstrations.* pp. 55–60.

Marcus, Mitchell P., Mary Ann Marcinkiewicz, and Beatrice Santorini. 1993. "Building a large annotated corpus of English: The Penn Treebank." *Comput. Linguist.* 19(2):313–330.

Maron, Melvin Earl and John L. Kuhns. 1960. "On relevance, probabilistic indexing and information retrieval." *Journal of the ACM (JACM)* 7(3):216–244.

Mason, Winter and Siddharth Suri. 2012. "Conducting behavioral research on Amazon's Mechanical Turk." *Behavior Research Methods* 44(1):1–23.

Mayhew, David. 1974. *The Electoral Connection*. New Haven: Yale University Press.

Mcauliffe, Jon D. and David M. Blei. 2008. "Supervised topic models." In *Advances in Neural Information Processing Systems*. pp. 121–128.

McCants, William, Jarret Brachman, and Joseph Felter. 2006. "Militant Ideology Atlas: Research Compendium." Technical report Military Academy West Point NY Combating Terrorism Center.

McGhee, Eric, Seth Masket, Boris Shor, Steven Rogers, and Nolan McCarty. 2014. "A primary cause of partisanship? Nomination systems and legislator ideology." *American Journal of Political Science* 58(2):337–351.

McLachlan, Geoffrey and David Peel. 2004. *Finite Mixture Models*. John Wiley & Sons.

McQueen, Alison. 2018. *Political Realism in Apocalyptic Times*. Cambridge University Press.

Melzer, Arthur M. 2014. *Philosophy between the Lines*. University of Chicago Press.

Mihalcea, Rada and Carlo Strapparava. 2009. "The lie detector: Explorations in the automatic recognition of deceptive language." In *Proceedings of the ACL-IJCNLP 2009 Conference Short Papers*. Association for Computational Linguistics pp. 309–312.

Mikolov, Tomás, Ilya Sutskever, Kai Chen, Greg S. Corrado, and Jeff Dean. 2013. "Distributed representations of words and phrases and their compositionality." In *Advances in Neural Information Processing Systems 26*, ed. C. J. C. Burges, L. Bottou, M. Welling, Z. Ghahramani, and K. Q. Weinberger. Curran Associates, Inc. pp. 3111–3119.

Mikolov, Tomás, Kai Chen, Greg Corrado, and Jeffrey Dean. 2013. "Efficient estimation of word representations in vector space." In *1st International Conference on Learning Representations, ICLR 2013, Scottsdale, Arizona, USA, May 2-4, 2013, Workshop Track Proceedings*, ed. Yoshua Bengio and Yann LeCun.

Mikolov, Tomáš, Wen-tau Yih, and Geoffrey Zweig. 2013. "Linguistic regularities in continuous space word representations." In *Proceedings of the 2013 Conference of the North American Chapter of the Association for Computational Linguistics: Human Language Technologies*. pp. 746–751.

Miller, George A. 1995. "WordNet: A lexical database for English." *Communications of the ACM* 38(11):39–41.

Mimno, David, Hanna M. Wallach, Edmund Talley, Miriam Leenders, and Andrew McCallum. 2011. "Optimizing semantic coherence in topic models." In *Proceedings of the Conference on Empirical Methods in Natural Language Processing*. Association for Computational Linguistics pp. 262–272.

Mimno, David and Andrew McCallum. 2008. "Topic models conditioned on arbitrary features with Dirichlet-multinomial regression." In *Proceedings of the Twenty-Fourth Conference on Uncertainty in Artificial Intelligence*. AUAI Press pp. 411–418.

Mitchell, Margaret, Simone Wu, Andrew Zaldivar, Parker Barnes, Lucy Vasserman, Ben Hutchinson, Elena Spitzer, Inioluwa Deborah Raji, and Timnit Gebru. 2019. "Model cards for model reporting." In *Proceedings of the Conference on Fairness, Accountability, and Transparency*. pp. 220–229.

Mohr, John W., Christopher A. Bail, Margaret Frye, Jennifer C. Lena, Omar Lizardo, Terence E. McDonnell, Ann Mische, Iddo Tavory, and Frederick F Wherry. 2020. *Measuring Culture*. Columbia University Press.

Monroe, Burt and Ko Maeda. 2004. "Talk's cheap: Text-based estimation of rhetorical ideal points." 21st Annual Summer Meeting of the Society of Political Methodology.

Monroe, Burt, Michael Colaresi, and Kevin Quinn. 2008. "Fightin' words: Lexical feature selection and evaluation for identifying the content of political conflict." *Political Analysis* 16(4):372.

Montgomery, Jacob M., Brendan Nyhan, and Michelle Torres. 2018. "How conditioning on posttreatment variables can ruin your experiment and what to do about it." *American Journal of Political Science* 62(3):760–775.

Moretti, Franco. 2013. *Distant Reading*. Verso.

Morgan, Stephen L. and Christopher Winship. 2015. *Counterfactuals and Causal Inference: Methods and Principles for Social Research*. Cambridge: Cambridge University Press.

Mosteller, Frederick. 2010. *The Pleasures of Statistics: The Autobiography of Frederick Mosteller*. Springer Science & Business Media.

Mosteller, Frederick and David L. Wallace. 1963. "Inference in an authorship problem: A comparative study of discrimination methods applied to the authorship of the disputed Federalist Papers." *Journal of the American Statistical Association* 58(302):275–309.

Mozer, Reagan, Luke Miratrix, Aaron Russell Kaufman, and L. Jason Anastasopoulos. 2020. "Matching with text data: An experimental evaluation of methods for matching documents and of measuring match quality." *Political Analysis* 28(4):445–468.

Mueller, Hannes and Christopher Rauh. 2017. "Reading between the lines: Prediction of political violence using newspaper text." *American Political Science Review* pp. 1–18.

Mullainathan, Sendhil and Jann Spiess. 2017. "Machine learning: An applied econometric approach." *Journal of Economic Perspectives* 31(2):87–106.

Mulvenon, James. 2015. "The yuan stops here: Xi Jinping and the 'CMC Chairman Responsibility System.'" *China Leadership Monitor* 47:1–14.

Munger, Kevin. 2019. "Knowledge Decays: Temporal Validity and Social Science in a Changing World." Working Paper The Pennsylvania State University.

Murphy, Kevin P. 2021. *Probabilistic Machine Learning: An Introduction*. MIT press.

Nassirtoussi, Arman Khadjeh, Saeed Aghabozorgi, Teh Ying Wah, and David Chek Ling Ngo. 2014. "Text mining for market prediction: A systematic review." *Expert Systems with Applications* 41(16):7653–7670.

Nay, John J. 2017. "Predicting and understanding law-making with word vectors and an ensemble model." *PloS One* 12(5):e0176999.

Nelson, Laura K. 2020. "Computational grounded theory: A methodological framework." *Sociological Methods & Research* 49(1):3–42.

Neuendorf, Kimberly A. 2016. *The Content Analysis Guidebook*. Sage.

Ng, Andrew, Michael Jordan, and Yair Weiss. 2001. "On Spectral Clustering: Analysis and An Algorithm." In *Advances in Neural Information Processing Systems 14: Proceeding of the 2001 Conference.* pp. 849–856.

Ng, Andrew Y. and Michael I. Jordan. 2002. "On discriminative vs. generative classifiers: A comparison of logistic regression and naive Bayes." In *Advances in Neural Information Processing Systems.* pp. 841–848.

Nguyen, Viet-An, Jordan Boyd-Graber, Philip Resnik, and Kristina Miler. 2015. "Tea party in the house: A hierarchical ideal point topic model and its application to Republican legislators in the 112th Congress." In *Proceedings of the 53rd Annual Meeting of the Association for Computational Linguistics and the 7th International Joint Conference on Natural Language Processing (Volume 1: Long Papers).* pp. 1438–1448.

Nielsen, Richard A. 2017. *Deadly Clerics: Blocked Ambition and the Paths to Jihad*. Cambridge University Press.

Nigam, Kamal, Andrew Kachites McCallum, Sebastian Thrun, and Tom Mitchell. 2000. "Text classification from labeled and unlabeled documents using EM." *Machine Learning* 39(2-3):103–134.

Nissenbaum, Helen. 2020. *Privacy in Context*. Stanford University Press.

Nsoesie, Elaine O., Sheryl A. Kluberg, and John S. Brownstein. 2014. "Online reports of foodborne illness capture foods implicated in official foodborne outbreak reports." *Preventive Medicine* 67:264–269.

O'Connor, Brendan, Brandon M. Stewart, and Noah A. Smith. 2013. "Learning to extract international relations from political context." In *Proceedings of the 51st Annual Meeting of the Association for Computational Linguistics (Volume 1: Long Papers)*. Sofia, Bulgaria: Association for Computational Linguistics pp. 1094–1104.

O'Connor, Brendan, Ramnath Balasubramanyan, Bryan R. Routledge, and Noah A. Smith. 2010. "From tweets to polls: Linking text sentiment to public opinion time series." *ICWSM* 11(122-129):1–2.

Olteanu, Alexandra, Carlos Castillo, Fernando Diaz, and Emre Kßcßman. 2019. "Social data: Biases, methodological pitfalls, and ethical boundaries." *Frontiers in Big Data* 2:13.

O'Neil, Cathy. 2016. *Weapons of Math Destruction: How Big Data Increases Inequality and Threatens Democracy*. Broadway Books.

Owoputi, Olutobi, Brendan O'Connor, Chris Dyer, Kevin Gimpel, Nathan Schneider, and Noah A Smith. 2013. "Improved part-of-speech tagging for online conversational text with word clusters." In *Proceedings of the 2013 Conference of the North American Chapter of the Association for Computational Linguistics: Human Language Technologies.* pp. 380–390.

Paisley, John, Chong Wang, David M. Blei, and Michael I. Jordan. 2015. "Nested hierarchical Dirichlet processes." *IEEE Transactions on Pattern Analysis and Machine Intelligence* 37(2):256–270.

Pan, Jennifer and Kaiping Chen. 2018. "Concealing corruption: How chinese officials distort upward reporting of online grievances." *The American Political Science Review* 112(3):602–620.

Paul, Michael and Mark Dredze. 2012. "Factorial LDA: Sparse multi-dimensional text models." In *Advances in Neural Information Processing Systems.* pp. 2582–2590.

Pechenick, Eitan Adam, Christopher M. Danforth, and Peter Sheridan Dodds. 2015. "Characterizing the Google Books corpus: Strong limits to inferences of socio-cultural and linguistic evolution." *PloS One* 10(10):e0137041.

Pena, José M., Jose Antonio Lozano, and Pedro Larranaga. 1999. "An empirical comparison of four initialization methods for the k-means algorithm." *Pattern Recognition Letters* 20(10):1027–1040.

Pennebaker, James, Martha Francis, and Roger Booth. 2001. *Linguistic Inquiry and Word Count: LIWC 2001.* Mahway, NJ: Erlbaum Publishers.

Pennebaker, James W. and Anna Graybeal. 2001. "Patterns of natural language use: Disclosure, personality, and social integration." *Current Directions in Psychological Science* 10(3):90–93.

Pennington, Jeffrey, Richard Socher, and Christopher D. Manning. 2014. "GloVe: Global vectors for word representation." In *Proceedings of the 2014 Conference on Empirical Methods in Natural Language Processing.* pp. 1532–1543.

Perry, Patrick O and Kenneth Benoit. 2017. "Scaling text with the class affinity model." *arXiv preprint arXiv:1710.08963* .

Perry, Walt L. 2013. *Predictive Policing: The Role of Crime Forecasting in Law Enforcement Operations.* Rand Corporation.

Peters, Matthew, Mark Neumann, Mohit Iyyer, Matt Gardner, Christopher Clark, Kenton Lee, and Luke Zettlemoyer. 2018. "Deep contextualized word representations." In *Proceedings of the 2018 Conference of the North American Chapter of the Association for Computational Linguistics: Human Language Technologies, Volume 1 (Long Papers).* New Orleans, Louisiana: Association for Computational Linguistics pp. 2227–2237.

Piper, Andrew. 2018. *Enumerations: Data and Literary Study.* University of Chicago Press.

Pitman, Jim and Marc Yor. 1981. "Bessel processes and infinitely divisible laws." In *Stochastic Integrals.* Springer pp. 285–370.

Platt, John C. 2005. "Fastmap, MetricMap, and Landmark MDS are all Nyström algorithms." *Proceedings of the 10th International Workshop on Artificial Intelligence and Statistics* pp. 261–268.

Poole, Keith and Howard Rosenthal. 1997. *Congress: A Political-Economic History of Roll Call Voting.* Oxford University Press.

Poole, Keith T. and Howard Rosenthal. 1985. "A spatial model for legislative roll call analysis." *American Journal of Political Science* 29(2):357–384.

Popkin, Samuel L. 1994. *The Reasoning Voter: Communication and Persuasion in Presidential Campaigns.* University of Chicago Press.

Porter, Martin F. 1980. "An algorithm for suffix stripping." *Program* 14(3):130–137.

Powell, Eleanor Neff. N.d. *Where Money Matters in Congress: A Window into How Parties Evolve.* Cambridge University Press.

Preis, Tobias, Helen Susannah Moat, Steven R. Bishop, Philip Treleaven, and H. Eugene Stanley. 2013. "Quantifying the digital traces of Hurricane Sandy on Flickr." *Scientific Reports* 3:3141.

Pritchard, Jonathan K., Matthew Stephens, and Peter Donnelly. 2000. "Inference of population structure using multilocus genotype data." *Genetics* 155(2):945–959.

Quinn, Kevin M., Burt L. Monroe, Michael Colaresi, Michael H. Crespin, and Dragomir R. Radev. 2010. "How to analyze political attention with minimal assumptions and costs." *American Journal of Political Science* 54(1):209–228.

Ranganath, Rajesh, Linpeng Tang, Laurent Charlin, and David Blei. 2015. "Deep exponential families." In *Artificial Intelligence and Statistics*. pp. 762–771.

Reilly, Shauna, Sean Richey, and J. Benjamin Taylor. 2012. "Using Google search data for state politics research: An empirical validity test using roll-off data." *State Politics & Policy Quarterly* 12(2):146–159.

Resnik, Philip, Anderson Garron, and Rebecca Resnik. 2013. "Using topic modeling to improve prediction of neuroticism and depression in college students." In *Proceedings of the 2013 Conference on Empirical Methods in Natural Language Processing*. pp. 1348–1353.

Rheault, Ludovic and Christopher Cochrane. 2020. "Word embeddings for the analysis of ideological placement in parliamentary corpora." *Political Analysis* 28(1):112–133.

Ribeiro, Marco Tulio, Sameer Singh, and Carlos Guestrin. 2016. "'Why should I trust you?' Explaining the predictions of any classifier." In *Proceedings of the 22nd ACM SIGKDD International Conference on Knowledge Discovery and Data Mining*. pp. 1135–1144.

Riffe, Daniel, Stephen Lacy, Brendan R. Watson, and Frederick Fico. 2019. *Analyzing Media Messages: Using Quantitative Content Analysis in Research*. Routledge.

Roberts, Margaret E., Brandon M. Stewart, Dustin Tingley, Christopher Lucas, Jetson Leder-Luis, Shana Kushner Gadarian, Bethany Albertson, and David G. Rand. 2014. "Structural topic models for open-ended survey responses." *American Journal of Political Science* 58(4):1064–1082.

Roberts, Margaret E., Brandon M. Stewart, Dustin Tingley, and Edoardo M. Airoldi. 2013. "The structural topic model and applied social science." In *Advances in Neural Information Processing Systems Workshop on Topic Models: Computation, Application, and Evaluation*. Vol. 4 Harrahs and Harveys, Lake Tahoe.

Roberts, Margaret E., Brandon M. Stewart, and Dustin Tingley. 2016. "Navigating the local modes of big data: The case of topic models." In *Computational Social Science: Discovery and Prediction*, ed. R. Michael Alvarez. New York: Cambridge University Press chapter 2, pp. 51–97.

Roberts, Margaret E., Brandon M. Stewart, and Dustin Tingley. 2019. "stm: An R package for structural topic models." *Journal of Statistical Software* 91(1):1–40.

Roberts, Margaret E., Brandon M. Stewart, and Edoardo M. Airoldi. 2016. "A model of text for experimentation in the social sciences." *Journal of the American Statistical Association* 111(515):988–1003.

Roberts, Margaret E., Brandon M. Stewart, and Richard A. Nielsen. 2020. "Adjusting for confounding with text matching." *American Journal of Political Science* 64(4):887–903.

Rodman, Emma. 2020. "A timely intervention: Tracking the changing meanings of political concepts with word vectors." *Political Analysis* 28(1):87–111.

Rodríguez, Pedro and Arthur Spirling. N.d. "Word embeddings: What works, what doesn't, and how to tell the difference for applied research." *Journal of Politics*. Forthcoming.

Rodríguez, Pedro L., Arthur Spirling, and Brandon M. Stewart. 2021. "Embedding Regression: Models for Context-Specific Description and Inference." Working Paper Vanderbilt University.

Rosen-Zvi, Michal, Thomas Griffiths, Mark Steyvers, and Padhraic Smyth. 2004. "The author-topic model for authors and documents." In *Proceedings of the 20th Conference on Uncertainty in Artificial Intelligence*. AUAI Press pp. 487–494.

Roweis, Sam T. and Lawrence K. Saul. 2000. "Nonlinear dimensionality reduction by locally linear embedding." *Science* 290(5500):2323–2326.

Rule, Alix, Jean-Philippe Cointet, and Peter S. Bearman. 2015. "Lexical shifts, substantive changes, and continuity in State of the Union discourse, 1790–2014." *Proceedings of the National Academy of Sciences* 112(35):10837–10844.

Rumelhart, David E., Geoffrey E. Hinton, and Ronald J. Williams. 1986. "Learning representations by back-propagating errors." *Nature* 323(6088):533–536.

Rybicki, Jan and Maciej Eder. 2011. "Deeper Delta across genres and languages: Do we really need the most frequent words?" *Literary and Linguistic Computing* 26(3):315–321.

Salakhutdinov, Ruslan and Geoffrey Hinton. 2009. "Replicated Softmax: An undirected topic model." In *Proceedings of the 22nd International Conference on Neural Information Processing Systems*. NIPS'09 Red Hook, NY, USA: Curran Associates Inc. p. 1607–1614.

Salam, Sayeed, Lamisah Khan, Amir El-Ghamry, Patrick Brandt, Jennifer Holmes, Vito D'Orazio, and Javier Osorio. 2020. "Automatic event coding framework for Spanish political news articles." In *2020 IEEE 6th Intl Conference on Big Data Security on Cloud, IEEE Intl Conference on High Performance and Smart Computing, and IEEE Intl Conference on Intelligent Data and Security*. IEEE pp. 246–253.

Salganik, Matthew. 2018. *Bit by Bit: Social Research in the Digital Age*. Princeton University Press.

Schnabel, Tobias, Igor Labutov, David Mimno, and Thorsten Joachims. 2015. "Evaluation methods for unsupervised word embeddings." In *Proceedings of the 2015 Conference on Empirical Methods in Natural Language Processing*. pp. 298–307.

Schofield, Alexandra and David Mimno. 2016. "Comparing apples to apple: The effects of stemmers on topic models." *Transactions of the Association for Computational Linguistics* 4:287–300.

Schofield, Alexandra, Måns Magnusson, and David Mimno. 2017. "Pulling out the stops: Rethinking stopword removal for topic models." In *Proceedings of the 15th Conference of the European Chapter of the Association for Computational Linguistics: Volume 2, Short Papers*. Vol. 2 pp. 432–436.

Schonhardt-Bailey, Cheryl. 2013. *Deliberating American Monetary Policy: A Textual Analysis*. MIT Press.

Schonhardt-Bailey, Cheryl. 2017. "Nonverbal contention and contempt in UK parliamentary oversight hearings on fiscal and monetary policy." *Politics and the Life Sciences* 36(1):27–46.

Schrodt, Philip A. 1986. "Predicting international events." *BYTE* 11(12):177–192.

Schrodt, Philip A. 2006. "Twenty years of the Kansas event data system project." *The Political Methodologist* 14(1):2–8.

Schrodt, Philip A. 2012. "Precedents, progress, and prospects in political event data." *International Interactions* 38(4):546–569.

Schrodt, Philip A. and Deborah J. Gerner. 1994. "Validity assessment of a machine-coded event data set for the Middle East, 1982–1992." *American Journal of Political Science* 38(3):825–854.

Schütze, Hinrich. 1993. "Word space." In *Advances in Neural Information Processing Systems*. pp. 895–902.

Schwartz, H Andrew, Johannes C Eichstaedt, Margaret L Kern, Lukasz Dziurzynski, Stephanie M Ramones, Megha Agrawal, Achal Shah, Michal Kosinski, David Stillwell, Martin E.P. Seligman, and Lyle H. Ungar. 2013. "Personality, gender, and age in the language of social media: The open-vocabulary approach." *PloS One* 8(9):e73791.

Sebeok, Thomas A. and Valdis J. Zeps. 1958. "An analysis of structured content, with application of electronic computer research, in psycholinguistics." *Language and Speech* 1(3):181–193.

Sennrich, Rico, Barry Haddow, and Alexandra Birch. 2016. "Edinburgh neural machine translation systems for WMT 16." In *Proceedings of the First Conference on Machine Translation: Volume 2, Shared Task Papers*. pp. 371–376.

Shank, Daniel B. 2016. "Using crowdsourcing websites for sociological research: The case of Amazon Mechanical Turk." *The American Sociologist* 47(1):47–55.

Shannon, Claude E. 1949. *The Mathematical Theory of Communication*. Urbana-Champaign: University of Illinois Press.

Shao, Li. 2018. "The dilemma of criticism: Disentangling the determinants of media censorship in China." *Journal of East Asian Studies* 18(3):279–297.

Sheng, Victor S., Foster Provost, and Panagiotis G. Ipeirotis. 2008. "Get another label? Improving data quality and data mining using multiple, noisy labelers." In *Proceedings of the 14th ACM SIGKDD International Conference on Knowledge Discovery and Data Mining*. ACM pp. 614–622.

Shih, Victor. 2008. "Nauseating displays of loyalty: Monitoring the factional bargain through ideological campaigns in China." *The Journal of Politics* 70(04):1177–1192.

Shor, Boris and Nolan McCarty. 2011. "The ideological mapping of American legislatures." *American Political Science Review* 105(3):530–551.

Silge, Julia and David Robinson. 2017. *Text Mining with R: A Tidy Approach*. O'Reilly Media, Inc.

Simmons, Joseph P., Leif D. Nelson, and Uri Simonsohn. 2011. "False-positive psychology: Undisclosed flexibility in data collection and analysis allows presenting anything as significant." *Psychological Science* 22(11):1359–1366.

Slapin, Jonathan B. and Sven-Oliver Proksch. 2008. "A scaling model for estimating time-series party positions from texts." *American Journal of Political Science* 52(3):705–722.

Smith, David A., Ryan Cordell, and Elizabeth Maddock Dillon. 2013. "Infectious texts: Modeling text reuse in nineteenth-century newspapers." In *2013 IEEE International Conference on Big Data*. IEEE pp. 86–94.

Snow, Rion, Brendan O'Connor, Daniel Jurafsky, and Andrew Y Ng. 2008. "Cheap and fast—but is it good?: evaluating non-expert annotations for natural language tasks." In *Proceedings of the Conference on Empirical Methods in Natural Language Processing*. Association for Computational Linguistics pp. 254–263.

Snyder, David and William R. Kelly. 1977. "Conflict intensity, media sensitivity and the validity of newspaper data." *American Sociological Review* pp. 105–123.

Snyder Jr., James M. 1992. "Committee power, structure-induced equilibria, and roll call votes." *American Journal of Political Science* 36(1):1–30.

Socher, Richard, Alex Perelygin, Jean Wu, Jason Chuang, Christopher D Manning, Andrew Ng, and Christopher Potts. 2013. "Recursive deep models for semantic compositionality over a sentiment treebank." In *Proceedings of the 2013 Conference on Empirical Methods in Natural Language Processing*. pp. 1631–1642.

Spirling, Arthur. 2012. "US treaty making with American Indians: Institutional change and relative power, 1784–1911." *American Journal of Political Science* 56(1):84–97.

Stevens, S. S. 1946. "On the theory of scales of measurement." *Science* 103(2684):677–680.

Stewart, Brandon M. and Yuri M. Zhukov. 2009. "Use of force and civil–military relations in Russia: an automated content analysis." *Small Wars & Insurgencies* 20(2):319–343.

Strauss, Leo. 1952. *Persecution and the Art of Writing*. Free Press.

Strubell, Emma, Ananya Ganesh, and Andrew McCallum. 2019. "Energy and Policy Considerations for Deep Learning in NLP." In *Proceedings of the 57th Annual Meeting of the Association for Computational Linguistics*. Florence, Italy: Association for Computational Linguistics pp. 3645–3650.

Taddy, Matt. 2013. "Multinomial inverse regression for text analysis." *Journal of the American Statistical Association* 108(503):755–770.

Tatman, Rachael. 2017. "Gender and dialect bias in YouTube's automatic captions." In *Proceedings of the First ACL Workshop on Ethics in Natural Language Processing*. pp. 53–59.

Tausanovitch, Chris and Christopher Warshaw. 2017. "Estimating candidates' political orientation in a polarized congress." *Political Analysis* 25(2):167–187.

Tausczik, Yla R. and James W. Pennebaker. 2010. "The psychological meaning of words: LIWC and computerized text analysis methods." *Journal of Language and Social Psychology* 29(1):24–54.

Tavory, Iddo and Stefan Timmermans. 2014. *Abductive Analysis: Theorizing Qualitative Research*. University of Chicago Press.

Tetlock, Paul C., Maytal Saar-Tsechansky, and Sofus Macskassy. 2008. "More than words: Quantifying language to measure firms' fundamentals." *The Journal of Finance* 63(3):1437–1467.

Teune, Henry and Adam Przeworski. 1970. *The Logic of Comparative Social Inquiry*. New York: Wiley-Interscience.

Thurstone, L.L. 1954. "The measurement of values." *Psychological Review* 61(1):47–58.

Thurstone, Louis L. 1927. "A law of comparative judgment." *Psychological Review* 34(4):273.

Timmermans, Stefan and Iddo Tavory. 2012. "Theory construction in qualitative research: From grounded theory to abductive analysis." *Sociological Theory* 30(3):167–186.

Tkachenko, Nataliya, Stephen Jarvis, and Rob Procter. 2017. "Predicting floods with Flickr tags." *PloS One* 12(2):e0172870.

Torres, Michelle. 2019. "A visual political world: Determinants and effects of visual content." Working Paper Rice University.

Turney, Peter D. and Michael L. Littman. 2003. "Measuring praise and criticism: Inference of semantic orientation from association." *ACM Transactions on Information Systems* 21(4).

Turney, Peter D. and Patrick Pantel. 2010. "From frequency to meaning: Vector space models of semantics." *Journal of Artificial Intelligence Research* 37:141–188.

Underwood, Ted. 2019. *Distant Horizons: Digital Evidence and Literary Change*. University of Chicago Press.

Vafa, Keyon, Suresh Naidu, and David Blei. 2020. "Text-based ideal points." In *Proceedings of the 58th Annual Meeting of the Association for Computational Linguistics*. Online: Association for Computational Linguistics pp. 5345–5357.

Van Atteveldt, Wouter, Jan Kleinnijenhuis, and Nel Ruigrok. 2008. "Parsing, semantic networks, and political authority using syntactic analysis to extract semantic relations from Dutch newspaper articles." *Political Analysis* pp. 428–446.

van der Vaart, Aaad W., Sandrine Dudoit, and Mark J. van der Laan. 2006. "Oracle inequalities for multifold cross validation." *Statistics and Decisions* 24(3):351–371.

Vaswani, Ashish, Noam Shazeer, Niki Parmar, Jakob Uszkoreit, Llion Jones, Aidan N. Gomez, Lukasz Kaiser, and Illia Polosukhin. 2017. "Attention is all you need." In *Advances in Neural Information Processing Systems*. pp. 5998–6008.

Veitch, Victor, Yixin Wang, and David Blei. 2019. "Using embeddings to correct for unobserved confounding in networks." In *Advances in Neural Information Processing Systems*. pp. 13792–13802.

Vikram, Sharad and Sanjoy Dasgupta. 2016. "Interactive Bayesian hierarchical clustering." In *International Conference on Machine Learning*. pp. 2081–2090.

Wainwright, Martin and Michael Jordan. 2008. *Graphical Models, Exponential Families, and Variational Inference*. Now Publishers.

Wallach, Hanna M., David M. Mimno, and Andrew McCallum. 2009. "Rethinking LDA: Why priors matter." In *Advances in Neural Information Processing Systems*. pp. 1973–1981.

Wallach, Hanna M., Iain Murray, Ruslan Salakhutdinov, and David Mimno. 2009. "Evaluation methods for topic models." In *Proceedings of the 26th Annual International Conference on Machine Learning*. ACM pp. 1105–1112.

Wallach, Hanna, Shane Jensen, Lee Dicker, and Katherine Heller. 2010. "An alternative prior process for nonparametric Bayesian clustering." In *Proceedings of the Thirteenth International Conference on Artificial Intelligence and Statistics*. pp. 892–899.

Wang, Chong and David M. Blei. 2009. "Decoupling sparsity and smoothness in the discrete hierarchical Dirichlet process." In *Advances in Neural Information Processing Systems*. pp. 1982–1989.

Wang, Chong and David M. Blei. 2013. "Variational inference in nonconjugate models." *Journal of Machine Learning Research* 14(Apr):1005–1031.

Ward Jr., Joe H. 1963. "Hierarchical grouping to optimize an objective function." *Journal of the American Statistical Association* 58(301):236–244.

Wieting, John, Mohit Bansal, Kevin Gimpel, and Karen Livescu. 2016. "Charagram: Embedding words and sentences via character n-grams." In *Proceedings of the 2016 Conference on Empirical Methods in Natural Language Processing*. Austin, Texas: Association for Computational Linguistics pp. 1504–1515.

Wilkerson, John, David Smith, and Nicholas Stramp. 2015. "Tracing the flow of policy ideas in legislatures: A text reuse approach." *American Journal of Political Science* 59(4):943–956.

Wilkerson, John and Andreu Casas. 2017. "Large-scale computerized text analysis in political science: Opportunities and challenges." *Annual Review of Political Science* 20(1):529–544.

Williamson, Ben. 2016. "Digital education governance: data visualization, predictive analytics, and 'real-time' policy instruments." *Journal of Education Policy* 31(2):123–141.

Williamson, Sinead, Chong Wang, Katherine A. Heller, and David M. Blei. 2010. "The IBP compound Dirichlet process and its application to focused topic modeling." In *Proceedings of the 27th International Conference on International Conference on Machine Learning*. ICML'10 Madison, WI, USA: Omnipress p. 1151–1158.

Wittgenstein, Ludwig. 1953. *Philosophical Investigations*. John Wiley & Sons.

Yano, Tae, William W. Cohen, and Noah A. Smith. 2009. "Predicting response to political blog posts with topic models." In *Proceedings of Human Language Technologies: The 2009 Annual Conference of the North American Chapter of the Association for Computational Linguistics*. Association for Computational Linguistics pp. 477–485.

Yao, Limin, David Mimno, and Andrew McCallum. 2009. "Efficient methods for topic model inference on streaming document collections." In *Proceedings of the 15th ACM SIGKDD International Conference on Knowledge Discovery and Data Mining*. ACM pp. 937–946.

Ying, Luwei, Jacob M. Montgomery, and Brandon M. Stewart. 2019. "Inferring concepts from topics: Towards procedures for validating topics as measures." PolMeth XXXVI@ MIT, Cambridge, MA. Society for Political Methodology.

Young, Daniel Taylor. 2012. "How do you measure a constitutional moment: Using algorithmic topic modeling to evaluate Bruce Ackerman's theory of constitutional change." *Yale Law Journal* 122:1990.

Young, Lori and Stuart Soroka. 2012. "Affective news: The automated coding of sentiment in political texts." *Political Communication* 29(2):205–231.

Zeng, Jinghan. 2016. "Changing manners of displaying loyalties through ideological campaigns in post-Deng China." *Journal of Contemporary China* 25(100):547–562.

Zhang, Han and Jennifer Pan. 2019. "CASM: A deep-learning approach for identifying collective action events with text and image data from social media." *Sociological Methodology* 49(1):1–57.

Zhang, Yian, Alex Warstadt, Haau-Sing Li, and Samuel R. Bowman. 2021. "When do you need billions of words of pretraining data?" In *Proceedings of the 59th Annual Meeting of the Association for Computational Linguistics*.

Zhang, Yuchen, Xi Chen, Denny Zhou, and Michael I. Jordan. 2014. "Spectral methods meet EM: A provably optimal algorithm for crowdsourcing." In *Advances in Neural Information Processing Systems*. pp. 1260–1268.

Index

CPSIA information can be obtained
at www.ICGtesting.com
Printed in the USA
JSHW031234140123
36191JS00007BA/9

9 780691 207544